Tales from the Marketplace

The Chartered Institute of Marketing/Butterworth-Heinemann Marketing Series is the most comprehensive, widely used and important collection of books in marketing and sales currently available worldwide.

As the CIM's official publisher, Butterworth-Heinemann develops, produces and publishes the complete series in association with the CIM. We aim to provide definitive marketing books for students and practitioners that promote excellence in marketing education and practice.

The series titles are written by CIM senior examiners and leading marketing educators for professionals, students and those studying the CIM's Certificate, Advanced Certificate and Postgraduate Diploma courses. Now firmly established, these titles provide practical study support to CIM and other marketing students and to practitioners at all levels.

**The Chartered
Institute of Marketing**

Formed in 1911, The Chartered Institute of Marketing is now the largest professional marketing management body in the world with over 60,000 members located worldwide. Its primary objectives are focused on the development of awareness and understanding of marketing throughout UK industry and commerce and in the raising of standards of professionalism in the education, training and practice of this key business discipline.

Books in the CIM series

Tales from the Marketplace

Stories of Revolution, Reinvention and Renewal

Nigel F. Piercy

Sir Julian Hodge Chair in Marketing and Strategy,
Cardiff Business School, Cardiff University

OXFORD AUCKLAND BOSTON JOHANNESBURG MELBOURNE NEW DELHI

To my mother, my wife Nikala and my son Niall

Butterworth-Heinemann
Linacre House, Jordan Hill, Oxford OX2 8DP
225 Wildwood Avenue, Woburn, MA 01801-2041
A division of Reed Educational and Professional Publishing Ltd

℞ A member of the Reed Elsevier plc group

First published 1999

British Library Cataloguing in Publication Data
Piercy, Nigel F.
   Tales from the marketplace: stories of revolution,
   reinvention and renewal –
   (CIM professional development series)
   1 Marketing – Case studies
   2 Strategic planning – Case studies
   I Title   II Chartered Institute of Marketing
   658.8

ISBN 0 7506 4265 3

Composition by Genesis Typesetting, Rochester, Kent
Printed in Great Britain

Contents

PART IV REFLECTIONS ON THE STORIES

About the author

Professor Nigel F. Piercy BA, MA, PhD, FCIM holds the Sir Julian Hodge Chair in Marketing and Strategy at Cardiff Business School in the University of Wales, Cardiff. His mother wants to know why he cannot have a desk to go with the chair. He has also been visiting professor at Texas Christian University, the University of California, Berkeley, Columbia Graduate School of Business, the Fuqua School of Business, Duke University, and the Athens Laboratory for Business Administration. His mother wants to know why he can never hold down a job in the same place for long. He has managerial experience in retailing and was in business planning with Amersham International plc. He has extensive experience as a consultant and management workshop speaker and facilitator with many organizations throughout the world, specializing in issues of market strategy development, planning and implementation. Recent client companies have included: British Telecom, Allied Dunbar, Ford Cellular, AT&T, Honeywell, AIB Group, ICL, Yellow Pages and other smaller companies. He has also run strategy courses for the Chartered Institute of Marketing, the Institute of Direct Marketing, the Chartered Institute of Management Accounting and the Institute of Chartered Accountants in England and Wales. He has worked with managers and management students in the UK, Europe, the

USA, Malaysia, Hong Kong, Greece, Slovenia, South Africa and Zimbabwe. His mother wants to know when he will settle down and stay at home (and his wife says she has not even started on that subject yet). Professor Piercy has written nine books – the most recent being *Market-Led Strategic Change: Transforming the Process of Going To Market* (Oxford: Butterworth-Heinemann, 1997) and *Marketing Strategy and Competitive Positioning* (with Graham Hooley and John Saunders) (Hemel Hempstead: Prentice Hall, 1998). He has also published approximately 200 papers in the management literature throughout the world, including contributions to the *Journal of Marketing*, the *Journal of the Academy of Marketing Science*, the *Journal of World Business* and the *Journal of Business Research*. His son regularly lectures him on wasting paper. He has also written on business issues for *The Sunday Times* and *The Independent*.

Preface

This is an unusual book (I hope). It is a book describing company strategies and experiences in times of industry and market revolution. It claims not to be a 'cases' book. The rationale for this is explained more fully in Part I. In short, I believe that many 'cases' produced for managers are boring, tedious, out of date, and potentially disastrously misleading. I also think that the way cases are used on many management training courses is positively harmful to managers, and should come with a government health warning. That is why this is definitely a book of stories. I also hope the stories are interesting enough to be read as stories by managers, and that they contain insights into strategy building which may be important to reinventing businesses.

There is the important question of what this book has to do with my managerial text: *Market-Led Strategic Change: Transforming the Process of Going To Market* (Oxford: Butterworth-Heinemann, 1997). There is no reason why people should not use the two books together – in fact, there are excellent reasons why they should because the stories told here are good illustrations of what is meant by 'transforming the process of going to market' and the imperative of 'market-led strategic change', which is what the earlier book was about – and that way I get more royalties and even better lunches from the publisher. Equally, this book stands just as well on its own. A brief perspective on market-based strategic management is given in Part I of the book, which should make these linkages clearer.

The other question I have been asked is whether this is a book about strategy or a book about marketing. The answer to this is 'yes'. This is also explained further in Part I, although it is a question that bothers academics far more than managers.

Naturally, thanks are owed to many people for different kinds of assistance in getting this work completed. However, I propose to ignore them all and take the credit myself, unless there is something wrong in which case it was their fault.

The potentially guilty therefore include my wife Nikala, and my son Niall* who both read the stories; my colleague Professor Leyland Pitt who is a great management case teacher and gave grudging approval to my efforts; Professor James Mac Hulbert at Columbia Business School for his encouragement in writing for managers, and for letting me use the new material with his students and executive education participants at Columbia; my colleague Professor Costas Katsikeas who rushed to take my stories into his classroom (and even asked for more!); and most particularly Professor David W. Cravens at Texas Christian University who inspired my search for a better understanding of the realities of market-based strategic management and much else besides. I would also like to thank my mentor, Professor Roger Mansfield, Director of Cardiff Business School, who provided the time and space for this project, and the Sir Julian Hodge Foundation which funds my chair at Cardiff Business School. The Fuqua School of Business at Duke University in North Carolina was kind enough to invite me to be a visiting professor in the winter of 1999, and provided me with the opportunity to complete this project, for which I am grateful.

Lastly, I would like to thank Nikala Lane, Carolyn Strong and Niall Piercy for proofreading. This means that any remaining errors are their fault.

Nigel Piercy, Cardiff Business School, January 1999

---

* Mind you, this is the horrible child who sent me a copy of the Groucho Marx book review which reads 'From the moment I picked up your book I was convulsed with laughter. Some day I intend reading it'. This is not unlike my friend Malcolm McDonald who once wrote to me that 'The thing about Nigel Piercy's books is that once you put one down, you just can't pick it up again'. Everyone's a critic these days!

PART I

Stories and Strategies

CHAPTER 1

Why a book of stories for managers?

I hope that the contents of this book will be of interest to a number of different audiences:

- Perhaps most important of all, I hope that the book will be useful and stimulating to *managers* who want to read about the experiences of many different organizations in developing strategies to cope and achieve success in a rapidly changing world.

  'read about the experiences of many different organizations in developing
- I hope also that the book will be useful to *management trainers and teachers* in providing them with up-to-date examples and teaching material for use with management students. However, they should know from the outset this is not a conventional decision-oriented 'case study' book. The reasons for this perversity are explained below.

  strategies to cope and achieve success in a rapidly changing world'
- Thirdly, I hope that stories included here will be of interest to *management students*, providing them with the chance to compare the real world with the theory they learn, and with examples and illustrations for their projects.

But most of all, I hope that the stories told here will be a good read for *anyone* who is genuinely interested in the excitement of business and the fascinating revolution taking place in so many markets throughout the world.

As a general rule, I loathe case study books in management and marketing. They are mind-blowingly boring and tedious. People do not *choose* to read books like that. They have them *imposed* by management teachers and trainers, who seem to think that things are not 'academic' unless they are incredibly boring. There is no reason why the fantastic excitement of the marketplace should be made boring. One of the recurring themes in the stories is that managers who create revolution are inspiring, and they seem to have great fun in doing what they do.

I will win no friends in some academic quarters, when I say that I have come almost to despise those who use 'Harvard cases' and their ilk, as a way of filling time in courses for managers and students, and as a substitute for doing something more useful which might involve making more effort. It may be that some managers like these sessions and find them entertaining, but the point is – what do they learn from them that will directly change how they run their own businesses? Experience and observation suggests that many participants in training and education courses find cases shallow, time-wasting, and too artificial to have any real instructive value. It does not have to be this way. Incidentally, this is not how the superb Harvard Business School uses cases – far from it. At Harvard, people learn from cases big time. However, some are critical even of this pinnacle of case teaching in management education. John Hunt of London Business School writes:

> Nearly a century ago, Harvard Business School tried to overcome the problem of linking theory and practice by stealing the case method from its law school. Cases simulated the real world of managing and subsequently every business school around the world copied this method for discussing managerial decision-making. And although 90 students sitting in a tiered lecture theatre discussing a pre-written, post-event case and being graded simultaneously for their contribution to an inconclusive discussion may not be ideal, it was certainly more popular with the students . . . than yet another lecture. (Hunt, 1998)

However, for those of us who are *not* at Harvard, and who may be more concerned with impacting on how managers think and act instead of just entertaining and grading them, I am changing the rules in the following ways.

First, I refuse to use case material with managers that consists of thirty or so densely packed pages of obscure historical facts and figures, where the main goal seems to be that the reader benefits in some obscure way from playing the game of teasing out the story that the case writer has hidden away in the middle of the facts and figures. This is just plain silly, and largely a waste of time. It is also wrong-headed. In the real world, the big problems tend to be blindingly obvious – they do not have to be discovered from a mass of irrelevancy. I think this is one of the reasons people are fed up with conventional cases. I am especially unenthusiastic about management teachers who use cases that are twenty-five years old because they 'make a point' that nothing newer does – this may very occasionally be true. However, if that is what you say, my suspicion is that you have not bothered to look for something more up to date that makes that point, or the point in question is no longer worth making.

'In the real world, the big problems tend to be blindingly obvious – they do not have to be discovered from a mass of irrelevancy'

Second, I see no reason why the stories of how different industries and markets are re-shaping and how companies are coping (or not) should be made inaccessible to readers. This book does its best to provide interesting stories that people can read just because they are interesting stories.

Third, my further observation is that executives and students alike positively prefer to read and hear about companies doing interesting things and facing interesting challenges, that they have actually heard of before. At its simplest people seem to get value from reading, talking and thinking about a fascinating company such as Dell, rather than an obscure mid-western engineering company in the USA, the yak industry in Outer Mongolia, or the sale of human urine to drug users to beat employer drug testing (just in case you wondered, these are all case studies published to instruct managers in strategy). Not least among the reasons for this preference, I suspect, is that there is more real revolution and reinvention in places such as Dell or Amazon than most others.

This leads to my *fourth* point. I truly believe that we do managers a huge disservice by giving them rigid, conventional 'structures' to analyse case studies (let alone rigging case data so that they conveniently fit some analytical tool). The challenge to managers is to reinvent businesses, design new business models, create revolution in their industries, and cope with massive step changes in how things are done to create value for customers and shareholders, as the only way to survive. I suggest that clinging to inflexible, analytical frameworks to analyse the past to death has a somewhat limited value for managers or students. People: the issue is the future, and the future is not contained in the Boston Matrix or anything similar. Yet worse is the idea that there is a 'right' answer, or even a 'right' approach to looking at company strategy. Generation X managers think differently and more creatively to develop radically new business designs because they know about Generation Y customers. This is the real challenge to us all.

Increasingly, the really devastating competition for a company or product does not come from the expected and anticipated sources – the traditional, 'me-too', same-technology competitor – it comes from someone you never even heard of, let alone thought could take your business away from you. Do we think that the banks really expected to be competing with supermarkets, car companies, and Internet-based operations? Do we think that traditional booksellers really expected Amazon.com to happen and to work? Providing managers with rigid, mechanical structures for strategy and competitive analysis does not seem a good way to prepare for strategic surprises like these – in fact, quite the reverse.

'the really devastating competition for a company or product does not come from the expected and anticipated sources – it comes from someone you never even heard of'

A similar point has been made much better recently by Thomas Stern of New York University, about conventional approaches to cases and management development in strategy:

> They are all addicted to left brain number crunching, but we won't need our financial MBAs twenty years from now. Managers of the future must be systems thinkers, who see patterns and loops; who do not just think in a linear way. (Thomas Stern in Bradshaw, 1997)

So, why 'stories', not case studies? I think we started talking about 'cases' in business to sound as 'academic' and 'professional' as doctors and lawyers. I prefer the word 'stories' for a number of reasons. Stories provide us with examples, which are useful for all sorts of things. We tend to use examples all the time. In talking about management issues in a company, in writing about management, in trying out new business theories, in trying to understand our own problems better – the first thing most of us do is to try to think of real-life examples. Even more important, when we are trying to argue the case for something with managerial colleagues, we usually try to convince people by giving them some real examples – even if we call them models, reference sites, or pilots.

Actually, this book is really just a bunch of stories and examples. I hope they will be useful to teachers, trainers and lecturers in exploring things with people by reference to real, topical company experiences. I hope they will be useful to management students in writing papers and projects, and in testing the relevance of the theories they are learning, but there is a much bigger test of whether the book works or not. That test is whether the book provides a 'good read' for managers – maybe on the train or plane rather than just on the training course. Passing this test would suggest that I had succeeded in writing a set of stories about business that were interesting and insightful, and this is the real goal of the book.

Incidentally, I was truly shocked recently by an academic colleague in the USA who innocently inquired if I was writing a book for British managers. I was so surprised, I had no answer. In fact, I do not see the value in management thinking that is restricted by international boundaries – I find it hard to believe that anyone still believes that they matter and protect you from 'foreign' competition. Such beliefs from the past seem a good way to blind managers to competitive invasion by people they never even considered as competitors. National identity was not an issue in choosing the stories for this book. The book is for managers everywhere.

So, finally to answer the question posed at the start of this chapter – why a book of stories for managers? We look to business stories for a number of possible insights: they may tell us about the strategic dilemmas faced by companies, from which we may learn more about our own companies' problems. Stories illustrate the revolutions taking place in markets driven usually by innovative rule-breaking business models, and how some companies decline and others reinvent the way they go to market to succeed in those same markets. Stories provide us with compelling evidence to win the support of others in the decision-making process in a company, and to defy colleagues to ignore the changes that are taking place around them.

'Stories illustrate the revolutions taking place in markets driven usually by innovative rule-breaking business models'

The structure of the remainder of the book is as follows. The next chapter is a brief discussion of the new era of market-based strategic management, driven by the search to create superior value, as some of us see it. This leads to the core of the book: a set of stories about markets and companies, grouped into stories of revolution and reinvention, and tales of obsolescence in conventional business models and the search by companies for renewal. The last part of the book is my commentaries on the stories – my thoughts about the major strategic questions that each story raises and illustrates.

My suggestion is that if you are reading the book just for the heck of it (and I hope many readers are doing just that), read a story and then have a look at the commentary to see if we agree about what can be learned from that company's experiences. On

CHAPTER 2

A new era of market-based strategy*

The title of this book suggests the stories told here are about revolution, reinvention and renewal:

- *revolution* – in the way industries and markets operate and the sources of competition which become important, and consequently in the strategies that successful organizations pursue;
- *reinvention* – in the creation of new business models that make traditional ways of doing business obsolete as routes to delivering and sustaining superior customer value;
- *renewal* – in the strategies of change and repositioning by companies whose business models have become outdated, as they seek to rebuild and respond to change. Increasingly the real strategic issue for companies is not just short-term performance but building the robustness to bounce back, to change, to survive, to turn things around, when the bubble bursts, as it surely will.

---

* This chapter leans heavily on the articles: David W. Cravens, Gordon Greenley, Nigel F. Piercy and Stanley Slater (1997), 'Integrating Contemporary Strategic Management Perspectives', *Long Range Planning*, Vol. 30, No. 4, pp. 493–506, and by the same authors, 'Mapping the Path to Market Leadership', *Marketing Management*, Fall 1998, pp. 29–39. I would like to fully acknowledge this debt to David W. Cravens in particular, who led this team of writers of which I was privileged to be a member.

'many of the traditional approaches to analysis and strategy development, and the hidden assumptions on which they are based, are quite simply obsolete'

It is important from the outset to accept that many of the traditional approaches to analysis and strategy development, and the hidden assumptions on which they are based, are quite simply obsolete and misleading in situations of radical change. Managers who do not grasp this reality are unlikely to survive and their companies are unlikely to prosper. The reality is simply that the rules have changed. The argument is that we are in the midst of a new era of market-based strategic management, which centres on developing better ways to achieve superiority in value in the marketplace.

Market-based strategy

In fact, management thinking about strategy has gone through a number of phases or eras. Some of the changes in the dominant emphasis of management theory and practice in different times are summarized in Figure 2.1, as a number of phases where different approaches to the strategy issue have preoccupied top management and have been the main focus of attention.

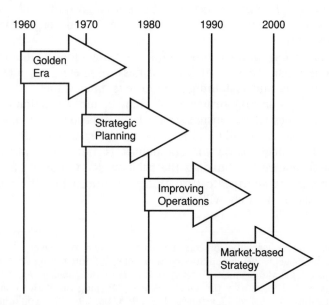

Figure 2.1   Eras of management theory and practice. Source: Adapted from Cravens *et al.*, 1998.

The 'Golden Era' of the 1950s and 1960s, when demand outstripped supply in many industries, and the global economy was recovering from the Second World War, has long since ended for most of us. In the late 1960s and 1970s the issue was strategic planning – business had become tougher and the environment less predictable, and we thought the answer was to produce better strategic plans: complex systems, techniques and models for planning were developed.

The broken promises of strategic planning

The results of strategic planning were all too often disappointing – strategies of little more than incremental change from previous years, and strategic planners separated from line management, producing plans that were frequently ignored. This latter point may explain why strategic planning systems were not more damaging than they actually were – no-one took much notice of the plans produced. The popular management writer, Tom Peters, famously offered $100 to the first executive who could demonstrate that a successful company strategy had resulted from strategic planning. He has yet to be obliged to part with the $100. An emerging view about the blind alley of strategic planning is:

'The results of strategic planning were all too often disappointing – strategies of little more than incremental change from previous years'

> The answer to developing a good strategy is not new planning processes or better-designed plans. The answer lies in managers' understanding of two fundamental points: the benefit of having a well-articulated, stable purpose, and the importance of discovering, understanding, documenting, and exploiting insights about how to create more value than other companies do. (Campbell and Alexander, 1997)

Deming

Underpinning the problems we face in many companies is the fact that these tools and techniques of strategic planning still dominate much MBA-style management education and training – this appears to be an excellent way to set managers up to be destroyed by the radical, unconventional revolution they are likely to face in the real marketplace.

Further recognition of the importance of strategic clarity comes from the 1998 *Financial Times* survey of the 'world's most

Table 2.1   Attributes that will make a company most respected in the future

Rank	Attribute
1	Strong, well thought-out strategy
2	Maximizing customer satisfaction and loyalty
3	Business leadership
4	Quality of products and services
5	Strong and consistent profit performance
6	Robust and human corporate culture
7	Successful change management
8	Globalization of business

Source: *The World's Most Respected Companies*, Financial Times Report, 1998

respected companies'. This study collated the views of 650 chief executive officers (CEOs) in a worldwide survey to gather peer-group judgements about which were the 'most respected' companies in the world (General Electric and Microsoft were the answers). These CEOs were also asked which attributes will make a company most respected in the future. The surprising results are shown in Table 2.1.

'the highest ranked attribute, respected by CEOs across the world, is strategic clarity'

Clearly the highest ranked attribute, respected by CEOs across the world, is strategic clarity – not short-term profit, cost control/reduction, operational efficiency, or share value. The suggestion is that strong and appropriate strategy will drive all the other good things that a company wants and needs.

The quest for operational efficiency

On the other hand, the 1980s and 1990s have been dominated by the global pursuit of operational efficiency – total quality management programmes, the implementation of new technology for automation, business process re-engineering initiatives, value engineering, the focus on core competencies, and most recently the 'lean enterprise' model of supply chain collaboration to remove stockholding and other waste throughout the supply chain (e.g. Womack and Jones, 1996).

The pursuit of operational efficiency has had enormous benefits in improving product and service quality in numerous sectors, and reducing unit costs. Of that, there is no doubt whatever. However, in many situations, the trap has been that strategy seems to have been driven by the search for greater operational efficiency. For example, the 'lean thinkers' in supply chain management have offered chief executives awesome reductions in cost by eliminating 'waste' in a co-ordinated supply chain of linked suppliers, manufacturers, distributors and customers. Unfortunately, it turns out that some of the 'waste' they have attacked is what produces customer choice and the flexibility for companies to respond to change, and they have built an edifice relying on inter-company collaboration, which it turns out is somewhat fragile (Piercy, 1998).

However, the most important point is that operational efficiency is not the same thing as strategy. Strategy is about competitive advantage and continuous innovation to sustain that advantage. Michael Porter of Harvard Business School wrote of this dilemma in 1995, with great insight and simplicity:

'the most important point is that operational efficiency is not the same thing as strategy'

> A company can outperform its rivals only if it can establish a difference that it can preserve. It must deliver greater value to customers or create comparable value at a lower cost or do both. (Porter, 1995)

Indeed, the 'rapid diffusion of best practices' means that industries have become more efficient without individual companies becoming more profitable, because benchmarking and best practice just make companies more similar not more differentiated:

> Operational efficiency means you're running the same race faster, but strategy is choosing to run a different race because it's the one you've set yourself up to win. (Porter, 1999)

'Operational efficiency means you're running the same race faster, but strategy is choosing to run a different race because it's the one you've set yourself up to win. (Porter, 1999)'

This logic leads us away from the search simply for internal efficiencies in the company, or even the supply chain, to focus on the general management responsibility for strategic positioning – defining the value provided to customers compared to competitors as the basis of competitive advantage and superior performance.

Strategy versus planning

Similarly, Gary Hamel (1996) writes about the difference between planning and strategy – planning is scheduling, strategy is revolution. For example, Hamel has described these routes to industry 'revolution' as the basis for strategy:

- *Reconceiving the product or service* – Radically improve the value equation – Hewlett-Packard built domination of the global market for laser printers by driving prices low enough to transform the printer from a capital equipment purchase to a consumable item. Separate function and form – the issue is the need the product meets not its form – people generally have little interest in how financial packages are constructed or by whom, they simply want to buy the car (Ford Motor Company currently earns more profit from selling financial services than selling cars). Achieve joy of use – marketing people's obsession with customer satisfaction has been largely unproductive in retention and strategic positioning, only absolute customer delight pays off. The strength of Richard Branson's Virgin brand extended over areas as diverse as airlines, financial services, music and drinks is a good illustration – though there is a major question about how well that brand strength will survive in an emerging era of value-focused competition.
- *Redefining market space* – Push the bounds of universatility – for example, the disposable camera transformed an adult product into a child's toy and opened new markets for a mature, specialized product. Strive for individuality – the challenge is to mass-produce products which are customized to the individual buyer, such as the Levi Strauss 'Personal Pairs' approach to providing customers with made-to-measure Levi jeans. Increase accessibility – the direct marketing of financial services by companies such as Direct Line and Virgin has transformed the financial services sector for ever.
- *Redrawing industry boundaries* – Rescale industries – take a local business national (e.g. national funeral firms) or make a larger business local (microbreweries and microbakeries). Compress the supply chain – Intel is opening up the computer processor market in China but holds no inventory for this market – the warehouse is the Federal Express aircraft taking the product to the market. Drive convergence – traditional industry and sector boundaries may become irrelevant as new competitors exploit their core competencies – consider the impact of supermarkets acting as banks on blurring the boundaries of the traditional financial services sector.

Strategy or marketing?

One problem is that as soon as you mention things such as customers, markets and value, some strategy people throw their hands up in horror and say that what you are actually talking about is 'marketing', and that is a job for the marketing department. This is actually more of a problem with academics than with managers. None the less, one way of looking at this is shown in Figure 2.2 (Piercy *et al.*, 1997).

If we consider organizational level and management focus as varying in the way shown in Figure 2.2, then we can separate:

- *Strategic planning* – primarily concerned with company-wide issues of portfolio management, resource acquisition and internal resource allocation.
- *Operations management* – mainly involved with the internal production, logistics and administrative systems needed to produce goods and services and operate the organization.
- *Marketing management* – focusing externally but at an operational level, involved with promotion, selling and operational customer service.
- *Market-based strategy* – the externally focused strategy of competitive positioning and sustaining competitive advantage. (It actually makes very little difference what you call this. The important point is that the issues here are not neglected. In many

'In many companies market-based strategy is neglected because it falls in the cracks between strategic planning and marketing management'

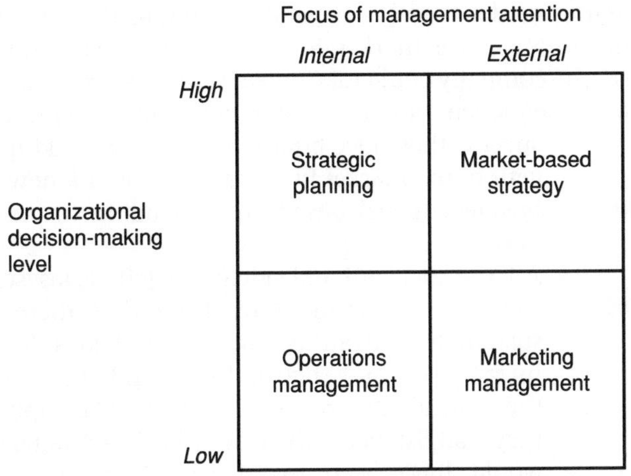

Focus of management attention

	Internal	External
High	Strategic planning	Market-based strategy
Low	Operations management	Marketing management

Organizational decision-making level

Figure 2.2 Marketing or strategy? Source: Piercy *et al.*, 1997.

companies market-based strategy is neglected because it falls in the cracks between strategic planning and marketing management. If you do not believe me – test this model in your own company, and stand by to be surprised at how many of the most important strategic issues are neglected because of lack of ownership. It does not matter what you call it – just do it.)

The death of the old ideas

In addition, increasingly it is being suggested that the strategy paradigms of the last three decades have actually become obsolete. David Cravens of Texas Christian University identifies fundamental shifts, as companies face not traditionally defined markets and sectors but networks of interlinked product–markets, and as they move from traditional functional organizations to process designs and strategic alliances to achieve the needed flexibility and rapid organizational innovation.

In fact some of the familiar strategy-making approaches of the recent past are not merely obsolete they are positively dangerous:

- Strategic planners cling to models like the Boston Matrix to identify appropriate strategy on the basis of relative market share and market growth rate – yet the success of companies such as Virgin in taking small but profitable market shares in mature markets denies the validity of the conventional model.

- A company such as Daewoo would have been advised by conventional planners never to invest in the UK automotive market – conventional analysts would have run a business screening model to prove beyond any doubt that this was a highly unattractive market in growth and competitiveness, where the company could take only a small market share – and as a consequence Daewoo would never have achieved the success they have built in that market, taking 1 per cent of the market in record time with a new direct business model based on responding to customer needs.

'All the conventional advice to Jeff Bezos starting Amazon.com would have been that there is no sustainable advantage in selling books from an Internet site'

- All the conventional advice to Jeff Bezos starting Amazon.com would have been that there is no sustainable advantage in selling books from an Internet site, and Michael Dell would have been told the same about direct sales of personal computers. If they had listened (which is unlikely actually), there would have been two fewer billionaires in the world.

- Many traditional strategy models – like the Boston matrix referred to above – have been obsessed with market share as the key lever for enhancing profitability. What the stories of companies such as Microsoft and the 'no-frills' airlines tell us is that for them the issue is not market share at all – it is *market growth*, because that is the real leverage on earning power. For example, since its founding in 1970, Airbus Industries vowed to overtake Boeing in aircraft manufacture, and Boeing responded by fierce competition to retain market leadership, including deep price cuts to win orders. In 1998 that battle ended – the companies both changed their focus from competition for market share to an emphasis on profitability.

You can run, but you can't hide . . .

Perhaps most touching is those managers who seem to think that the marketplace revolution does not include them. There are many examples of the democracy of new models and new competitors:

- Medical practitioners have always been fond of seeing themselves as somehow above the vulgar commercial world – and any customers who did not like it could do the other thing, and risked being struck off the doctor's list if they got awkward! This may be why there are now more alternative therapists in the UK (40 000) than registered general medical practitioners (36 000) – chiropractors, osteopaths, hypnotherapists, and so on, who seem to offer customers what they want. It may also be why in the late 1990s under a socialist government we are seeing the previously unthinkable relaunch of a private GP service, where the doctors will see you when you want, not when it is convenient for them.
- Public services, for example the police, have often laughed at words such as 'customer' and 'value' in their organizations. Perhaps that is why there are now more private security workers in the UK than there are police officers. It is the same for everyone – your service can be replaced by those with a new way of doing things that creates superior value for customers in their terms. In 1998, the London police called in 'security experts' to advise them about public order and safety in the Millennium celebrations – what happened to the old idea that the police were the security experts?

- Managers in the utilities, for example gas, electricity and water, have also been introduced to some harsh realities through privatization and the introduction of competition to their sectors. And only a few years ago, water industry managers were saying that competition was not a relevant concept in their business. By 1998 the dominant issue in the British water industry was competition between alternative water distribution companies, and pressure was about getting prices lower instead of just water through pipes.
- Even that traditional bastion of conventional brand-based marketing – the detergents industry – is on the brink of revolution. 1998 saw the invention in South Korea of the washing machine that does not need detergents to clean clothes, and the prospect of sonic clothes cleaning systems that do not use detergents or conventional washing machines is on the near horizon.

'if your prosperity depends on the belief that your customers have no choice but to deal with you, and to do so in the way you prefer because it is convenient for you – you had better be very sure'

The truth of the matter seems to be that if your prosperity depends on the belief that your customers have no choice but to deal with you, and to do so in the way you prefer because it is convenient for you – you had better be *very* sure of your grounds, or you too may be in for a nasty surprise. It may even be that in the revolutionary marketplace, 'monopoly' is a redundant word. Peter Martin recently put forward a yet stronger view:

If there is a long-term threat to Microsoft and Intel, it will come from the first instance from within. Just at the moment their dominance seems most assured, the curse of monopoly will be gradually eating away at the company's success. The desire to preserve compatibility with previous products at all costs; the belief in a divine right to market share; a profound mistrust of the bona fides of competitors – these are the penalties that the gift of monopoly brings. (Martin, 1998)

The competitive box

One of the most pernicious tendencies is for managers to build a fixed mental map of the industry in which they compete – they create a myopic competitive box (see Figure 2.3). The competitive box ring-fences familiar competitors using similar technology to produce similar products and services for a shared customer base

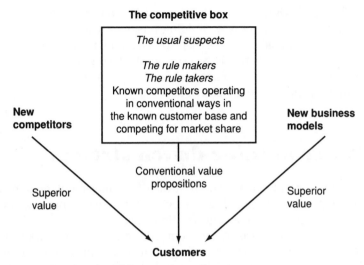

Figure 2.3   The trap of the competitive box

– these are the 'usual suspects' we mean when we talk about our competitors. Competition is probably based on brands and the measure of success is probably market share in the familiar customer base, with great excitement about percentage point changes in that market share for a brand. The fences we build – the competitive box – are what blinds us to the real sources of competition – new competitors with new technologies and new business models. It is becoming more and more true for managers that your most deadly competitor is not the person you sat next to at this year's trade convention – it is probably someone you never even heard of and do not take seriously when you do.

'the competitive box – are what blinds us to the real sources of competition – new competitors with new technologies and new business models'

The examples are numerous – banks who still do not believe that grocery retailers and Internet sites can be retail banks; booksellers who did not believe that Amazon could sell books; airlines who did not believe that business travellers would use a 'no frills' service with no 'free meals'. The competitive box is deadly.

In fact, it can be even worse. In some companies, by taking conventional advice and following industry rules, you see managers taking an operation that has an unconventional business model outside the competitive box and forcing it back inside the box. The 'rules' say that you cannot combine manufacturing or retailing, so you have to choose one or the other – so if the stock market says you are a retailer, we must make you into a conventional retailer (even if it destroys your competitive advantage).

The underlying truth is that those who can produce superior value through a new way of doing business will almost always come from outside the competitive box and revolutionize the familiar stable industry. This too is worth testing out when you look at how a company plans and develops its strategy – is it only thinking inside the competitive box?

Power of value-driven strategy

The new era of market-based strategic management demands new approaches to building strategies that reinvent markets and create revolution in conventional industries.

'The basis of new competition in modern markets is clear – it rests on offering superior value in the eyes of the customer'

The basis of new competition in modern markets is clear – it rests on offering superior value in the eyes of the customer. This is not, however, the simple and obvious truth it may seem. Different customers and different markets buy different types of value. Also, the basis of value changes or 'migrates', as customer priorities change – last year the laptop computer had to have more memory and a colour screen, but this year superior value is the same specifications in a lighter package. One of the biggest mistakes made in the 'total quality revolution' and other approaches to enhanced operational efficiency was the belief that customer value was easily measured and remained stable over time, and was a matter of rational cost/benefit analysis by customers. Value is more complex than this.

In Fremont, California General Motors and Toyota operated a car plant as a joint venture, producing very similar cars. The cars were branded as the Geo Prism and the Toyota Corolla. As these near-identical vehicles left the plant, the Toyota was worth a 10 per cent higher price. After five years, as a second-hand vehicle, the Corolla was typically worth 20 per cent more than the corresponding Geo Prism. The value-creating power of a 'master brand' such as Toyota is awesome and unavoidable.

The airline business provides another case in point. Traditional 'hub and spoke' routing approaches by large airlines have been undermined by the new 'no frills' city-to-city packages provided by companies such as Southwest in the USA, and Ryanair, easyJet and the new British Airway's 'Go' airline in Europe. Flying passengers from the city where they *are* to the city where they *want to be*, strangely enough seems to be better value to customers than flying to a hub (convenient for the airline not the passenger). The vastly cheaper fares on offer help too.

One of the hardest and bitterest pills for managers to swallow is that increasingly customers have wised up, and simply will not accept anything less than world-class service and value. Figure 2.4 suggests a rationale for this statement – which can be tested out against any business and its competitors. The scenarios for doing business seem to have progressed something like this:

'increasingly customers have wised up, and simply will not accept anything less than world-class service and value'

- *Transactional business* – This is where most of us started out – the issue was the 'deal', the contract, or the sale, and once made, there was little further interest in the customer. The customer was the enemy, and we used all those pseudo-military words to describe how to 'beat' the customer. If this sounds unreal – try having a look at the contents of some sales training courses and how some salespeople deal with their customers. This approach works fine as long as the customer is unsophisticated, and as long as customer loyalty does not matter to the seller.
- *Brand-based competition* – When we realized how much impact customer retention had on profitability, we changed our approach. We still treated customers as though they were stupid, but instead of just settling for a single transaction, we wanted loyalty. So, we did our best to tie customers to a brand (that is, take away their choices or make them think we had). By adding brand values and associations (just about anything but cutting price), we tried to take customers

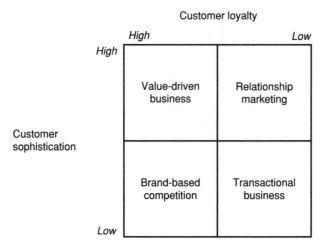

Figure 2.4   From transactions, brands and relationships to value

hostage. In some cases, this was more blatant than others: the warranty invalidated if the customer uses a competitor's supplies; barriers to interfacing equipment from different suppliers; the sheer hassle involved in changing bank accounts; and so on. The trouble is that ultimately customers tend to see through the bad deals and look for something better. In fact, successful branding is not easy (and for cattle can be quite painful).

- *Relationship marketing* – Where many of us ended up was believing that the failure of brand to deliver long-term customer loyalty, meant we had to emphasize improving customer relationships. The 1990s have been awash with customer loyalty programmes, loyalty bonuses, customer satisfaction measurement, customer care policies, complaint response systems and the like. There is nothing wrong with any of these things, and some have been fantastic sales promotion devices – for example in grocery retailing. However, as customers get smarter, these approaches do not buy loyalty. The smart customers are in *all* the loyalty programmes – they get the benefits, whichever supermarket they visit or airline they choose. Smart customers are happy to take all the benefits on offer and report high levels of satisfaction – they just do not give long-term loyalty in return. The truth is that most companies do not really want satisfaction as such, what they want is customer retention, because that drives profitability up dramatically. And that is what they are not getting.

'Smart customers are happy to take all the benefits on offer and report high levels of satisfaction – they just do not give long-term loyalty in return'

- *Value-driven business* – Achieving customer loyalty with sophisticated customers is the new challenge and we are only just beginning to realize what it means. It means transparency – but you try telling used car salespeople that they should always show the customer the invoice so the customer knows what the dealer paid for the vehicle (I did, and they were not happy). It will mean integrity and trustworthiness. It will mean innovative ways of doing business. It will mean a focus on value in customers' terms not ours. It will require new types of organization and technology to deliver that value. It is going to be tough for many of us. We are already seeing radical changes in consumer spending patterns that do not follow past patterns. These changes have developed from the freedom of more sophisticated consumers, with the result for consumer goods firms that: 'Predictions of consumer behaviour are being thrown into disarray by the chaos that this new freedom is causing' (Buckby, 1998).

In short, the challenge for the future is a constant search for new and better ways of delivering value to customers, because that seems to be the most important source of competitive differentiation that exists. Value does not stand still, and neither do successful companies.

'the challenge for the future is a constant search for new and better ways of delivering value to customers'

However, the trouble is that when managers look for support in meeting this challenge – conventional theory lets them down. The management literature and consultants have produced countless models of how to develop and plan strategy – to the point that it is hardly surprising if the manager confronted by the challenge of 'strategizing' simply reverts to the more familiar issues of internal organization and efficiency.

In fact, it is possible to see some clear and important trends emerging in how we are beginning to think about strategy, and how we understand organizations with robust strategies that deliver solid shareholder value that is sustained.

The picture of value-driven strategy in Figure 2.5 is a way of summarizing that new understanding of the sources of an organization's strategic strength or vulnerability. This model describes a strategic pathway that has three purposes. We can use the model as a checklist to stimulate and develop strategic thinking in our own organization, as a way of moving from strategic planning to real 'strategizing'. The picture also provides a structure for understanding the strengths of current or potential competitors, and a way of gathering together the insights that come from the stories told here.

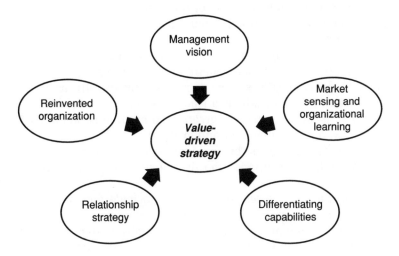

Figure 2.5   The sources of value-driven strategy

'value-driven strategy provides us with a way of pulling together and integrating the huge number of strategy paradigms and models'

Lastly, value-driven strategy provides us with a way of pulling together and integrating the huge number of strategy paradigms and models on offer to make sense of the most important issues in the new competitive realities we are all confronting.

The goal of the strategic pathway is to reduce confusion about strategic issues, and to make market-based strategy operational as a basis for management action. The building blocks for this integration of strategy can be described in the following terms.

Management vision

'wherever you see radical innovation and revolutionary change, whenever a business is reinvented, there is always someone driving that change'

One of the things that the stories in this book underlines is that wherever you see radical innovation and revolutionary change, whenever a business is reinvented, there is always someone driving that change – whether it is Jeff Bezos at Amazon, Michael Dell at Dell Computers, Anita Roddick at the Body Shop, or Lord Blyth at Boots. There is always someone with a sense of purpose, who makes the unconventional happen, and who shares that vision across an organization.

Hamel and Prahalad (1994) suggest that we should evaluate the performance of the management of a company in the following areas, to judge if they are forward looking and visionary:

- Senior management's view of the future compared to that of competitors (conventional and reactive versus distinctive and far-sighted).
- What absorbs most senior management time (re-engineering core processes versus regenerating core strategies).
- How do competitors view our company (mostly as a rule follower versus mostly as a rule maker or rule breaker).
- What is our company's greatest strength (operational efficiency versus innovation and growth).
- What is the focus of our company's attempts to build competitive advantage (mostly catching up versus mostly getting out in front).
- What has mainly set our company's agenda for change (our competitors versus our foresight).
- Do we spend most of our time monitoring the status quo (acting as a 'maintenance engineer') or designing the future (acting as a 'strategic architect').

That visionary strategic architect is not always the CEO. There is a saying that 'the fish rots from the head', which suggests the reason why visionaries may not always be solely those at the top of the organization. The trouble is traditional organizations seem to do their best to stifle the visionaries. Charles Handy recently noted:

> There is a poverty of imagination at the top of some British companies. Companies need people with passion and integrity who can inspire trust in those working for the organization. At present such characters find it difficult to flourish.

Effectively managing talent, not hierarchy, is the first step in building the capability to survive in the revolutionary market-place. One test of failing in this area is the number of a company's key personnel who leave to become competitors.

Market sensing and organizational learning

Increasingly, it seems that in effective organizations the market is pivotal in shaping strategic direction, and positioning on the basis of customer value produces stronger performance than the finance-driven and technology-driven strategies of the past. Value has become the central focus of effective strategy. Superior company performance is based on the continuous search for understanding of the markets where a company has to make its living, and that new understanding has often to break free of corporate culture and industry conventions.

'*Superior company performance is based on the continuous search for understanding of the markets where a company has to make its living*'

This is less about complex business analysis, market research and sophisticated information systems, and far more about the ability of managers to listen and learn from their markets. The failure of the Disney Corporation's EuroDisney venture to achieve success at launch was not caused by a lack of information and conventional market research but from the refusal of management to accept that the European marketplace was fundamentally different from the USA or Japan, with dire consequences for that project which has struggled through to profitability. The success of Daewoo Cars in taking 1 per cent of the British car market in six months (a feat never equalled by their more traditional competitors) was based on sensing the existence of a large market segment that would buy cars in a different way, if given the chance. Encyclopaedia Britannica did not fail to respond to the impact of CD-ROMs on the encyclopaedia business because no-one told them about CD-ROMs – they just did not believe the business could change in this way, with catastrophic effects on the company's market position.

'learning is more about listening and building insights that can produce innovative strategies'

It is fashionable to talk about achieving the status of a 'learning organization', and to interpret this as the need for ever-larger computer systems or spending more on training. This misses the real point – learning is more about listening and building insights that can produce innovative strategies, than it is about storing data and 'mining' it for understanding. Research and data mining produce facts and figures (which may be incredibly useful – see the stories about Amazon.com and Dell Computers, for example). The difference is that market sensing and the capacity to learn produce understanding. Facts and figures are good in plans. Understanding is the basis for new strategy.

Differentiating capabilities

Much of the 1990s thinking about strategy has been dominated by two conflicting goals. One school of thought urges us to focus on core competencies – the five or six areas where our organization can achieve world-class excellence. The critical management task is seen as identifying, cultivating and exploiting those core competencies. Examples of such core competencies include: Sony – the capacity to miniaturize; Philips – optical-media expertise; 3M – competence with sticky tape; BT – microprocessing (handling massive numbers of small accounts).

The implications have been great: water companies attempting to enter telecommunications (one of their core competencies is IT not simply water management); BT marketing gas and electricity to exploit their microprocessing capability. Indeed, this approach is the basis for much of the divestment and strategic alliance strategies of recent years.

'the issue is what activities an organization does better than the rest, that create superior value for customers'

By contrast, as we saw earlier, other advice is that strategic strength only comes from competitive differentiation – doing the things that matter in the market different from competitors, or doing different things. The idea of *differentiating capabilities* combines these two approaches – the issue is what activities an organization does better than the rest, that create superior value for customers.

An example is the success of Avis Europe in driving that company's 'We Try Harder' theme through all its processes and operations, to outstrip its competitors in customer satisfaction and market share. Avis rents the same cars from very similar locations to its competitors – the differentiation lies in that company's ability to link employee and customer satisfaction and to focus its processes on driving those two critical factors.

Relationship strategy

The new era of market-based competition is also one where many of the traditional rules of competition with which we are familiar and comfortable are being replaced by collaboration, alliance and new forms of network or 'hollow' organization.

Relationship marketing has become a dominant approach in many consumer markets and partnering has replaced many traditional buyer–seller relationships in industrial markets. In many business-to-business buyer–seller situations, customer pressure for partnership is drawing sellers from the traditional 'bow-tie' relationship to the integrated 'diamond' relationship, as shown in Figures 2.6 and 2.7. The implications for management and organization design of these types of changes are huge.

Strategic alliances have become the dominant basis for competition in industries such as airlines, IT and telecommunications. Supply chain collaborations are replacing traditional relationships between competitors and their suppliers and

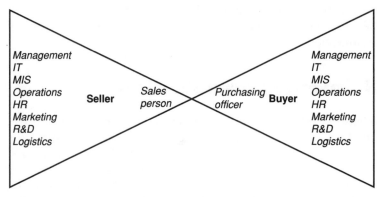

Figure 2.6 The traditional bow-tie relationship between buyers and sellers

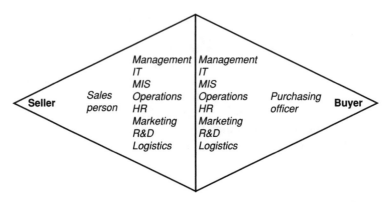

Figure 2.7 The new diamond relationship between buyers and sellers

distributors. Market complexity and risk drives organizations towards partnering to cope, but making good skills and resource gaps that result from the 'leaning' to focus on core competencies also motivates alliances.

'There has been a fundamental shift in interorganizational relationships that should not be underestimated in its importance'

There has been a fundamental shift in interorganizational relationships that should not be underestimated in its importance. Not all organizations will partner with others, but in many industries, collaborations will radically alter the competitive realities faced. Understanding our organizations will increasingly depend on analysing the underlying, but often hidden, relationship structure.

The stories of Dell Computers and British Airways are particularly good illustrations of the power of a strong relationship strategy and the strategic vulnerability created by a weak relationship strategy.

One effect of collaborative relationship-based strategies is that we are seeing the emergence of highly flexible new forms of organization.

Reinvented organization

'the organizational forms of the past will not survive, because they cannot deliver the strategies of the future'

It follows that the organizational forms of the past will not survive, because they cannot deliver the strategies of the future. Traditional hierarchies and functional specializations are being abandoned by companies searching for the speed and flexibility, the learning capacities, the process orientation and the relationship management focus required by new strategies.

There are no models for what these reinvented organizations are going to look like, or for how we will manage in them. We are already seeing the move from function to process, from professional specialists to multifunctional teams, from integrated to 'hollow' organizations, and from traditional goal setting and evaluation to the 'balanced scorecard'.

Indeed, not least among the challenges faced by managers in new-style organizations will be meeting the demands of the 'balanced scorecard' – already operationalized in companies such as BT. The balanced scorecard represents a 'stakeholder' view of the organization and defines the areas for setting objectives, defining measures, forming targets and developing initiatives. Vision and strategy might be turned into goal setting areas such as:

- *Financial* – to succeed financially, how should we appear to our shareholders?
- *Internal business processes* – to satisfy our shareholders and customers, at which business processes must we excel?
- *Learning and growth* – to achieve our vision, how will we sustain our ability to change and improve?
- *Customers* – to achieve our vision, how should we appear to our customers?

However, the chances are that this is only the start of the change in the organizational forms and new criteria of performance we will have to design and manage to drive market-based strategy.

The characteristics of robust strategy

Interesting insights into effective strategy come from the research at Warwick Business School (Doyle, 1998). This work distinguishes between radical, rational and robust strategies to give us some basis for answering the perennial question – what type of strategy actually works?

Radical strategies produce spectacular short-term results, but not sustainable performance for customers or shareholders. Alan Sugar's Amstrad computer business was awesomely successful in selling cheap PCs, imported from low-cost suppliers in the Far East – challenging IBM and ICL in the British marketplace. There was no long-term competitive advantage and Amstrad has crumbled. The explosive growth achieved through acquisition, marketing and PR creates temporary heroes for the business press, but no sustainable competitive advantage.

Rational strategies may also achieve impressive growth by bringing genuine increases in customer value through innovation, but not sustainable competitive advantage. Direct Line pioneered the direct selling of financial services and changed that sector forever. But once the model had been proved – it was easy for just about every competitor to launch their own direct sales on the telephone, which is exactly what they have done.

Robust growth strategies, by contrast, are characterized by companies consistently showing the following attributes:

- they focus continually on superior customer value
- they are based on continuous learning and innovation not on a single innovation or an inflexible strategy
- they make investments in long-term relationships with supply chain partners (supported by world-class information technology), with collaborators, with customers and with employees
- they have a clear strategy of customer focus, and emphasize retaining existing customers
- they achieve world-class competitive performance, not just in their own sectors but against the best in any sector
- they are strong on delivering long-term shareholder value

Examples include companies such as Johnson & Johnson, Dell, 3M, Toshiba, Sony and Toyota (though losing track of these prerequisites can result in the loss of robustness – for example see the story of Marks & Spencer).

The new challenge is about developing robust strategies and this is the purpose of the strategic model described here. Often interesting insights come from comparing the players in a marketplace and trying to identify the robust strategies for the future.

'The need for the new approach is underlined by the obsolescence of the strategies and the strategic thinking of the past'

The need for the new approach is underlined by the obsolescence of the strategies and the strategic thinking of the past. Perhaps one of the best statements of the nature of the modern strategy problem facing companies was that made by the inimitable Peter Drucker in 1993:

A company beset by malaise and steady deterioration suffers from something far more serious than inefficiencies. Its 'business theory' has become obsolete.

The powerful and painful accuracy of this observation is underlined when we look at companies who are suffering from the lack of a robust strategy for the future and are in decline.

The market-based strategy model attempts to provide managers with an operational tool for testing and rebuilding the fundamental business theory that drives their organizations, and for understanding that of their competitors, and it provides the context for reading the stories that follow.

The new principles

For readers who insist on a theoretical basis for the approach taken in the stories that follow and my commentaries on them, the discussion above leads me to lay down the following new strategic principles:

1 *There are (probably) no principles*
   There are almost certainly no enduring or all-encompassing laws that guide strategic decision making. It would be a lot easier if there were. For just about any principle you can formulate, there will be new examples that disprove it. The issue has become one of challenging any assumptions and preconceptions we have about a business and searching out new business models. This is about understanding and innovation, not programming. It is probably the main difference between strategizing and planning.

   'There are almost certainly no enduring or all-encompassing laws that guide strategic decision making'

2 *The myths of monopoly*
   Many of the areas that looked like monopolies were not – they can be attacked and broken, as we saw. Much traditional strategy has been about building monopolistic positions – dominating a geographical market or a product market, or building a unique brand – and these strategies have crashed around managers' ears. The concept may be obsolete – if we say that every company has 100 per cent of its own market, then the issues become clearer (look, for example at the Marks & Spencer story). However, being judged to be 'abusing' market position in an era of unprecedented transparency and openness is getting to be too risky (look, for example, at the BT International and British Airways stories).

3 *The myopia of market share*
   A lot of traditional strategic thinking has been dominated by the importance of market share – high share equals high profit. In some situations this is true – in others it is not. The danger in obsessing about market share is that we forget

   'The danger in obsessing about market share is that we forget something more important – market growth – and we become tied to traditional market definitions'

something more important – market growth – and we become tied to traditional market definitions and wake up to find that the market has changed and new competitors have taken the best parts away from us.

4 *The magic of competition*

'competition has magical powers – it makes the impossible become possible'

Notwithstanding the points above, competition has magical powers – it makes the impossible become possible. British Gas discovered when its 'monopoly' was taken away, that spookily they were suddenly able to make a 10–15 per cent price cut, which had not previously been possible. Magic. When Iceland started to make home deliveries of groceries in the UK, amazingly supermarkets such as Tesco, Sainsbury and even Marks & Spencer suddenly discovered that they could make home deliveries as well, even though it has previously been quite impossible. Magic. Competition also appears magically from nowhere. There you are, quite happily treating your customers badly and overcharging them, because you reckon you are safe from competition, and all of a sudden the impossible happens: alternative therapists displace doctors; supermarkets become banks; books and music sell from the Internet; or direct selling by new competitors displaces those who cling to traditional methods of distribution. Magic.

5 *Revolution and reinvention rule and only robust strategy survives*

The types of market and industry change that we see in the stories are fundamental – they amount to revolution. The winners are those who develop new business models that produce robust strategies, which often fly in the face of the conventional wisdom and strategy models. This is reinvention. Companies which deliver solid shareholder value are those which can sustain robust strategies of superior customer value, relationship management capabilities, and constant learning and innovation.

'The winners are those who develop new business models that produce robust strategies, which often fly in the face of the conventional wisdom and strategy models. This is reinvention'

6 *The most important principle*

If you:

agree with Principles 2 to 5 – then go back to Principle 1;

are in doubt about Principles 2 to 5 – then go back to Principle 1.

Having declared the underlying approach – it is time to let the stories speak for themselves. You may want to re-read this part of the book after you have looked at some of the stories.

References

Buckby, Simon (1998), 'Consumer Choices Fox Marketers', *Financial Times*, 11 November.

Campbell, Andrew and Marcus Alexander (1997), 'What's Wrong With Strategy?', *Harvard Business Review*, November–December, 42–51.

Doyle, Peter (1998), 'Radical Strategies for Profitable Growth', *European Management Journal*, **16**(3), 253–261.

Drucker, Peter (1993), 'A Turnaround Primer', *The Wall Street Journal*, 2 February.

Hamel, Gary and C. K. Prahalad (1994), 'Competing for the Future', *Harvard Business Review*, July–August, 122–128.

Hamel, Gary (1996), 'Strategy As Revolution', *Harvard Business Review*, July–August, 69–82.

Handy, Charles (1998) quoted in Ruth Sunderland and Richard Halstead, 'Executive Crisis Hits Top Firms', *Financial Mail on Sunday*, 27 December.

Martin, Peter (1998), 'Dangerous Gifts', *Financial Times*, 12 December.

Piercy, Nigel F. (1998), 'Marketing Implementation: The Implications of Marketing Paradigm Weakness for the Strategy Execution Process', *Journal of the Academy of Marketing Science*, **26**(3), 222–236.

Piercy, Nigel F., Lloyd C. Harris, Linda D. Peters and Nikala Lane (1997), 'Marketing Management, Market Strategy and Strategic Management: Domain Realignment and Redefinition', *Journal of Strategic Marketing*, **5**(1), 50–62.

Porter, Michael E. (1995), 'What Is Strategy?', *Harvard Business Review*, November–December, 61–78.

Porter, Michael E. (1999) quoted in Surowiecki, James, 'The Return of Michael Porter', *Fortune*, 1 February, 135–138.

Womack, James P. and Daniel T. Jones (1996), *Lean Thinking: Banish Waste and Create Wealth in Your Corporation*, New York and London: Simon and Schuster.

PART II

Stories of Revolution and Reinvention

CHAPTER 3

British Airways

The next generation?*

Our focus here is on the story of British Airways in the period from 1997 to 1999. The tenth anniversary of BA's privatization in 1997 has been taken by company executives, under the leadership of controversial chief executive Robert Ayling, as the start of a new era in the company's strategic development. Changes in the company and reactions to the company's new strategies have been varied and frequently dramatic.

'Changes in the company and reactions to the company's new strategies have been varied and frequently dramatic'

Specifically, the company has undertaken a major rebranding and repositioning strategy and has continued to pursue the sale of assets (although the 'virtual airline' concept remains controversial in the company), and the aggressive pursuit of strategic alliances to create a global network of airlines. The reactions from customers, employees, competitors, regulatory authorities and shareholders have not been wholly favourable, and its current performance is relatively weak in a number of important areas.

---

* This material has been prepared by Nigel F. Piercy, Cardiff Business School, Cardiff University, UK from published material and interviews with company executives. This story follows on from 'British Airways: Where Now for the 'World's Favourite Airline'', published in Nigel F. Piercy (1997), *Market-Led Strategic Change: Transforming the Process of Going to Market* (Oxford: Butterworth-Heinemann), pp. 555–654. © Nigel F. Piercy, 1999.

By late 1998, in common with other airlines, BA was suffering from the world economic crisis, with traffic slowing and unused capacity rising. In the summer of 1998 BA management warned staff of the adverse effects of a slow down in the British economy on business and leisure travel (which was widely interpreted as a warning to staff to expect further cost cutting). The company explains its current disappointing profit results and share price by the impact of the high sterling, high interest rates and the financial crisis in Asia.

Although they are interrelated, we can examine in turn the company's new branding and positioning strategy, launched in 1997, and its underlying rationale; the alliance and networking strategy underpinning the company's globalization; the cost-cutting and outsourcing approaches taken; and the effects on relationships with customers, regulators, competitors and employees. This last context is important – the launch of the company's new branding/positioning strategy in 1997 was followed within months by industrial action by cabin crew which took BA out of the air for three days of peak business.

Branding and positioning

The BA brand remains the central platform for Ayling's strategy and 1997 saw one of the most widely publicized rebranding launches ever.

BA's 'second transformation'

'BA's 'first transformation' was from a state-owned airline, to a successful commercial business after ten years of privatized operation'

BA's ' first transformation' was from a state-owned airline, to a successful commercial business after ten years of privatized operation. On 10 June 1997, BA launched its new corporate identity (code named 'Utopia'), unveiling a portfolio of new visual images, created by a team of international artists, at 136 events in 63 countries around the world. BA's global party included African witch doctors, fireworks in Sydney harbour, and a scale model of Concorde which closed down Time Square in New York. The most overt sign of the new branding was the innovative tail-fin decoration with abstract designs from different cultures, intended to symbolize the company's global reach and cultural empathy. The rebadging cost some £60 million, as paintings of jackals from Africa and wave designs from Japan replaced the traditional

Union Jack motif on BA's aircraft (except on Concorde), to portray the company as a 'caring citizen of the world'.

The launch of the new identity was accompanied by bold new television advertising which aimed to overcome BA's staid and nanny-like image and to replace the traditional 'world's favourite airline' message. The new advertisements (each with a £1 million production budget) presented multicultural images that 'convey the universal joy of shared experience' – excited Italians at a wedding; an American footballer enjoying applause; a Chinese woman being handed her grandchild; an African boy enjoying the rain.

'BA's global party included African witch doctors, fireworks in Sydney harbour, and a scale model of Concorde which closed down Time Square in New York'

The rebranding exercise was BA's response to consumer research that suggested that the company's reputation for professionalism, safety and service has been increasingly qualified by perceptions of starchiness, aloofness, 'masculinity' and arrogance. The research suggested that customers wanted a more personal, culturally diverse and empathetic approach.

Part of the company's goal is to be positioned in the customer's mind not as *British* Airways, but as British *Airways*. The goal is underpinned by the fact that forecasts suggest that by 2000 fewer than 20 per cent of BA passengers will be British. This follows directly from the globalization of the BA brand, and some defensiveness at the company. Robert Ayling commented: 'We don't want to ram our Britishness down people's throats. There's no more empire. We're just a

'Part of the company's goal is to be positioned in the customer's mind not as British Airways, but as British Airways'

small nation on an offshore island trying to make our way in the world.' Indeed, the new branding has been accompanied by a cabin crew retraining programme called 'Kaleidoscope' with the goal of making crew appear 'less British' and 'more informal' and to 'bring out their personalities' – the goal is for cabin crew to 'become the customer's friend for the flight'.

The rebranding followed the launch by BA management in February 1997 of the company's new 'mission, values and goals':

- *The mission* – to be the undisputed leader in world travel.
- *The values* – safe and secure, honest and responsible, innovative and team-spirited, global and caring and a good neighbour.
- *The goals* – 'Customers' Choice' (to be the airline of first choice in key markets); 'Inspired People' (to have inspired teams of people building and benefiting from the company's success); 'Strong Profitability' (meeting investors' expectations and securing the future); and 'Truly Global' (global network, global

outlook, recognized everywhere for superior value in world travel).

'It was more than a new paint job, it is all to do with changing the spirit and ethos of the organization'

Martin George, BA's marketing director described the new identity as 'a symbol of the company we want to be, a promise of a new BA the visual representation of the new mission and values and goals . . . It was more than a new paint job, it is all to do with changing the spirit and ethos of the organization.'

Reactions to the launch

It was unfortunate that the new branding launched in June 1997, was followed by industrial action by cabin staff a month later which kept BA on the ground for three days of the summer season. This action cost £125 million, a narrowly avoided strike by ground staff and weeks of internal disruption, recrimination and bitterness within the company.

Public reactions to the launch – and particularly the move from 'Britishness' to a multicultural identity have been very mixed indeed.

'Fly British Airways, the airline ashamed to be British'

Initial press comment included suggestions that the new BA advertising slogan should be 'Fly British Airways, the airline ashamed to be British'. Some embarrassment also occurred when former Prime Minister Margaret Thatcher (whose government created the privatized BA), was filmed at the design launch objecting to the new tail-fin on a model aircraft at a BA exhibition stand, covering the new design with a folded paper handkerchief, and muttering 'That's better!' for the benefit of the cameras.

Full advantage of the criticism was also taken by BA's traditional enemy, Richard Branson's Virgin Atlantic. After the BA design launch, Virgin painted British flags on its aircraft, and undertook an advertising campaign using BA's former slogan 'Fly the Flag'. Branson has ruled out putting the flag permanently on his aircraft tail fins, but plans to make bigger use of the flag in his new livery, to attempt to cut BA off from using it again.

BA employees have been less than supportive in some cases. *The Log*, a British pilots' magazine, 'reported' an incident when a passenger in a BA plane was sick over the seats in front of him. When asked what should be done the first officer replied 'Let it dry, and tell everyone it's part of the new colour scheme'.

Another BA employee suggested that given the nature of the new ethnic colour scheme, BA should stand for 'Baboon's A***'. Another press story was that when air traffic control ordered a pilot to take second place behind a BA aircraft, he replied that he was happy 'to follow the vomit comet'.

Staff reactions to the new uniforms designed to reflect the ethnic design initiative were hostile enough that the company decided to drop the new uniform designs in January 1998. Cabin crew reactions to the Kaleidoscope training programme focusing on informality have also often been unfavourable, with staff comments suggesting they are being asked to give up their distinctive 'Britishness' just to be fashionable.

More seriously, Ayling faced revolt at the 1997 BA share-holders' meeting, much of which focused on the new 'ethnic' look and image. Ayling was booed and jeered from the floor when he said the idea was to give the airline a more international look and to get rid of the 'aloof' British image. Ayling was accused of being unpatriotic and wasting money.

'Ayling was booed and jeered from the floor when he said the idea was to give the airline a more international look and to get rid of the "aloof" British image'

By May 1998, the BA executive responsible for winning support for the new design initiative championed by Robert Ayling, had 'decided to leave' his post as communications director after less than two years. Industry comments centred on the phrase 'shooting the messenger'. It has also been noted that while Ayling rushed the changes through and personally oversaw the new designs commissioned from international artists, he suffers from colour-blindness that prevents him from distinguishing blues and greens, and so is likely to have had little idea of the visual impact of the designs!

In July 1998, it was apparent that BA was preparing to drop the controversial ethnic art designs from tail-fins on its most popular routes (mainly transatlantic flights), and to return to the type of 'red, white and blue' livery based on the British flag, used on Concorde.

The reasons for the decision are a backlash from the USA in particular, where both customers (and perhaps most significantly partner airlines) want Britain's flagship airline to look more British. This has been underlined by the fact, conceded by Robert Ayling in September 1998, that the majority of BA's business class travellers (who provide half the company's fare revenue on many routes) were unhappy with the multicultural, psychedelic look.

The prospective alliance with American Airlines (AA), and the views of American's CEO, is thought to have been a particularly decisive factor on this issue.

The move towards a global brand

'Ayling is totally committed to globalization, as a key component of his strategy for BA'

In spite of these problems, Ayling is totally committed to globalization, as a key component of his strategy for BA, and the creation of an effective global identity – not just for BA as a company brand, but also for the international network of allied airlines of which BA is a part.

While the BA/American Airlines alliance has been held up by regulators for more than two years (see below), Ayling has been working on the establishment of a single global brand for the alliance. The umbrella brand will apply to the cluster of airlines gathered around BA and AA – possibly including Japan Airlines, Iberia, Lot Polish Airlines, Deutsche BA, Finnair, and all nine BA franchise airlines, but initially comprising Cathay Pacific, Quantas and Canadian Airlines. The working name for the brand was 'World Alliance'. Importantly, Cathay and BA hold 83 per cent of the London/Hong Kong market, and with Quantas will dominate the Australian market. The five member airlines will mount joint advertising and marketing initiatives, and virtually all their 220 000 employees will take part in joint training programmes.

In September 1998 the brand was announced to the press as 'Oneworld' – a network serving 632 destinations in 138 countries with 300 airport lounges, and code-sharing and linked loyalty programmes between member airlines. This umbrella branding is central to Ayling's view that future competition will be driven by global networks of partners, not individual airlines. He was quoted in 1997 as saying:

> Strong competitive pressures are transforming the industry from one of national carriers and a few entrepreneurial interlopers to a smaller number of global players who will be kept on their mettle by an ever-changing fringe of low-cost niche players. To succeed in this world, airlines must find ways to combine maximum system-wide efficiency with individualized care for customers.

'The "second transformation" at BA has been dominated by the company's attempts to build an alliance with American Airlines'

BA's alliance and network strategy

The 'second transformation' at BA has been dominated by the company's attempts to build an alliance with American Airlines. This strategy has been blocked for two years by regulators in the USA, the UK and the European Commission, but its success is central to Ayling's Oneworld brand.

The BA and American Airlines alliance

BA's partnering with airlines in the USA got off to a bad start. Its initial choice of partner was USAir, an industry laggard. Even so, the partnership with USAir generated additional annual revenue of $100 million for BA. The collapse of the relationship with USAir was triggered by the June 1996 announcement of a BA alliance with American Airlines. It appears that when the BA and AA CEOs posed for pictures with the Stars and Stripes draped over their shoulders, they believed that the US authorities would wave the alliance through in a matter of months, while the European Commissioner in Brussels had no jurisdiction and could not interfere. If they believed this, then they were wrong on both counts. More than two years later, the alliance has not received the approval it requires to operate in Europe and the USA. When approval had not been achieved by November 1998, the alliance missed out for the third time on the international airline scheduling conference when slots are allocated for the summer 1999 season.

Reactions from regulators and competitors to the proposed alliance have been problematic. Richard Branson of Virgin displays a 'No Way BA/AA' slogan on his aircraft and on the side of trucks paraded outside BA press meetings, and Gordon Bethune, CEO of Continental Airlines has commented 'With BA and AA together, you have the guys that own Heathrow getting into bed with the guys that own JFK.' In effect, the BA/AA alliance would control over 60 per cent of UK/US flights.

'Richard Branson of Virgin displays a 'No Way BA/AA' slogan on his aircraft and on the side of trucks paraded outside BA press meetings'

The critical issues for regulators have been the number of landing and take-off slots that BA and AA should sacrifice at Heathrow as a price for the alliance, and a variety of protections for competitors, given the size of the proposed alliance. The milestones in the progress towards alliance have been:

- June 1996 – BA and AA announce alliance and their expectation of swift regulatory approval.
- July 1996 – European Commission says it will investigate this and other airline partnerships.

- December 1996 – UK Office of Fair Trading says the alliance should give up 168 weekly take-off and landing slots at Heathrow.
- July 1997 – European Commission says alliance must give up 350 Heathrow slots.
- May 1998 – US Justice Department regards the alliance as anti-competitive and says alliance should be blocked unless the airlines give up 336 Heathrow slots.
- July 1998 – European Commissioner recommends alliance be allowed to go ahead if the alliance gives up 267 slots at Heathrow and Gatwick (on specified routes, so no airline can control more than half the flights on a route), but denied the companies the ability to operate a joint frequent flyer programme unless they allow other airlines to participate. Approval by UK Trade and Industry Secretary and US Department of Transportation still required.
- August 1998 – British Trade Secretary and European Commissioner are not agreed on whether BA will have to give up slots at Heathrow and Gatwick, or can sell them (for around £530 million).
- September 1998 – the European Union transport commissioner, Neil Kinnock, says that under EU law, airlines are not allowed to buy and sell slots, although the British Office of Fair Trading disagreed.
- October 1998 – the BA/AA alliance was threatened with further postponement after the USA walked out of talks with the UK authorities on 'open skies' because of lack of progress, with the US authorities maintaining that an open skies agreement is a precondition for them to approve the BA alliance.
- November 1998 – unwilling to give up slots at Heathrow without compensation, BA announced it was scaling down its full alliance plans and would pursue a looser code-sharing and marketing agreement with AA (also involving Quantas, Cathay Pacific and Canadian Airlines), to meet the immediate response from US regulators that this link with AA would generate further investigations likely to last beyond year 2000 (they still want 'open skies' as a prerequisite).
- November 1998 – BA suggests that the US authorities cannot block the code-sharing plan, further straining relationships.
- December 1998 – BA asks the British government to delay its final decision on the planned alliance until the dispute with the US government on open skies is resolved.

Ayling is committed to alliance to enable BA to compete with the other airline partnerships already operating. These include the

KLM/Northwestern partnership, the Star Alliance (led by Lufthansa and United Airlines), and the partnership between Delta, Swissair, Austrian Airlines and Sabena in Belgium. Ayling has also accused the EC Commissioner of bias in allowing these alliances to proceed and operate, while blocking BA and AA for two years. However, while the full-scale merger of BA and AA was seen as a possibility in 1996, Ayling has made it clear that if the price demanded by regulators for alliance is too high, then the companies will revert to a simple code-sharing and joint marketing relationship, allowing joint collaboration in selling seats but precluding collaboration on schedules or fares. Meantime, BA has suspended flights from several UK regional airports to the USA on the grounds that the routes are not profitable without AA participation, with the consequent prospect of job losses in those locations. High profile BA orders for new aircraft have also been placed astutely. Abandoning BA's record of buying only from Boeing, Ayling placed a £5 billion order with the European Airbus consortium for 188 short-haul jets, while placing a £3 billion order with Boeing for 777 long-range twin-jets from the USA in August 1998.

The 'Oneworld' alliance

From the base of the proposed BA/AA alliance, BA is committed to a larger network operating under the new Oneworld umbrella brand. Progress towards this goal has continued while the alliance with AA has been blocked. Key stages in this building process, leading to the announcement of the Oneworld brand in 1998, have been:

'From the base of the proposed BA/ AA alliance, BA is committed to a larger network operating under the new Oneworld umbrella brand'

- August 1997 – Richard Branson of Virgin makes a surprise press announcement that BA has a 'secret global deal' involving BA/AA with Japan Airlines and KLM, which should be stopped.
- September 1997 – plans to include Iberia of Spain in the alliance fall through, but by January 1998 a looser code-sharing agreement with BA and AA holding equity in Iberia is being discussed with BA and AA each taking a 10 per cent stake.
- October 1997 – BA and Finnair announce a marketing and network alliance in Scandinavia to challenge the Scandinavian Airlines System (part of the Star alliance) dominance.
- January 1998 – BA and Lot Polish Airlines announce a partnership to counter Lufthansa's strength in Poland.

- May 1998 – news breaks of an imminent end to the dispute between BA and USAir, as a prelude to USAir joining the BA/AA alliance (AA and USAir already have a marketing agreement).
- September 1998 – BA/AA widen their alliance to include Cathay Pacific in Hong Kong, Australia's Quantas and Canadian Airlines.
- September 1998 – the Oneworld alliance branding is announced by BA.
- September 1998 – although designed specifically to avoid regulatory issues, the European Commissioner announces that he is scrutinizing the plans and may take action.
- December 1998 – Finnair, the state-controlled Finnish carrier joins Oneworld.
- January 1999 – Japan Airlines plans to introduce code-sharing flights with BA and Cathay Pacific, seen as a move by Asia's largest carrier towards alliance.

Winning and losing the hearts and minds of BA employees

However, in spite of the importance of rebranding and global alliances, closer to home, relationships between management and employees at BA have also been high on the agenda during this period.

Industrial action looms

Even the threat of industrial action by staff is severely damaging to an airline. The threat of disruption is enough to persuade many passengers to travel with another airline. Actual industrial action is worse. One industry executive describes the situation for an airline experiencing industrial action: 'they watch their reputation die every day this drags on . . . Travellers do not wait for a dispute to be settled, they just book a flight with a different carrier.'

In the summer of 1996, BA pilots voted for strike action because company cutbacks had reduced their attractive allowances. In spite of his reputation as a New Labour-voting friend of Tony Blair, Ayling's reaction was abrupt and confrontational. He raised the stakes by threatening to shut down much of BA's

'they watch their reputation die every day this drags on . . . Travellers do not wait for a dispute to be settled, they just book a flight with a different carrier'

Gatwick Airport operation if the strike went ahead. The strike did not happen.

However, a year later BA was facing a second 'summer of discontent'. In June 1997, baggage handlers, catering staff and cabin crew were all voting on whether to stage industrial action. The protest by 9000 ground staff and 8000 cabin staff was over BA's efficiency plans, cost cutting and job losses planned, and the company's imposition of restructuring without negotiation.

On 9 July 1997 between 2000 and 3000 BA cabin crew stopped work, bringing most of BA's Heathrow traffic to a halt. (A large proportion of the absent staff stayed home 'sick' rather than confront the dilemma whether to strike or not.) Two days into the cabin crew stoppage, 9000 ground staff threatened to join the industrial action (mainly in protest at the sale of BA's catering business).

The strategies adopted by Ayling and BA management in the period leading up to the strike and during the industrial action have been described as the confrontational actions of 'bully-boys', on a par with nineteenth-century mill-owners. Company actions and threats included the following:

- In June, Ayling announced that ground staff joining walk-outs would receive dismissal notices because they would be breaching a 'no-strike' agreement, and began press advertising for 1000 new recruits to replace dismissed strikers.
- The company also leaked plans in June to use 'any tactics available' to keep services flying, including using foreign cabin crew, training management staff to replace strikers and calling on partner airlines to provide their off-duty staff to BA.
- BA formed a 'strikebusting force' secretly recruited and trained before the strike.
- Staff were sent warning letters suggesting if they went on strike, they would lose travel perks and be disqualified for promotion, and might lose pension rights.
- Strikers were warned they could be sued personally for damages.
- Strikers' picket lines were conspicuously filmed by BA surveillance officers (indeed, the picket lines were said to be the prettiest ever seen in Britain, and it is rumoured that attending police officers enthused about persistent offers of boiled sweets and blankets from the striking cabin crew).
- Staff absent on sick leave during the strike were told they would be presumed to be on strike, unless they produced doctors' letters.
- In the midst of the strike, BA threatened to sue the union for major damages.

'The three-day stoppage is estimated to have cost BA £125 million, and a lot of goodwill from staff and customers'

The stakes in the cabin crew strike were substantial. BA stood to gain: savings of £42 million a year from cabin crew; more efficient roster patterns and lower starting salaries; and a more favourable climate for pushing through further savings in the future. The costs were also large. The three-day stoppage is estimated to have cost BA £125 million, and a lot of goodwill from staff and customers.

The aftermath of the strike

Ayling achieved the implementation of his cost-saving plan for cabin staffing. However, the £125 million cost of the strike was largely responsible for an 8.5 per cent fall in BA's 1997 profits. The most direct effects were reduced aircraft occupancy levels, as well as falling ticket prices and sales for first and business class seats on BA. BA's passenger numbers fell nearly 5 per cent following the strike, but with many business travellers in the first and club class group transferring to other airlines, there was a 9 per cent fall in BA's premium traffic.

However, the hidden costs to be paid are in weakened employee relations in the company, damage to BA's reputation and widespread criticism of Ayling's aggressive 'macho-management' style, and the long-term impact of these issues on customer service and retention. Indeed, in September 1997 there were still threats of renewed industrial action before negotiations reached a peaceful conclusion.

Winning BA people back

BA executives admit they did not expect the strike to actually happen and they were wrong-footed when it did. In the aftermath managers were asking themselves why they had failed to sell their vision for the company's future to thousands of staff. By the autumn of 1997, BA had started an intensive 'hearts and minds' drive to improve staff morale, and particularly the damage done by the cabin crew strike. At a weekend meeting Robert Ayling pledged to be more 'caring', and to put people back at the top of the BA management agenda. In a message to staff, Ayling said 'today is the day when I put a stake in the ground and re-involve everyone in this company'.

Ayling established a 'Way Forward' group led by Martin George, BA marketing director, to learn lessons from the dispute with staff and to produce a 'new spirit of co-operation'. Three subgroups were created to look at how morale and motivation could be rebuilt, to find ways to mend customer relationships and repair the damage to BA's reputation, and to ensure the airline gets the 'basics of customer service right'.

Ayling received a boost to his plans in January 1999 when his 2000 pilots' union backed his cost-cutting plan and recommended to its members that they spend more time flying.

But is BA still Ayling?

Some executives have suggested that the cabin crew strike was not just about the pay restructuring deal but was caused by much deeper concerns about the direction in which BA is being taken by Robert Ayling. It is suggested that Ayling's change strategy, and particularly his way of managing it, has sown confusion and loss of morale within BA, and the real cost of the confrontational stance during the strike will be a bitter internal war of attrition. He is widely seen to have failed to carry the workforce with him in rebuilding BA.

The striking cabin crew were incensed at the way they had been treated by the company and especially at what they saw as the CEO's arrogance. A former BA executive observed 'Morale within the airline is terrible. People think he is doing the right thing, but the timing and tactics have been a disaster'.

'Morale within the airline is terrible. People think he is doing the right thing, but the timing and tactics have been a disaster'

Certainly, Ayling's stance during the strike has been regarded by many in the industry as heavy-handed in the extreme, and he was given a very rough ride by shareholders at the 1997 annual general meeting, and was severely criticized for alienating the staff of BA (many of the shareholders are past or present BA staff).

Indicative of the strength of feeling is the fact that Ayling has also been vilified in an Internet 'cyberspace smear campaign' accusing BA management of serious irregularities and suggesting that BA's board want to dismiss the CEO. More seriously, in May 1998 *Sunday Business* reported that Ayling's departure from BA was 'on stand-by', suggesting that chairman Sir Colin Marshall and the BA board was waiting only for the right opportunity to present Ayling's departure as a smooth transition, and that interim candidates were already slated in the company. A BA executive was quoted as saying 'It's not a matter of if, it's a matter of when. Ayling won't go unless it can be seen to be his choice. He needs to have the right job to go to – he's not going to be pushed out.' Since then Ayling has repeatedly denied this and other reports that he has been offered a post in Prime Minister Tony Blair's administration, or that he has any interest in such a career move. By November 1998, Lord Marshall again insisted to the City that Ayling's job was not at risk. City opinion is that 1999 is 'make or break' year for Ayling.

Divestment and outsourcing – the 'virtual airline'?

In addition to global branding and alliance, Ayling's strategy relies on a large and effective cost-cutting strategy – his goal is to reduce BA's cost structure by £1 billion by 2000. He has recently admitted that this is proving more difficult to achieve than anticipated, but that success is essential to avoid the company moving into loss by the end of the decade. By the end of 1998, Ayling's savings had reached £600 million.

'Ayling becomes angry when it is suggested he is building a "virtual airline" that consists primarily of a brand and core staffing'

Ayling becomes angry when it is suggested he is building a 'virtual airline' that consists primarily of a brand and core staffing. None the less, his strategy involves major cost-cutting programmes, the sale of many assets replaced by outsourcing, creating innovative financing deals to lease aircraft instead of buying them and franchising the BA brand to other airlines.

Indeed, it has been noted that this slimming by BA may be a major strength if there is a general downturn in the airline business.

Cost cutting

Ayling's tenure as CEO at BA has been associated with massive cost cutting from the start. Indeed, one sticking point triggering the 1997 cabin crew strike was the £42 million savings demanded from this part of the business. In May 1997 it became apparent that economies were going to lead to the loss of 5000 jobs, as part of the company's Business Efficiency Programme. BA also continues to seek a way of reducing the commissions paid to travel agents. Relationships between BA and travel agents (who sell 85 per cent of all air tickets in the UK) remain strained. Most controversial has been the sale of many BA assets, and their replacement with outsourced services. For example, in 1998 this involved the decision to close all US retail ticket offices and the substitution of Internet-based sales for retail customers.

Divestment and outsourcing

By the end of 1997, Ayling announced that the sale of its in-flight catering operation to Gate Gourmet (a Swissair company) for £65 million, marked the end of his restructuring and asset disposals plan (although he did not rule out future disposals). Gate Gourmet has a ten-year contract to produce BA's in-flight meals at Heathrow. (The threatened protest strike by catering workers was averted by allowing catering employees to retain BA conditions of employment including cheap flights to Asia, highly valued by the largely Asian workforce.)

Ayling's stated view is that BA should sell any and all subsidiary businesses that could be operated more cheaply by third parties. Since 1996, in addition to the catering business, he has sold BA's wheels, brakes and gear overhaul units, and a large part of its stake in the Galileo International computerized reservation system.

'Ayling's stated view is that BA should sell any and all subsidiary businesses that could be operated more cheaply by third parties'

BA is also continuing involvement in franchising its brand to numerous low-cost and regional operators, particularly for low-margin charter holiday flight business. These carriers normally fly in BA colours but are operated independently and pay lower wages to cabin crew and pilots. One example is the company Flying Colours (which runs the Club 18–30 holiday resorts), which is operating BA Boeing 777s out of Gatwick, flying as Aircraft Management Ltd, a joint venture with BA. In other cases, independent operators fly small aircraft on low volume regional routes as BA franchisees.

Financing new aircraft

Ayling's policy of outsourcing extends to the aircraft. In February 1998, he told Boeing and Airbus Industrie, the aircraft manufacturers, to devise 'innovative' ways of funding aircraft acquisition to allow BA to reduce substantially the capital assets it owns. He said then that:

> Airlines are operating companies. Our strength is in our network and in our ability to manage and distribute [aircraft] capacity. If we can find a way of not having some of the risk of ownership, that would be an advantage.

His view is that BA is too dependent on assets and is looking to other companies to assume ownership of aircraft. The current BA fleet has 219 aircraft on the balance sheet and a further 89 operated under off-balance sheet leases.

As a result, in the 1998 deal for the Airbus supply of £600 million of short-haul jets, Airbus retains ownership of the aircraft with BA leasing them back through its Irish-based finance company. BA is said to favour the option of leasing the planes by the hour when they are in the air, leaving the manufacturers liable for everything from maintenance and repair costs to the residual values when the aircraft reach the end of their working lives.

Similarly, BA is negotiating a deal with General Electric (supplier of Boeing engines), to sell GE a package of older Boeing aircraft in the BA fleet and then to lease the aircraft back.

Customer relationships

The effects of the new BA strategy have not been well received by all customer groups. Clearly, the 1997 strike has left a problem of disgruntled passengers, some of whom have not brought their business back to BA after the end of the strike.

The most visible signs of BA's problem in winning back customers have been a series of low-price campaigns. In September 1997, the company launched a series of deep price cuts on flights to more than a hundred cities. While BA fares had traditionally been slightly higher than the competition, the problems associated with the strike led in the direction of discount pricing. Inevitably, leading competitors such as Virgin Atlantic and United Airlines retaliated with their own price discounts. In January 1998, following Virgin's launch of price reductions, BA produced further deep price cut special offers, e.g. taking the London/New York fare down from £329 to £189 and London/Johannesburg from £727 to £399. In the summer of 1998, BA launched a surprise 'summer sale' of two million cheap tickets, though with disappointing sales results. The summer season of 1998 also saw BA urging staff to sell cheap tickets to relatives and friends with a message in the in-house newsletter that 'here's the chance to bring out the salesperson in everyone'. Complaints about BA staff touting tickets to strangers in clubs and pubs are accompanied by rumours that seats to Asia in particular are being off-loaded through staff travel clubs and bucket shops.

'By late 1998, however, the loss of BA's position with business class passengers was a major cause for concern'

By late 1998, however, the loss of BA's position with business class passengers was a major cause for concern for the BA board of directors. Aside from general damage to BA's reputation for customer service, BA figures showed a loss of £50 million in

revenue because long-haul Club World customers were transferring to rival airlines to receive better service.

At the same time, an internal BA survey of Gold Card members
(the most frequent BA flyers), showed 48 per cent now prefer to
fly with BA's business class competitors.

While Club World accounts for only 5 per cent of BA's
passengers, it generates 25 per cent of the airline's revenue. On its
own, the £50 million drop in sales is a small change in sales of £2
billion in BA's Club World, but the emergence of a brand-
switching issue is a major concern. In particular, suggestions that
competitors have overtaken BA in customer service, that BA's
frequent flyer programme is less attractive than others, and the
possibility that BA has been wrong-footed by major corporate
customers trading down to economy travel pose serious threats.

BA plans a new Club World service in 1999 with improved
catering, quicker check-in, new in-flight entertainment, quicker
luggage delivery and better seats. However, this may only be
enough to catch up with the standards now set by rivals such as
Virgin and Singapore Airlines who have invested heavily in
innovative upgrades to their business class services.

In November 1998, BA – the 'world's favourite airline' – had
the humiliation of seeing itself beaten by Virgin Atlantic winning
the 'Best British Airline' title in the prestigious Daily Telegraph
Travel Awards. Indeed, BA narrowly missed the further insult of
being beaten by Go, its own budget airline subsidiary.

By 1998 there was also some hostile comment emerging about
the type of service provided by airline alliances. Corporate travel
buyers have expressed concerns about the reduction in choice,
higher prices and variation in quality between alliance partners,
which are possible threats from airline networks. There have also
been suggestions that code-sharing, where a passenger books a
seat with one airline and ends up being carried by another,
amounts to 'a fraud on the consumer' (the words of Robert
Crandall, American Airlines' chairman speaking *before* the BA/
AA alliance was mooted). Corporate travel buyers in 1999
complained that the alliances do not keep the promise of seamless
service because of lack of integration and co-operation between
diverse alliance member airlines, and that there is no sign yet of
the promised reduction in long-haul fares.

Robert Ayling's City briefing in January 1999 saw BA shares
fall further as he revealed that he had been unable to stop the
erosion in premium passenger numbers – down 2.4 per cent in
October and 2.9 per cent in November 1998 – and that yields
(the amount earned per seat) were still falling. From a summer
peak of 703p, BA shares settled at 405p – giving a market value
for the company down to £4.2 billion. Ayling is sending cabin

'each employee is expected to become a "sales deputy" and sell a first or business class ticket'

crew to small companies and travel agents to try to rebuild business class sales – each employee is expected to become a 'sales deputy' and sell a first or business class ticket.

Competition and BA's performance in 1997–98

The Virgin situation

There is no doubt that BA's most persistent, vocal and highly publicized source of competitive pressure is Richard Branson and his Virgin Atlantic airline. Branson has achieved the notable position of simultaneously attacking BA for abusing its market position through *high* prices, and abusing its market position to drive out competitors through *low* prices. Every move made by BA is publicly and noisily opposed by Virgin, for example:

- Branson has vocally opposed the BA alliance with American Airlines with his 'No Way BA/AA' slogan, funding from his 'war chest', and personal appeals to the Civil Aviation Authority and the European and US authorities. He has attacked on the basis that the alliance will force prices up and act anti-competitively.
- Branson has equally noisily attacked BA's price-cutting campaign and new 'no-frills' European operation as predatory and designed to remove competitors by pricing them out of the market.
- Branson has also organized a campaign to force BA and AA to give up Heathrow slots rather than being allowed to sell them.
- It was Branson who accused BA of a 'secret global deal' ahead of the Oneworld announcement, to 'destroy competition', unhelpfully timed to reach the ears of the European Commissioner while he was still examining the BA/AA alliance proposal.
- The long-running battles between Virgin and BA in the US courts continued through 1998, with Virgin claiming $1 billion in damages from BA.
- Even BA's tactical marketing programmes, like the joint promotion with the Sainsbury supermarket chain for Christmas 1997, attract immediate 'spoiling' tactical responses from Virgin.

- Branson's complaint to the European Commission triggered the 1998 threat of a £900 million fine to be paid by BA as a penalty for 'dirty tricks' through its loyalty discount scheme with travel agents and discounts to corporate customers. (BA cut basic commission to travel agents from 9 per cent to 7 per cent, and offered 3 per cent extra if they increased the sale of tickets, with the effect that agents must increase the number of tickets sold each month or suffer reduced commission. Since the agents can only achieve this by transferring business from other carriers, the European Commissioner has to decide if this is an abuse of market power by BA. Interestingly, in May 1998 it was apparent that the effect of the scheme was that sales of BA tickets through travel agents had, in fact, fallen 10 per cent because of the agents' hostility to the scheme.)
- In January 1999, Branson, together with his ally Stelios Haji-loannou of easyJet, were vocal in their attack on BA's 'back-door price increases' of up to 15 per cent created by transferring passenger service charges from airline costs absorbed in the ticket price to the additional 'taxes' paid by the passenger on top of the ticket price.

BA's management has had to learn to live with the fact that every move they make will be scrutinized and attacked personally by Richard Branson.

'BA's management has had to learn to live with the fact that every move they make will be scrutinized and attacked personally by Richard Branson'

New products

In addition to plans to upgrade the services provided to first and business class passengers, BA has a number of new product and service directions.

Spring 1998 saw the launch of 'Go', a new low-cost airline to compete with easyJet, Debonair and Virgin Express, in offering a 'no-frills' service from the UK to Europe with ultra-low fares. This operation is run by Barbara Cassani as a separate entity to the main BA airline.

In 1998 plans were being developed between BA and BAA (the airports' operator) to develop a railway route through South London to link with the Channel Tunnel, as well as other ways of making Heathrow airport a major rail hub. This would counter the dual threat of travellers from UK to Europe using 'no-frills' air operators, and passengers transferring travel plans from air to rail by using the Eurostar rail service through the Channel Tunnel. BA is also attempting to take a 40 per cent stake in the British arm of Eurostar from London & Continental, with a further 40 per cent to be taken by the bus and rail operator National Express.

The prospect is new products combining air and rail travel on the same ticket.

In January 1999 BA bid £75 million to buy Cityflyer Express – one of its short-haul franchisee airlines flying to fifteen European destinations out of Gatwick under BA colours. Cityflyer has 12 per cent of the Gatwick slots, compared to BA's 32 per cent. With 44 per cent of the Gatwick slots under its control, BA plans to move some of its less profitable routes out of Heathrow. Amid claims by Virgin that it should have been allowed to bid for Cityflyer and was not given the chance, the BA bid was referred to the Mergers and Monopolies Commission for investigation. The US regulatory authorities warned that further restrictions in access to Gatwick for US airlines would be an impediment to BA's alliance plans.

'the company aims "to become as successful in global financial services as we are in world travel"'

BA has also said that the company aims 'to become as successful in global financial services as we are in world travel'. The airline is expanding its travel insurance, foreign currency and credit card services under a single brand and initially targeting its 600 000 Executive Club members.

These areas reflect Ayling's aspiration to compete by offering a broader package of service in an 'A to Z' positioning.

In fact, BA's financial performance over this period has been mixed, as shown in Table 3.1.

The full year results announced in May 1998 showed a 9.4 per cent cut in pre-tax profits to £580 million. Without the support of lower fuel prices and the BA cost-cutting programme, the fall in profits would have been substantially larger. Staff numbers actually rose by 2.6 per cent in the year, though total employee costs fell by 1.6 per cent, as a result of the deal for lower starting salaries. The efficiency programme has produced savings of £250 million, translating into annual savings of £700 million by 2000–2001, leaving a further £300 millions of savings to be

Table 3.1   British Airways Financials 1995–99

Year to March	1995	1996	1997	1998	1999 (estimated)
Turnover	£6.60 bn	£7.18 bn	£7.76 bn	£8.66 bn	£9.20 bn
Pre-tax profit	£280 mn	£327 mn	£585 mn	£580 mn	£429 mn
Earnings per share	27.6p	24.5p	44.2p	42.0p	34.0p
Dividend per share	11.1p	12.4p	13.6p	16.6p	18.0p

Source: *Daily Telegraph*, 10 November 1998

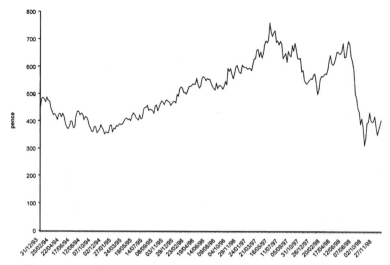

Figure 3.1 BA's share value, 1993–98 (unadjusted prices). Source:
Datastream

made, to reach Ayling's goal of £1 billion out of the cost
structure. However, BA reported poor first quarter results in
September 1998, with pre-tax profit down to around £100
million. Blame was placed on the strong sterling, high
interest rates, and the financial crisis in Asia, with the   *'By the end of*
company performing reasonably well in the USA and   *1998, Ayling was*
Europe but very badly in Asia. By the end of 1998,   *cutting his*
Ayling was cutting his expansion plans dramatically –   *expansion plans*
plans for 9 per cent growth were reduced to 2 per   *dramatically'*
cent.

The performance of BA's shares through the late-1990s is
shown in Figure 3.1.

Sources

Alexander, Andrew (1998), 'BA Trims its Alliance Plans as Watchdogs Set
    Too High A Price', *Daily Mail*, 31 October.
Anderson, Simon (1998), 'BA Poised to Unveil Global Alliances', *Daily
    Telegraph*, 21 September.
Eakin, Jan (1998), 'BA Buffeted From Several Sides At Once', *Daily Telegraph*,
    10 August.
Hill, Michael (1998) '"Aloof" BA Stewardesses Learn To Be Less British',
    Daily Telegraph, 6 July.

Lynn, Matthew and Edward Welsh (1997), 'Air Sick', *Sunday Times*, 13 July.

Mazur, Laura (1997), *Marketing Business*, September.

O'Connell, Dominic (1998), 'Ayling Departure "On Stand-By" At BA', *Sunday Business*, 25 May.

O'Connell, Dominic (1998), 'BA Morale and Figures Dive', *Sunday Business*, 8 November.

O'Connell, Dominic (1998), 'BA Rethink As Ayling Tries To Fill From the Front', *Sunday Business*, 6 December.

O'Connell, Dominic (1998), 'BA Turns Staff Into Sales Army', *Sunday Business*, 16 August.

Parsley, David (1998), 'BA Alliance Prepares for Take-Off', *Sunday Times*, 12 July.

Parsley, David (1998), 'BAnnus Horribilis', *Sunday Times*, December.

Parsley, David (1998) 'Business Passengers Desert BA', *Sunday Times*, September 20.

Randall, Jeff (1999), 'Ayling's Judgement Year', *Sunday Business*, 3 January.

Simms, Jane (1997), 'Flight of Fantasy', *Marketing Business*, October.

Skapinker, Michael (1997) 'BA Flies Through Turbulent Skies', *Financial Times*, 6 November.

Skapinker, Michael (1998), 'BA Profits Hit By Strike and Strong Pound', *Financial Times*, 29 January.

Skapinker, Michael (1998), 'BA Tries To Propel Its Shares Through the Cloud Layer', *Financial Times*, 9 September.

Skapinker, Michael (1998), 'Alliances: Passengers not Convinced', *Financial Times*, 19 November.

Taylor, Robert (1997), 'Flying in the Face of Partnership', *Financial Times*, 10 July.

CHAPTER 4

Dell Computers*

The Dell direct business model

If our goals are to uncover processes of revolution and reinvention, it is impossible to get far without examining one of the most amazing stories of business achievement in the last twenty years – Michael Dell's creation and continual reinvention of the process by which personal computers go to market. Dell has built,

'one of the most amazing stories of business achievement in the last twenty years'

since 1984, a Fortune 500 company operating globally and achieving sales of around $17 billion by 1998, and with profit results constantly outstripping market expectations. He did this be reinventing the way in which personal computers (PCs) are bought and constantly refining his company's processes to deliver superior value to customers.

The rate of change in this company quickly outdates historical financials, but Table 4.1 shows the key performance achievements for recent financial years up to the year ending 1 February 1998.

---

* This material has been produced by Nigel F. Piercy from secondary sources and discussions with industry executives. © Nigel F. Piercy.

Table 4.1 **Dell's key financial results, 1994–98**

	1994	1995	1996	1997	1998
Turnover	$2873 mn	$3475 mn	$5296 mn	$7759 mn	$12327 mn
Operating profit (loss)	$(39) mn	$249 mn	$377 mn	$714 mn	$1,316 mn
Earnings per share*	$(0.07)	$0.23	$0.36	$0.75	$1.44
Total shareholder equity	$471 mn	$652 mn	$973 mn	$806 mn	$1293 mn

* Adjusted to allow for 2-for-1 splits of common stock in March 1998 and July 1997.

The origins of Dell Computers

By the age of twelve, Michael Dell had obtained a licence to sell postage stamps to collectors and was organizing auctions for stamp enthusiasts. However, in the 1980s Dell was planning to follow in his father's footsteps and become a doctor, and he had started a degree in biology at the University of Texas, Austin in 1983. The early 1980s in Texas saw the growth of enthusiasm and interest in PCs – then mainly sold by specialist electronics retailers, who knew little about computers or computing. Interested in the hardware, Dell spent time playing with an IBM PC in his student bedroom, and made some interesting discoveries.

The IBM PC then sold in the retail store for around $3000, and was bought in by the retailer for around $2000. Dell's reasoning was that it was unreasonable for the retailers to get $1000 when they knew less about the computer than he did. He also worked out that the same PC probably cost IBM $600–700 to make, and that most of the components and technology were not even IBM's, but came from companies such as Intel and Microsoft and other technology suppliers. This reasoning led to the two critical elements in the Dell Computer Corporation's business model: selling direct to computer users instead of through retailers or distributors who wanted a mark-up; and buying components and technology direct from producers to assemble a better PC than IBM.

'Dell Computer Corporation's business model: selling direct to computer users instead of through retailers or distributors who wanted a mark-up; and buying components and technology direct from producers'

The immediate result was that Dell started a computer business from his student dormitory, buying IBM PCs on the 'grey market', upgrading them, and reselling them direct to companies and home users. This operation turned into a business selling between $50 000 and $80 000 from the student dorm. His parents hated the idea of him running a computer business instead of becoming a doctor, so he had to hide the evidence on family visits to the university. Eventually they conceded to the inevitable.

Dropping out of university, Michael Dell used $1000 of savings to acquire a 1000 square foot office. The business outgrew the office in its first month.

Dell's present position

Michael Dell's simple business insight was that he could bypass the dealer channel through which PCs were then being sold, by selling direct to customers and building products to order, instead of guessing what people would want and producing stock while waiting for sales. This was the origin of what has become known as Dell's 'direct business model'.

The results have been spectacular. From a standing start in 1984, at thirty-three Michael Dell's personal worth in 1998 was estimated as $5.5 billion, and he owns 16 per cent of the Dell Computer Corporation, which has a market value by now pushing $50 billion. He has some claim to being the wealthiest Texan ever – richer than Ross Perot or the Hunt brothers. In fact, some estimates make Michael Dell the fourth-richest man in the USA. An intense and edgy man, he appears something of a 'computer geek', and dislikes travelling, preferring to stay home with his family in his $45 million castle in Austin, Texas.

The business went public in 1988. In 1990 a Dell share was worth 39 cents, by 1998 it was around $114, giving a growth rate that is almost 30 000 per cent. To put this in context: an investment of $10 000 in Dell shares in1990, would be worth just under $3 million at the end of 1998. In the latter part of the 1990s Dell was growing at an average of 55 per cent a year, and in the third quarter of 1997, Wall Street was stunned by an awesome 71 per cent profit growth. In the worldwide PC market, Dell claims to be outselling IBM and to be rapidly catching the market leader, Compaq. Dell's sales at the end of 1998 were consistently growing at six times the industry rate and this with the lowest cost structure of any of the major firms in the industry.

This has been achieved in a marketplace that is highly concentrated and aggressively competitive. The

'Dell's sales at the end of 1998 were consistently growing at six times the industry rate and this with the lowest cost structure of any of the major firms in the industry'

top four suppliers hold around 70 per cent of the world market and only the big PC makers can achieve economies of scale. The cost advantage achieved by Dell's business model is that overhead costs amount to just 11.6 per cent of sales compared to 15 per cent for Compaq, not least of the difference is Dell's ability to consistently turn over its inventory in eight days.

As the market prices of PCs have tumbled during the 1990s, this is the marketplace where players such as Packard-Bell and AST Research have been losers in the USA, and Apple has seen its market share halved. In Europe, several PC makers, including Escom in Germany, have gone bust. Others have withdrawn from the PC market altogether, for example ICL in the UK, or become specialist niche suppliers, for example Olivetti in portables and business servers. At the same time, Dell has grown in volume, profit, market share and international presence. Following launch in the UK in 1987, Dell now manufactures in Round Rock, near Austin, Texas; in Limerick, Ireland, in Penang, Malaysia, and in Xiamen, China, and is able to offer a 'Global Enterprise Program' to meet the worldwide needs of its largest customers by operating in 150 countries. By 1998, Dell employed around 23 000 people worldwide.

In fact, things have not always been so rosy for Dell. The company has been through what Michael Dell admits were 'very scary times'. For example, in 1990 a problem with the supply of memory chips caused a sharp decline in Dell's profits, and in 1993 the company had to issue a profit warning and withdrew a

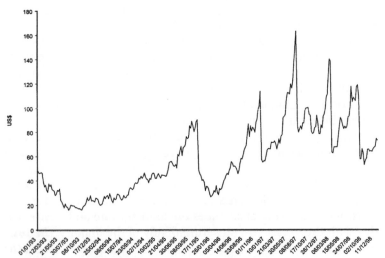

Figure 4.1 Dell's share value, 1993–98 (unadjusted prices). Source: Datastream

share issue, after intense competition in the industry had caused a fall in profits. Dell has not always been right. In 1989 Dell went into the retail PC business, thinking that the direct business would not grow enough to support the company, and entered computer superstores and warehouse clubs. Low profits resulted, the company realized that it has made a mistake and exited from the retail market.

None the less, Dell's performance through the 1990s has been impressive, and it is based on a simple business model. The performance of Dell's shares is shown in Figure 4.1 (these figures are not adjusted for the stock splits in July 1997 and March 1998).

A fall in Dell's share value in December 1998/January 1999 was associated with the seasonal selling of stocks by company insiders disposing of stock acquired in options packages.

The Dell direct business model

Dell describes its business model in the following terms:

- *Price for performance* – By eliminating resellers, retailers and other intermediaries, coupled with the industry's most efficient procurement, manufacturing and distribution process, Dell offers customers more powerful and more enhanced systems for the price than competitors.
- *Customization* – Every Dell system is built to order, so customers get exactly and only what they want.
- *Service and support* – Dell uses the knowledge gained from direct contact with customers, before and after the sale, to provide tailored customer service which has won many industry awards.
- *Latest technology* – The newest technology is introduced into product lines faster and more cheaply than in other distribution channels.
- *Superior shareholder value* – The performance of the direct model produced a stock that doubled in value during 1998.

At its simplest, the Dell business model is direct selling of PCs, primarily to business customers as shown in Figure 4.2.

The business relied on the telephone ordering of PCs by business users, adding a salesforce in the late 1980s to handle big corporate clients. Although the pioneer of the direct model, Dell accepts that major corporates require personal sales contacts as well. For example, Boeing has around 100 000 Dell PCs and buys

Traditional business model in the personal computer industry
Arm's-length transactions from one level to the next

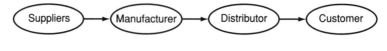

Dell's direct business model
Takes out the time and the cost of third-party distributors

Figure 4.2 Dell's direct business model v. traditional business model

'Boeing has around 100 000 Dell PCs and buys around 160 Dell products a day, and Dell himself admits: "Boeing you go to see"'

around 160 Dell products a day, and Dell himself admits: 'Boeing you go to see'.

Dell notes that more than 80 per cent of all computer purchases are made by businesses and other organizations, and businesses prefer to buy straight from the manufacturer. He expects that direct selling will become more than half the computer market. At the end of the 1990s, 90 per cent of Dell's sales are to businesses and institutions, and 70 per cent to very large customers that buy at least $1 million of PCs a year.

'the customer's order is what triggers the production of the PC'

However, what is also important to the Dell model is that from the outset PCs were made to order, that is the customer's order is what triggers the production of the PC. In this way of doing business the customer's specifications determine what is produced (from the components available), and the company does not have to keep a large stock of PCs which have been produced in anticipation of the customer's requirements. However, Dell has also reduced the time between order to a few days, not the weeks that conventional suppliers take to build a customized computer. For example, in October

'The direct business model as operated by Dell can get stockholding down to 7–10 days, as opposed to the 2–3 months of stock held in the conventional distribution system'

1997 the Asian financial crisis resulted in 20 million hits on Nasdaq's web site on Wall Street – to avoid a catastrophic traffic jam, one phone call to the account representative at Dell produced 11 new Dell servers for Nasdaq within 72 hours.

The leverage on performance from reducing inventory in this model is massive in an industry where materials depreciate at 50 per cent a year, and rapid product transitions can make components obsolete overnight. The direct business model as operated by Dell can get stockholding down to 7–10 days, as opposed to the 2–3 months of stock held in the conventional distribution system. (Dell has taken the day's supply in stock down from around 32 days in 1995 to around 7 days in 1998.) Dell consistently undercuts its rivals' prices both in PCs, and now in workstations and servers.

Not least among the strengths of the direct model is that it is difficult for competitors to imitate. Companies with an established reseller channel face the problem that selling direct would place them in competition with their own distributors and disrupt and weaken established selling channels. As Dell has noted: 'It's hard to go direct just a little bit . . . Balancing resellers and direct sales is very, very tough.' This has provided Dell with some considerable protection from competitive attack by Compaq and IBM, its leading competitors.

However, direct selling alone does not explain Dell's success or the strength of the business model – otherwise it would have been much easier for competitors to imitate. It is unlikely that Dell himself realized at the outset that the direct model builds a relationship with the customer that creates unique information, which can then be used to change the direct seller's relationship with suppliers (and then in turn with the customer). Three factors stand out in the way Dell has refined and extended its business model, that underpin the company's spectacular performance:

'the outset that the direct model builds a relationship with the customer that creates unique information, which can then be used to change the direct seller's relationship with suppliers'

- the direct model put Dell in the near-perfect position to exploit the *Internet* and become the leading electronic commerce supplier of PCs
- Dell has developed what is, in effect, a new organizational form through what the company calls '*virtual integration*', and
- Dell has developed processes of *learning and responsiveness* to the market which incorporates the company's technology, and the human processes of listening to customers and learning from them.

A rocket boost from the Internet

It would be difficult to overestimate the impact of Internet-based sales on Dell's business. The Dell web site went live in June 1997. In that year, Dell became the first company to sell $1 million of products on the Internet in a single day, and Michael Dell admitted that in December that year the company had a couple of '$6 million days', which was 'pretty exciting'. Dell's view of the

'Dell's view of the Internet at that time was that: "It's essentially rocket fuel for the direct-sell engine"'

Internet at that time was that: 'It's essentially rocket fuel for the direct-sell engine. We couldn't have asked for anything better. It enhances the productivity of our entire organization. The customer finds it easy to get information, to buy and to find support.'

In the course of 1998, the power of *www.dell.com* became even clearer. In January 1998 Dell's Internet sales were running at around $2 million a day. By March this had risen to $4 million a day. In September the company was achieving $6 million a day, and by the end of 1998, Dell was reporting Internet sales as $10 million a day. The company estimates that by 2000, Internet sales will account for more than half the total Dell business (and this excludes customers who visit the web site for information, and then place orders over the telephone, because they want to talk to someone about their purchases – Dell estimates that customers who visit the web site and then phone are twice as likely to buy products).

The customer web site allows the customer to pick the performance details of the computer on-screen, as well as peripherals and software, calculating the cost as the package builds up. For the 'educated' or knowledgeable customer, this is much faster than talking through menus and choices with a telephone operator. Once the customer has entered an address and credit card number, an e-mail comes back confirming the order, and the custom-built computer arrives with the customer a few days later. Meanwhile, the customer can visit the web site to track the progress of the on-line order. Dell has established 'e-tailing' for computers, but the next stage is 'e-service'. If there is a problem with the computer, the customer will click onto 'support' and the state of the problem machine will be captured and sent to a Dell server for analysis, to tell the customer what is wrong and help to fix it (for simple configuration or software problems the two computers may just sort it out between themselves).

'Dell has established "e-tailing" for computers, but the next stage is "e-service"'

For big customers, Dell operates 'Premier Pages' – each is a site dedicated to the specific corporate customer with details of orders, pricing and deliveries, as arranged by the account executive. Dell operates almost as the customer's IT department in implementing its IT strategy.

Scott O'Hare is president of Dell Canada, and took fewer than eight months to build the on-line business in Canada – his on-line sales were built from zero to $2.5 million a week in this time. O'Hare explains: 'There is no magic in all this. The Internet is just another way of turbo-charging our direct sales engine . . . It's just the next natural extension of how to build a relationship with a customer.' The Canadian web page gives specific information for Canadian customers, rather than the US information from competitors' web sites. The Internet offers special potential in expanding internationally also – when Dell introduced a new product line in Japan in 1997, 20 per cent of orders in the first week came in on-line.

The beginning of 1999 saw an important alliance between Dell and America Online, the largest Internet service provider in the USA. Under this deal, Dell computers will be delivered with pre-installed software to connect users with AOL, and AOL is joining Dell's ConnectDirect service which guides computer buyers through the process of linking to the Internet.

Underlying the impact of Internet selling on Dell's business is a natural compatibility with the company's business model. While conventional sellers are faced with the challenge of reinventing their ways of doing business to incorporate the Internet and direct contact with customers, Dell had no such problems.

A strategy of virtual integration

In an insightful interview for *Harvard Business Review* in March 1998, Michael Dell discussed the 'power of virtual integration' underpinning the strength of his direct business model. His conclusion was that the direct model has offered unique opportunities to build different types of relationship with suppliers and customers, not based on ownership (vertical integration) or simple buyer–seller contracts, but on virtual integration (see Figure 4.3).

Dell sees this as the evolution of the direct business model, and the hidden source of its strength. This evolution has some important characteristics.

Dell's direct business model
Partnering with suppliers and customers
Linked by processes of 'virtual integration'
not vertical integration

Figure 4.3   Dell's direct business model – 'virtual integration'

Growth through added-value not vertical integration

From the outset, Dell rejected what he saw as the 'we-have-to-develop-everything' view of the world that was associated with IBM, Compaq and Hewlett-Packard. Instead of investing in developing and producing computer chips and motherboards (which is not very profitable anyway), the Dell strategy has been to invest capital in activities that can add value for customers, such as the fast assembly of built-to-order computers exploiting components and software produced by other suppliers.

'Dell's rapid growth has been underpinned by the freedom to choose superior components suppliers and the flexibility of a small workforce'

This offers a strong market position and allows fast growth. Dell's rapid growth has been underpinned by the freedom to choose superior components suppliers and the flexibility of a small workforce with no factories for components production. For example, Dell has around 10 000 service technicians in the field servicing products, but most are employed by contractors not Dell.

From outsourcing to partnering

At first appearance this may just look like outsourcing of supplies and services, but in the Dell model it goes much further. Dell argues that conventionally in the IT industry outsourcing has simply been a way for a company to get rid of a problem it cannot solve itself. With Dell's virtual integration approach suppliers work to Dell's quality measures and through information linkages that enable Dell to see in real time when parts are dispatched or service requests handled.

Suppliers are treated as partners, agreeing to meet a proportion of Dell's requirements for a component even when it is in short supply in the industry and allocating engineers to Dell's design team to work in Dell's plants. However, Dell admits to wanting as few partners as possible, and that partnership with suppliers lasts only as long as they maintain their leadership in technology and quality. The real difference is treating external suppliers as though they were internal to Dell's organization – sharing information and plans freely – but maintaining the ability to shop around for something better. The dramatic improvement Dell has gained in time to market is supported by sharing design databases and methodologies with suppliers.

The benefit to the supplier?

The gain for the supplier is that Dell pulls product through the channel in a consistent and predictable way, because the distance between demand and the source of supply is much shorter. Dell's customer mix (no single customer represents more than 1–2 per cent of total sales) means that its demand for computers is stable (though growing). Dell believes that the benefit he delivers to his suppliers is less variability in orders, less stockholding for everyone, and thus lower costs and less risk.

The critical issue for Dell is velocity

Central to the Dell virtual integration philosophy is changing management focus from how much inventory is held, to how fast it is moving – *inventory velocity.* Accounts receivable is not a problem for Dell – in fact, because of the way they operate they get paid by customers before they have to pay suppliers. However, inventory which rapidly depreciates in value, and slows down the ability to exploit new technological advances is seen as a large risk. As Dell explains it, if he has eleven days stock and his competitor has eighty, when Intel comes out with a new chip, he can take the new product to market sixty-nine days earlier than his competitor can.

'Central to the Dell virtual integration philosophy is changing management focus from how much inventory is held, to how fast it is moving – **inventory velocity'**

Inventory velocity gives Dell such leverage that with some suppliers no stock at all is necessary. For example, with a supplier of the calibre of Sony providing monitors, Dell is happy to have its name on them and does not even need to take them out of the box to test them. This means there is no reason to transport the monitors to Austin on a truck, just to give them a tour of the warehouse, and then put them back on the truck. Dell says 'That's just a big waste of time and money, unless we get our jollies from touching monitors, which we don't.'

Instead Airborne Express or UPS collect the monitors from Sony's Mexico factory on a daily basis as determined by customer orders received. The courier also collects the same number of computers from Dell's plant in Austin, matches up the computers with the monitors, and delivers to the customers.

This requires the supplier to adjust to selling a constant flow of product, instead of large batches, but they sell more because Dell takes it faster. It relies on sophisticated data exchange between Dell and its collaborators, but the Dell model effectively substitutes information for stockholding, and ships only to real demand from end-user customers not to distributors.

'The Dell challenge to its suppliers is to collaborate in finding ways to enhance speed in every part of the business'

The Dell challenge to its suppliers is to collaborate in finding ways to enhance speed in every part of the business, directly by improving logistics or indirectly by improving quality. For example, customers pay for service and support and Dell contracts with third-party maintainers (TPM) to make the service calls. Customers call with problems, and that triggers two electronic communications: one to ship spare parts from Dell to the customer site, and one to send the TPM to the customer. Dell acts as information broker to facilitate the TPM's work. However, because poor quality slows things down, defective components go back to Dell for diagnosis, and the diagnosis goes back to the supplier to redesign the component.

The same principle applies within Dell as well: salespeople travelling to Austin for product training pointed out how time expensive this was. The company fine-tuned its web site to include an internal page from which salespeople can learn many of their new product presentations wherever they are located.

The benefit to the customer?

'Virtual integration means the same types of links between Dell and its customers as between Dell and its suppliers'

Customer benefits from the Dell business model go far beyond low prices. Virtual integration means the same types of links between Dell and its customers as between Dell and its suppliers.

Sales account managers work closely with large corporate customers to analyse future PC needs by department or function and to provide technical advice. With smaller business customers telesales provide real-time information about purchase patterns (as well as a link for steering customers towards what is available to fine-tune the balance between supply and demand).

The Dell customer relationship is dominated by numerous information links. For example, Dell will help a global customer to standardize its PC purchasing worldwide, to reduce the problems created through diverse configurations and software at the user level. Selling direct means Dell has full information about that global customer's total PC purchasing country by country, which can be fed back to the company to manage its IT strategy.

With a customer such as Boeing, with 100 000 Dell PCs, some thirty Dell staff work permanently on-site at Boeing's plants, operating almost as Boeing's PC department, closely involved in planning PC needs and network configuration. Similarly, users and internal help-desk personnel at a customer such as MCI can access Dell's internal support tools on-line in the same way that Dell's own technical support teams do.

Around 200 Dell customers have 'Premier Pages' on the Internet, giving the customer secure and direct access to purchasing and technical access to the specific configurations they buy from Dell. The page acts as an interactive catalogue for customer employees to select approved PCs and to order – drastically reducing paperwork for Dell and the customer organization.

Close customer relationships and information sharing uncover new opportunities for adding customer value. For example, Dell now routinely pre-loads a customer's own software onto PCs in the factory. A company such as Eastman Chemical has a unique mix of licensed proprietary software and its own programs. Normally, the customer would pay $200–300 dollars a machine for a technician to visit the user's desk to load the company's software from diskettes and CD-ROMs. For $15–20 Dell will pre-load the unique software mix in the factory in a few seconds. Dell will also put asset labels on the machines and keep an asset register for the customer, to save someone having to do this manually at the customer's premises.

Michael Dell's conclusion about the operation of his business model is that it relies on this kind of 'virtual integration'. He says that: 'If our customers didn't work with us as partners, managing to eleven days of inventory would be insane . . . We simply couldn't do it without customers who work with us as partners.' It is the tight linkages that result which make Dell's model difficult for competitors to imitate – it is not just about direct selling, it is about forecasting demand, product design and information for co-ordination.

'If our customers didn't work with us as partners, managing to eleven days of inventory would be insane . . .'

Learning and innovation

Less obvious, but equally significant to Dell's success, is maintaining and extending the company's ability to learn and improve constantly. This characteristic is even more difficult for competitors to imitate than direct selling. Learning and responsiveness is implicit in the Dell business model – it is what the technology-driven information linkages and data exchanges with suppliers and customers are all about. For example, when a problem with a product occurs anywhere in the world, the information

'Learning and responsiveness is implicit in the Dell business model'

about the problem enters the Dell knowledge base and technicians throughout the world have access to it. But learning is exhibited throughout the company's processes, based both on technology and more simply on listening to customers.

Continuous improvement

For example, we saw earlier that Dell has achieved rapid and spectacular success in the Internet sales operation. However, Michael Dell worried about the fears that customers seemed to have about credit card security on the Internet. These worries translated into the 1998 introduction of the 'Dell online secure shopping guarantee', offering customers enhanced protection from credit card theft, misuse or fraud. All information customers put onto the site is encrypted and Dell offers reimbursement of liability charges for fraudulent card use. Similarly, customer fears about information being passed to other companies has been met with Dell's privacy policy that prohibits the release of customer information to any outsider.

An evolving customer strategy

Dell's customer strategy is another element of the business model that has evolved during the life of the business. In the early stages, Dell did not differentiate much between different customer types, but has developed finer and finer market segmentation over the years.

For example, for a long time Dell did not actively pursue the consumer market because it did not offer the level of profit the company required – competitors drove prices and profits down to get high volume sales. However, the direct selling information advantage is that Dell found that while the industry average price to consumers was going down, Dell's average price to consumers was going up. The effect was caused by consumers becoming more knowledgeable about PCs and when they moved on to their second or third computer, they were buying from Dell. This had produced a billion-dollar consumer business for Dell, which was profitable. In 1997 the company responded by forming a group to serve that segment.

'while the industry average price to consumers was going down, Dell's average price to consumers was going up'

In fact, Dell's market segmentation strategy has developed in the type of way shown in Figure 4.4.

This finer approach to segmentation as Dell developed, grew and learned more from the database provided by the direct selling

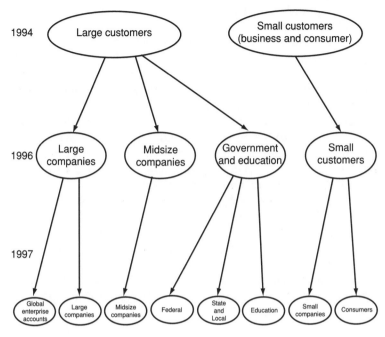

Figure 4.4   Market segmentation strategy

operation underpinned the company's ability to forecast demand and to co-ordinate strategic information from each customer segment back into the supply chain. Segment groups focus on the opportunities emerging in each segment of the market.

Listening to customers

Michael Dell's leadership has been characterized as continuously looking for small improvements – e.g. putting asset labels on machines – that eventually add up to a major value shift for the customer. He aims to spend about 40 per cent of his time with customers. He says one of his major challenges is to find managers who can sense and respond to rapid shifts in the market.

The listening philosophy of 'virtual integration' is also built into the company's formal customer relationships. Dell's Platignum Councils are regional meetings of large customers every six to nine months, where senior technologists share views about where the technology is going and the practical issues faced by customers. Each meeting reviews what the

'The listening philosophy of "virtual integration" is also built into the company's formal customer relationships'

customers told Dell at the previous meeting, and what Dell has done about those issues.

Listening can throw up disagreements between engineering experts and customers. Dell's desktop PC engineers were operating on the theory that corporate customers wanted state-of-the-art performance from PCs – the faster the better. What customers said they wanted was a stable product that did not change – what mattered to them was not small increases in speed but stability. Dell overruled the engineers to build a product with inter-generational consistency over many years. Different brands offer greater stability to corporate customers, as opposed to the fast technology changes demanded by consumers.

Customer requests for a laptop computer that lasts the whole day, instead of running out in the middle of an airplane journey, were translated into a collaboration with Sony to put lithium ion batteries into notebook computers. These were the first notebooks that lasted 5–6 hours, i.e. the time it takes to fly from New York to Los Angeles. Dell is constantly on the lookout for shifts in value – the customer who says 'Hey, I don't care about that any more, now I care about this . . .'

Wrongfooting the competition

Dell has performed spectacularly well in a marketplace dominated by major companies such as IBM, Compaq and Hewlett-Packard, who are able and aggressive competitors. In the early stages the conventional business models were unable to imitate the direct model – the major players were committed to traditional distribution channels and unable effectively to exploit the direct approach and were not well positioned to move into Internet-based sales in the way that Dell was. However, industry relationships are strained and changing fast and counter-attacks against Dell are underway.

'In the early stages the conventional business models were unable to imitate the direct model'

Dell now has a direct competitor in the form of Gateway. Gateway has imitated the direct selling of PCs and has launched PC server products, aiming to undercut the prices of Dell and Compaq to gain a foothold in the corporate market, although it has struggled to meet profit targets.

Gateway is the number two direct seller of PCs operating telephone sales and Internet-based selling, it has followed Dell's example of manufacturing in the USA, Ireland and Malaysia. Gateway was founded by Ted and Norm Watt in 1985 (then as Gateway 2000), and 1997 sales were $6.3 billion – one-third to consumers. 1997 sales grew 25 per cent on the previous year, but quarterly net profits were running between 3 per cent and 5 per cent and moved into loss in the final quarter of 1997.

Michael Dell is not popular in the industry. He is fond of annoying his peers by reminding the world that he is the longest-serving CEO in a major US computer manufacturer, and continues to irritate Compaq and IBM with public claims to market leadership (which are only true if you carefully pick the right part of the market to consider). Dell also refused to retract his public statement that he believed the ailing Apple Computer company should be shut down and the money returned to the shareholders. Apple co-founder Steve Jobs, on returning as Apple CEO declared 'war' on Dell, displaying a huge image of Michael Dell at an employee meeting in 1997 with a target superimposed on the face, and uttering the threat 'We are coming after you, buddy'. Theatrics aside, actually Apple probably has more problems than Michael Dell, but the story is illustrative.

More seriously, there has been some regrouping of major competitors that may impact on Dell. Michael Dell's goal of overtaking Compaq's share of the market was postponed for the time being by Compaq's purchase of Tandem Computers in June 1997 to take Compaq from its strong base in PCs into the high performing PC servers market. This purchase doubled the size of Compaq's salesforce to 8000 and in worldwide sales put Compaq/Tandem in third place behind IBM and Hewlett-Packard, with a 1996 sales value of $20 billion (compared to $76 billion at IBM and $38 billion at Hewlett-Packard). This move put Digital Equipment into fourth place with 1996 worldwide sales of $15 billion.

Seven months later, Compaq moved a rank higher in the global IT industry by a $9.6 billion purchase of Digital. This acquisition added large-scale servers used for big business applications to Compaq's product line, and gave it entry to the growing computer services market. The deal also brought closer ties to Microsoft, with whom Digital had a networking alliance. The combination of Compaq's marketing and sales expertise with Digital's heritage of engineering and technology innovation was seen as creating an effective rival to IBM in enterprise computing, with high-level entry to some of the world's largest corporate customers. What remains to be seen is the impact that the new Compaq/Digital business may have on Dell's corporate customer base.

'during 1998 it certainly seemed Dell's low prices were continuing to provide protection against its conventional customers' distribution'

However, during 1998 it certainly seemed Dell's low prices were continuing to provide protection against its conventional customers' distribution. Compaq tried to clear stocks by cutting business PC prices by around 20 per cent, and Hewlett-Packard moved high volumes of products but mainly at a loss in the first half of 1998. In the consumer market the continuing shift of attention to sub-$1000 dollar machines was also a problem for these companies. Dell's ability to turn stock over in 7–8 days continues to avoid the retailer's problem of having weeks or months of unsold inventory while prices are falling.

'Dell's success in consistently undercutting their PC prices and now prices of servers, through the direct business model has become increasingly difficult for his bigger rivals to live with'

Dell's success in consistently undercutting their PC prices and now prices of servers, through the direct business model has become increasingly difficult for his bigger rivals to live with.

Late in 1997, both Compaq and Hewlett-Packard had moved to adopt a modified version of the direct sales model – some resellers are allowed to assemble and configure PCs in response to customer preferences, in an attempt to get closer to Dell's 'made to order' capability with customers.

The end of 1998 saw Compaq announcing its launch of on-line sales operation on the Internet. Specifically, Compaq is targeting small businesses, which is also a key Dell target segment. It remains to be seen if a distributor-based company such as Compaq will be able to sell direct from the Internet without disrupting conventional distribution and selling channels. Indeed, even by the start of 1999, the Compaq strategy was generating resistance and protest from its conventional resellers. There have been rumours that Compaq might be looking to buy Gateway – the second place direct marketing PC seller, smaller but based on Dell's direct model.

Certainly, IT industry commentators continue to talk about the need for further consolidation, because there is no end in sight to the price crash of PCs. Forecasts are of fewer brand names and even lower prices.

The future for Dell?

It is difficult, even as Dell continues an unbroken period of declaring profits that beat expectations, to believe that growth rates and performance can continue at the present level. None the less, an industry facing falling prices, uncertainty about technology development, and customers switching to Internet-based purchasing are probably the ideal conditions for the direct business model. Certainly, Michael Dell remains publicly committed to making his company the market leader.

'Michael Dell remains publicly committed to making his company the market leader'

Dell's growth strategy includes extending its product range. The first expansion was from desktop and portable PCs into servers and workstations, and it is developing data storage products and services. Dell is also committed to further international expansion, and to organizing around specific market opportunities, such as education, small business and government markets.

Sources

Brown, John Murray (1998), 'Dell To Expand Irish Operation', *Financial Times*, 23 January.

Jackson, Tony (1998), 'Interview: Michael Dell', *Financial Times*, 5 November.

Kehoe, Louise (1997), 'Tandem Deal Puts Compaq in Global League', *Financial Times*, 24 June.

Kehoe, Louise, (1997), 'Apple Chief Has Dell In His Sights', *Financial Times*, 12 November.

Kehoe, Louise (1998), 'Compaq To Buy Digital for £5.7 bn', *Financial Times*, 27 January.

Kehoe, Louise (1998), 'Dell Tops Corporate Sector of PC Market', *Financial Times*, 11 September.

Kehoe, Louise and Paul Taylor (1998), 'Compaq Achieves Goal of Joining Top Three Ahead of Time', *Financial Times*, 27 January.

Kehoe, Louise and Paul Taylor (1998), 'Long and Winding Download', *Financial Times*, 12 March.

Levy, Doug (1998), 'Dell's Earnings Jump 62 per cent', *USA Today*, 19 August.

Lynn, Matthew (1998), 'PC Whiz-Kid Piles Up the Billions', *Sunday Times*, 26 April.

Magretta, Joan (1998), 'The Power of Virtual Integration: An Interview With Dell Computer's Michael Dell', *Harvard Business Review*, March–April.

Martin, Peter (1998), 'Time For New Trade-Offs', *Financial Times*, 12 November.

'Michael Dell's Plan for the Rest of the Decade', *Fortune*, 9 June 1997.

Stewart, Anna (1998), 'Compaq Goes Online In Battle of the Giants', *Mail on Sunday*, 11 November.

Stewart, Anna (1998), 'Rocket Trip To Riches on the Net', *Mail on Sunday*, 11 January.

Taylor, Paul (1998), 'Big Name Suppliers Tighten Their Grip', *Financial Times*, 4 March.

Wheelwright, Geoffrey (1998), 'Dell's Online PC Sales Surge Ahead', *Financial Times*, 2 September.

CHAPTER 5

New marketing channels

E-commerce, E-fficiency and E-volution?*

One area where marketplace revolution is most apparent is in marketing channels, and it is seen most particularly with the impact of e-commerce or e-tailing (electronic retailing, where a customer orders products from an Internet web page using electronic mail). The most difficult strategic question is whether these changes, and the reinvention of business processes that goes along with them, just represents increased efficiency (doing the same things cheaper) or a more fundamental evolutionary change in the nature of the businesses concerned.

The following company and industry stories provide some basis for answering this question.

- *Car distribution* is in the process of transition based on the use of the Internet and other processes of reinvention in ways not even understood by most of the existing players in this sector because new business models are being created.
- *Calyx & Corolla* is the business which reinvented the process of flower buying in the USA (interestingly based on technology no more advanced than the telephone and fax until relatively recently).

---

* This material has been produced by Nigel F. Piercy from secondary sources and discussions with industry executives. © Nigel F. Piercy.

- *Amazon.com*, the Internet bookseller, is probably the best-known Internet-based business in the world, which is evolving from an electronic retailer into something new, for which no category name currently exists.
- *The music business* looks like it faces a fundamental change firstly in the channels of distribution for tapes and CDs, but maybe in the product itself as a result, and provides a telling example of how change in channels can lead to much more fundamental reinvention.

We can consider these examples in turn.

Car distribution systems

Generally speaking, the only people the public trusts less than journalists, politicians and lawyers are second-hand car dealers. A recent press comment is illustrative: 'Visiting a car dealer appeals to people about as much as a trip to the dentist. It may not hurt so much, but the near certainty that you will be greeted by smarmy salesmen, surly service and bloated bills is enough to set the teeth grinding.'

'the only people the public trusts less than journalists, politicians and lawyers are second-hand car dealers'

A *Financial Times* report in 1998 summarizes the problem for those who make a living by selling cars in the following terms: 'The developed world's way of buying cars cannot survive in the face of widespread consumer dissatisfaction and the emergence of rival sales channels' (*The Future of Automotive Distribution*, Financial Times Business Ltd, 1998). Consultants AT Kearney report that only 25 per cent of buyers in the USA and Japan are satisfied with the car-buying process through traditional franchised dealers, and even in Europe where consumers regard franchised dealers more favourably, only 30 per cent of German, 40 per cent of French and 43 per cent of British buyers want to buy their next car through a franchised outlet. The FT report identifies six new channels opening up in the USA:

- direct sales by manufacturers, most notably through the Internet
- independent traders and brokers dealing in a variety of ways from 'grey' (i.e. unofficial) markets and parallel imports
- manufacturer-owned dealer outlets, including manufacturer-branded 'megastores'
- non-automotive supermarket chains

- 'unbundled' franchised car dealers with new cars, used cars, parts and service franchised separately to increase competitiveness

'Car manufacturers are dissatisfied as well. The distribution channel accounts for 20 to 30 per cent of the retail price of the car, and manufacturers do not believe that dealers are earning this margin'

Car manufacturers are dissatisfied as well. The distribution channel accounts for 20 to 30 per cent of the retail price of the car, and manufacturers do not believe that dealers are earning this margin and delivering the value to customers that their brands require. Manufacturers adopt the view that: 'Distribution will see the third car revolution of the past 20 years'. As a consequence, the leading car manufacturers are cutting their dealer networks, buying back dealerships to run them direct, awarding fewer franchises, and making bigger demands on those distributors who remain. The National Franchised Dealers Association in the UK says, 'any profits you make are immediately challenged by the level of investment required by the franchiser . . . Words like partnership are used a lot but mean very little'. The manufacturers' problem is to reduce order to delivery time and stockholding in the channel at the same time, so cars are built almost to order.

Developments in the distribution channel extend far further than these attempts by manufacturers to make their existing distribution networks more efficient, and are moving progressively further away from traditional forms of distribution.

New style car distributors – supermarkets

In spite of falling demand, 1996 to 1998 saw the launch of 'car supermarkets' in the used-car marketplace in the UK. Car Group was the first such venture floated in November 1996 and aiming to sell 250 000 'nearly-new' cars a year from 12 sites within 4–5 years. It plans to treat the used vehicle as a commodity – 'cars as bean cans on wheels' – and building brand strength for the retailer instead of the car. By mid-1998, the company issued its first profit warning and its survival is in question. This was followed by the launch of CarLand also aiming to bring the national 'supermarket chain' concept to used-car retailing with a national group of fixed-price, indoor, user-car stores.

'It plans to treat the used vehicle as a commodity – "cars as bean cans on wheels" – and building brand strength for the retailer instead of the car'

A similar development is National Car Supermarket, again claiming to sell cars using the same principles as supermarkets – wide choice, fixed prices and lower prices than competitors. Profits have been significantly below expectations in the first years of operation.

The first similar move in the new car market was the 1998 announcement by Tesco, the food supermarket, that it planned to enter the car business in the course of the following two years, as part of its move from the core food business into key non-food areas.

The 'Blockbuster' arrives in the car business

A more radical shift from traditional channels for cars is Wayne Huizenga's Republic Industries AutoNation USA chain (initially selling used cars but now with franchises for new vehicles also), which is interested currently in setting up retail parks in the UK and Ireland.

Huizenga is the US entrepreneur who has created three multibillion dollar businesses: Waste Management, the Blockbuster video chain and Republic Industries. He is also a man who kept a pet alligator at college until it died of whisky poisoning, has waterskied on a rocking chair, a stepladder and a dustbin lid and who collects sports teams as a hobby. Republic Industries includes car hire, car retail, electronic security firms and outdoor advertising businesses. However, in one year's trading the company became the largest car dealer in the USA, based on the vision of making the purchase of a car as straightforward as buying a fridge, by building huge outlets with facilities for children and a ban on haggling. Republic is already the largest car hirer in the UK, by virtue of its purchase of Eurodollar in 1997.

The AutoNation chain set out to develop a new business model and to change the way Americans buy cars – new or used. There is no price haggling, the sales staff are not paid on commission and all used cars get a thorough overhaul. Computer terminals in the showroom guide customers through the stock of cars; they can visit the coffee bar and then be taken in a golf cart to view vehicles, while the children stay in the play centre. Huizenga says he is aiming to do for cars what McDonald's did for hamburgers – to consolidate the industry by creating a national brand.

'The AutoNation chain set out to develop a new business model and to change the way Americans buy cars'

Underlying Huizenga's strategy are two aims. One is to become the dominant force in new and used-car sales by delivering customer-friendly service with no-haggle pricing and money-back guarantees. The second aim is to control the car throughout its useful life and earn a profit every time it changes hands. The plan is to establish integrated sales operations in the top fifty US markets. Each market will have up to a dozen Huizenga new-car dealerships and several AutoNations selling used cars. These operations will be supported by Alamo and National car hire outlets and ValuStop outlets for older used cars, and large reconditioning centres, shared by the other businesses. Taking maximum earnings from a vehicle can involve the following sequence:

1 lease a new car to a customer for 12–18 months from a new-car dealership
2 take it back at the end of the lease, or as a trade-in, and recondition it
3 send it to Alamo or National as a hire car for up to four months
4 take it back and recondition it
5 put it up for sale or lease on an AutoNation lot
6 if it does not move quickly, send it to a ValuStop outlet
7 if it does not move, send it to the reconditioning centre for spare parts and scrap value.

The company's calculations suggest this would give Huizenga a $1000 additional profit per car, which is a massive increase in the margin earned from a vehicle in conventional US new-car selling.

Huizenga is also looking at ways to let customers swap from one car to another under one lease plan, e.g. a sports car in the summer, a four-wheel drive in the winter, a small car for commuting, a large car for a family trip. Customers are enthusiastic about such plans, but there remains the barrier of the lease costs that are high in the first year of any vehicle. An integrated operation where 'swaps' can come from your own car hire firms or used-car lots could overcome this.

The US car makers in Detroit are co-operating with Huizenga, while trying to consolidate their own networks, but the Japanese are suing. Toyota, Nissan and Honda are so nervous about the innovation they are trying to stop Huizenga acquiring more dealerships than their 'rules' allow.

Implementing this strategy has involved delays and adjustments, but the general belief is that Huizenga will have the leverage to permanently change the factory-dealer relationship in the car business by his new business model.

By January 1999, Republic had become the world's largest car retailer in the space of two years' growth through acquisition. It owned around 450 dealerships in twenty of the US states, including new car dealerships as well as used car outlets, and

1999 sees the planned opening of the first AutoNation location in Dublin. The Autonation's chain has expanded to forty-three outlets, and moved into profit in the third quarter of 1998. Through this period, the Autonation's outlets have seen some change in direction – average stocks have been cut from 1000 to 600 vehicles per store, salaried salespeople were put on salary plus commission, and the company substantially scaled back its refurbishing of used cars, but the haggle-free, one price concept has survived.

The end of this first phase of expansion is signalled by the 'Mile High' project linking seventeen dealerships in Denver, Colorado, and is a pilot for the implementation of the new business model and where adjustments are being made to it, prior to launch across the whole of the USA. The goal is to take market share from 20 per cent to 30 per cent in the first year.

The Denver development is based on seventeen dealerships acquired from local sports hero John Elway. This is the first Republic venture with a grouping of dealerships in one urban area.

Employees have been trained in a new way of selling vehicles and in how to provide a wide range of services, including information through an Internet web site. For example, the web site allows consumers to view the stock of 3000 new and used vehicles available in all seventeen dealerships, to determine price and finance terms and apply for credit, to schedule an appointment for a test drive, and print out a map of directions to the dealership with the vehicle of interest. All dealerships have a one-price, no-negotiations sales policy, and for trade-ins a one-price estimate/offer good at any of the dealerships. Repairs are guaranteed and all used vehicles come with a 99-day warranty regardless of age and condition. Oil changes are carried out in half an hour or the service is free.

The new model also includes a customer loyalty programme – never before applied to this sector. The new business model emphasizes 'customer for life', to obtain multiple purchases of vehicles and service. The programme is called Autorewards and awards points to customers buying or leasing cars – a new car purchase gets 5000 points, a trade-in gets 1500 and bringing a car in for service gets 1250 points. The highest levels of points offer members discounts off fuel, priority in servicing, a free loan car if needed, and discounts off car rentals with Alamo and National. The perks of offer include:

- 5000 points – $5 off oil change
- 10 000 points – free oil change and tyre rotation
- 12 500 points – one day free car rental with Alamo or National

- 25 000 points – $250 towards purchase of a new or used car
- 50 000 points – $500 towards purchase of a new or used car

However, the refurbishing centres have not been effective – they are being closed and sold and the refurbishing work downscaled to be carried out at the service departments of the dealerships and Autonation sites.

The impact of the web

Early in 1998, KPMG motor industry analysts estimated that more than 20 per cent of new and used cars will be bought on the Internet within two years. Later that year, the Economist Intelligence Unit estimated that the majority of car purchases (new and used) will *involve* the Internet within five years (this includes information search and price comparisons not necessarily purchase). This would mean that traditional dealers would be cut out from the purchase process altogether or become involved far later when the customer has chosen the model to buy and knows what price to pay. The trade remains sceptical.

While traditional distributors fail to see the Internet as an effective trading tool, Car Shop, Virtual Showroom and Auto Trader have launched Internet sites. Auto Trader, for example, has moved from magazine publishing to offer what it claims to be the biggest car showroom in the world with a database of 100 000 cars with full specifications and pictures, and it is looking to provide integrated car insurance and financing as well. If this were not enough, Auto-by-Tel, the largest US-based Internet car seller is entering the UK market.

In addition, Microsoft has launched MSN Carpoint in the USA to compete with several other Internet car-buying services. MSN Carpoint has developed a network of more than 2000 dealers in the USA and collaborates with Reynolds and Reynolds, a company that trains car dealers to work successfully with Internet customers. To participate in the MSN Carpoint network, dealers must attend a two-day training session and commit to abiding with Carpoint's seven participation requirements (e.g. responding to customer requests within 48 hours and offering a no-haggle deal by stating their best price from the outset), pay a flat monthly fee averaging $1000 and agree to have a dedicated Carpoint service person on site. JD Powers estimates that in the USA, as soon as 2000 14 per cent of new car purchases will be made through an online car buying service, while others put this figures as high as 25 per cent.

Carpoint has focused on removing the unpleasantness that its research showed some consumers experience in buying cars: the hassle in getting all the information needed to make the choice; and dealing with the customer-unfriendly traditional distributor. Carpoint does not aim to give the customer a wide range of alternative purchasing outlets or chase down the lowest possible price – the Carpoint model provides value for the customer who wants to find a good price with no work or search time. By the end of 1998, Carpoint was driving car sales of $300 million.

The impact of online car sellers and networks has not escaped the attention of the car manufacturers. General Motors plans to launch its own online service, 'GM BuyPower' in 1999.

The Internet already provides more sophisticated UK buyers access to the lower new car prices in near European countries. The revolution in how cars are bought is going way past friendlier conventional outlets into new integrated offers and electronic commerce, and the existing trade seems to be struggling to find ways to respond effectively.

'The revolution in how cars are bought is going way past friendlier conventional outlets into new integrated offers and electronic commerce'

Calyx & Corolla – the flower lover's flower company

Calyx & Corolla (C&C) is the US pioneer of the direct marketing of fresh flowers, founded by Ruth Owades in 1988 after her graduation from Harvard Business School in 1975 and experience in the mail-order business. The company is named after the botanical terms for the outer leaves and petals of a flower. C&C achieved sales of $25 million in the $14 billion US flower market by 1998, having moved into profit in 1991.

Owades and C&C have become the subject of one of the best-selling Harvard Business School case studies, which is ironic since the last thing she set out to be was an entrepreneur, having seen her father's struggle to run a family bookstore in San Francisco. Owades graduated in liberal arts in 1966 and was a Fulbright scholar to France. She worked briefly on economic development issues for the Mayor of Los Angeles before marrying a beer industry consultant. Her goal was a career in broadcasting and she went to Harvard Business School in the hopes of gaining an executive management position in the media.

After graduation, media opportunities not being forthcoming, she worked for United Brands, and then as marketing director for

CML Inc., a Massachusetts-based company with seven mail-order businesses. In researching and developing customer profiles with CML, Owades reached the conclusion that the gardening industry was a good target for a new direct mail operation. CML did not agree and she left in 1978 to found Gardener's Eden, the first mail-order house specializing in gardening accessories. She had single-handedly raised the capital for this venture, located merchandising sources and developed a capital and after four years sold it to Williams-Sonoma for $1 million – at the time a sum greater than annual sales. She continued to run the company for five years, based in San Francisco, opening Gardener's Eden retail stores alongside the catalogue business to develop a $15 million business.

'I wondered if it would be possible to market fresh flowers through a catalog, despite the fact that they were so perishable.'

In 1987 Owades decided she was ready for a new venture and took a year off to think. Her inspiration was the busy San Francisco flower market near her office, which led her to the point where: 'After numerous visits, I wondered if it would be possible to market fresh flowers through a catalog, despite the fact that they were so perishable. An idea came to me during a tennis match: shortcut the distribution system and deliver the flowers to the consumer faster and fresher.'

Traditional flower distribution

The horticulture industry was highly fragmented – many small family businesses operated as flower growers, distributors, wholesalers and retail florists. A typical distribution channel would be from growers to distributors located in the growing region, to geographically dispersed wholesalers, who sold to florists, supermarkets and other retailers in their catchment areas. Small retailers generally shopped around for the best products from the wholesalers in their area, for example at the flower markets seen in most major cities. Retailers provided added-value services like making up displays and bouquets and delivering the product to the end-customer. In the 1980s, US consumer spend on fresh flowers was only around $36 a year, around half the level normal in Europe. Year-round fresh flower purchase was still developing at this time in the USA.

A key issue was perishability, although it varies between different flowers, the quality of the product deteriorates steadily from the moment the flower is picked. In the traditional distribution system, a flower could easily be 7–10 days old before it was available for purchase in the retail store. Also there was no guarantee that a customer ordering a flower display would necessarily receive the freshest flowers in the retail store – the retailer had to rotate stock.

The Calyx & Corolla reinvention

C&C was an entirely new concept which revolution-ized the distribution of flowers, directly linking cus-tomers with growers (through Federal Express) to shorten the distribution channel and reduce the time to get flowers from grower to consumer. C&C typically delivered roses to the consumer within one to two days of the time they were cut. The conventional channel would typically deliver roses one to two weeks after cutting. The C&C business model took the form shown in Figure 5.1.

'C&C was an entirely new concept which revolutionized the distribution of flowers, directly linking customers with growers'

At the core of this model are three critical relation-ships: with the growers – Owades wanted the best available; with Federal Express – the number one air carrier; and with the flower consumer ordering from the catalogue, whose emotional attachments to flow-ers were the central focus.

'At the core of this model are three critical relationships'

Owades started C&C, with Fran Wilson, a former employee of Williams-Sonoma who became operations vice president, joined a

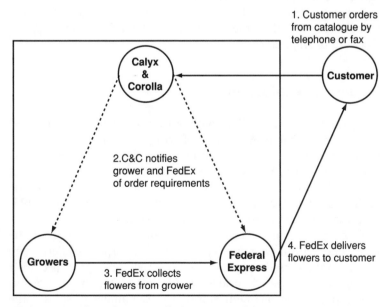

Figure 5.1 The Calyx & Corolla business model

year later by Ann Hayes Lee bringing long experience as a catalogue retailer as vice president of marketing. Modest offices in downtown San Francisco were supplemented with nearby warehouse space – for storage of vases, wreaths, dried flowers, non-perishables and packaging supplies. Initially, core sales/ customer service staff numbered five, although this could be expanded to as many as sixty in the holiday seasons.

Owades' first major problem was to recruit growers. She could offer them a new outlet for their product to compete with imports and increased supply in the industry and to offset the seasonality of demand, but they had to accept new operating methods – high quality packaging of individual customer orders instead of large shipments sent to distributors. Her efforts resulted in a network of around thirty quality flower growers, located mainly in California, Florida and Hawaii, of which eight supplied 80 per cent of C&C's products. Contracts prohibited them from dealing with other mail-order companies. Orders were transmitted from C&C by computer to the grower, where orders would be made up using packaging materials supplied by C&C. C&C paid the grower wholesale prices, plus a surcharge for packaging and administrative labour. None the less, C&C was able to achieve gross margins of 80 per cent.

The second key relationship was with Federal Express. Initially, C&C was no more to FedEx than a small account with special needs, but this relationship matured into one of partnership: FedEx trailers being left at growers to be filled and collected; delivery drivers aware of the problems in delivering flowers; FedEx computer terminals in major growers and at C&C to allow on-line tracking of shipments.

Customer relationships

The main communication with customers were the six C&C catalogues a year (now seven), offering a selection of fresh and dried flowers, plants, vases and other floral accessories. The catalogue also provides for continuity programmes such as 'a Year of Orchids' offering monthly deliveries of the chosen flowers, which countered some of the seasonality in the market. In 1991, C&C mailed more than 12 million catalogues.

Seventy per cent of C&C sales revenue were direct from the catalogue, with a further 20 per cent from corporate clients and promotional links (for example links to wedding supply specialists selling to prospective brides; a Mother's Day promotion in Bloomingdales department store). The remainder of sales came from telemarketing to previous and existing customers.

C&C now maintains an Internet web site (in partnership with FedEx who provided the expertise to develop the site), where buyers can order from an on-line catalogue.

Ann Lee's information was that active buyers were those who purchased at least twice a year – though some bought as often as ten times a year, 85 per cent of these customers were female, mostly in the 30–55 age groups, mainly working and with substantial disposable income. The largest group of potential buyers were those who used florists and other retailers, but were unaccustomed to buying anything by mail order.

C&C has chosen to position itself as 'The Flower Lover's Flower Company', focusing on the active buyers described above. Owades says, 'We consider ourselves the Mercedes-Benz of the flower business, offering quality, style, and service'.

'C&C has chosen to position itself as "The Flower Lover's Flower Company"'

C&C is distinguished from other flower sellers because it has reinvented the distribution channel – shipping direct from growers to customers, cutting out costly middlemen and providing fresher flowers. Others have also tried to sell flowers by mail order – Floral Gift Express failed around the time of C&C's launch, and C&C acquired some of its assets. Stillwater entered the market at about the same time. The conventional flower sellers co-operative FTD sells 'same-day delivery' flowers from the Internet also. An Internet site is also operated by 'FreshFlowerSource' selling cut-price flowers direct from Californian growers.

However, C&C's operation is based on a focus on 'flower lovers' and partnering with growers and FedEx, in a hollow or networked organization, and this seems more difficult for competitors to emulate. It sells $25 million of flowers direct to consumers without owning the flowers, let alone owning a fleet of vehicles to distribute the flowers. This has been achieved with a core workforce of only sixty employees (though expanding up to 260 for holiday seasons). Many competitors are able to imitate the direct selling aspect of the C&C business model, but C&C's unique strength is in the 'flower lovers' market'.

'Many competitors are able to imitate the direct selling aspect of the C&C business model, but C&C's unique strength is in the "flower lovers' market"'

Amazon.com – the world's largest bookstore

Amazon.com has received huge amounts of publicity for its performance as the first online bookseller. More importantly, *'there can be no company that has done as much to overturn conventional assumptions about traditional distribution channels'*

there can be no company that has done as much to overturn conventional assumptions about traditional distribution channels.

Briefly, Amazon.com was started by Jeffrey P. Bezos on three floors above an art gallery on a seedy Seattle street, furnished cheaply, with computer monitors balanced on piles of books and Bezos's golden retriever wandering around (all employees get stock options which have made dozens of Amazonians millionaires, to compensate for the squalid working conditions). Employees tend to have green hair, body piercing, strange clothes, often work around the clock and usually have no prior experience of book retailing. Bezos' own experience was in investment banking, though he says, 'I've always been at the intersection of computers and whatever they revolutionize.' Bezos named his business after the river with the greatest volume of water and has a goal of building a $10 billion business. When launched in the online book-selling business in 1994, Amazon.com was dismissed by established booksellers as a cult venture with limited appeal.

'Amazon.com was dismissed by established booksellers as a cult venture with limited appeal'

Quite simply Amazon.com uses its Internet site to sell books from 3.1 million available titles. It also sells music and has quickly become the leading online music retailer, as well as videos, and is moving into other Internet-based services. During the Christmas period of 1998, Amazon also offered a range of 185 children's toys – disconcerting new entrant eToys, which thought its main problem was Toys 'R' Us. Amazon.com sells books at discounts of up to 40 per cent, which are mostly ordered directly from distributors after the customer makes a selection and delivered two or three days later (although obscure titles may take up to six months). Customers are offered free e-mail notification of new books and recommendations in specific areas depending on customer interests.

The performance of Amazon.com shares is shown in Figure 5.2.

In 1998 Amazon.com had some 4.5 million customers and sales of around $540 million (compared to $148 million in 1997). At its initial public offering Amazon.com shares were valued at $9, but by the end of 1998 the shares were trading at around $209, giving a market value of $11.1 billion. Founder, 34-year-old Jeff Bezos's stake was valued at $4.4 billion. In December 1998, an analyst at CIBC Technology forecast a $400 price over the following twelve months, which drove the stock up to $243 (going through the $300 barrier for a short time), valuing the company at $14.6 billion and Bezos's

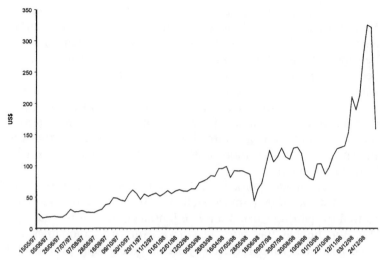

Figure 5.2   Amazon's share value, 1997–98 (unadjusted prices).
Source: Datastream

holding at $5.7 billion. This made Amazon twice the value of Barnes & Noble, the USA's largest conventional bookstore chain.

It should be noted that this valuation has been achieved by a company that has yet to make a profit. Explosive sales growth has been followed by the same rate of growth in the company's losses – selling more books means losing more money. Quarterly sales in mid-1998 of $153.7 million brought a loss of $45.2 million. Even optimistic forecasts are that the company will not move into profit until 2001 at the earliest and profitability remains a big question mark in a marketplace where price-cutting is making margins even slimmer.

'this valuation has been achieved by a company that has yet to make a profit. Explosive sales growth has been followed by the same rate of growth in the company's losses'

Bubble.com?

This valuation of Amazon should be placed in the context of a controversial boom in the value of a whole range of Internet-related stocks in late 1998 and early 1999 – the so-called 'e-icons'. Many analysts see this stock value driven by small investors, who are keen to get into Internet stocks, as insanely high.

For example, in January 1999, Rupert Murdoch of the global News Corporation media empire lashed out at the stock market enthusiasm, claiming that many Internet companies were heavily overvalued and would not produce profits. He may have been stimulated by the fact that the market values his lifetime achievement of building the News Corporation at $24 billion, while Yahoo! (the Internet version of a media company) had just reached a market value of $40 billion after a few years of operation. Murdoch was quoted worldwide as accusing that the Internet will 'destroy more businesses than it creates', and he may have a point.

However, while January 1999 saw some falling back in Internet stock values (Amazon fell back 30 per cent from its peak, as well as splitting stock 3-for-1 in January), there is no real sign that the bubble has burst as far as Internet companies are concerned. The value is driven by sensationally rapid growth and the fact that the stock market has no traditional measure to value these new business forms.

'1998 saw the first e-Christmas, with $4 billion of Internet sales in the USA alone'

In fact, 1998 saw the first e-Christmas, with $4 billion of Internet sales in the USA alone, giving $10 billion for the year according to a Boston Consulting Group study. While still less than 1 per cent of total retail sales in the USA, the Internet is the fastest growing sales medium in history. The driver for this spectacular sales growth, according to the Boston study is simply that a sizeable and growing minority of consumers *loathe* shopping in conventional stores.

The Amazon.com business model

The impact of Amazon.com in redefining the book business should not be underestimated. It has forced traditional book retailers to rethink whether their traditional advantages of size, mass-media branding and the attractions of store-based shopping will be enough to survive in the reshaped business.

Obviously the basis of the model is direct selling of books (and now other products) from an Internet site. Amazon.com has simply made it incredibly easy for customers to buy books, and has built a 'community' of book buyers – reading reams of reviews about books, receiving e-mail notifications of new books and related purchases, participating in book reviewing, having online chats with authors and suggesting endings to short stories started by major authors. After the information is collected in the first purchase – further buys involve just a mouse click. By 1998, 64 per cent of sales were from repeat customers and that

Table 5.1   Amazon versus Barnes & Noble

Amazon		Barnes & Noble
1 web site	Number of stores	1011
3.1 million	Titles per superstore	175 000
2%	Book returns	30%
306%	Sales growth (1998)	10%
1600	Number of employees	27 000
$375 000	Sales per employee (annual)	$100 000
24 times	Inventory turnovers per year	3 times
Low	Long-term capital requirements	High
High	Cash flow	Low

proportion is rising, and Amazon was gaining an average of 9000 new customers a day. While traditional booksellers offer discounts on the top 100 titles or so, Amazon discounts 400 000 titles.

The strength of the model lies in its advantages over the traditional book distribution channel. For example Table 5.1 shows a comparison with the major US book retailer Barnes & Noble.

While traditional channels require large investments in bricks and mortar, staff and stocks of books to offer customers a relatively limited choice, Amazon's site offers the customer the chance to browse a huge number of book titles without the overhead of sales staff, physical facilities or stock holding. The model succeeds only by getting large numbers of people to visit the Internet site (Amazon's customer number in 1998 was around 4.5 million), which involves a large marketing spend – $200 million in 1998. There is also a large initial investment in computer systems and editorial staff. However, while conventional retailers can grow sales only by building more stores to reach more people, Amazon has only to get more people to visit the Internet site.

'while conventional retailers can grow sales only by building more stores to reach more people, Amazon has only to get more people to visit the Internet site'

The technology supporting the Amazon.com business model also offers other advantages. Amazon was the first Internet trader to use 'collaborative filtering technology' to analyse customer purchases and visits on the site to suggest purchases (based on what people with similar interests have bought). This provides very accurate targeting of marketing. It also provides a database of customers and indications of what they might buy in the future. The technology also facilitated Amazon's partnering with

'Amazon Associates' – other Internet sites providing links to Amazon.com for their visitors and paid a commission on resulting sales. (Amazon has around 140 000 sites in the Associates programme.)

Recently, Amazon has made moves towards further exploiting its capabilities of becoming an information broker or shopping service by the purchase of Junglee (a shopping search engine) – providing technology to search the Web for products and to compare prices. Bezos sees a future in becoming a broker who helps people find things being sold elsewhere on the Web, and takes a commission from those sellers as reward for putting them in touch with buyers. Ultimately the purchases of partner companies' products may be made through the Amazon site where the customer's information is stored. This is linked to PlanetAll – a service where customers register their personal information and facts such as key birthdays and anniversaries, friends they want to stay in touch with and their interests. The service prompts customers on key dates and alerts them to new products that match their interests (and gift-buying obligations).

'Bezos sees a future in becoming a broker who helps people find things being sold elsewhere on the web, and takes a commission from those sellers'

The business model also has advantages in cash flow. Physical bookstores must stock up to 160 days worth of books to provide the kind of in-store selection customers want. They have to pay distributors 45–90 days after they buy the books, so on average they carry the costs of the books for three to four months. Amazon carries only about 15 days worth of stocks (high volume titles only) and is paid almost immediately by credit card, so getting about a month's use of interest-free money. That float provides a large part of what is needed to cover operating expenses.

The flaws in the business model?

'If there is a major flaw in the model, it is that it is relatively easy for conventional competitors to open their own web sites'

If there is a major flaw in the model, it is that it is relatively easy for conventional competitors to open their own web sites as well and this is exactly what has happened – the entry costs are low and the technology is easily accessible. Barnes & Nobles' entry also signalled the start of an online price war. Amazon.com faced major competition from Barnesandnoble.com and Borders, and its 1998 launch of a UK page and a German page, faces competition from Waterstones/ Dillons, the collaborative web site The Bookplace, and WH Smith's The Internet Bookshop in Britain and Bertelsmann (with ownership of half of Barnes & Nobles' Internet operation) in Germany. In fact, there are estimated now to be some 500 online booksellers. Conventional retailers are also fighting back by upgrading stores with reading areas and coffee bars to improve the customer's experience of book buying, and moving to out-of-town locations for customer convenience.

In 1997, CEO of Forrester Inc., George F. Colony promised that the Internet revolutionary would soon be made 'Amazon.toast'. In the context of books, Amazon's Jeff Bezos says that the question is 'Can Amazon.com establish a world-class brand name before Barnesandnoble.com buys, builds, acquires or learns the competencies it needs to be excellent online retailers?'. Amazon's fear is that if the critical element of the offer to online customers is speed of delivery – then the advantage goes to the retailer with the biggest stock of books, and for conventional retailers such as Barnes & Nobles, the physical stores act as a giant wholesaler for their online selling. The conventional retailer may even equal Amazon's online operation, by treating its web site as a loss-making shop window for the conventional stores.

'CEO of Forrester Inc., George F. Colony promised that the Internet revolutionary would soon be made "Amazon.toast"'

In 1998, Barnes & Noble also made moves towards the $600 million purchase of Ingram Books – the biggest book distributor in the USA. Ingram supplied 58 per cent of the books sold by Amazon.com in 1998. This purchase would give Barnes & Noble a further edge in speed of delivery.

Building the Wal-Mart of the web?

Amazon's marketing and promotion costs are high – $29 per sale compared to $2.50 in conventional stores. A 1998 Boston Consulting Group study concludes that typically cyber-retailers spend 65 per cent of revenues on marketing and advertising, compared to an average 5 per cent spend by conventional retailers. This places pressure on profitability unless revenue per sale can be levered upwards. Amazon's business model leads in the direction of extending the product range on offer – already from books to music and videos. However, the market situation may be different in these new areas. Amazon has become the leading online bookseller and was the first entrant, but its sales are small in the total world market for books of $82 billion. Amazon's music sales reached $14.4 million in the first three months of selling, outselling the former leader CDnow, in a market worth $38.1 billion worldwide, but CDnow and N2K are merging and margins on CDs are even lower than books.

The video market is worth $16 billion worldwide, but the quick shipments that customers demand require large stockholdings.

Amazon is already testing for entry into areas such as consumer electronics, games and toys. Possible areas beyond that are software, health supplies, clothing, flowers, magazine subscriptions and travel arrangements. However, in all these areas there are established competitors online, and a 1998 Boston Consulting Group study found that almost two-thirds of electronic commerce revenues were generated by companies that also sell through conventional channels and have an established brand.

Moreover, the logistics of delivery look like a major constraint. While books, music and computer hardware and software fit the e-tailing model because these industries have large, efficient distributors and can ship products overnight, other businesses do not have the same logistics coverage. For example, eToys has found in the toy business in the USA, with no dominant distributors, the company has to buy from more than 500 manufacturers, hold high stocks of products and arrange direct delivery to consumers. Based on his experience in this type of market, founder of eToys, Toby Lenk, believes: 'The original notion of Internet retailing was that you never need to touch the product, you outsource everything, and you run an empire with hardly any people. That's totally wrong. The virtual company simply doesn't work.'

Moreover, in case the comparison of Amazon with Wal-Mart seems fanciful, in 1998 the giant Wal-Mart sued Amazon, accusing the upstart Internet trader of poaching its executives to gain merchandising and distribution trade secrets and claiming that Amazon had caused it 'economic damage' and continues to do so.

'When asked if Amazon is a retailer or a technology company, Jeff Bezos's answer is "Yes"'

When asked if Amazon is a retailer or a technology company, Jeff Bezos's answer is 'Yes'. He says, 'In physical retail, the three most important things are location, location, location. At Amazon.com, the three most important things are technology, technology, technology.' It is also interesting that Amazon's founder, Jeff Bezos, is himself unwilling to give up the experience of buying books through conventional channels: 'I still buy half my books in bookstores and the reason is I like it. I like hearing the bindings creak and smelling the pages and having a tactile sensation. I have a lifelong habit of going to bookstores and I'm not going to change it!' None the less, be believes that Amazon.com can take 15–20 per cent of the book market.

The music business

Along with pornography, air tickets, software and books, recorded music has been one of the main categories of product sold on the Internet. The Internet can provide music consumers with wide choice and easy access for a relatively inexpensive product with little risk, and the chance to sample the music on a multimedia computer at home or work, prior to purchase. However, the interaction between the Internet and the music business illustrates how fundamental change in distribution channels may become in making the established business model obsolete.

'the interaction between the Internet and the music business illustrates how fundamental change in distribution channels may become in making the established business model obsolete'

Traditional music distribution

Since the 1980s, nearly 80 per cent of the global recorded music market has been controlled by six record companies: PolyGram, Sony, Warner, EMI, Bertelsmann and Seagram's Universal Music subsidiary. In 1998, the big six became the big five when Seagram spent $11 billion to acquire Polygram, creating a business holding nearly 24 per cent of the global music market. This is a strategy assuming that size will provide the critical leverage on costs and enhancing profitability in the conventional business model.

The underlying business model pursued by these companies is very simple. The record companies locate, fund and promote recording artists – putting the successful under contract and abandoning the unsuccessful. The branded product is essentially the artist. Recordings reach the consumer as CDs, tapes or records through conventional retail outlets, specialist record/music stores, general book/record stores and general outlets such as supermarkets and departmental stores. In addition, there has been an active mail-order record business selling recordings from catalogues.

The Internet arrives

The Internet is particularly well suited to selling music in the form of CDs and tapes, and has quickly become a major new distribution channel offering an alternative to conventional shops. Market Tracking International estimated in 1998 that the Internet already accounted for 0.1 per cent of the global market, with sales of $87 million, and forecast that this share is growing far faster than previously expected. They estimate that Internet sales will exceed 7 per cent of the total market by 2005 with sales in excess of $3.9 billion.

The leading Internet record stores have been CDnow and N2K, which have merged.

CDnow was the result of the Olim twins' frustration in not being able to obtain an obscure Miles Davis album. They borrowed $20 000 to set up CDnow from their parents' home in Philadelphia in 1994. CDnow stocks around 250 000 albums, videos and CDs and takes around a third of online music sales.

Larry Rosen founded N2K, using funds from the sale of his jazz music label GRP to establish Music Boulevard in 1995. Distribution by these companies has been by mail in the USA, and by air mail and courier to customers outside the USA. Rosen's goal is to turn Music Boulevard into a worldwide chain of virtual music and video stores, with regional marketing and distribution systems – Japan and Europe are targeted as markets where local subsidiaries will tailor the product range to local tastes and provide fast local delivery. Both companies have exclusive placement rights with Internet sites or web pages, so consumers click on their logos to go direct to the Music Boulevard and CDnow sites – Music Boulevard is partnering with American Online, and CDnow with Yahoo and Excite search engines. By late 1998, both companies were still loss making. They offer substantially lower prices than conventional retailers. A *Daily Telegraph* 'shopping basket' of five popular CDs in November 1998, found a CDnow price of £33.49 (including postage) compared to £55.95 on the British high street.

'Traditional music and video retailers were initially very sceptical about online retailing'

Traditional music and video retailers were initially very sceptical about online retailing. However, the impact of CDnow and Music Boulevard has been to bring conventional music retailers to the Internet.

Tower Records, the world's largest music retailer, Camelot Music and other conventional US record retailers have set up Internet stores. In the UK, Virgin Megastores and HMV (the record chain owned by the EMI music group until 1998) have also announced their plans for Internet stores. Tower Records has a UK site as well as a US page. Pricing has been a problem for conventional retailers launching on the web – comparisons between European and US prices are much easier for consumers to make on the Web, and there is the complicated issue for the companies of whether to sell cheaper than their own traditional retail outlets.

The large record companies were even more constrained – operating on the Internet and selling direct to consumers would put them in direct competition with their traditional retail customers. Direct selling would enable the record company to avoid retailer profit margins and costs, but at what cost to their traditional distribution channels? In addition, record companies do not have strong corporate brands – their branding has been the performers.

The ranks start to break

In mid-1997, Sony was the first of the big six record companies to break ranks and to sell records direct to consumers from 'thestore', a subsite on its US web page.

'Sony was the first of the big six record companies to break ranks and to sell records direct to consumers from "thestore"'

Sony's strategy has been aggressive. It has positioned 'thestore' as a rival to other Internet sellers, all its artists are represented there and their albums are sold below list price.

Other record companies have followed Sony's lead but more cautiously. Warner Music and BMG (Bertelsmann's music division) have launched Internet direct selling but with strategies designed to avoid harming relationships with retailers. Warner's pilot sold only 200 albums from its artists' promotional sites, and its sales subsite is low key, all albums are sold at full list prices to avoid accusations of undercutting its retail customers – they are consequently priced substantially higher than CDnow. BMG has also opted for full list prices. In the UK, Island and Polydor labels (part of the PolyGram group) sell from their web sites but have not actively promoted this activity.

More aggressively, in 1998 when Creation Records (49 per cent owned by Sony), for which the band Oasis records, launched its Internet operation, the chairman, Alan McGee, made no secret of his belief that a time was coming when bands would rather sell their music over the Internet than through record stores. The Creation site transmits live performances by artists as well as selling CDs. At the end of 1998, Creation defied the industry rules again by cutting the wholesale prices of its back catalogue albums as well as deep discounts on music sold from its Internet site – its plan is to progressively reduce the prices of CDs.

In January 1999, the record companies' worst nightmare started to come true. Chuck D, a best-selling US rap artist, chose to post a new recorded track to his band's web site instead of releasing it as a CD. This was the first artist to use the new MP4 technology, developed by Global Music Outlet, providing superior quality to the MP3 files commonly used by consumers to

'In January 1999, the record companies' worst nightmare started to come true'

download music (see below). The likelihood is that other artists will quickly follow this precedent to free themselves from the restrictions imposed by conventional record companies.

The rules start to change

One of the characteristics of technology-based channels is that they may bring new competitors drawn in by the technology rather than expertise in the product or service concerned.

For example, in 1997 Wal-Mart, the powerful general retail chain in the USA, began selling chart albums from its web site, priced at $11.88 compared to $14.99 in normal stores. The music business is likely to attract other investors with no history in the traditional business.

'Another example, of the blurring of traditional boundaries was the planned launch in 1998 of an Internet record store by Capital Radio'

Another example, of the blurring of traditional boundaries was the planned launch in 1998 of an Internet record store by Capital Radio (as a joint venture with Telstar, the UK's largest independent record company). Capital's radio stations have a weekly audience of 5.8 million, and its Internet sites receive more than a million monthly page requests, providing a music customer base and the radio station's broadcasts provide the promotional channel.

The traditional record companies have been constrained in their response by fears of Capital Radio dropping their new releases from the radio playlist.

The product changes

'the Internet music channel may not merely damage irreparably the traditional retail music sector, it may remove the need for much of the traditional product as well'

It is quickly becoming apparent that the Internet music channel may not merely damage irreparably the traditional retail music sector, it may remove the need for much of the traditional product as well. Music can be downloaded from the Internet as digital signals by the consumer onto a PC or other recordable medium – there is then no need for prerecorded CDs, tapes or records.

For example, MP3 is a PC file format which compresses audio files to a size where transferring them on the Internet is feasible. The MP3 file is downloaded, it can then be played on the PC, copied onto a recordable CR-R drive to make a CD or copied to a minidisk player. MP3 'Walkman' units that download direct from the computer and are then portable are already on the market. A lively Net music community based on MP3 has quickly emerged, mainly offering home recordings by amateur musicians, with its own 'Top Ten'. MP3.com and Internet Underground Music Archive have developed into Internet jukeboxes. MP4 technology is now available, offering superior quality.

Internet Underground Archive was started by Jeff Patterson, a student in Santa Cruz, California, posting unrecorded bands to help people hear new music. By 1998, five years later, more than a million people a month log on to listen to music by about 2500 acts. It is a small operation by record company standards, but as the highest-profile digital jukebox it is a prototype of some importance. Anyone can post music on the site, after paying an annual fee of $240. Consumers can listen to the music free, or pay 99 cents to download as an MP3 file, and some acts sell disks and tapes by mail order.

Personal MP3 players are freely available for as little as £200 in portable versions.

In fact, initially, apart from some experiments, downloading music from the Internet has been the preserve of pirate jukeboxes posting unauthorized copies of albums, which can be illegally downloaded, and legal Internet sites like those above dealing with unrecorded performances.

However, the 1998 Internet launch by Creation Records aims to start digital distribution within a year, so consumers can download music onto their computers from the Creation site.

The fears for the traditional record companies are that the legal and technical safeguards do not protect their music from piracy, even though direct downloading would give them reduced manufacturing and distribution costs. More significantly in the longer term, digital downloading is likely to encourage the entry of new competitors from other sectors diversifying into music – telecommunications companies, technology specialists and electricity suppliers are likely candidates.

The reaction of the conventional recording companies has been predictable. They have sued for breach of copyright where music has been found on the Internet and have lobbied (unsuccessfully) to have MP3 recording devices made illegal. In December 1998, Warner Brothers, EMI, BMG and Sony announced their collaboration, the 'Secure Digital Music Initiative', to develop an alternative to MP3, which is as easy to use but more 'secure', i.e. consumers pay the record companies for the music they download. The recording companies would like to distribute music over the Internet (it is cheaper than paying record shops) but want to protect their income.

A major landmark in 1998 was the agreement reached between Sony, Warner, EMI, Universal and other US record companies to participate in the Madison Project, organized by IBM. The Madison Project is to develop a commercial digital distribution system for music. AT&T is marketing its A2B music distribution system against IBM's.

The industry changes

'if music can be downloaded digitally, then the role of record companies may be replaced by direct contacts between musicians and consumers with the Internet site as broker'

More fundamental, if music can be downloaded digitally, then the role of record companies may be replaced by direct contacts between musicians and consumers with the Internet site as broker.

Quite simply, musicians may increasingly choose to bypass record labels by releasing their own material over the Internet. This is, after all a sector with a strong anti-establishment tradition – Frank Zappa and The Grateful Dead successfully launched their own self-run record labels in the 1970s, operating on a mail-order basis and making millions from the operation.

In fact, thousands of young, unsigned acts already bypass the traditional music industry by selling music direct from their own Internet sites, and this has proved a fertile hunting ground for the record companies to locate new acts. However, if established, major recording stars choose to sell direct, then the situation becomes very different. George Michael, for example, already distributes other people's music over the Internet through Aegean Records, a label he founded in 1996, but not his own music. However, he is one of the recording stars who has made no secret of his misgivings about traditional record companies.

'developments in classical music underline the new model which sidelines conventional products and distribution channels'

Somewhat different developments in classical music underline the new model which sidelines conventional products and distribution channels. Mastervision is a closed circuit cable system in the USA to link schools and libraries with sources of performance and instruction. The school can listen to an original musical performance, but as interactive participants who can talk to the musicians and ask advice about their own performing. As well as linking audiences and artists, the same system can link writers, production teams and performers to rehearse and perform through the electronic system. This is a precursor to the 1998 launch of the Global Music Network Internet site. GMN is an Anglo-US joint venture that has started a daily offering of live and 'as-live' performances of classical music from festivals and concerts throughout the world. Listening to the performances is free. Payment is only made for downloading a recording or ordering it through the post, which may also be a compilation of favourites from the offerings on the site. The site also offers interviews with the artists and feedback or 'chat' facilities for listeners. Many of the performers are major stars released by major record companies. The significance of these developments is that they provide direct communication between musician and audience with no intervention by middlemen, that is record companies, retailers or even the broadcast media.

Sources

'Car Wars: Wayne Huizenga vs Everybody', *Fortune*, 9 June 1997.

Akre, Brian S. (1998), 'Restructure of Dealer Networks Will Change Retailing', *Marketing News*, 26 October.

Blackwell, David (1998), 'A Metal-Moving Chain for Treating Cars As Bean Cans On Wheels', *Financial Times*, 2 February.

Dwek, Robert (1998), 'By The Book', *Marketing Business*, November.

Eldridge, Earle (1998), 'New Leases May Allow Car Swaps', *USA Today*, 13 August.

Franklin, Carl (1998), 'Amazon Boss Makes Rivals Eat Their Words', *Sunday Business*, 22 November.

Franklin, Carl (1998), 'Amazon Defies Gravity As Investors Pile in Blindly', *Sunday Business*, 20 December.

Griffiths, John (1998), 'Car Dealers Warned of Rise in Internet Sales', *Financial Times*, 2 February.

Griffiths, John (1998), 'Car Supermarket Chain Launched', *Financial Times*, 5 January.

Griffiths, John (1998), 'Rival Car Sales Outlets Threaten Status Quo', *Financial Times*, 12 December.

Hof, Robert D., Ellen Neuborne and Heather Green (1998), 'Amazon.com: The Wild World of E-Commerce', *Business Week*, 14 December.

Jackson, Tim (1998), 'Coming Up Trumps With Card Sales', *Financial Times*, 15 December.

Lebrecht, Norman (1998), 'Click Here For the Future of Music', *Daily Telegraph*, 9 December.

Martin, Peter (1998), 'Exposed Links in the Established Value Chain', *Financial Times*, 15 October.

Mitchell, Alan (1998), 'Cutting Out the Middleman', *Marketing Business*, July/August.

O'Connell, Dominic (1998), 'Air Miles To Sell Holidays Online', *Sunday Business*, 15 November.

Pellegrini, Frank (1998), 'Amazon.com's Uncertain Future', *Time Digital*, 12 December.

Pretzlik, Charles (1998), 'This Old Man's A Dustman and He Wears A Baseball Cap', *Daily Telegraph*, 16 August.

Price, Christopher (1998), 'Fashion Suits the Internet Shopper', *Financial Times*, 24 June.

Rawsthorn, Alice (1997), 'Online Music Shops Send Record Retailers Into A Spin', *Financial Times*, 8 August.

Rawsthorn, Alice (1997), 'Sony Sounds Discordant Note', *Financial Times*, 11 August.

Rawsthorn, Alice (1997), 'Sleepy Booksellers Get Wake Up Call', *Financial Times*, 10 October.

Rawsthorn, Alice (1997), 'Internet Music Retailers Hear An Upbeat Tempo', *Financial Times*, 5 December.

Rawsthorn, Alice (1998), 'Internet Sales Could Become Key To Music Industry', *Financial Times*, 6 June.

Rawsthorn, Alice (1998), 'Capital Plans Online Record Store', *Financial Times*, 28 July.

Rawsthorn, Alice (1998), 'Digital Musicbox Makes Sweet Sound of Music on the Internet', *Financial Times*, 11 November.

Rawsthorn, Alice (1998), 'IBM To Test Internet Music Delivery', *Financial Times*, 26 November.

Rawsthorn, Alice (1998), 'Record Companies See Their Stars Fly Away To The Net', *Financial Times*, 27 November.

Rawsthorn, Alice (1998), 'Record Label Plans Digital Distribution on Internet', *Financial Times*, 30 November.

Rawsthorn, Alice and Frederick Studemann (1998), 'Traditional Booksellers Move To Thwart Online Amazon', *Financial Times*, 8 October.

Rees, Jon (1998), 'Creation Sells Music on the Net', *Sunday Business*, 20 September.

Sellers, Patricia (1999), 'Inside the First E-Christmas', *Fortune*, 1 February.

Simonian, Haig (1998), 'Dealing With the Car Dealers', *Financial Times*, 4 March.

Stross, Randell E. (1997), 'Why Barnes & Noble May Crush Amazon', *Fortune*, 29 September.

Taylor, Paul (1998), 'Middle Men Delted As the Word Spreads', *Financial Times*, 27 October.

Taylor, Roger (1998), 'Driving A Harder Bargain in the Motor Showroom', *Financial Times*, 7 August.

Tomkins, Richard (1998), 'Busy Tills At High Street Shops Are Outshining Online Sales', *Financial Times*, 11 November.

Uhlig, Robert (1998), 'Christmas Shopping Costs Less on the Internet', *Daily Telegraph*, 30 November.

Waters, Richard (1998), 'Steering Through A Car Sales Revolution', *Financial Times*, 8 July.

Waters, Richard (1999), 'Bubble.Com', *Financial Times*, 17 January.

Waters, Richard and John Labate (1998), 'Brought To Book', *Financial Times*, 10 November.

Wice, Nathaniel (1998), 'Amazon Adding 9000 New Customers A Day', *Time Digital*, 23 July.

Wice, Nathaniel (1998), 'Amazon Outgrowing Books', *Time Digital*, 7 December.

Wylie, David (1995), 'Calyx & Corolla', Harvard Business School Case Study 9–592–035, October.

Younger, Rod (1998), 'New Structures Will be Required', *Financial Times*, 1 December.

CHAPTER 6

Reinventing the airline business*

If you want dinner, go to a restaurant!

'the airline industry has experienced a revolution in the last decades as governments have introduced deregulation'

Throughout the world, the airline industry has experienced a revolution in the last decades as governments have introduced deregulation to allow companies greater freedom in the way they operate. However, while the major airlines have been pursuing 'hub and spoke' strategies (you are in Cardiff and want to be in Dallas, so the airline naturally enough offers to fly you from London to Detroit and then to Dallas/Fort Worth), and global alliances, something new has emerged – the 'no-frills' airlines and flights from regional airports.

There are some interesting questions to be raised about this reinvented airline concept and whether the 'no-frills' strategy is robust enough to achieve long-term success.

The airline industry

Traditionally, the airline industry was hemmed in by severe regulation by governments on where and how they could compete. Landmarks were 1978 in the USA when the domestic skies were

---

* This material has been produced by Nigel F. Piercy from secondary sources and discussions with industry executives. © Nigel F. Piercy.

opened up to competition and 1997 in Europe when the EU wrapped up its own programme of deregulation, allowing any EU airline to start domestic operations in another member state. (This is, however, a long way from free-for-all competition in 'open skies', but it is a start.) At the same time, many state-owned airlines have become commercial organizations.

This limited revolution in the freedom for airlines has led to many new entries to the industry, and some considerable carnage. Between 80 and 85 per cent of the new carriers launched in the USA after deregulation have already gone out of business, and in the tough times of 1993–96, sixty out of eighty new European airlines failed. Developing robust new strategies in this business is easier said than done. However, one approach to reinventing the airline business which stands out is the 'no-frills' airline, with a value proposition which is radically different to the branding and service offer of the conventional airlines. The model for the 'no-frills' airline is Southwest Airlines in the USA.

'one approach to reinventing the airline business which stands out is the "no-frills" airline, with a value proposition which is radically different to the branding and service offer of the conventional airlines'

The Southwest model

Southwest Airlines started operations in Texas in the early 1970s, and it has declared a profit every year for the past twenty-five years – which is a boast that no other US airline can make. By 1997, Southwest was the seventh largest carrier in the USA, with revenues of $3.8 billion and operated a fleet of 250 aircraft. It is the low-cost airline against which its countless imitators are judged.

After a shaky start in 1971, Southwest captured the Texas market with its 'no-frills' concept, flying between Dallas, Houston and San Antonio. The large carriers, more concerned with their intercontinental business, did not take the competition seriously. This left Southwest space to build a cash-pile, which then enabled it to attack prime markets such as California. By the time it expanded, Southwest was no longer a small start-up operation.

The 'no-frills' offer Southwest makes to its customers has been the model for many others. The essential elements are:

- very low fares – with the effect of filling the aircraft with people who might not otherwise have flown at all
- cattle-car boarding with no assigned seating or classes of seat
- no in-flight service apart from a soft drink and a bag of nuts

From the outset, the airline drew attention to itself by being weird. The company takes the idea that work can be fun to extremes, led by a remorseless practical joker – Herbert Kelleher as chief executive. For example, at its launch targeting a predominantly male Texas clientele, Southwest adopted a 'love' theme: air hostesses wore hot pants and white PVC go-go boots; drinks were called 'love potions'; peanuts were 'love bites'; and tickets came from 'love machines'. (The inspiration was that Southwest flies out of Dallas' Love airport.) In a broader market than Texas and an era of rabid political correctness in the USA, the love campaign was replaced by a mission to deliver 'positively outrageous service at unbelievably low fares'.

'Southwest adopted a "love" theme: air hostesses wore hot pants and white PVC go-go boots; drinks were called "love potions"; peanuts were "love bites"; and tickets came from "love machines"'

The fun elements persists, however, and practical jokes and wisecracks are almost compulsory:

'sometimes flight attendants play tricks on passengers by hiding in the overhead luggage bins and leaping out at unexpected moments'

- sometimes flight attendants play tricks on passengers by hiding in the overhead luggage bins and leaping out at unexpected moments
- safety announcements turn into comedy routines: 'Those of you who wish to smoke will please file out to our lounge on the wing, where you can enjoy our feature movie presentation 'Gone With the Wind' . . .'
- routinely in-flight announcements are not spoken but sung

There are more serious sides to the Southwest strategy, however.

Southwest has made huge efforts to build and sustain a highly motivated workforce. The 'fun' theme is pervasive and is backed by recognition for good service, greetings cards and parties for birthdays and special occasions and a large investment in training and personal development.

The result of almost fanatical dedication to the CEO and the company is that employees show exceptional levels of productivity compared to the rest of the industry. For example, Southwest has got turnaround time between arrival and departure for its aircraft down to twenty minutes – less than half the time other carriers take to get the plane back in the sky. One reason is that flight attendants and even pilots are ready to help out in cleaning the passenger cabin, loading the bags or doing anything else needed to get back in the air.

Southwest has driven other elements of the cost structure for getting in the air to very low levels:

- operating mainly on short-haul flights with high traffic densities
- the fleet is standardized on Boeing 737s, simplifying the spare parts inventory and reducing training needs
- regional airports have substantially lower charges for airlines

As well as the low cost base and the 'no-frills' offer, there is something else striking about Southwest – its aggressive customer service strategy. In 1997 Southwest ranked first in customer service among major US airlines in a *Money* magazine survey. Lorraine Grubbs, manager of Southwest's training programme the 'University for People' says 'the frills are not what's important for most people, it's the compassion and caring and the people'.

Currently in the US market low-cost carriers account for about 30 per cent of the domestic air travel market. Southwest is the most successful, but other operators include Tower Air and ValuJet (renamed AirTran after a much-publicized DC9 crash in Florida). The other low-cost entrants did not survive the retaliation of the large airlines who reduced prices and increased capacity until the newcomers disappeared – the failure rate was 85 per cent.

'No-frills' flying in Europe

Following EU policies of aviation liberalization, several European 'no-frills' airlines started with the Southwest model: low fares, no on-board meals, no allocated seats, often using regional airports and lower staffing costs. Initially expected to attract mainly leisure travellers, much of the demand has turned out to be from business travellers who resent paying premium fares to travel within Europe. Estimates suggest that almost half the customers for the low-cost carriers are price-conscious business travellers. One executive was quoted in the national press, 'I've given up paying £100 for breakfast' to explain his choice of flying to Glasgow with easyJet for £68, compared to the £198 quoted by British Airways for the same trip. The low-cost flight market from the UK to Europe grew from zero to 5 per cent in just two years.

'Estimates suggest that almost half the customers for the low-cost carriers are price-conscious business travellers'

The 'no-frills' operators undercut the big carriers by as much as 50 per cent and focus mainly on high volume, short-haul, point-to-point trips. Low fares are achieved by exploiting several important levers to achieve low cost (the alternative of low fares *'"no-frills" operators can get costs per seat down to half those of the major network carriers'*

with high costs is clearly unattractive). A recent report by the Civil Aviation Authority of the UK notes that the 'no-frills' operators can get costs per seat down to *half* those of the major network carriers. Savings come from:

- *Distribution costs* – it has been estimated that as much as 25 per cent of the cost of conventional air tickets comes from distribution, e.g. travel agent commissions and promotion, the computerized reservation system shared by major airlines and the coupon exchanges to reconcile passenger switches. Direct selling and ticketless travel avoid most of these costs.
- *In-flight catering and staffing* – conventional airlines provide 'free' meals and drinks in their ticket prices. Removing these services saves money (and a lot of waste when passengers turn down the food because they want to sleep). However, easyJet estimates that while it has three cabin crew on a short-haul flight, the equivalent BA flight will have six cabin crew, because that is the only way to distribute and collect hot towels and serve all passengers with drinks and food and another round of drinks on a short flight.
- *Fleet uniformity* – a fleet standardized on a single aircraft type drastically reduces maintenance and spares costs and crew training.
- *Regional airports* – using regional airports instead of the major hubs has several important implications. It gives access to the underserved regional population in the regional airport's catchment area; fees are lower; less congestion allows the operator to be more efficient and to get better utilization from the aircraft (because they stay on the ground for less time).

The major players in establishing and growing this market in Europe are the following companies.

easyJet

easyJet was started by Stelios Haji-Ioannou, heir to a Greek shipping fortune, in 1995. Haji-Ioannou joined his father's shipping business after graduation and then set up his own shipping line, Stelmar Tankers, in 1992. He caught the 'airline bug' after meeting Richard Branson, founder of Virgin. He started the easyJet operation in Luton with little more than an office, a booking system and sub-contractors to provide the rest of the services. By the end of 1998 he was operating seventeen

European routes with a rapidly expanding fleet of owned aircraft. The easyJet operation has much in common with the Southwest model: point-to-point flights, short haul only, scheduled flights not charters, no frills, low fares and low costs.

Haji-Ioannou's thinking is dominated by two things: keeping in touch with the customer and driving out bureaucracy in the business. In spite of his personal shyness, he flies his own aircraft three or four times a week to talk to the passengers and he delights in customer letters thanking him for making air travel affordable, saying things like 'You've saved my love life, you made it more affordable for me to go and see my other half!' He believes in motivating his staff by example – focusing on the external enemy by holding 'war meetings', standing up to signal urgency.

The easyJet mission is stated as 'To Make Flying Affordable' and Haji-Ioannou says the goal is that more people will fly, and the same people will fly more often. He describes his target customers as everyone who pays for travel out of their own pockets (including leisure travel but also business), with the exception of 'fat cats who want airmiles'.

'The easyJet mission is stated as "To Make Flying Affordable"'

His frustration with the formality and bureaucracy in his father's company has turned into a quest for informality and the paperless office in his own company. He describes easyJet as a 'socialist company' in which 'there are no secrets', because all employees have access to the computer system on which all information is stored. He says easyJet has a 'unique people culture', no neck-ties, no fuss, no formality, no secretaries for executives, no private offices, and no paperwork, but plenty of parties, including a regular Friday afternoon barbeque at the back of the Luton office. Haji-Ioannou says he aims to recruit people with talent and character who will enjoy working in the easyJet culture and this counts for more than experience in the traditional airline business.

In fact, easyJet was modelled directly on the Southwest Air approach from the very beginning, boasting that flights from the Luton-base to Scotland would 'cost as little as a pair of jeans' – starting from £29 one-way. At this time, the London to Scotland fare with conventional airlines was more than £100. Route extensions include Amsterdam, Nice, Athens and Barcelona as well as Scotland. It has established a second hub in Liverpool with flights to Amsterdam and Greece. In 1998 plans were announced for a massive increase in easyJet's fleet with orders placed for fifteen new generation Boeing 737–700s, in addition to a 1997 order for twelve older generation 737–300s. This will increase the fleet from seven to thirty-five aircraft in five years.

In 1998, easyJet bought a 40 per cent stake in TEA Switzerland, a Swiss chartered carrier with four leased Boeing aircraft, with the option to increase the stake to 90 per cent. The goal is to relaunch TEA as easyJet Switzerland as a 'no-frills' airline and to ease pressure on the Luton Airport base. A major attraction of this purchase was that TEA operated the same aircraft as easyJet, so the fleet increased but remain standardized.

'easyJet's founder is fond of reminding his customers, "If you want a meal, go to a restaurant"'

Costs have been contained, Southwest-style, from the outset. easyJet's founder is fond of reminding his customers, 'If you want a meal, go to a restaurant'. Passengers are fed jokes instead and also have to face recycled boarding passes, no first or business class privileges, and the trek out to secondary airports such as Luton. Luton is the alternative to London Heathrow, Liverpool is the alternative to Manchester, and the purchase of TEA makes Geneva a third base (recently vacated by Swissair pulling out).

In addition, easyJet is a 'ticketless' airline. By refusing to honour competitors' tickets, easyJet avoids the paperwork of exchanging coupons to get paid for carrying other people's passengers and the need to issue tickets. Mr Haji-Ioannou says, 'Your right to fly comes from the fact that your name is in the computer – not from any document you hold. That's the paradigm shift.' easyJet runs its own call centre and reservation system and does not have to pay to participate in the reservation systems operated by the full-cost airlines.

For similar reasons, easyJet does not pay commission to travel agents; it relies on direct sales made by telephone booking clerks, paid 80p per seat sold. Pursuing the same logic, easyJet emphasizes online booking by customers visiting the easyJet Internet site – the web address is painted on the side of the aircraft in giant orange characters. By the end of 1998 Internet sales were already 10 per cent of total revenue and growing – the company hopes to take 30 per cent of its booking through the web site by the end of 1999. Indeed, Haji-Ioannou plans to open a chain of Internet cafes, easyEverything, which will enable consumers with no home Internet access to book tickets online, as well as accessing e-mail and Internet-based shopping.

In late 1988, easyJet was the first no-frills airline to feature in *Company Barclaycard's* annual survey of business travel. It was rated higher in reliability than BA or KLM and the majority of business travellers in the survey reported that the small airlines gave better service. Of the business travellers who had used a no-frills airline, an impressive 86 per cent said they would do so again.

The aggressive attack on BA's European business travel market by easyJet is illustrated by the copy of a national press advertising campaign launched in November 1998.

RECESSION?

In a boom, nobody worries about the travel budget. In a recession everyone with shareholder value at heart should question the cost of flying BA Club Europe. A Harris Poll, commissioned by easyJet, proves that one of the reasons executives refuse to fly with easyJet is that they don't get any air miles. Air miles is just a bribery scheme and the greatest enemy of the travel budget.

Other excuses used by 'fat cats' can be dealt with as follows:

1 **The corporate travel agent does not book easyJet!** ... because easyJet does not pay them any commission. You or your secretary can book direct over the phone or via the Internet. Alternatively, if your company is big enough, get the travel agent to do it anyway!
2 **Luton is too far away!** It takes about an hour from central London to any of the London airports.
3 **Bookings are not flexible!** Rubbish! First you can buy one way, none of these idiotic minimum stay rules. Also ask for the £10 change fee for a truly flexible fare at one third of Club Europe.
4 **Not enough flights in a day!** 3–5 flights a day on most business routes must be enough.
5 **Surely the aircraft must be old!** An all-Boeing fleet, one of the youngest in the industry. Another 40 brand new ones will be delivered over the next few years.
6 **But easyJet is a Mickey Mouse airline!** So, why did Bob Ayling (the CEO of BA), having failed to buy easyJet, create a carbon copy of it?

easyJet
0870 6 000 000
www.easyJet.com

---

easyJet's UK operating company lost £3.3 million in 1997, but in January 1999 announced annual pre-tax profits of £2.3 million, based on a 65 per cent increase in passenger numbers producing turnover of £77 million. Haji-Ioannou has no immediate plans to float the company.

Debonair

Luton-based Debonair flies to and between six European destinations. It mixes direct selling with travel agency bookings, and keeps costs low by contracting out everything from check-in to maintenance. Over half its customers are business travellers. Large companies such as Xerox and Rover routinely book all but their most senior executives on Debonair, if they have a choice of carrier.

'Large companies such as Xerox and Rover routinely book all but their most senior executives on Debonair, if they have a choice of carrier'

Debonair is slightly different to the other operators. It offers a free snack and tea and coffee, for which the others charge, and has introduced a business class section. Debonair also operates conventional seat allocation. Chairman Franco Mancassola believes that the European traveller is too sophisticated for the complete 'no-frills' approach and the chairman denies that his company is a 'no-frills' operator. The company is expected to move into full profit in 1998–99 and announced its first quarter's profit in December 1998, after two years of heavy losses.

Mancassola has tried to insulate Debonair from some of the stresses of the low-cost market by signing contracts to fly on behalf of larger airlines, including Lufthansa and Air France. With low operating costs, Debonair is positioning as a subcontractor for conventional airlines, to fly cheaply on low-yield routes.

In 1998 Debonair looked set to double the size of its fleet with an order for 10 new Boeing 717s. Debonair has started a joint venture with AB Airlines at Gatwick and is looking at adding routes to Eastern Europe.

Ryanair

Ryanair was originally a conventional full-service airline started by Tony Ryan to compete with Aer Lingus, by offering lower prices. The results were a disaster – Ryanair lost £18 million in four years and went through five CEOs. Current CEO, Michael O'Leary, adopted the Southwest model and extended services from Dublin to London to the rest of Britain and now some Continental Europe routes. An aggressive competitor, O'Leary was accused by the Irish premier of 'tooth and claw capitalism'.

'O'Leary was accused by the Irish premier of "tooth and claw capitalism"'

Now one of Europe's most experienced low-cost carriers, while easyJet remains a private company, Ryanair shows that low-cost airlines can currently make profits in Europe, showing 1997 pre-tax profits of I£24.5 million on turnover of I£136 million. The airline is renowned for constant 80 per cent load factors. Ryanair has been skilful in avoiding direct competition by taking on underdeveloped routes from Dublin to UK regional cities. Analysts judge that Ryanair has created more of a market than it has taken away from traditional airlines. When it started flying Dublin to London in 1985, the route carried one million passengers a year, but by 1998 this had reached four million at a one-way fare as low as £19.99.

In 1998, Ryanair held an autumn seat sale cutting fares as low as £16.99 one-way to Europe. Floated in May 1997, 1998 saw passenger volumes rise 35 per cent on the previous year. Floatation funded the expansion of the fleet from twelve to eighteen aircraft.

Virgin Express

Virgin operates from Gatwick and Heathrow and is priced between easyJet and the big carriers and flies from Brussels to seven destinations, including Rome, Barcelona and Nice. A relative newcomer, Virgin achieved break-even in 1996 and a small profit in 1997. Based in Brussels, Virgin partners with Sabena to fly the Belgian carrier's passengers into Heathrow – Sabena sells the tickets and their passengers sit in a separate business class section on the Virgin plane. By 1998, in a drift away from the 'no-frills' concept, Virgin was increasing passenger leg-room and looking at launching a frequent flyer programme. In 1997 the company announced plans to become a publicly quoted company with a dual listing in the USA and Belgium. Plans also involved increasing the fleet to eighteen aircraft by 1998. Virgin Express issued a profits warning in August 1998, and the third-quarter results issued in December that year showed that escalating operating costs (mainly caused by leasing expensive fully-crewed aircraft to overcome pilot shortages) had resulted in a 77 per cent fall in profits. Shares have fallen from $15 to $7.06. The company has applied for an Irish air operator's licence to shift some of its base to Ireland and reduce some operating costs.

In spite of this initial success for the low-cost airlines, industry commentators have been predicting a phase of rationalization and consolidation, as happened in the USA, with the weaker operators closing.

However, the most dramatic event in this sector has been the response of British Airways in launching its own low-cost 'no-frills' airline in 1998 – Go.

The nightmare begins . . .

'BA has been forced to respond in a dramatic way, because it was hurting, and in spite of the clear risk to the value of its main brand'

Perhaps the most dramatic proof of the impact of the 'no-frills' model is that BA has been forced to respond in a dramatic way, because it was hurting, and in spite of the clear risk to the value of its main brand.

As the dominant UK airline, BA's first response to the 'no-frills' operators' impact on its business was to discuss a take-over with easyJet. BA had earlier talked to Ryanair. BA backed off from the easyJet purchase, apparently concerned that move would be blocked anyway by the UK regulators. A possible alliance was also discussed with Debonair.

easyJet reacted with hostility to the rumour BA was entering the 'no-frills' market, apparently concerned that BA would use the information gained in their acquisition discussions and legal action was threatened. Less worried at the rumour was Michael O'Leary, CEO of Ryanair, who simply observed, 'If British Airways think they can set up a discount airline, they must be smoking too much dope.' Debonair and Richard Branson both threatened action on the grounds that entry by BA would be a blatant attempt to destroy the low-cost competition.

'If British Airways think they can set up a discount airline, they must be smoking too much dope'

In fact, entering the 'no-frills' market represents a major risk for BA. It faces a difficult industrial relations problem with lower wages and could end up simply cannibalizing its own customer base, i.e. transferring full-fare passengers from BA's Heathrow flights to discounted fares out of Stansted. It could also damage BA's brand and its new positioning unveiled in 1998.

None the less, in November 1997 BA announced the launch of its new European airline offering reduced in-flight service and lower fares at around a 30 per cent discount against BA's regular prices. Initial plans were to fly to Italy, Spain, Scandinavia, France and Germany out of Stansted airport. The new operation is a separate structure from BA, with its own brand, headed by Barbara Cassani, formerly BA's general manager in the USA. From the outset, Go had a different physical location to BA headquarters, to reinforce its 'separateness' from the main airline. Seats can be purchased over the telephone, with no tickets issued, streamlined check-in and no free in-flight food and drink. Rumoured to have been given a start-up budget of £25 million, Cassani described her vision as transforming the low-cost airline business: 'We will be the IKEA of the airline business. What IKEA did to make cheap furniture tasteful, we will do to the low-fare market. There will be more style to this market than has been seen before.' The new brand is Go.

'We will be the IKEA of the airline business. What IKEA did to make cheap furniture tasteful, we will do to the low-fare market'

Go attacked the market in May 1998 with a £100 fare to Rome, Milan and Copenhagen. easyJet and Debonair accused BA of subsidizing the new operation, because this level of fare could not make a profit. Go sold 18 000 bookings in its first month. However, Go increased its fares by around 80 per cent within two weeks of launch, to a level where it was more expensive than other operators such as Virgin Express, Debonair and KLM UK on its main routes. Go still faces court action on its possible subsidies from BA.

The war continues

The result of the Go entry has been to trigger an unprecedented level of competition in this part of the air travel business.

The commencement of hostilities

BA's Go operation launched in 1998 with a London to Edinburgh flight priced at £70 for a standard return and £100 for a fully flexible return. The result was that this route was competed by five airlines (including BA itself along with the low-cost carriers and KLM UK). On this route the easyJet fares ranged from £68 to £228, KLM UK's fares were between £68 and £288, BA from Heathrow and Gatwick was charging between £69 and £276.

In answer to the question of whether the low-cost airlines can compete with this attack, Haji-Ioannou of easyJet says:

The short answer is that we can compete with them if they play fair. Fair competition means they are exposed to the same costs and risks of failure that we are. In other words, they get their aircraft, fuel and insurance at the same price, and not BA prices which are substantially lower. The second thing is the pressure to make money. My first reading of the situation is that I don't believe Go is run with the intention of making money. I don't believe that anyone can make money at the prices they have just announced.

easyJet's Stelios Haji-Iaonnou promised that there would be 'the mother of all fare wars' as a result of Go's attack. Some of his aircraft carry the message in giant orange characters along the fuselage: 'Stop BA, Stop GO'. By September 1998 in response to Go's launch and the BA summer sale of tickets, Ryanair hit back with seats from London to Scotland, France, Italy and Sweden priced at £16.99 single, from all UK ports to Dublin at £29.99 single, and from London to other European destinations charging £29.99 single. Michael O'Leary of Ryanair commented, 'If BA wants a fares war, they have come to the right place. We have the financial clout to be able to do this.' The Ryanair seats were priced below cost to fill unused capacity.

The response from KLM UK concentrated on adding additional flights on the routes competed by Go in an attempt to have departures around the Go flights and to increase capacity. Similarly, Virgin Express has started operations from Gatwick (not currently available to Go, which has to use the less convenient Stansted airport), by purchasing Sabre, a charter airline for £8 million in April 1998.

Aggressive advertising by easyJet in the national press focused on antagonism towards BA. For example, one full-page ad included the following copy:

Does the world's favourite airline really want a low cost carrier?

1 They will screw it up and lose a fortune
2 They will confuse their customers who won't know what to expect
3 They will cannibalise their main business with passengers switching to the new airline
4 They will turn up the heat with the unions already sensitive from a summer of discontent
5 A direct sales strategy will stir up travel agents who may boycott their long haul flights
6 They will open the door to legal action from existing low cost airlines

If they're not doing it for the money the only possible reason is to eliminate smaller competitors like easyJet and then put their fares up again!

Source: *Financial Times*, 28 October 1997.

Interestingly, these messages were clearly designed to reach BA shareholders and airline regulators, rather than customers. Other ads placed by easyJet characterized Barbara Cassani and Robert Ayling as 'Beauty and the Beast', and congratulated Cassani for promotion from BA's 'Dirty Tricks Department' to the 'BA Cheap Tricks Department' (referring to Cassani's alleged role in the BA campaign against Richard Branson and Virgin Atlantic for which BA has been fined by the British courts).

'ads placed by easyJet characterized Barbara Cassani and Robert Ayling as "Beauty and the Beast"'

High court actions in May 1998 accused BA of 'classic predatory behaviour' and a 'lack of transparency' in launching Go to kill off the low-cost airlines in breach of European competition rules. easyJet claimed BA was illegally cross-subsidizing Go by guaranteeing its aircraft leases to get more favourable rates and exploiting BA's brand image to associate Go with higher standards of reliability and safety. By October 1998, easyJet was urging the European Commission to bar Go's £15 single fare from London to Edinburgh, because it was a 'cheap trick' subsidized by BA and designed to crush the competition.

Debonair also took BA to the European Commission accusing Go of abusing its dominant position on the London–Rome route by predatory pricing and dumping excess capacity on the route. This claim was rejected by the Commission, but it is just one of many to be decided.

It is interesting to note the exploitation of the European regulators as a competitive weapon. Haji-Ioannou claims that the European regulators are far more prepared to protect the new airlines than were their counterparts in the USA. He says that when the European Commission began investigating his earlier complaints against KLM trying to drive him off the London–Amsterdam route, the Dutch carrier behaved less aggressively towards him. European Commission officials raiding KLM's offices for evidence may explain this. He says 'The European authorities are much more on the ball'.

What happens next?

The growth of the low-cost 'no-frills' operators in Europe has been highly successful and profit performance has generally been good. The major issue is whether this performance can be sustained.

Certainly the US experience has been that most of the low-cost airlines have failed. While some of the conventional carriers such as Delta have low-cost off-shoots, the only really successful low-cost operator is Southwest. The US transportation department explains that when the new low-cost entrants started services, the large airlines responded by cutting prices and offering more seats. Once the new carrier was forced out of business, the big airline raised prices and withdrew the extra seats. One analyst notes that where Southwest flies, fares are low, but where it does not operate fares are not low. The computerized reservation systems make it relatively easy for an airline to find what competitors are doing and adjust prices accordingly.

'the moment of truth is approaching for the low-cost operators'

Sir Michael Bishop of British Midland suggests that the moment of truth is approaching for the low-cost operators. He argues that the low rates they have been offered by airports will end and move to market rates; the profits from duty-free sales are about to end; and several of the low cost carriers will have to buy new aircraft to comply with new EU noise regulations. He picks Debonair as the likely first casualty.

The biggest threat, however, is the BA Go strategy.

In the past, BA has removed independents by acquisition – it took over both British Caledonian and Dan-Air. Attempts to buy easyJet or Debonair floundered. There is no doubt that Go is intended to retrieve the business lost to the 'no-frills' airlines, as well as to participate in the travel market growth that can be achieved by low fare strategies.

'"When is a no-frills airline, not a no-frills airline?" The answer is: "When it adds the frills back again"'

In addition, industry analysts are asking the question: 'When is a no-frills airline, not a no-frills airline?' The answer is: 'When it adds the frills back again'. There are several signs that a number of the low-cost airlines are finding it difficult to sustain the 'no-frills' strategy and are drifting back to become cheaper versions of the full-fare airlines.

Many expect that the European experience will follow the US model, with a phase of consolidation, leaving only the strongest low-cost brand as survivor.

Certainly, 1999 opened with special offers and price cuts predicted to lead into the lowest fares ever. Ryanair offered free seats to passengers buying already-discounted tickets – London to Glasgow was discounted to £29.99 – and receive an extra seat for free. Go responded with deep price cuts – bringing the return fare from London to Rome down to £70. Airline executives anticipated that the New Year ticket sales signalled the start of a price war likely to continue through the year. All the budget airlines have new aircraft arriving during 1999 with a lot of capacity to sell at a time of customer uncertainty adversely affecting travel. Rumours of a merger between easyJet and Virgin Express have been noted.

Sources

Ashworth, Jon (1998), 'BA Goes In Search of Blue Skies With No-Frills Travel Operation', *The Times*, 18 November.

Gresser, Charis (1997), 'Taking A Ticket To Fly Without the Thrills or the Frills', *Financial Times*, 22 October.

Kaydo, Chad (1998), 'Riding High', *Sales & Marketing Management*, July.

Leathley, Arthur and Steve Keenan (1997), 'BA Flies Into Europe With No-Frills Service', *The Times*, 18 November.

Maitland, Alison (1998), 'No Frills and Lots of Feedback', *Financial Times*, 18 September.

Marston, Paul (1998), 'BA Accused Of Being "A Classic Predator"', *Daily Telegraph*, 12 April.

Marston, Paul (1998), 'Basic Instincts', *Daily Telegraph*, 12 November.

Marston, Paul and Tarquin Cooper (1998), 'Watchdog Attacks BA After 80 Per Cent Rise in Go Fares', *Daily Telegraph*, 31 June.

Martin, Peter (1998), 'Paperless Darts', *Financial Times*, 4 August.

Nicoll, Alexander and Charis Gresser (1997), 'BA Sets Up A No-Frills Airline', *Financial Times*, 18 November.

Parsley, David and Ricky Dalton (1998), 'BA Go-Ahead Sets Scene For Airline Battle', *Sunday Times*, 5 April.

Parsley, David (1997), 'BA Ruffles Rivals With Discount Airline Plan', *Sunday Times*, 2 November.

Skapinker, Michael (1998), 'All Go in the No-Frills Sector', *Financial Times*, 7 May.

Skapinker, Michael (1998), 'Low-Cost, No-Frills Airlines Tighten Seatbelts', *Financial Times*, 22 October.

Skapinker, Michael (1998), 'Airline Warns BA Against Cut-Price Move', *Financial Times*, 27 October.

Tomkins, Richard (1998), 'No Take-Offs for Start-Ups', *Financial Times*, 7 May.

Tomkins, Richard (1998), 'Wackiness on the Wing', *Financial Times*, 7 May.

Upton, Gillian (1998), 'Flying High With Cheap Frills', *Financial Times*, 19 October.

Upton, Gillian (1998), 'Costs Win Over Creature Comforts', *Financial Times*, 24 November.

CHAPTER 7

Treasure Island*

Paradoxes in supermarket and car pricing

'Treasure Island' is the somewhat fatuous name given to the UK market for consumer goods by executives in some sectors.

'UK consumers are being charged higher prices than those in immediately neighbouring countries, as well as elsewhere in the world, for a huge range of consumer products'

The reason is simple. UK consumers are being charged higher prices than those in immediately neighbouring countries, as well as elsewhere in the world, for a huge range of consumer products. The implications for higher company profits are clear. The implications for customer value are pretty clear too. This is a good game for those who can get away with it, for as long as they can get away with it. However, of particular interest is the trade-off between brand strength and customer value, and the effect of changing balance of power in the supply chain, which offer broader insights.

The UK is a relatively small market, but if this market can be isolated in various ways, profit margins are boosted way above those that can be earned elsewhere, and it becomes a very attractive market. This is mainly about the ability of companies to

---

* This material has been prepared by Nigel Piercy, Cardiff Business School, from published secondary sources. All statistics and quotations come from the sources listed at the end of the study. © Nigel F. Piercy, 1999.

create artificial 'monopolies' around retail stores and brands, which reflects much of the classical marketing approach to strategy. The underlying issues are: can this very profitable strategy be sustained and at what long-term cost to the companies concerned if they do sustain it?

'can this very profitable strategy be sustained and at what long-term cost to the companies concerned if they do sustain it?'

Is the UK really Treasure Island?

Well – it really does look like it! There is a huge range of areas where it has been shown that prices paid by consumers in the UK are substantially higher than those paid for the same products in other countries.

An internal report at the British Treasury prepared for government ministers and recently leaked to the *Sunday Times* in 1998 suggests that British consumers are paying more than US consumers for virtually all high street goods and blames high mark-ups by retailers. The report found that on average prices in Britain were:

- 56 per cent higher for furniture and carpets
- 54 per cent higher for hotels and eating out
- 31 per cent higher for sporting goods
- 29 per cent higher for cars and motorcycles
- 22 per cent higher for electrical goods

These findings fit the general observation that goods in the USA ranging from computers to cars to music tapes to CDs to food seem to be priced on a dollars-for-pounds basis. That is a computer that costs $2000 in the USA will cost £2000 in the UK. This is especially amusing for consumers when the goods in question have been produced in Europe and exported to the USA!

Further evidence comes from a range of sources including the following:

- Computer industry executives from PC manufacturers including Compaq and Fujitsu claim that high retailer margins and lack of competition mean that home computer purchasers in the UK in 1998 pay 25 per cent more than prices in Germany and France, while other estimates are that UK buyers pay 40 per cent more than those in Germany, much hidden in the 'extras' purchased with the PC. Retailers such as Dixons and Currys offer an extended warranty on a standard computer for

Table 7.1   Prices of electrical goods in the UK and the USA

Branded electrical products	Prices in stores (£)					
	Dixons	John Lewis	Comet	Currys	Harrods	USA
Sony Playstation	129.99	129.99	129.99	129.99	130.00	90.30
Sharp Viewcam VLE 34mm	549.99	n/a	549.99	549.99	n/a	412.10
Philips TV/VCR 14PV 162	369.99	n/a	n/a	369.99	n/a	241.60
Hitachi video VTF 545	329.99	n/a	n/a	329.99	n/a	181.20
Sony TV KV29X1	599.99	599.99	599.99	599.99	600.00	303.00
Aiwa Mini Hi-Fi NSX F9	449.99	n/a	449.99	449.99	n/a	296.40

Source: Poulter, Sean (1998), 'TV Prices To Tumble As Cartel Is Crushed', *Daily Mail*, 25 May.

£299, while the same cover from an insurance company costs £89.

- During 1998 the uncovering of high prices for PCs and computer games became yet more pointed. Dominant retailer Dixons was accused of using its market power to enforce excessive prices and profits by the magazine *Computeractive*, by Intel, the world's largest microchip manufacturer, and by the Consumers' Association. Dixons' response was to threaten to sue anyone who said its prices were artificially high.
- In 1998 the government reacted to a Monopolies Commission report on the pricing of electrical goods such as washing machines, refrigerators and televisions by announcing an open market from September, where manufacturers will not be able to impose minimum prices on retailers. The scale of the difference on electrical goods between the USA and the UK and the complete lack of price differences among UK retailers is illustrated in Table 7.1.
- British prices for CDs are claimed by the Consumers' Association to be up to three times higher in the UK than other countries, with average price comparisons in store prices in different countries summarized in Table 7.2.
- Well-known brands of cameras in the UK were reported to be priced 50 per cent higher than in the USA and the Far East.
- Mortgage loans in the UK are more expensive than in the USA, with British banks and building societies taking twice as much profit from these loans as their US counterparts.

However, of all the areas where high pricing for the UK market has been uncovered, there is no doubt that two have achieved

Table 7.2 Prices of CD recordings

	CD recordings		
	Titanic soundtrack (£)	Bob Dylan: Blonde on Blonde (£)	Schumann: Complete Works (£)
UK	14.49	10.89	16.05
Switzerland	13.22	7.97	14.42
New Zealand	10.49	3.48	8.74
Holland	11.66	7.28	13.12
Hong Kong	8.03	8.43	9.09
Australia	12.06	6.02	12.06
Finland	13.23	6.56	14.34

Source: 'A Compact Disgrace', *Daily Mail*, 2 July 1998.

highest profile: grocery pricing in supermarkets and motor car pricing by distributors.

The price of food

Making price comparisons across countries is fraught with problems. How do you allow for differences in what are 'typical' grocery items? How do you account for exchange rate movements? How do you account for differences in local taxation, and so on? For these reasons retailers reject 'grocery basket' comparisons as meaningless. If the differences found between the prices of groceries in different countries was in any way marginal these would be fair points. However, the differences are not marginal, they are massive.

For example, a comparison between prices for twenty-two supermarket items conducted by a national newspaper in 1998 is shown in Table 7.3. On this comparison, the goods purchased in a Tesco store in the UK are 39 per cent more expensive than in Holland, 38 per cent more expensive than Belgium and 26 per cent more expensive than in Italy.

An earlier comparison by this newspaper using the same approach had found a basket of groceries costing £82.05 in Britain could be purchased for £60.14 in France, £53.31 in Germany and £56.48 in the USA.

In spite of retailer protests – of which there are many – there is little real doubt that supermarket prices in the UK are substantially higher than in other

'there is little real doubt that supermarket prices in the UK are substantially higher than in other European countries or the USA. This is why it is called "Treasure Island"'

Table 7.3   **Supermarket prices in the UK and Europe**

Product name	Quantity	Prices in £			
		Tesco	Holland	Belgium	Italy
Sirloin steak	1 kg	11.49	7.18	6.71	7.53
Chicken breast	1 kg	11.94	5.83	6.46	6.10
Smoked salmon	1 kg	23.00	9.14	9.31	16.20
Heineken cans	4 × 440 ml	3.25	1.93	2.60	2.28
Deep pan frozen pizza	425 g	2.36	1.17	1.02	0.72
Standard pack grated cheese	1 kg	6.45	4.57	3.86	4.21
Coca-Cola	1 litre	0.65	0.47	0.55	0.63
Heinz tomato ketchup	460 g	1.05	0.82	0.91	1.26
Mars bar 'fun size'	346 g	1.74	1.40	1.56	2.26
Haagen-Dazs ice cream	500 ml	3.59	3.04	3.17	3.09
Potatoes	1 kg	0.55	0.37	0.49	0.30
Carrots	1 kg	0.55	0.46	0.65	0.67
Olive oil	500 ml	2.09	2.14	2.00	1.19
Nescafe instant coffee granules	100 g	1.89	1.17	3.17	2.59
Kellogg's Cornflakes	500 g	1.15	1.21	0.99	1.75
Tuna fish, tinned	185 g	0.55	0.49	0.51	1.36
Butter	250 g	0.98	0.83	0.83	0.69
Large eggs	6	0.82	0.30	0.50	0.98
Milk, semi-skimmed	1 litre	0.42	0.33	0.50	0.66
Mayonnaise	500 ml	0.96	0.89	0.79	0.94
Fresh squeezed orange juice	1 litre	2.25	1.84	1.66	1.53
Gillette Sensor razors	5 pack	3.86	3.97	2.43	3.26
Basket price		**81.59**	**49.55**	**50.67**	**60.20**
% difference between Tesco in the UK and each country			+39%	+38%	+26%

Source: Smith, David (1998), 'Supermarkets Use Bogus Claims To Justify High Prices', *Sunday Times*, 30 August.

European countries or the USA. This is why it is called 'Treasure Island'.

This happens in a market that is dominated by a handful of companies. The five major supermarket groups in the UK are Tesco, Sainsbury, Asda, Safeway and Somerfield/Kwiksave. These five control half the £53 billion a year food retail business in the UK, with the rest split between Marks & Spencer, William Morrison, the Co-op, Iceland, discounters such as Aldi and smaller independent supermarkets. In 1997/98 the big five retailers made total operating profits of £2.75 billion, which was up 35 per cent from 1993/94. Recent Office of Fair Trading reports suggest that net margins in large British supermarkets have risen sharply and are roughly three times higher than in France, Germany, Italy and Spain. It is increasingly being suggested that although they can negotiate low prices from suppliers because of their market domination, these discounts are simply not being passed on to consumers as lower prices in the store.

The price of cars

Even more emotive than the price of the food and household products bought in the UK is the price of the motor car.

In July 1998, the European Commission released a study showing that sixty out of seventy-four best-selling cars cost more in the UK than in the rest of Europe. The largest disparity was the Ford Mondeo which was 58.5 per cent more expensive in Britain than in Spain. Prices of Alfa Romeos, Citroens, Fiats, Fords, Renaults, Rovers, Seats and Volkswagens were *'sixty out of seventy-four best-selling cars cost more in the UK than in the rest of Europe'* all at least 30 per cent more expensive in Britain than in the cheapest EU country. Some illustrations of the differences found are shown in Table 7.4. Naturally, the Society of Motor Manufacturers and Traders denied that prices were high and blamed the strong pound if they were. This is an interesting explanation for why British-produced Rovers should be 50 per cent more expensive in Britain than in Holland!

More straightforwardly, a study by KPMG suggests that the reason for the higher prices is the 'Great British mark-up' or pure profit. As the only European country driving on the left, the UK

Table 7.4 Car prices across Europe

Vehicle	UK price (pre-tax) (£)	Lowest European price (pre-tax) (£)	Difference (£)	% saving for European buyer
VW Polo	6836	4428 (Portugal)	2408	35.2%
Fiat Bravo	8450	5669 (Holland)	2781	32.9%
Alfa 145	9367	6284 (Holland)	3083	32.9%
Ford Escort	9138	6281 (Portugal)	2857	31.2%
Land Rover Discovery	19,447	13,430 (Italy)	6017	30.9%
Peugeot 306	9544	6611 (Holland)	2933	30.7%
Mazda 323	11,232	7812 (Belgium)	3420	30.4%
Toyota Starlet	6661	4644 (Luxembourg)	2017	30.2%
Renault Laguna	12,850	9127 (Portugal)	3723	28.9%
Citroen Saxo	6370	4662 (Portugal)	1708	26.8%

Source: Fraser, John (1998), 'Car Firms Cashing In', *Daily Mail*, 14 February.

market can be differentiated from the rest, if it is 'difficult' for British buyers to acquire right-hand drive vehicles in cheaper countries.

Recently, Marc Firome of Peugeot, interviewed by *Sunday Times* journalists posing as car buyers, commented with disdain on the notion that the British should pay less for cars:

> In France, Peugeot will never sell right-hand drive cars . . . Because the level of price in Britain is, er, very, very much higher than the market in Europe, I think all the manu-facturers – and I will speak only for Peugeot – are very satisfied with this situation . . . The gross margin in the British market is very comfortable for us.

Other comments from car company executives approached by the same reporters were similar:

> Us and the other premium manufacturers are trying to persuade the public to pay more money than the car is worth . . . It's wonderful, we are making more out of England per unit than ever. (Peter Hornby, Saab)

> I don't think there is any European car maker that is able to lose this big (profit) margin that is in Great Britain . . . no way. (Ricardo Nicolucci, Fiat)

'British consumers pay too much for cars simply because of an "unholy alliance" of manufacturers and European politicians'

One analyst has recently concluded that British consumers pay too much for cars simply because of an 'unholy alliance' of manufacturers and European politicians, who have granted them the right to dictate the terms on which cars may be sold. This has ensured that motor distributors remain weak and fragmented. None has the strength to take on a manufacturer for fear of having his precious franchise withdrawn.'

It seems that car prices are substantially higher in 'Treasure Island' and that the manufacturers are really quite happy about this!

So, retailers are rogues and robbers?

So, why are prices in British supermarkets higher than most other countries, when retailer strategy is dominated by aggressive 'competition' and 'value pricing' (or so the retailers claim)? The real answer to that question is that British retailer strategies focus on competition and pricing only *against each other.* This is why 'grocery basket' price comparisons between the big five supermarket firms show so little real difference and why product choices are almost identical which-ever store you go to. This is the illusion of competition, not the reality. Firms with market dominance and high profits have little incentive to enter genuine price wars or disrupt the status quo. It is far easier to compete for marginal (and probably relatively temporary) changes in market share between friends than to risk disruption in the market.

'British retailer strategies focus on competition and pricing only against each other'

The strategies of the dominant British supermarket companies are similar and are based on exploiting their market power in a number of important ways.

- *Access to market* – big retailers negotiate the best deals from suppliers, because no supplier can afford not to supply one of the big chains. A current joke in the food supply industry is illustrative:

Question: What is the difference between a super-market and a terrorist?
Answer: You can negotiate with a terrorist!

'Question: *What is the difference between a supermarket and a terrorist?* **Answer:** *You can negotiate with a terrorist!'*

- *Special offers* – loss leaders are used to create an impression of value, with heavy promotional expenditure, while high margins are made on the other products the consumer selects on the same purchase trip. While many consumers know what is a good price on a small number of items – because they are 'barometer' products – they tend to have far less idea about a good price for the vast majority of the items they buy in the total assortment that makes up the week's grocery shop. For instance, David Proud, formerly sales and marketing director of one of Britain's big drinks firms claims the four leading supermarket firms have doubled the profit they make on products such as soft drinks and snacks in the past ten years, so current margins are generally over 40 per cent and often above 50 per cent, and says, 'Unless the supplier submits to the margin demands made by supermarkets, they risk having their product de-listed'.

- *Value pricing* – the impression of cheapness is maintained by having a very narrow range of products – the so-called 'known value items' (KVIs) such as bread and baked beans for which most shoppers have a good idea of what the price should be – priced very low. In fact, figures released by beleaguered suppliers to the *Sunday Times* suggest than many own-label products earn massive gross margins as high as 60 per cent over the price the store pays the supplier. An own-label product priced a few pence less than a brand leader may look a bargain to the consumer, even though it could be priced much lower and still be profitable.

- *Own-label brands* – by avoiding development and promotional costs, and looking like the brand leader products, own-labels free-load on the leading brands and can earn high margins.
- *Limiting local competition* – small town-centre competitors have largely been beaten now, but the big firms also tend to avoid competing head to head with each other by selecting new sites with a catchment area which does not overlap too much with those of rival stores.
- *Loyalty offers* – for the cost of around a 1 per cent discount on purchases, loyalty schemes provide huge amounts of customer data to target customers better. Loyal customers tied in by discounting schemes are also less sensitive to prices and will pay more.
- *Blocking new competitors* – Treasury research has shown how Britain's dominant retailers are highly effective in limiting entry to the market by new competitors. This is partly because of the barrier to entry in terms of advertising and promotional spending, but also because they can outbid potential competitors for new sites (for which new entrants may also find it more difficult to get planning permission than the big five). It is also possible that the big five might suggest to suppliers (as part of their collaborative 'partnering' in supply chains) that they would be happier if new competitors found it difficult to get supplies.
- *Cross-subsidy* – British supermarkets have taken the profits enhanced through market control in the grocery business to fund developments into new areas such as toiletries, branded clothes, petrol and financial services. The high earnings from grocery margins allow predatory pricing in the new areas to establish a foothold where this is necessary.

> *'British supermarkets have taken the profits enhanced through market control in the grocery business to fund developments into new areas'*

What do the retailers say?

Obviously, they deny everything! For example, Tesco's immediate response to the 'grocery basket' comparisons mentioned above was that they were 'simplistic' and ignored the fact that 'labour and distribution costs are more expensive in Britain'. This is an interesting response for two reasons: the shopworkers' trade union USDAW was under the impression that wages for shopworkers in Britain were lower than in Europe and the USA; and Tesco's massive investment in an integrated supply chain makes it one of the world's most efficient retailers. Indeed, McKinsey study figures suggest British supermarkets sell up to twice as much per square foot of selling space as do their European and US counterparts.

Tesco and Sainsbury both blame the high pound for high food prices. In fact, as a net importer of food, a high exchange rate should mean cheaper food in Britain. Indeed, figures from the Office of National Statistics suggest in the twelve months up to August 1998, the cost of basic food bought by Britain's food manufacturers has fallen by 7.2 per cent, while the price of food products leaving factories has fallen by 1.1 per cent, but retail food prices have risen by 0.6 per cent.

High prices are said to be what pays for the things that British shoppers want – convenience, attractive shopping environments, shorter checkout queues, good parking, wide choice and so on. Retailers say if British consumers want 'no-frills' retailing provided by European-style discounters and hypermarkets, then why have stores like Aldi only been able to take about 6 per cent of the market?

Besides, look at the gestures that the big retailers make to show their social responsibility:

- In the summer of 1998, at a time of accusations of profiteering, Tesco announced its 'penny for the poor' scheme for cutting the prices of selected staple food products in up to 300 of its 1250 stores serving poorer customers.
- As a response to charges that supermarkets have driven small village shops out of business, Sainsbury has announced plans to allow these types of independent outlets to carry some of Sainsbury's own-brand products.
- As supermarkets have been charged with holding meat prices high, even though British farmers' can sell only at frighteningly low prices, Asda announced it would sell only British lamb.

However, these gestures should be put in the context of more serious muscle-flexing by these companies.

Hey, these guys don't play nice!

The large British supermarket firms are extremely well-connected politically. That nice Lord Sainsbury has become a minister in the Blair government, after Sainsburys donated £3 million to help Labour fight the last election; Asda's cheeky-chappie Archie Norman is

'The large British supermarket firms are extremely well-connected politically'

a high-level advisor to leader of the opposition William Hague (they used to work together at McKinseys); Labour party delegates at the 1998 conference had the pleasure of wearing identity badges adorned with the Somerfield name; and those nice people at Tescos have been ever so helpful about putting some money into the government's Millennium Dome project (about £12 million actually). One commentator notes that the Labour party's policy generally against new shopping centres has matured into a Labour government's studied neutrality on the issue, coincidentally after a meeting in Tony Blair's office with the supermarket chiefs.

Another coincidence is that in spite of the wishes of the British food minister to launch a new food safety body to regulate the industry, supermarket lobbying persuaded Prime Minister Tony Blair to shelve such plans. One of the lobbyists involved is quoted as saying 'We hijacked this from the start!'.

The consumer affairs programme *Watchdog*, fronted by Anne Robinson, became the target for a secret 'battle plan' agreed by large companies (not just retailers actually), who believed that the programme's criticisms of companies should be stifled.

It has also been rumoured that the academic authors of some of the research criticizing supermarket prices have since found that their research grants are under threat and their invitations to nice overseas conferences have been cancelled.*

'an officially inspired media and government campaign against retailing'

The chairman of the British Retail Consortium launched a public attack on what he called 'an officially inspired media and government campaign against retailing'. Certainly, late 1998 saw the emergence of a 'war cabinet' of leading retailers within the British Retail Consortium with the goal of mounting a propaganda offensive to undo the harm caused by the criticisms of their pricing policies. The BRC chief executive said, 'We need to show that people value the range of goods, convenient car parking, extended trading hours and home delivery services that retailers offer. This is long overdue.'

Muddying the pool

Simple denial of the evidence was followed by the supermarkets orchestrating a more elaborate denial. The brainchild of the BRC war cabinet was their own Shop Price Index, to prove grocery prices were not high. The retailers' new index when first

---

* This present writer would like to make it known that he totally disbelieves *any* criticism of British retail firms, because they are run by some of the nicest and kindest people in the world, at whose feet he is not worthy to kneel. . . .

published in December 1998 suggested that food prices had fallen 1 per cent in a year. In the same month, Labour peer Baroness Thornton had been recruited by BRC to lead a campaign to prove that the British consumer gets a good deal on food prices. She led in with a new MORI survey showing that most consumers were satisfied with supermarkets and believed they got value for money, saying, 'Shoppers want convenience, short queues and a wide range of quality products that European consumers simply don't expect. Price is not the only factor.'

Also in the same month, the research agency, Verdict (a specialist market research firm in the retail sector), produced a report suggesting that British supermarkets did not earn higher profit margins than firms in other countries and that Britain had one of the most competitive food markets in the world.

1999 saw a flurry of promotional activity by the leading firms, described by one analyst as creating a 'promotional fog' and by the National Consumer Council as 'confusion marketing'.

'1999 saw a flurry of promotional activity by the leading firms, described by one analyst as creating a "promotional fog" and by the National Consumer Council as "confusion marketing"'

Changing the battleground

It is also notable that after a summer of press lobbying about high grocery prices, the debate switched mysteriously to the prices of personal computers (PCs). Peter Mandelson – the champion of the Millennium Dome and then Trade and Industry Secretary – wrote to the Director-General of the Office of Fair Trading to express concern about the pricing policies of the electronics retailing giant, Dixons. The Consumer Affairs Minister, Kim Howells, added his weight to the pressure on the OFT. Coincidentally, the supermarket Tesco had stocked low-price computers from Fujitsu and Siemens Nixdorf from July that year and Asda launched a cheap PC for £499. In November 1998, the OFT launched its enquiry into PC prices, while Dixons was still threatening to sue its detractors. In the process, grocery prices have dropped out of public attention. Tesco's unfriendly intentions towards Dixons became even clearer in February 1999, with Tesco's launch of free Internet access for its Clubcard holders to challenge Dixon's huge success with a similar offer to consumers.

So, what will happen?

Feelings have run high. In November 1998, British management guru, Sir John Harvey-Jones appeared on national television to accuse supermarkets of causing long-term damage to the food industry, by irresponsibly ignoring the long-term viability of the food supply chain and blighting many small businesses. However, it remains to be seen what, if anything, will happen as a result of the exposure of high supermarket pricing policies. However, a lot of possible solutions have been discussed, many involving government intervention in some form.

- Paul Dobson, co-author of the OFT report argues that the big four supermarket firms should be forced to sell some of their stores to smaller, low-cost competitors, in a form of monopoly 'break-up' used in other sectors.
- Dobson also proposes as an alternative that where one of the big four has bought up leases on premises surrounding a superstore, it should be forced to let to another food retailer
- There has been some talk of the appointment of a regulator for supermarket retailers, similar to those employed as watchdogs over the utilities and phone companies.
- Farming groups have lobbied for a 'windfall tax' to be levied on supermarkets to be invested in supporting British farmers.
- There has been some lobbying for supermarkets to be obliged to label products with the wholesale price they have paid, as well as the retail price at which they sell.
- A Treasury document outlines the plans of Gordon Brown, Chancellor of the Exchequer and a political rival of Tony Blair, to set up a 'price-busters web site' on the Internet, which will post constantly updated price lists, with the Treasury acting as an 'honest broker' to ensure that people have access to accurate price information via their computers. The report suggests, 'Lack of information allows firms to charge high prices if they think consumers are unlikely to see the prices of rivals . . . If we can increase the effective search of consumers [for the best deal], markets are likely to become more competitive'.
- A consortium has emerged of brand-name producers, including Cadbury-Schweppes, Unilever, Bass and Kimberly-Clark and accounting for thirty of the top 100 products sold in supermarkets, called the Consumer Needs Consortium. The goal is to exploit direct marketing tools to sell direct to consumers and reduce the degree of supermarket control of the market. However, by mid-1998 this consortium was reported to be struggling.

'Late in 1998, it was rumoured that Wal-Mart, the world's largest and toughest retailer, was planning entry to the UK supermarket business'

- Late in 1998, it was rumoured that Wal-Mart, the world's largest and toughest retailer, was planning entry to the UK supermarket business, possibly by the purchase of Asda or William Morrisons, which would be a major force in disrupting the present status quo. Wal-Mart's retail model does not offer consumers a choice between low prices and high service, it provides both. In December 1998, Wal-Mart bought a German supermarket chain with seventy-five outlets and appointed a British executive as director of European operations with an objective of advising on how best to enter the UK.

'Wal-Mart's retail model does not offer consumers a choice between low prices and high service, it provides both'

All right, then the brand owners are the real bully boys?

Let's go back to the retailers' argument that they are powerless in the face of the suppliers of branded products. It is certainly not true for food products. It may be truer with other non-food branded products.

Branded consumer goods of this type do seem to show the same characteristics of price fixing, but this time enforced by manufacturers, though still to the disadvantage of the British consumer. For example, Table 7.5 looks at a 1998 comparison of US and UK prices for a range of branded consumer products, showing UK prices up to 40 per cent higher. Analysts suggest 'high prices for branded goods in Britain appear to be the product of tacit collusion ... between manufacturers and retailers'. Company attitudes are illustrated by what their salespeople say about lowering UK prices to the US level for their brands:

'high prices for branded goods in Britain appear to be the product of tacit collusion ... between manufacturers and retailers'

It would crucify the market and devalue all the brands' (Rockport salesperson)

Britons don't know about American prices. What we don't know doesn't hurt us. (O'Neill salesperson)

We don't want to work with people who play around with our prices. (Polo Ralph Lauren salesperson)

Although it is sometimes not legal, the reality has been that any retailer tempted to cut prices, particularly on designer brands has faced being shut off from supplies of the product in question.

However, the mid-1990s have seen a new phenomenon: British supermarkets attempting to stock non-food branded goods and sell at cut prices.

Table 7.5 Prices of branded non-food products

	Typical UK price (£)	Typical USA price (£)	Price difference (£)
Timberland boots	129.00	89.98	**39.22**
Wrangler jeans	35.00	12.96	**22.04**
Tommy Hilfiger jacket	139.00	83.58	**55.42**
Ralph Lauren Polo Sport sweatshirt	85.00	46.44	**38.56**
Levi's 501 jeans	59.95	32.20	**27.74**
Nike Air Zoom trainers	99.99	61.91	**38.08**
Sony Playstation	129.00	92.96	**36.04**
Sharp Viewcam VLSE10	599.99	352.93	**247.06**
Compaq PC Presario 5030	1599.00	988.23	**610.77**
Microsoft Windows 98 upgrade	69.99	55.66	**14.33**
Revlon Lipcolour	7.95	5.52	**2.43**
Gillette shaving gel 200ml	2.79	1.78	**1.01**
Rockport 'Benny' shoes	99.00	80.42	**18.58**
Ray-Ban Wayfarer sunglasses	59.00	30.94	**28.06**
O'Neill board shorts	45.00	18.57	**26.43**
Estee Lauder eau de toilette 50 ml	27.50	23.84	**3.66**
McDonald's Big Mac	1.84	1.35	**0.49**
Harley-Davidson Sportster 1200	6495.00	5579.00	**916.00**

Source: Smith, David (1998), 'Overpriced Over Here', *Sunday Times*, 5 July.

- In 1997 Tesco stocked Levi 501 jeans, cutting to a price of £30 compared to the 'recommended price' of £50. Although Levi and Polo Ralph Lauren have refused to supply their products to Tesco, the supermarket got supplies of Levi's from a middleman in Mexico. Levi Strauss threatened legal action following a European Court decision that lower priced goods could not be imported from outside Europe without permission. Levi Strauss has also banned any US mail-order catalogues from accepting orders from UK consumers (the US price for 501s is £27).

- Tesco has pursued a similar policy for Adidas sports clothes, buying a stockpile of supplies in the USA from a secret supplier and selling at around half-price. This won praise from the government's consumer affairs minister and reluctant acquiescence from Adidas.

- Tesco is launching half-price contact lenses to be sold from an in-store kiosk, expecting legal action from high street opticians to ensue.

- Nike is threatening legal action against Sainsbury's to prevent the stocking of Nike polo shirts, while Tesco is selling Nike clothes and trainers at 50 per cent savings.

- Following its sales of cut-price designer sunglasses and jeans at 30 per cent below recommended prices, Asda is buying cheap supplies of Calvin Klein CKOne fragrance through the overseas 'grey market', and is threatened with legal action by Unilever, the owner of the brand.
- Two leading computer manufacturers – Fujitsu and Siemens-Nixdorf – have trialled sales of cheap computers through Tesco supermarkets, because other retailers will not cut prices. Tesco sold 10 000 machines in the first three months from twelve stores.
- Late in 1998, Asda launched a high-value mobile telephone offer in partnership with Cellnet, involving pre-payment by vouchers bought in-store, signalling its entry into this market.

Amazingly, the media view of British retailers does a complete U-turn, when we consider attempts by the major supermarket firms to cut prices on leading designer and branded goods such as clothes, shoes and cosmetics, only to be met by fierce resistance by the owners of the brands in question. They change from over-charging rogues to the consumer's best friend, in one fell swoop. Or so it would seem . . .

In fact, the leading British supermarkets are desperate for further growth and this is not likely to come from the food business at home. One avenue for growth is branded non-food goods such as clothes and cosmetics. Currently it seems that the major supermarkets are using their protected and enhanced earnings in the food business as a way of financing entry into a variety of new markets with low price offers.

'the leading British supermarkets are desperate for further growth and this is not likely to come from the food business at home'

The reasons why brand owners such as Levi-Strauss, Nike, Calvin Klein and the rest do not want supermarkets to sell their brands at cut prices fall into two categories: what the firms say and the truth.

Brand owners talk about their huge product development and advertising investment in creating a brand with a particular identity and hence intangible added-values for the consumer – we wear Levi jeans or CK clothes to be associated with an advertised image and life style. They believe that cutting prices and selling the products in 'undesirable' locations that detract from the brand image will reduce the value of the brand to consumers and hence the companies' brand equity. This is the type of garbled nonsense we had to swallow from advertising agency executives in

'This is the type of garbled nonsense we had to swallow from advertising agency executives in the 1970s. The world has moved on. The issue is value, not brand image'

the 1970s. The world has moved on. The issue is value, not brand image.

The real reasons why brand owners do not want supermarkets stocking their products and cutting the prices are four. First, this will reduce the number of people willing to pay the full price for the brand and the brand owner's overall profits and sales will suffer, particularly if the retailer uses the brand leader as a positioning mark for its own-label equivalents. Second, many of the brand owners want to exploit 'diffusion ranges', i.e. using their brand names on cheaper products to spread downmarket and this will not work if the supermarkets have already dragged prices of the main brand down. Third, the brand owners of things such as designer clothes dispose of 'last year's' surplus stock through factory outlets, so they can protect the higher prices of 'this year's' products. Fourth, if supermarkets achieve the same market dominance in these new areas as they have in food, petrol and so on, then the brand owners' profits and sales income will be permanently reduced by powerful distributors.

Perhaps the most interesting question is what can a brand owner do to protect brands from predatory retailers seeking to extend their dominance? The European Court decision to prevent retailers selling 'parallel imports' (i.e. branded goods bought from middlemen outside Europe) has not yet been lifted despite British government protests to Brussels.

Does Arthur Daley* run the British motor trade, or what?

A special case of brand-owner control of product prices which does seem to work is the British motor trade, where we saw earlier that UK prices are maintained at substantially higher levels than in other European countries and the USA.

The traditional price-fixing arrangement, where manufacturers dictate minimum prices to distributors, only works if you can stop buyers gaining access to cheaper cars (the same brands) from lower price markets – 'grey' imports. It also only works if governments let you do it – the 'block exemption' under EU law allows car manufacturers to dictate prices charged by distributors.

---

* Arthur Daley was a fictional character in a British TV series called *Minder*, selling second-hand cars of dubious value and quality, on the fringes of legality.

Manufacturers have long argued that British car prices were higher because the market was different – big fleet sales distort the private car market and drivers demand higher specifications. The reality is that car manufacturers have made it as difficult as possible for British buyers to import cheaper right-hand drive cars from Europe or elsewhere. Sometimes there has been a 'shortage' of right-hand drive vehicles for British purchasers to buy in European countries. More extreme actions have also been taken – a confidential memo issued by Fiat instructed dealers on mainland Europe to add a 'surcharge' to prices for British buyers, as a way of making importing less attractive. Such practices to restrict supplies within Europe are on the edge of illegality under European law. In 1998 Volkswagen was fined more than £60 million by the European Commission for restricting cross-border shopping by Austrian and German consumers looking for a bargain price on a VW car in Italy.

'Manufacturers have long argued that British car prices were higher because the market was different'

'a confidential memo issued by Fiat instructed dealers on mainland Europe to add a "surcharge" to prices for British buyers'

Manufacturers have also tried to make life difficult for those who have purchased 'grey imports' through surcharges on servicing and repairs and 'scare tactics', calling unofficial imports 'unroadworthy'. In the summer of 1998, a letter from Mitsubishi's official importer, The Colt Car Company, told dealers they should 'charge owners of grey imports extra for services, repairs and parts', that is 'charge them for the privilege of ignoring our contractual rights as the sole UK importers'. Mercedez-Benz dealers were instructed to report all 'grey' cars brought in for service and Subaru has sacked dealers selling 'grey' cars alongside their official allocations.

The isolation of the UK car market was also underpinned by government safety inspection regulations for individual cars imported into in Britain and a limit on inspections to fifty cars in each model. In effect, the government was making cheap imports difficult for individuals or independent traders. This may be related to the level of employment and investment giving the motor manufacturers a powerful lobby with the government. In September 1998, the British Independent Motor Trade Association won a judicial review to challenge this government policy. Government reaction has been to look at changing the rules about imports and in October 1998 the government revealed plans to allow non-franchised dealers to sell potentially hundreds of thousands of 'grey' imports, much to the disgruntlement of the conventional car trade.

By the summer of 1998, estimates of the number of 'grey market' imports to the UK (selling up to 30 per cent cheaper than official imports) ranged from 30 000 to 100 000, with a rising number of used cars coming in from Japan via Dublin, in a British market which registers around 2 million new cars a year.

It may be worth noting that in the much smaller motorcycle business, independent importers now hold 30 per cent of the UK market. By late 1998 official dealers were making deep price cuts on motorcycles to get their prices closer to those of 'grey' imports. However, by the end of 1998, in response to losing 25 per cent of its business to parallel imports, Honda was fighting back by taking legal action against parallel importers and suing for compensation.

Another crack in the status quo is illustrated by the demand by the Rover Group late in 1998 that their dealership network should take £50 million out of the cost structure to get retail prices lower.

Investigations ensue

Renewed public attention to car pricing in 1998 led to a report from the House of Commons Trade and Industry Committee at the end of the year. More extreme views of the members of the committee included jail sentences for executives caught rigging prices 'as a mark of the weight of public anger'. The report threatens the continuation of the block exemption beyond 2002 and challenges the right of fleet buyers to get 35 per cent discounts on cars at the expense of the consumer.

An Office of Fair Trading enquiry into car distribution continues in 1999 and is expected to lead to a full-blown referral to the Mergers and Monopolies Commission.

The ultimate irony

Recovering their position in the consumer's mind, late 1998 saw the ultimate irony of the supermarkets adopting the position of consumer champion against brand owners by announcing plans to enter car distribution.

Tesco announced its intention to enter the car business offering at least 30 per cent off list prices and has entered negotiations with leading manufacturers, although has not decided whether to act as a distributor or franchise parts of its sites to car manufacturers. The Society of Motor Manufacturers remained sceptical and Professor Garel Rhys (the SMMT-sponsored professor of motor industry economics) suggested that manufacturers would not be likely to supply Tesco if they cut prices.

(This would put car manufacturers in the same category as cigarette producers, book publishers and the many others who thought they could refuse to supply Tesco because it cuts prices.)

The strategic dilemma

At first sight groceries and cars may not seem to have a lot in common. In fact, both the markets described above share an important characteristic: control of the market by powerful companies and brands forming 'pools of monopoly' (around stores for retailers and around car brands for the motor trade). That monopoly enables the dominant to charge higher prices to customers who are persuaded that they have no choice. In the grocery business the dominant are the big four or five super-market firms, while in the car trade, distributors lack market power and are dominated by the large car manufacturers who own the brands. Your view of the desirability of this situation will depend whether you take a consumer perspective, a social policy viewpoint or own shares in the companies concerned. However, these companies face some very real problems for the future.

Defending the status quo

In the short term our dominant retailers and car manufacturers are trapped – they are committed to the current style of operation. It is unlikely that the supermarkets will unilaterally reduce prices and profits for groceries, because collapsing share values put executives out of work. The car companies are limited in changing how cars are priced and distributed for a similar reason, but also because they are tied to traditional channels of distribution. Freedom of strategic manoeuvre for these companies is actually quite limited.

The problem they face is that the conditions that allow them their monopolistic positions are in the process of change. Will the existing players be able to cope?

Revolution

For the big retailers the problem is that customers are changing. These companies conform to the conventional wisdom of business strategy – the retailers are following a classic portfolio strategy of milking the grocery 'cash cow' to move into new product areas and the car companies cling to conventional branding strategies. However, there are signs that as consumers become more sophisticated and learn that they are being 'ripped off', they become unhappy. You may say, 'so what, they can't do anything about it?', and in the short term you would probably be right. However, there are two issues. First, the large retailers rely on a brand identity and customer relationship that allows them to expand into new areas. If you damage the brand value and customer relationship, you may reduce the scope for profitable expansion. Second, consumers may not be able to do anything now, but what about when they can ... people have long memories.

For the car companies, the controls that prevented 'grey imports' are crumbling fast and it may be difficult to maintain higher prices as they do.

Reinvention

The biggest danger for the existing companies in both these trades is that new entrants may design new ways of doing business, that are not available to the existing competitors, that increase transparency in the market and offer value-oriented consumers higher value in their terms. It is possible that regulators may give this process a nudge to introduce more competition. It is impossible to predict how new competitors can fundamentally reinvent traditional businesses – if you could, you would probably do it yourself.

For example, in the grocery business there have already been attempts (as yet largely unsuccessful) by brand manufacturers to develop direct marketing strategies to bypass traditional retailers. Maybe the scenario for the future weekly grocery shop might be like this:

It is time to stock up on food and household essentials. You make a list. Then you log onto your computer and scan the shopping list into memory. The computer says 'Hi' and asks you how you are today, you say 'Shut up and get on with it'. Unlike your partner, the computer does not sulk when you say this; it asks your permission to e-mail the suppliers of your toilet tissues, detergents, cleaners and toiletries to place an order, which will be delivered to the house later in the day. You agree. The computer checks the best prices for heavy frozen and canned goods and offers to e-mail various retailers and suppliers to have these delivered. You agree. This leaves the interesting stuff on the list. The computer checks the online price lists of the local stores (you have loyalty cards for them all) and comes up with the best deal on your exact mix of goods. It reminds you that you always pick up some chocolate as well even though it is never on the list and factors this into the choice. The computer asks you whether you want these products delivered but you decide to go to the store yourself because you like a bit of shopping …

The technology to create this situation already exists – it simply needs application. It is the start of what Bill Gates of Microsoft calls 'frictionless capitalism', where companies lose the ability to make money from knowing that people cannot or will not comparison shop and many traditional business models simply do not make sense.

In the motor trade, the Economist Intelligence Unit estimates that within the next ten years, the majority of car purchases will involve the Internet. This does not necessarily mean that cars will be purchased directly from a web page, but that product and price search will involve the Internet. This is a fundamental process of reinvention that is already happening.

'the Economist Intelligence Unit estimates that within the next ten years, the majority of car purchases will involve the Internet'

The dilemma for the existing dominant players in these industries is how to break free from the status quo and survive the revolution and reinvention that is on the way.

Sources

Alderson, Andrew and Paul Nuki (1998), 'Car Giants Keep British Prices High', *Sunday Times*, 10 May.

Alexander, Alex (1998), 'Harsh Supermarket Study Is Well Past Its Sell-By Date', *Daily Mail*, 24 September.

Barrow, Rebecca (1998), 'KPMG Leads New Car Pricing Investigation', *Daily Telegraph*, 6 July.

Becket, Michael (1998), 'Snap Decision That Camera Retailers Face', *Daily Telegraph*, 27 July.

Bevan, Stephen (1998), 'Supermarkets Conceal 50 per cent Profit Margins', *Sunday Times*, 4 October.

Bevan, Stephen and David Smith (1998), 'A Raw Deal', *Sunday Times*, 20 September.

Cochrane, Peter (1998), 'Power to the Customer Cartel', *Daily Telegraph*, 27 August.

Derbyshire, David (1998), 'Store Chains Accused Over PC Price Gap', *Daily Mail*, 1 January.

'Farmers Call For Tax On Supermarkets', *Daily Mail*, 10 October 1998.

Fletcher, Matthew (1998), 'We're Such Good Value Say Stores', *Financial Mail on Sunday*, 18 October.

Fletcher, Matthew (1998), 'Shoppers "Happy About Prices"', *Mail on Sunday*, 20 December.

Gribben, Roland (1998), 'Grey Cars From Japan Via Dublin', *Daily Telegraph*, 7 August.

Griffiths, John (1998), 'Dealers Seek Legal Review of Grey Car Imports', *Financial Times*, 10 August.

Griffiths, John (1998), 'MPs Say 'Cosy' Car Deals Must be Exposed', *Financial Times*, 9 December.

Halstead, Richard (1998), 'Big Brands Bypass the Supermarkets', *Financial Mail on Sunday*, 2 February.

Halstead, Richard (1998), 'Big Four Flop in Fight Against Own-Brands', *Financial Mail on Sunday*, 14 June.

Halstead, Richard (1998), 'Is Choice Being Devoured By the Food Monsters?', *Financial Mail on Sunday*, 9 August.

Helm, Toby (1998), 'British Paying More To Buy New Cars Than The Rest of Europe', *Daily Telegraph*, 7 July.

Jaggi, Rohit (1998), 'Motorcycle Buyers Are Driving A Parallel Market', *Financial Times*, 14 August.

Johnson, Boris (1998), 'Why Tony Worships In The Temple of Gammon', *Daily Telegraph* 14 October.

Massey, Ray (1998), 'A Dirty War Hits Cut-Price Car Sales', *Daily Mail*, 8 August.

Mitchell, Alan (1999), 'Evolution', *Marketing Business*, January.

'Motorcycle Makers Cut Prices To Get Ahead of Parallel Importers', *Daily Telegraph*, 19 October 1998.

Nuki, Paul (1998), 'British Homebuyers Get raw Deal', *Sunday Times*, 14 June.

Nuki, Paul and Andrew Alderson (1998), 'Revealed: Motor Firms Block Sale of Cheap Cars to Britain', *Sunday Times*, 10 May.

Nuki, Paul and Andrew Alderson (1998), 'Fiat Orders Secret Surcharge On Britain's Continental Bargain Hunters', *Sunday Times*, 24 May.

Nuki, Paul and Stephen Bevan (1998), 'Stores Mark Up 'Bargains' By 60 per cent', *Sunday Times*, 8 November.

Oldroyd, Rachel 'Minister's Move As New PC Price Gulf Is revealed', *Financial Mail on Sunday*, June 21 1998.

Oldroyd, Rachel (1998), 'Mandelson Joins Battle Over Dixons' High Prices', *Mail on Sunday*, 22 November.

Poulter, Sean (1998), 'Penny for the Poor Price Cuts at Tesco', *Daily Mail*, 31 August.

Poulter, Sean (1998), 'Supermarkets To Sell Cars', *Daily Mail*, 16 November.

Prescott, Michael and Jonathan Carr-Brown (1998), 'Treasury To Become A Shopper's Best Friend', *Sunday Times*, 10 October.

Roberts, Dan (1998), 'Researchers Back Supermarkets, *Daily Telegraph*, 7 December.

Rushe, Dominic and David Smith (1998), 'Retail Boss Lashes Out At Criticism Over High Prices', *Sunday Times*, 11 October.

Sheehan Maeve and Edin Hamzic (1998), 'Naive Britons Pay 40 per cent Extra for Computers', *Sunday Times*, 28 June.

Smith David and Stephen Bevan (1998), 'Official: High Street Prices Are A Rip-Off', *Sunday Times*, 19 October.

Smith, David (1998), 'Overpriced Over Here', *Sunday Times*, 5 July.

Taylor, Paul and Peggy Hollinger (1998), 'Home PC Buyers Forced To Pay Too Much', *Financial Times*, 25 September.

'Tesco Rejects Survey on High Prices', *Daily Telegraph*, 24 August 1998.

'Tesco and Asda Would Shine in the World of Car Retailing', *Daily Telegraph*, 7 August 1998.

'Warning Over the Computer Warranty Hard-Sell', *Daily Mail*, 22 October 1998.

Wheatley, Catherine and Richard Fletcher (1998), 'Wal-Mart Sets Its Sights Overseas', *Sunday Business*, 13 December.

Wright, Robert (1998), 'Customers Foot the Bill for Car Industry Squabbles on Pricing', *Financial Times*, 2 November.

CHAPTER 8

BT International*

The global adventure

British Telecommunications plc (BT) is a British telephone company. Until 1984, the telephone business in Britain was an offshoot of the state-owned Post Office. In 1984 BT was one of the earliest large-scale privatizations of the Margaret Thatcher government of the 1980s, with the highly successful issue of shares to the public and investment institutions.

The years following privatization were ones of a massive transformation in BT, from a sleepy and highly inefficient state-owned company to a large and profitable commercial enterprise, which prides itself on world-class customer service.

The British telephone service of the 1970s had been plagued with massive civil service bureaucracy, producer orientation, destructive trade unionism, vandalized phone boxes and poor customer service. Privatization brought a massive programme of streamlining, restructuring to remove layers of bureaucracy and large culture change to focus on customer service and quality.

The BT of the 1990s is a world player in digital communications. BT's key financial results in recent years are indicative of its successful transformation and the sheer size of the BT operation size (see Table 8.1).

---

* This material has been prepared by Nigel F. Piercy, Cardiff Business School, Cardiff University from published sources and discussions with executives. © Nigel F. Piercy, 1999.

Table 8.1 BT's key financials 1994–98

	1994	1995	1996	1997	1998
Turnover	£13.7bn	£13.9bn	£14.5bn	£14.9bn	£15.6bn
Pre-tax profit	£2.8bn	£2.7bn	£3.0bn	£3.2bn	£3.2bn
Earnings per share	28.5p	27.8p	31.6p	32.8p	26.7p*
Dividends per share	16.7p	17.7p	18.7p	54.35p**	19.0p

* After payment of a Windfall Tax of £0.51bn imposed by the incoming Labour government.
** Including special dividend of 35p.

The robustness of the company's development is also demonstrated by solid and consistent growth in its share performance during the 1990s (see Figure 8.1).

By mid-1998, BT was one of the top ten telecommunication groups globally (see Table 8.2), although the speed of formation of alliances and merger and acquisition activity quickly dates such comparisons.

'By mid-1998, BT was one of the top ten telecommunication groups globally'

The transformation of BT is largely associated with the leadership of Sir Iain Vallance. Son of a director of the Post Office in Scotland, Vallance followed his father into the Post Office, and was a senior manager there when BT was split off. He

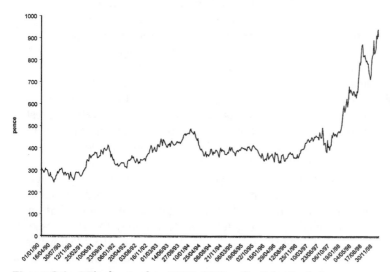

Figure 8.1 BT's share value, 1990–98 (unadjusted prices). Source: Datastream

Table 8.2 The top ten telecom groups
(July 1998)

	Market value
Nippon T&T	£84 bn
SBC Communications + Ameritech	£81 bn
AT&T Corporation	£59 bn
MCI Communications + WorldCom	£59 bn
British Telecom	£53 bn
Deutsche Telekom	£48 bn
Bell Atlantic	£42 bn
BellSouth	£41 bn
France Telecom	£40 bn
GTE	£34 bn

Source: *Sunday Business*, 26 July 1998.

became a director of BT at its inception, and in 1986 aged forty-three became chairman. More recently, the role of Sir Peter Bonfield has been decisive as a 'deal-making' CEO, working closely with Vallance. Bonfield joined BT in 1996, after fifteen years with Texas Instruments and fourteen years running the British computer company ICL.

The focus here is not the transformation of BT in the domestic market, but its progress in becoming a global player in the worldwide telecommunications industry, and in particular its strategy towards the large US marketplace in the 1990s.

'Almost from the moment of privatization, the BT board decided that one of its key global strategies should be a tie-up in North America'
Almost from the moment of privatization, the BT board decided that one of its key global strategies should be a tie-up in North America. Although BT has also developed an extensive network of alliances and partnerships in Europe, in spite of a problematic regulatory environment, to develop a pan-European communications network. By 1998 BT had invested nearly £2 billion in countries such as France, Germany and Italy, an investment showing losses running at £300 million a year.

A first attempt to develop the BT position in North America in 1986 involved buying a 51 per cent controlling stake in Mitel, a Canadian switchboards manufacturer, for £156 million. The goal of leading telecoms technology from the base in Mitel largely failed and BT sold its stake in 1992, showing a loss of £135 million on the deal. A second attempt was a £980 million investment for a 20 per cent minority stake in US-based McCaw Communications, a pioneer of mobile telephones. However, this time US regulators refused to allow BT to increase its stake, and the holding was sold in 1996 to AT&T for £1.2 billion. It was in the mid-1990s that the BT strategy for the USA became the dominating issue for the company.

The global telecommunications industry

The worldwide industry for telecommunications is large (estimated to be worth $600 billion in 1997), turbulent and technologically emergent. It is also experiencing the paradoxes of deregulation and liberalization on a global level. The regional division of the global market is shown in Table 8.3.

Several key characteristics of the global telecommunications industry are important to understanding BT's global strategy.

Market liberalization

For most of the twentieth century telecommunications operators have behaved as monopolists in their home markets and enjoyed comfortable, often co-operative, relationships with their fellow monopolists in other countries. Indeed, most operators were state-owned and governments took far-reaching precautions to ensure that what they classified as 'strategic' national assets remained under government control. The USA and the UK were

Table 8.3 World telecommunications revenues

	1997	2012
North America	37%	34%
Europe (including the UK)	35%	31%
Africa/Middle East	3%	3%
South America/Caribbean	4%	5%
Developing Asia	4%	10%
Developed Asia/Australasia (includes Japan, Australia, New Zealand, Singapore, Hong Kong, Taiwan, South Korea)	17%	17%

Source: *Financial Times*, 27 July 1998.

among the earlier countries to break free from this model through market liberalization policies and in the UK privatization.

In 1997, the World Trade Organization negotiated an international agreement that opens around 90 per cent of global telecoms services revenue to competition by 1998 (compared to the then existing 40 per cent). For example, in January 1998 the European Union opened its telecoms markets to full competition in fixed and mobile telephony for both voice and data, and in services and infrastructure, as well as allowing the full foreign ownership of national carriers. This has happened in an area which until recently regarded privatization as something unpleasant that had travelled from the USA and found a home in the UK.

'the US and UK experience suggests that true market liberalization may be relatively slow'

However, the US and UK experience suggests that true market liberalization may be relatively slow. For example, while there are now more than fifty licensed operators in the UK, and BT's market share is falling, BT still has 90 per cent of the local calls and 60 per cent of international calls. At the rate of attrition in BT's market share in the UK current in 1998, it would take forty years for BT to lose half its domestic market. Most countries have also maintained strong interventionist regulatory bodies to oversee telecommunications companies. There have also been many accusations that the incumbent operators (who own the network linking from the final exchange to the customer) have overcharged for interconnections and are obstructive – the possibilities for delays, 'misunderstandings' and technical failure that impact poorly on customer service are many. MCI, for example, blamed its 1997 profits warning on the costs of dealing with anti-competitive tactics by the local phone companies in the USA – the 'Baby Bells'.

Indeed, in the USA much of the deregulation intent that led to the split of AT&T – 'Ma Bell' – to create the seven 'Baby Bells' as local phone companies, leaving AT&T as a long-distance carrier, has been eroded by merger and acquisition. The 'Baby Bells' were down to five by 1998 because of mergers and expected to become four. The Bell Atlantic $52.5 billion merger with GTE combines a dominant local phone carrier with a long-distance carrier again.

Alliances

As telecommunications operators have faced up to the problems of defending home markets against new rivals at the same time as attempting to sustain revenues by competing successfully abroad, the industry has been dominated by a huge number of alliances and partnerships. These groupings include:

- *AT&T/Unisource* – an alliance between AT&T in the USA and Unisource owned by KPN of the Netherlands, Swisscom and Telia of Sweden.
- *Concert Communications* – owned and controlled by BT with minority stakes held by MCI, Telefonica and Portugal Telecom (MCI's stake has been bought out following its acquisition by WorldCom).
- *Global One* – a joint venture between Deutsche Telekom, France Telecom and Sprint of the USA.
- *Equant* – an international carrier owned by an alliance of international airlines.
- *Cable & Wireless* – less a conventional alliance than a network of telecoms assets, with special strengths in the Asia Pacific region.

However, as we will see these alliance groupings are proving fragile and difficult to sustain, and may fail to build 'supercarriers' with truly global reach and market power. For example, by 1998, Spain's Telefonica had managed to switch three times between different alliances in as many years.

'these alliance groupings are proving fragile and difficult to sustain, and may fail to build "supercarriers" with truly global reach'

The industry has become dominated by merger, acquisition and alliance. One investment bank suggested in mid-1998 that the global value of telecoms mergers and take-overs in the first half of 1998 had increased by 589 per cent from £15 billion to £101 billion. The combined effect of technological advances, deregulation, the need for cost savings and economy of scale and market invasion by new competitors has driven telecoms operators into merging and buying high-tech companies. The underlying logic is to assemble the components to offer customers complete communications solutions, encompassing voice, data and Internet services.

There are some signs of vigorous efforts in the industry to overcome the instability of the new alliance-based groupings by freezing the partnerships. Merging assets and increasing common ownership and structure are seen as the way to lock partners into the arrangement. The parallel is attempting to lock customers into a relationship with its carrier, for example if a corporate customer outsources internal communications to its telephone company, it will be much more difficult to sever the relationship.

Market invasion

'new competitors are entering from the computing industry instead of a telecoms background'

As 'Datawave' becomes more significant – data communications and networks obeying Internet protocol transporting data and voice traffic – new competitors are entering from the computing industry instead of a telecoms background. This has included WorldCom, America Online, PSINet and NetCom. The convergence of telecoms and computing may mean market control could pass to companies such as Microsoft and Netscape from the conventional suppliers. Indeed, one industry analyst in 1998 suggested that with a company like Microsoft providing more and more of the services customers need from their phone company, it could end up as the largest telephone company of all, and that there was no longer any reason for the existence of companies like AT&T selling what was no more than a 'commodity'.

The move to fibre optics as the basis for networks is a source of further potential disruption – the local carriers in Europe faced the threat of being undermined by trans-Europe fibre optic networks owned by WorldCom, Colt, Esprit and others.

Also, new inroads are being made by wireless and satellite service providers. In 1998 Motorola and Teledisc, a satellite venture, merged their projects for an 'Internet in the sky'. Others pursuing the same goal include Skybridge (owned by France's Alcatel) and Inmarsat, an international maritime satellite group. Others expected to join this movement are Iridium, Globalstar and ICO.

Customer demands

The way in which customers pay for telecoms is in the process of changing. Most operators have billed customers through a combination of time used and distances travelled, but with the growth of the Internet and the likely collapse of the accounting rate system for international calls, payment may have to change to subscriptions.

In addition, the transmission of voice conversations, the core business for most operators is declining in importance compared to the transmission of data – text, video and online information. By 1998, more than half the traffic carried on BT's networks comprised data that was not voice.

The Internet is also a major threat to traditional telephone businesses, for example in Internet telephony and faxes, sending information cheaply as packets of data. The larger operators are responding to this demand – BT, MCI, AT&T are all creating Internet provider products.

Customer expectations for suppliers to focus on their communications needs instead of selling technology, and to deliver against service promises is escalating, at the same time as the prices are falling rapidly and new competitors are redefining the boundaries of the market.

It is against this fast-changing environment that BT's global strategy should be judged.

Concert

Much of BT's international expansion has been through a complex set of alliances with local carriers.

However, the front-edge of the BT international strategy is Concert Communications – a global network servicing around 3800 large corporate customers globally.

Concert is a network management product. It centres on the creation of 'virtual private networks' for corporate customers with international operations. This provides an integrated, cost-efficient and highly secure telecoms service to a company. It replicates the sort of service a company would get from its own modern telecommunications network linking its worldwide offices, without that cost.

First under the name Syncordia and now as Concert, BT has invested around £1.5 billion into the service in four years. The operation reached break-even in mid-1998, with revenues of around £700 million. Concert is one of the most successful 'supercarriers'.

The critical target market is multinational corporations. Spending on telecoms by the top 5000 multinationals had reached around $100 billion in 1997, amounting to as much as 15 per cent of global telecom revenue and around 30 per cent of total profit. The key to this market is that 80 per cent of the top 1000 multinational are headquartered in the USA, Japan, Britain, Germany and France.

The MCI merger

Building up to a bid

The profit BT made on the sale of McCaw Communications to AT&T provided part of the funding for the next BT attempt to build a transatlantic link. In 1993, BT paid $4.3 billion for a 20 per cent stake in MCI, the USA's second largest long-distance phone company after AT&T. Vallance saw this as the effective entry point to the USA and established the 'Little Concert' joint venture, with BT owning 75 per cent and MCI the remainder of the joint venture. However, prevailing US competition legislation prevented a foreign investor from holding more than 25 per cent of a domestic telephone company. This changed in 1996, when deregulation meant that foreign ownership was allowed by companies whose own domestic market was open to overseas competition, opening the way to a full bid.

BT was by then looking at a £33 billion merger with Britain's other leading telephone company, Cable & Wireless. This would have taken BT into the Asian market rather than the USA. There were complications, however: UK monopoly law would have forced the sale of C&W's Mercury subsidiary (a small telephone carrier competing with BT in the UK market); BT would have had to buy out minority shareholders in C&W's Hong Kong Telecom subsidiary. After two attempts to negotiate a deal, talks broke off in late 1995.

Within a few months, BT made a $23 billion cash-and-shares bid for MCI, which was endorsed by Bert Roberts of MCI. The new business created would be Concert. BT began aggressively to add further international partnerships to support the Little Concert alliance with MCI – in support of the goal of creating an international telecoms infrastructure which will connect to regional carriers in local markets, to outmanoeuvre competitors such as AT&T and the C&W GlobalOne partnership. Bernard Vergnes, president of Microsoft Europe commented in June 1997 that, 'The best alliance today, the best working and most dynamic, is clearly BT and MCI'. In April 1997, for example, Telefonica chairman Juan Villalonga, joined Iain Vallance and Bert Roberts of MCI in a triple hand-shake photocall to celebrate Telefonica's entry into the Concert alliance.

Renegotiating the price

By summer 1997, while the BT bid was still being considered by the US government, the effects of deregulation of the US domestic market became apparent when MCI issued a profit warning, because of a forecast $800 million loss in its domestic operations, the value of its shares fell dramatically. Bonfield and Vallance turned back from the airport in New York to meet with Bert Roberts, MCI chairman.

Relationships between BT and MCI became increasingly strained, as a taskforce of senior BT executives carried out a six-week review of MCI's business operations in the USA. This culminated in BT claiming that MCI had concealed the extent of its domestic market problems, which MCI vehemently denied (pointing out that BT had three directors on its board, including Bonfield). Reservations about BT management taking charge of MCI re-emerged as negotiations continued, particularly regarding MCI's plans to invest heavily in the US local phone market conflicting with BT's goals for the multinational corporation market, and as BT attempted to pressure MCI into removing two senior MCI executives – Timothy Price, president and chief operating officer and Douglas Maine, chief financial officer. BT's claim that MCI had over-invested in expanding its local phone operations fuelled fears and uncertainties about the impact of BT strategy on MCI.

Meanwhile at home, in July 1997, Sir Peter Bonfield faced a hostile BT shareholders' meeting where there were loud calls for his resignation on the grounds of 'poor management and judgement'. He was accused of being 'suckered' by a smart US company, and investors demanded to know why MCI were in charge of the deal. BT was accused of being out of touch with its US partner and having been outsmarted by MCI's lawyers. Questions asked in the financial press were:

- Why did it take BT so long to realize that MCI's ambitious plans to enter the US local telephone market would cost so much more than originally envisaged, despite having senior BT executives, including Bonfield, on the MCI board?
- Why did Bonfield sign a schedule to the main agreement that ruled out renegotiation of the terms of the merger because of MCI's local phone market difficulties?
- Why did BT seek the resignations of two senior MCI executives and then deny it?

At a Scottish BT shareholders' meeting, one investor taunted Sir Iain Vallance as being 'An English muffin' because 'American companies eat you for breakfast'. Some institutional investors urged Bonfield to walk away from the deal.

'one investor taunted Sir Iain Vallance as being "An English muffin" because "American companies eat you for breakfast"'

Under pressure from its institutional investors, in August that year, and in spite of MCI's ferocious reputation for litigiousness, BT reduced the value of its offer for MCI by 22 per cent. The deal achieved final regulatory approval at around this time.

This was arguably in breach of the terms of the original agreement that explicitly ruled out renegotiating price based on

MCI's domestic performance. MCI executives were outraged, but reluctantly accepted the revised offer.

The man who shot 'Liberty Vallance'? – losing MCI to WorldCom

While agreeing to BT's revised offer, MCI directors were secretly talking to another US phone company – WorldCom.

WorldCom was a relatively little known Mississippi company run by Bernie Ebbers. Ebbers has grown WorldCom from an earlier business called LDDS by acquiring other small companies that were buying unused capacity from large network carriers and reselling it at a discount to smaller businesses. Ebbers' acquisition strategy extended to local and national fibre optics networks and integrated telecommunications companies. In 1996 he acquired MFS Communications for $14 billion, and thus (unwittingly) UUNet, a leading Internet network owned by MFS. WorldCom stock had appreciated at 57 per cent a year during the 1990s – $100 invested in 1989 would have been worth £3137 in 1997 (compared with $191 for a similar investment in BT). WorldCom had become the USA's fourth largest carrier (after AT&T, MCI and Sprint). Some analysts see WorldCom as a 'hot air balloon' that is due to burst.

WorldCom's brokers were Saloman Brothers, who had advised throughout Ebbers' acquisition strategy. Salomans had also lost about $100 million, when MCI's share fell as a result of the renegotiated price to be paid for MCI by BT.

In October 1997, WorldCom topped BT's bid by offering $30 billion in shares.

Ebbers' argument was that combining the domestic operations of WorldCom and MCI would offer massive cost savings – $800 million in the first year of operation – as well as providing economics in overheads and advertising – maybe a further $1 billion a year. MCI would save $500–800 million immediately by abandoning its expensive programme to build infrastructure for entry into local markets (that infrastructure can be provided by WorldCom's own networks).

On 15 October 1997, GTE counterbid $28 billion in cash. In November, WorldCom increased its offer to $37 billion, and MCI and BT accepted the terms.

Crawling out

Vallance and Bonfield spent forty-eight hours of intense negotiation with MCI and WorldCom to get a deal good enough to keep their shareholders happy. For each MCI share it bought for $32 in

1993, BT got \$54 – \$51 in cash and the rest as a kill-fee from MCI for calling off the deal. This gave an investment profit of around \$3 billion. Also WorldCom/MCI agreed to act as distributor for Concert for five years.

The post-MCI trauma

The most immediate impact of losing the MCI deal was that Vallance and Bonfield's international strategy appeared to be in ruins and the fall in BT's shares touched 500p. One analyst commented at the time, 'The cornerstone of BT's strategy for the past five years has just been bought by someone else'. Having failed to secure a deal with C&W, Vallance and Bonfield has failed to acquire MCI. In particular, without a US partner, Concert seemed to have no long-term future – because it could not service multinational US customers. The threat by WorldCom's Bernie Ebbers that his next move might be a bid for BT looked all too credible.

'Vallance and Bonfield's international strategy appeared to be in ruins and the fall in BT's shares touched 500p'

In fact, BT's share price grew dramatically in the aftermath of the MCI deal, for two reasons. First, many investors believed that the alliance with MCI was an extremely high-risk venture, and were relieved that risk had been avoided. Second, the prospect of BT selling its stake in MCI and returning cash to shareholders was welcomed.

In fact, WorldCom paid £3.8 billion for BT's stake in MCI, and BT's shares ended 1998 at 905p.

In February 1998, Sir Iain Vallance stepped down as BT chairman to become part-time chairman.

At this time, BT's attention turned its focus to Asia instead of America – purchasing a £230 million stake in the mobile phones arm of LG, the Korean *chaebol*, for example. This followed moves into Singapore and Malaysia and led to a doubling of the BT stake in the Indian mobile operator Bharti Cellular to 40 per cent. Moves also started to take a major holding in VSNL, the Indian national telecoms carrier. By the end of 1998, BT was also looking to invest in Japan with the forecast demerger of the national carrier, NT&T.

However, Bonfield continued the search for a US partner. He remained convinced that only this would give BT secure access to the lucrative US business market and sharing the costs and risks of developing new generations of products for multinational customers.

The unthinkable – alliance with AT&T

In spite of personal links between Iain Vallance of BT and Michael Armstrong, AT&T's incoming chairman in 1997, the two companies had been traditional rivals with no history of collaboration. Both had been dominant players in their domestic markets. Indeed, there had been some overt hostility between Robert Allen, AT&T chairman and CEO during the 1990s, and BT. Under Allen, the idea of collaboration between AT&T and BT would have been simply 'unthinkable' – as one analyst noted, 'about as likely as Coca-Cola and Pepsi-Cola co-operating to market a global drink'.

Once the by-word for corporate power, the AT&T of the 1990s had seen its base eroded by new competitors, though it still had 90 million customers, around half the US market for long-distance phone calls and revenues in excess of $50 billion in 1997. The challenges facing incoming chairman, Robert Armstrong in 1997 were to protect AT&T's core long-distance business while gaining a foothold in the larger local call market (now permitted under new legislation); to fill the vacuum that passed for its international strategy; and to use its resources to gain a technological lead in an industry where the economics are being transformed by innovation. Armstrong has started to reinvent the struggling giant, beginning by circumventing the high local access fees charged by the 'Baby Bells' by acquiring cable TV operator, Tele-Communications Inc., using its wires to bypass the local phone companies to reach potentially one-third of US homes, as well as buying Teleport, an independent local carrier.

'the "unthinkable" became a reality in 1998 when BT and AT&T agreed to an alliance' Significantly, the 'unthinkable' became a reality in 1998 when BT and AT&T agreed to an alliance, forming a joint venture to combine 'trans-border' operations – services they offer on a global rather than a country-to-country or national basis, with an initial sales base of £6 billion. The heart of the deal was BT's Concert – the network management business focusing on large corporate customers worldwide. The plan was for BT to buy MCI's 25 per cent stake in Concert (for $1 billion). The appeal was simple: Concert had the infrastructure and AT&T had lots of corporate customers to sell it to. AT&T gained presence in the European market, which it had previously not had. One of the attractions of the MCI deal had been to link with a US operation with a strong Internet backbone, which AT&T had previously lacked but had now acquired.

The new joint venture will be owned 50:50 by BT and AT&T and will offer a package of services to multinational customers, while investing in new technologies and networks. It was planned to comprise three parts:

- a global voice and data division containing both companies' international networks for domestic and business calls – undersea cables, satellite dishes, wires and substations – and will include BT's existing international operation, Concert
- packaging services for multinational companies, offering services such as video conferencing and global billing and initially targeting companies in the petroleum, financial and information technology sectors
- managing telecoms traffic for other carriers around the world

Although by the start of 1999, it still required regulator approval in the USA and Europe, the alliance quickly gained major customers in the UK, for example Imperial Chemicals Industries (ICI).

In fact, this left AT&T with the problem of unravelling its position in two other alliances – WorldPartners and Unisource. It has also to sell its £1 billion stake in TeleWest, a UK cable TV and telephone operator to placate the European competition regulators.

The expectation is that the alliance will develop further, while it is unlikely that BT will want to enter basic US telephony, it might join in collaborating with AT&T in some of its higher-growth domestic operations. By the early part of 1999, there was speculation about linking the mobile phone services of the two companies in a further alliance, to counter the new Vodaphone AirTouch operation.

A phoney war?

Reactions from competitors were predictably shock and then hostility towards the BT and AT&T alliance, suggesting the partnership would have an unfair lock on transatlantic and European traffic.

Partly in response to a formal objection lodged by Cable & Wireless, by November 1998 the European competition commissioner announced a decision to carry out an in-depth examination of the alliance proposals – introducing at least a four-month delay before a decision. C&W accused that the alliance could account for half the telecommunications traffic between the USA and UK and acquire 40 per cent of the multinational corporate customers it was targeting.

On similar grounds, Bert Reynolds, now chairman of MCI WorldCom demanded 'close review' by regulators in both Brussels and Washington.

Meantime, C&W entered negotiations with the Unisource alliance to take the place vacated by AT&T in the alliance.

Prospects for the future

BT ended 1998 in a strong position: the AT&T alliance was developing; there had been one spectacular success in France and progress made in Germany and Italy. Leadership had successfully passed to Bonfield, with Vallance's move to part-time chairmanship. BT's shares were sitting at 905p, close to their peak.

The biggest question lies over the effectiveness of the alliance with AT&T. BT and AT&T are seen to be closer in culture than BT and MCI. However, industry analysts speculate about whether AT&T can ever be a successful partner, particularly a junior one. Indeed, AT&T has yet to show it can operate successfully as anything other than a monopolist – since its 1984 break-up it has been losing long-distance market share to innovators such as MCI and WorldCom. Its previous attempt to build a global telecoms alliance, Unisource, foundered over its unwillingness to co-operate with its foreign affiliates or show commitment to new common investment.

The issue is underlined by the fact that BT carried out a 'cultural audit' to see whether executives in the two companies could work together.

However, the largest immediate issue for BT is at home – the potential purchase of Securicor's 40 per cent stake in Cellnet, the mobile phone operator, with the relaxation of government regulations about BT involvement in mobile telecoms. BT wants to buy Securicor's stake, but only if the price is right. However, summer 1999 is the date set for the British government's auction of licences for the next generation of cellular telephones, called UMTS. This will turn the mobile phone into a multimedia communication vehicle. There is a risk that British regulators will demand major concessions from BT in the domestic market as the price for allowing it to own the whole of Cellnet.

Late in 1998, BT had also looked for a partner to bid for AirTouch, the USA's largest independent cellular phone operator (it cannot bid alone because of an agreement not to compete with AT&T in the USA, and it cannot bid with AT&T because both are the top mobile phone suppliers in their domestic markets). The deal was lost to Vodaphone's takeover of AirTouch – creating a company larger than BT.

BT has also made some critical moves in the Internet arena. In November 1998, BT purchased 50 per cent of the UK business of Excite, one of the largest US Internet portal groups.

Relationships with one-time potential partner Cable & Wireless have soured. C&W has complained formally to the European Commissioner about the BT/AT&T alliance. C&W announced in November 1998 a £600 million investment on a European high-speed network for corporate customers, taking it into head-on competition with Concert and the BT/A&T alliance. WorldCom announced at the end of 1998 that it was spending £150 million to extend coverage of its network in the UK, in a direct challenge for BT's domestic business in the residential and corporate markets. The announcement came just two weeks after World-Com paid BT $7 billion for its 20 per cent stake in MCI.

'Relationships with one-time potential partner Cable & Wireless have soured'

Sources

Alexander, Garth (1997), 'BT Blown Out', *Sunday Times*, 5 October.

Alexander, Garth (1998), 'Telecoms Giants Rush for Global Alliances', *Sunday Times*, 2 August.

Cane, Alan (1998), 'Business As Usual Despite Phoney War', *Financial Times*, 17 March.

Cane, Alan (1998), 'Operators Race To Surf Datawave', *Financial Times*, 10 June.

Cane, Alan (1998), 'A Tale of Doubt, Fear and Uncertainty', *Financial Times*, 22 August.

Cane, Alan (1998), 'Finding Partners Becomes Priority', *Financial Times*, 30 September.

Cane, Alan (1998), 'Innovation Key In Fight for Survival', *Financial Times*, 10 September.

Cane, Alan and Tracy Corrigan (1998), 'BT and AT&T Unveil Link-Up', *Financial Times*, 27 July.

Cane, Alan and Emma Tucker (1998), 'BT-AT&T Alliance Attacked', *Financial Times*, 25 November.

Clark, Andrew and Andrew Cave (1998), 'BT Goes Global Via £6 bn AT&T Tie-Up', *Daily Telegraph*, 27 July.

Corrigan, Tracy (1998), 'Deal With BT Completes Reformation of Once-Lagging AT&T, *Financial Times*, 27 July.

Gribben, Roland (1997), 'The Day BT Got An $800m Alarm', *Daily Telegraph*, 23 August.

Gribben, Roland (1998), 'American BT Tie-Up Halted By Brussels', *Daily Telegraph*, 13 November.

Hall, Amanda (1998), 'BT Put On Hold', *Sunday Telegraph*, 16 November.

Jackson, Tony (1997), 'Internet Takes On the Phone', *Financial Times*, 2 October.

Lorenz, Andrew (1999), 'Bonfield Sets BT On Upwardly Mobile Path', *Sunday Times*, 3 January.

Lorenz, Andrew and Kirstie Hamilton (1999), 'BT Seeks US Ally for £36 bn AirTouch Bid', *Sunday Times*, 10 January.

Northedge, Richard (1998), 'After 12 Years of Crossed Lines, Britain's Telephone Giant Could Finally Make A Transatlantic Connection', *Sunday Business*, 26 July.

Pfeifer, Sylvia (1998), 'Nippon T&T Is Global Leader', *Sunday Business*, 26 July.

Pretzlik, Charles (1997), 'The Man Who Gazumped BT', *Daily Telegraph*, 4 October.

Pretzlik, Charles (1997), 'WorldCom Wins Battle for MCI', *Daily Telegraph*, 11 November.

Rushe, Dominic (1998), 'BT Architect Takes A Step Into History', *Sunday Times*, 2 August.

Schwartz, Nelson D. (1999), 'How Ebbers Is Whipping MCI WorldCom Into Shape', *Fortune*, 1 February.

Skeel, Shirley (1998), 'C&W and BT Clash in Europe', *Daily Mail*, 17 November.

Tucker, Emma (1997), 'Euro-Regulator Spectre Hovers Backstage', *Financial Times*, 19 December.

Waters, Richard (1997), 'High Achiever Reaches for MCI', *Financial Times*, 2 October.

Waters, Richard (1998), 'Ma Bell's Crash Diet', *Financial Times*, 29 January.

Waters, Richard (1998), 'Ma Bell On the Offensive', *Financial Times*, 25 June.

CHAPTER 9

Retail banks*

Who needs them?

'The world needs banking, not bankers.' (Bill Gates, Microsoft, 1997)

One of the most striking examples of revolution in the market-place which can totally disrupt traditional structures and conventional ways of doing business is the financial services sector. It is also a good illustration of traditional competitors going into 'denial' and being sidestepped by new competitors and new ways of doing business – hence the Bill Gates quotation above. The experiences of the traditional retail banks** in recent years raise major questions about their future. Conventional banks are unlikely to disappear in the near future, but their role is likely to be transformed and their market power will be far less than in the past.

The real point, however, is not simply to glory in the demise of companies that treat their customers badly (enjoyable though this revenge may be for bank customers), but to ask whether the

---

* This material was produced by Nigel F. Piercy, Cardiff Business School, Cardiff University, from published sources, personal prejudices and discussions with executives from the financial services industry. © Nigel F. Piercy, 1999.
** For simplicity, the term retail banks includes the demutualized building societies and the current building societies still maintaining mutual status.

same type of revolution and reinvention may take place in other industries and markets and how we can cope.

The present situation in this industry is summarized by a recent *Financial Times* report in the following terms:

'The financial services industry is a sector under siege' The financial services industry is a sector under siege, driven by the challenges of globalization, consolidation and new competition in a market where developments such as the rapid growth of the Internet, online banking and electronic commerce are re-writing the rule book for doing business.

The traditional rationale for having banks

The very word 'bank' conjures an image – probably the self-righteous, pompous, small-minded, judgemental, risk-aversive and old-fashioned little Captain Mainwaring* figure. This is drastically unfair to people who work in real banks, but whoever said life was fair? A couple of questions are worth considering: how did traditional banks come into being and who said they had a God-given right to ownership of the financial services business?

Banks originated at a time when they collected small savings from individual depositors, to provide capital to lend to business. The basis of 'maturity transformation' in banking is transforming a flow of short-term deposits into long-term loans. The traditional local bank manager was probably well equipped to attract savers and investors and to assess the creditworthiness of potential borrowers. However, to this has been added the retailing of a large number of financial services.

It is very advantageous from a bank's point of view to become a financial services conglomerate. This gives it the chance to use its retail deposits as the collateral for riskier activities in securities markets, such as trading, market making and placing, which can earn high speculative profits. Banks with large retail deposits also have competitive advantages in providing other financial services, although those advantages do not suggest they have unique skills

---

* Captain Mainwaring was the archetypal prig in the British television series *Dad's Army*, who was a local bank manager turned Home Guard commander.

or competencies in these areas. In fact, the reverse may be true.

The rationale disappears

The message from customers to banks seems very clear: 'We don't like you. We don't want you. And now at last, we don't need you'. This would seem to be the harsh reality that the traditional retail banks are doing their very utmost to ignore.

'The message from customers to banks seems very clear: "We don't like you. We don't want you. And now at last, we don't need you"'

Why don't people like banks?

An interesting question. Probably appallingly bad service, intransigence in the face of customer needs, overcharging and hints of racism go some of the way towards an answer.

Bad service. In one of the many surveys published on this issue, a 1997 report by Abbey National highlighted customer perceptions of banks as providing poor service, expensive overdrafts and no interest on accounts in credit (and even when interest is paid it is laughably minimal). Major causes of discontent for nearly one-quarter of all account holders include shoddy service standards, charges for statements and stopped cheques. The report estimated that some two million were considering changing banks. However, most will not because the banks have made it so difficult to transfer accounts to competitors – there is just too much 'hassle' involved. Bank staff also tell customers that it is 'illegal' for them to have accounts at more than one bank (it is not). There is also very little difference perceived between the 'competing' banks anyway.

Later the same year, the Consumers' Association reported that in spite of a succession of promises and charters 'guaranteeing' better service, its survey found that customers were still angry and frustrated about impersonal service, inadequate facilities, high charges and poor interest rates.

The 1990s have also seen a continuation of the policy of shrinking branch networks by the main retail banks. Datamonitor research suggests bank branch numbers will fall from 21,800 in 1985 to 13,500 by 2003. Notwithstanding the advent of postal and telephone banking and cash machines, to many customers who signed up at a local branch, this policy is a dramatic and unilateral reduction in the main customer service they were promised.

Sharp practices. In May 1998 the British government announced a crackdown on banks' treatment of customers, after it became apparent that Northern Rock had changed its savings rates and unilaterally switched customers into lower paying accounts. Many banks advertise high interest rates to attract investors, and then shortly afterwards reduce rates or launch a better account, leaving the first savers trapped in a lower interest rate account.

A bank auditing firm – Bankcalc – was one of those responsible for uncovering and making public the bank practice in cheque clearing of unnecessarily holding cheques for an extra day to earn the bank interest on the money. This practice was estimated to gain the banks £300 million a year at their customers' expense.

In 1997, Abbey National decided to 'fine' customers who cash cheques at the counter. They want Instant Plus account customers to use cash machines, so if they have the impertinence of troubling the bank's staff with their pathetic requests for service, they will pay a £1 penalty each time they do so.

Overcharging. So bad is the situation in Britain that there is a whole new emerging industry of bank and mortgage account checking firms. Those firms have claimed that 80 per cent of interest payments on overdrafts are incorrectly calculated and 50 per cent of mortgage borrowers are overcharged.

A *Sunday Times* survey in May 1998 concluded that the biggest cause of overcharging on overdrafts is branch managers manipulating customers' overdraft limits, to allow charging of penalty interest rates of more than 30 per cent. The bank-auditing firms report that 90 per cent of the refunds they secure – worth around £10 million a year – are the result of bank managers secretly lowering overdraft limits to below the overdraft balance, pushing the borrower into the penalty-interest zone. Less dramatic is the practice of allowing borrowers to exceed their limits without informing them, so that they pay penalty-interest rates – which raises an interesting question about how such borrowing can be 'unauthorized' when the bank allows it to happen.

The banks claim that they have no duty to prove that they have acted fairly – the burden of proof is on the customer. Customers brave enough to take banks to court for overcharging are faced with reams of bank figures to check – to uncover errors. Settlements when made usually come with 'gagging orders' that prohibit those involved publicizing outcomes.

Intransigence. British banks claim that it would be too expensive to provide customers with a full statement detailing the daily application of interest to overdrafts – instead of just the balance and the interest charged. Interestingly, BT seems to have no difficulty in producing itemized statements for phone calls, yet this is 'impossible' for banks. The response to customer complaints about service seems to have been to close branches (it saves money, and then the staff is spared the inconvenience of meeting customers).

Racism. This is a strong term. Yet a report produced in 1998 by the University of Nottingham demonstrated that black and Asian business customers get a poorer deal from banks than white customers – they pay higher interest rates on overdrafts and loans, even though their businesses are more profitable. Non-white managed businesses seem to be regarded as high risk. More generally, this may be part of the reason why the Grammen Bank of Bangladesh is planning to set up in the UK, offering 'micro loans' of up to £500 to help Britain's poor establish businesses, in the face of the traditional banks' preference for lending only to the affluent.

Excluding the disadvantaged. In January 1999 the Office of Fair Trading (OFT) drew attention to the fact that millions of people are excluded from essential financial services because banks prefer to deal only with affluent, low-risk consumers. The OFT's report into financial services for 'vulnerable' consumers – the six million people in the UK on low incomes, unable to work, disabled and ethnic minorities – says that there is a need for low-cost current accounts for poorer households currently without access to banking facilities. (To their credit, alone among the big retail banks, Lloyds TSB is working with other organizations to establish innovative community banks to bring mainstream financial services to deprived areas.)

All in all, it seems clear that the banks are not popular with their customers and have policies which are positively hostile towards many customers. If the banks need defence against change and new types of competition, then they would be unwise to depend on customer loyalty and brand equity, since there would seem to be none. Customers seem to be overwhelmingly disenchanted, not loyal. What may appear to be loyalty is probably no more than retention by inertia. Traditional banks may have underestimated the extent to which their only brand is the branch.

'banks are not popular with their customers and have policies which are positively hostile towards many customers'

How have the rules changed?

The most obvious reason why banks treat their customers they way they do is simple – because they can. Customers have had very little choice other than to deal with a bank (or they were *'it is possible for new types of competitor to reinvent this business and to develop "new-style" banking and financial services'*

encouraged to believe that this was so), if they want chequebooks, cashless payments and all the rest of the services on offer. At least, that is the way it used to be. Fundamental revolution has changed the rules: the reasons for the existence of banks have gone and the logic for banks being the suppliers of a bundle of financial services has changed. This is why it is possible for new types of competitor to reinvent this business and to develop 'new-style' banking and financial services. Not least of the banks' problems come from the growing sophistication of customers.

'the conventional label "banking sector" is probably redundant and meaningless'

What constitutes a 'financial institution' in the 1990s raises an interesting question – indeed the conventional label 'banking sector' is probably redundant and meaningless. A combination of deregulation, globalization and advancing technology means almost any competitor can establish a 'virtual bank' or insurance company, if they have access to capital and expertise in managing risk. In effect, what was once a nationally based market of well-established institutions has become wide open to new types of competition. What is more, traditional financial institutions are at a major disadvantage in the new global marketplace.

'This alone suggests that the whole rationale for linking together the traditional functions of the bank has simply gone – bundled services suited banks, not customers'

Historically, banks existed to take in deposits and to make loans. At its simplest, the reason for linking taking deposits and making loans disappeared with the securitization of markets. Besides, large businesses can access capital markets on better terms than their bankers. What is more, specific bank functions – retail marketing of financial services, financial advice to companies, monitoring the credit standing of large companies – are probably better done by specialists, and those specialists do not need to be bankers. This alone suggests that the whole rationale for linking together the traditional functions of the bank has simply gone – bundled services suited banks, not customers.

What this all adds up to is very simple: banks rely on 'bundling together' a range of financial services to hold their position in the market. The conditions that allowed them to achieve this have largely disappeared. They have held their dominant position also because they had a limited number of rivals and the cost to customers of obtaining the information necessary to make informed judgements was high (and was kept that way by shrouding charges and rates in mystery). Developments such as the Internet mean those conditions have changed forever – rivals can enter from abroad or outside the traditional sector altogether and customers can compare all competitors instantaneously. That is what is creating the revolution.

In fact, the cross-selling phenomenon may have been an illusion, writes John Authers in the *Financial Times* in 1998. The rewards of selling several products in one package may be spectacular, but relatively few companies have actually achieved this goal. It relies on a cross-selling culture and effective incentives, not just size and product availability. Being big has not guaranteed that customers will buy more products from the same company. 'Relationship banking' may have been a fiction for most banks.

'"Relationship banking" may have been a fiction for most banks'

The preoccupation of bankers

In this era of revolution and change in the customer marketplace for financial services, the major interest of banks in the late 1990s appears to be in merger to create even larger conventional banks. The underlying belief of bankers at the end of the 1990s appears to be that the world will be dominated by ten universal global banks, because big balance sheets are the best way to do modern banking and full service financial conglomerates will drive out the other players. Given their other obsessions with the Euro and the Millennium 'bug', it is perhaps no wonder that they have no time to worry about customers.

In fact, the insatiable herd instinct of bankers notwithstanding, size is almost certainly not the key to success in modern banking. Besides size in banking may just mean that you have lent out a lot of money – this makes growth relatively easy, though profitability will depend on whether the loans are serviced and repaid.

More positively, Datamonitor reported in 1998 that the major banks were re-assessing their strategies to focus on brand and client value. This has been manifested in such policies as: investing in cash machine networks to substitute for branches; a growth in telephone banking services; the launch of online banking services for customers; expenditures on image building through advertising, accompanied by closure of branch networks and a general impression of complacency and 'business as usual'.

New-style banking

At a time when Richard Branson's Virgin branded goods group sells pensions, the clothes retailer Marks & Spencer advertises loans on television and the supermarkets Tesco, Sainsbury and Safeway offer retail bank services, it is becoming apparent that there is no 'banking sector' any more, in the traditional sense. What we have seen is a variety of attacks on traditional providers of financial services from a variety of new competitors – some of which will fail, some are trivial, some are small, but some of which are permanent changes in the way customers buy financial services. Consider the following examples of the 'unthinkable' happening, while the big banks continue clinging to each other in new mergers.

Banking at the post office

In 1997, the Co-operative Bank launched a strategy of offering banking services through 15,500 post offices, to supplement its network of 150 branches and 'Handybanks' in Co-op retail grocery stores. The result is that a small bank now has in effect the largest banking network through collaboration, and incidentally has branches open longer hours. This may be a precursor to the 'hollow' bank organization. If this sounds trivial, bear in mind that in Japan the post office has become the largest retail financial institution in the country, offering better interest rates than the conventional banks.

By 1998, the Post Office itself was adding to this source of competition by offering six types of insurance under its own brand name – Everyday Cover. The Post Office is developing its business to take over the high street role of banks and building societies as they close their branches.

Virgin One

'the conventional banks were traumatized by the launch of the Virgin One bank account, by Richard Branson's Virgin financial services operation'

Also in 1997, the conventional banks were traumatized by the launch of the Virgin One bank account, by Richard Branson's Virgin financial services operation. Branson has attempted to reinvent the relationship between the customer and the institution that holds the customer's assets and makes loans to that same customer. At its simplest, the Virgin One account reduces all banking to a single account that incorporates: the customer's income and savings deposits, with the customer's long-term borrowing for house and car purchase and short-term borrowing for other purposes. The concept offers the customer the opportunity to avoid heavy interest changes on credit cards and mortgages and get good rates on savings, in fact, the same rate. The product is provided for Virgin by the Royal Bank of Scotland, with 24-hour telephone access. It is a sophisticated product that will probably appeal only to a small affluent segment of the market (but one that the conventional banks would very much like to keep).

The conventional bank reactions were: it will never work; if it does, then we could have done it anyway; and (mysteriously) Virgin's product signals the end of 'free' current account banking for everyone. Reinvention of products by new competitors is difficult to respond to.

The Prudential's Egg

When the Prudential, the UK's biggest life assurance company, launched Egg, a new direct banking operation, they ran into immediate problems. Those problems stemmed not from lack of interest, but because they were swamped with demand from customers wanting to transfer from conventional banks. Egg received 65 000 telephone inquiries in the first five days after launch (double their expectations), and more than a million web site hits. Egg is offering a substantially higher deposit rate than its traditional banking competitors.

DIY banking

Even more startling is that the 1990s have seen a small but growing trend towards 'do-it-yourself' banking in the form of credit unions – fuelled not just by customer dissatisfaction with conventional banks and building societies, but also by Labour government support for expanding and extending credit unions to replace the mutuality lost with the commercialization of building societies into banks.

'the 1990s have seen a small but growing trend towards "do-it-yourself" banking in the form of credit unions'

Credit unions are financial co-operatives of people linked by a common bond, e.g. neighbourhood, workplace or church. Police officers, taxi drivers and council staff are some of the groups that have formed credit unions. Savings are pooled and used as a common fund from which members can apply for loans. The maximum interest rate is fixed by law and the unions are non-profit making. There are no credit checks on members, which is important to those with 'bad' credit ratings, who otherwise would borrow at very high interest rates from conventional lenders or not be able to borrow at all. Bad debts can be pursued in the normal way. Any surplus income is distributed to members in the form of an annual dividend. New legislation is planned to give credit unions the ability to offer mortgages and interest-bearing savings accounts.

Currently, the UK has around 600 credit unions with 210 000 members and £104 million in assets. However, they are much more widely operated in Ireland, the USA and Canada. The proposed relaxation of the restrictions in the 1979 Credit Unions Act may dramatically change this picture and credit unions may move from simple loans to mortgages and insurance. Perversely, there are some suggestions that credit unions are popular with affluent middle-class consumers and cannot be dismissed as simply 'a poor man's bank'.

Non-bankers

Also at the edge of conventional banking has been the growth of high street cheque encashment businesses, such as Cash Centres and N&N Cheque Exchanges. No-one knows how many people in Britain manage their money without current accounts. Estimates vary from 14 per cent to 23 per cent of the total population (though many of these may have access to a savings account), and this group is dominated by the over-seventies and under-twenties. Cash centres will cash a company cheque for those without chequing accounts, giving money on demand (not after a 'clearing' period of 4–14 days operated by the conventional banks). In 1997 the two leading companies handled payments of £170 million. Their charges are high: 5–10 per cent of the value of the cheque plus handling charges of £2–3. None the less, for those without bank account, or who want fast access to a wages cheque, they provide an alternative and they are growing.

Even if traditionalists dismiss these non-bankers as trivial, at a wholly different international level there are interesting parallels. For example basic financial services and banking functions, once the sole preserve of banks, being offered by non-banks:

- General Electric is a big lender
- Fidelity is a big fund manager
- market data suppliers such as Reuters and Bloomberg are moving towards executing transactions between subscribers
- Discover manages a major credit card outside the banking system

- in 1998 in Britain, clothing retailer Marks & Spencer and branded goods company Virgin offered the cheapest Personal Equity Plan investment products
- by 2001, the car manufacturer Volkswagen may own four separate banks under the VW, Audi, Seat and Skoda brand names, and already Volkswagen Bank GmbH is one of the largest direct banks in Germany

'by 2001, the car manufacturer Volkswagen may own four separate banks under the VW, Audi, Seat and Skoda brand names'

New banks

The 1990s have seen the emergence of new companies offering products such as savings accounts in the British market – insurance companies and supermarkets. In a period of about eighteen months, these new-style banking operations had amassed around £6 billion in customer deposits.

'The 1990s have seen the emergence of new companies offering products such as savings accounts in the British market – insurance companies and supermarkets'

Insurance companies offering this type of 'bank' account include Standard Life Bank (raising £1 billion in eight months), Scottish Widows, Sun Bank, Legal and General and Prudential. Supermarket entrants include Safeways, Tesco (£800 million in deposits in eleven months), and Sainsbury (£1.4 billion deposits in the first eighteen months). In 1997, 2 per cent of people opening savings accounts in Britain did so with supermarkets, by 1998 this figure had risen to 15 per cent (compared to the traditional banks' 19 per cent share of these new accounts).

The new entrants have exploited their lower cost base, because they do not carry the cost of bank branch networks, and disenchantment of customers with traditional banks, to build this position quickly.

Traditional banks appear to view this development with some complacency – the new entrants may be taking a high share of new savings business, but the total impact on the savings business is still small – the Halifax alone has £75 billion of retail deposits. The

'Traditional banks appear to view this development with some complacency'

high street banks have tended to see the new-style bankers as a nuisance rather than a real threat. Industry opinion is that the new entrants are just 'cherry-picking' and do not offer the full range of banking services like 'real banks' – none provide a current account, for example. (As noted earlier, traditional banking relies on 'bundling services' together, although there is no evidence that this strategy remains sustainable. It is also possible that the traditional current account may have become obsolete.) Some also suggest that if the insurers and supermarkets move into other financial services such as loans and mortgages, they will become as unpopular as the other banks, and will give it up to avoid damaging their core brands.

However, while most banks are relying on their established position and customer inertia to protect them, until the new competitors give up and go away, most have also responded by offering postal and telephone accounts that offer higher interest rates than accounts at branches. The Halifax, for example, has gone for an instant saver account paying the same rates as Tesco and Sainsbury, because they see the new players as a greater threat than the high street banks and building societies.

The new banks are already expanding into mortgages, personal loans and credit cards. In fact, the supermarket entrants are taking an aggressive and long-term view of this market, as part of their 'share of customer' approaches (leveraging profitability by taking a growing proportion of the customer's total lifetime expenditure). For example, in October 1998, Stuart Sinclain, CEO of Tesco Personal Finance was quoted in the *Financial Times*:

> We are bringing the high street into the supermarket ...
> Supermarket banking is an extension of the new paradigm
> – non-branch based banking. We are contributing to the
> unbundling of financial services. We are not emphasizing
> relationships in the short term because we think a lot of
> customers simply want a good deal.

This apparently simple statement is actually a complete rejection of the fundamental principles of conventional retail banking.

The supermarkets have a number of advantages: low customer acquisition costs because they are selling to their own shoppers and no branch network to maintain. Tesco, Sainsbury and Safeways are all operating in partnerships – Tesco with the Royal Bank of Scotland (RBS), Sainsbury with the Bank of Scotland and Safeways with Abbey National. Back office functions are provided by RBS and Bank of Scotland, while the supermarkets focus on merchandising, customer acquisition and product design. The change in status for the conventional banks is underlined by the fact that Tesco has already broken its original partnership with National Westminster and moved to RBS. Tesco is offering savings accounts, credit cards, loans, home insurance, travel insurance and pensions (through a collaboration with Scottish Widows). Such supplier banks have had to learn that you cannot deal with major corporates such as Tesco and Sainsbury in the same cavalier 'take it or leave it' way that you traditionally treated customers.

Interestingly, the traditional banks anticipated that the super-markets' savings accounts would attract only the less affluent small saver. In fact, nearly three-quarters of the supermarkets' banking customers earn more than £20000 a year and are major middle-market targets for financial services products.

Online banking

Perhaps the most fundamental change in view is the impact of the Internet on banking. In 1997, the Centre for the Study of Financial Innovation, the think-tank sponsored by the Bank of England, reported its forecast that by mid-2002, most consumers will run their current accounts through the Internet. Access to the Net will not be just through personal computer, but through normal televisions via satellite, cable, telephone or radio waves. Electronic cash systems are likely to replace much of the need for physical cash and bank branches. The report notes that the cost of running a bank over the Internet will be at least 75 per cent cheaper than operating branches.

Part of the significance is that 'virtual banks' can be opened and operated by those currently not in the banking or financial services sector and they are not restricted by geography. The Internet can also provide the information and comparisons for customers that may break customer inertia. It is already possible to do personal banking, arrange mortgages and buy insurance, shares and pensions on the Internet – and the companies offering these services are new to the financial services market.

'"virtual banks" can be opened and operated by those currently not in the banking or financial services sector'

Conventional banks are still struggling to find a role in the mainstream of electronic commerce. Richard Lowrie, a senior consultant in IBM's banking group was quoted in the *Financial Times* in July 1998:

In traditional commerce, the banks have a critical part to play in transactions. But in electronic commerce it is the customers at the centre of the hub – such as Marks & Spencer, the retailing chain, or General Motors – which set the standards for how suppliers deal with them, providing the potential for the banks to be cut out of electronic trading networks.

'In traditional commerce, the banks have a critical part to play in transactions. But in electronic commerce it is the customers at the centre of the hub'

Later in 1998, an Ernst & Young report suggested that traditional banks 'lack a strategy on the Internet', and were generally pessimistic about being able to increase sales or retain customers via the Internet. The fundamental problem is that the rules of the game have changed. The technology infrastructure that makes it easier and cheaper to deliver a wider range of products and services valued by customers, is the same infrastructure that makes it easier for sophisticated customers to compare and contrast competitors and undermines customer retention.

Even if current volumes of 'virtual bank' customers remain low, the new entrants are targeting the most valuable customers. Typically, 70 per cent of the traditional banks' profits come from 20 per cent of customers – the new Internet services are designed to cut into this 20 per cent. For example, in 1998 Morgan Stanley, Dean Witter announced plans to start a direct banking business over the Internet, using its Discover credit card brand name (Discover is one of the best-known retail brands in the USA), aimed at younger, affluent banking customers – precisely the high net worth/high potential income consumers who provide a prime market segment for traditional retail banks.

What will become of the traditional banks?

Before we get carried away, it is worth remembering that banks are big companies with unique protection from regulators. They may, for example, be big enough to be too big to fail – because governments will not allow this to happen. (However, it is possible that the financial conglomerates into which traditional banks are developing may find the internal control and management problems they have built too difficult to handle.)

Peter Martin wrote in the *Financial Times* in 1998:

> Banks have no future. Their economic purpose is redundant. To survive they must find another role: adviser, speculator, fund manager. . . . Traditional banking is dying but the grieving throng around the deathbed face a long and expensive vigil.

He refers to this as 'the long goodbye'.

There is a central paradox in this sector in the UK. The banking sector has expanded rapidly with the addition of the demutualized building societies, with their enormous branch networks, at the same time that the existing banks are closing branches and emphasizing direct selling of services. This sounds like a recipe for painful and potentially radical rationalization. The current obsession with merger is the first sign of this process, but more radical changes in ownership and structure may follow.

However, it is also true that the future for conventional banks probably lies in two areas: imitating others in moving towards non-branch banking; and reinventing themselves as 'wholesaler' suppliers to those who operate retail banking and financial services (the banks may end up as 'content providers' for others, operating remote from the customer). However, 'wholesalers' lack market power and brand differentiation and have to compete on price to win business with 'retailers'. Dealing with powerful corporate customers as suppliers is very different to dominating a fragmented consumer market. As we saw, Tesco had no problem in dumping National Westminster to use RBS as its supplier; and similarly Virgin broke off its relationship with Norwich Union and selected another supplier for Virgin Direct financial services. Business-to-business branding may become a dominant issue with which banks have to struggle.

If you were looking for a way to compete in a global financial services marketplace driven by new technologies and more demanding customers, it is unlikely that you would start by building a widely spread network of expensive high street branches together with a cumbersome centralized administration. This is, of course, exactly what the conventional banks have.

One possibility is that contrary to the current moves towards a small number of global universal banks, the future may actually involve breaking up universal banks. Andre Levy-Lang, chairman of Paribus, sees the future of banking as specialized players with good control of technology in distribution, and investment banks with the ability to commit capital to take financial risks. He writes in the *Financial Times*:

> The universal bank must now justify itself beyond the monopoly it used to have in a regulated environment . . . [this is] a warning for believers in the current conventional wisdom that a few universal banks will soon dominate global finances. This new conventional wisdom is as dangerous as that of the 1970s, which said that a sovereign country cannot default, or that of the 1980s that real estate values will never collapse. Yet this view is held by many, as evinced by recent mergers. The belief in the value of gigantism may cost some banks as much as did

'The universal bank must now justify itself beyond the monopoly it used to have in a regulated environment . . . there cannot be consistent profits unless there is a creation of value for customers'

the previous conventional banking wisdoms ... Banking will have to play by the same rules as industry, and bankers will have to submit to the iron rule of business – there cannot be consistent profits unless there is a creation of value for customers.

Sources

Alexander, Andrew (1997), 'Banks' Future Lies in Phones Not Branches', *Daily Mail*, 23 July.

Authers, John (1998), 'Cross-Selling's Elusive Charms', *Financial Times*, 16 November.

'Bank of the Poor Heads for Britain', *Mail on Sunday*, 15 November 1998.

'Big Banks Charged With Failure', *Daily Mail*, 6 November 1997.

Bromwich, Neil (1998), 'High Street Revolution Cashes In On the Cheque', *Mail on Sunday*, 23 August.

Brown-Humes, Christopher (1998), 'A Small But Growing Threat From the Novices of Banking', *Financial Times*, 4 September.

Brown-Humes, Christopher (1998), 'Banks 'Lack Strategy on Internet'', *Financial Times*, 9 September.

Brown-Humes, Christopher (1998), 'Supermarkets Take On The High Street Leviathans', *Financial Times*, 15 October.

Brown-Humes, Christopher (1998), 'Prudential Warns of Long Delay on Egg Accounts', *Financial Times*, 19 October.

Brown-Humes, Christopher (1998), 'Banks Seen As Too Complacent About New Rivals', *Financial Times*, 16 November.

Brown-Humes, Christopher (1998), 'Movement Seeks a Loosening of Law's Shackles', *Financial Times*, 16 November.

Corrigan, Tracy (1998), 'Banks May Face Internet Attack from Outsider', *Financial Times*, 11 July.

Freeborn, Tim (1997), 'Net Banking Revolution "Within Next Five Years"', *Daily Mail*, 20 June.

Gardner, Nick (1998), 'Banks Guilty of Cheating', *Sunday Times*, 24 May.

Gardner, Nick (1998), 'Don't Take Bank Charges On Trust', *Sunday Times*, 24 May.

Hopegood, James (1997), 'Three and a Half Million Don't Rate Their Bank', *Daily Mail*, 20 August.

Kay, John (1998), 'The Key to the Banks', *Financial Times*, 14 October.

Levy-Lang, Andre (1997), 'Who Needs Bankers?', *Financial Times*, 26 September.

Manchester, Philip (1997), 'The Market Is Wide Open', *Financial Times*, 2 July.

Martin, Peter (1997), 'Ghost of Business Future', *Financial Times*, 11 December.

Martin, Peter (1998), 'A Long Goodbye', *Financial Times*, 24 November.

Montgomery, Emma-Lou (1997), 'Banks Are Relying More On Cashpoint Machines To Beat the Opposition', *Daily Telegraph*, 13 September.

Moran, Nuala (1998), 'Banks Face A Threat From On-Line Start-Ups', *Financial Times*, 1 July.

Parsley, David (1998), 'Banks Look At Ways of Spying On Customers', *Sunday Times*, 22 November.

Prestridge, Jeff (1997), 'Mortgages in Virgin Territory', *Mail on Sunday*, 26 October.

Sunderland, Ruth and Henrietta Lake (1998), 'Banks Dearer for Blacks and Asians', *Mail on Sunday*, 20 September.

Taylor, Paul (1998), 'A Sector Under Siege', *Financial Times*, 1 July.

Vincent, Clare (1998), 'All Credit to the New Do-It-Yourself Bankers', *Daily Mail*, 5 August.

PART III

Stories of Obsolescence and Renewal

CHAPTER 10

M&S

Has Marks lost its Sparks?*

Marks & Spencer (M&S) is a British institution with a worldwide reputation as a high quality retailer – nicknamed 'Marks and Sparks' by the irreverent British consumer. It is also a global business with operations in Canada, the USA and Caribbean, Europe, North Africa and Southeast Asia, and owns Brooks Brothers and Kings Super Markets in the USA. The 'Britishness' of M&S is such that when Princess Diana died in France, it was the Paris M&S store on which thousands of Parisians converged to pay their respects.

M&S has consistently been Europe's most profitable retailer. Group sales exceeded £8 billion in 1998 and group pre-tax profit was greater than £1 billion for the first time in 1997. Market capitalization was £12 billion. Although seen by many as a dull and sluggish company that is poor at coping with radical change, in the five years up to 1997 M&S doubled its profits – far outperforming any other company in the sector.

'M&S has consistently been Europe's most profitable retailer'

The core product area for the company is clothing, and it has dressed a substantial proportion of the men, women and children in the UK for five generations, from their underwear outwards.

---

* This material has been complied by Nigel F. Piercy, Cardiff Business School, Cardiff University from published sources and discussion with executives. © Nigel F. Piercy, 1999.

M&S has around 25 per cent of the UK £15 billion clothing market. Traditionally a fiercely British retailer, in the 1960s M&S sourced 99 per cent of its products from the UK, and even by the 1990s still sources 70 per cent of its products domestically, spending around £5.7 billion a year.

The company is renowned also for its high quality grocery selection – it has become the UK's largest butcher, fishmonger and greengrocer – taking 3–4 per cent of the £60 billion UK food market, traditionally concentrating at the high margin end. M&S also sells a range of household products and furnishings, as well as becoming a major financial services supplier – it has 5.5 million charge card holders – and the consumer trust in its brand is so high that it can sell investment products alongside clothing and food. The company operates 373 M&S stores, 85 M&S franchises with partners outside the UK, 173 Brooks Brothers stores and 40 Kings Super Markets stores, as well as operating some direct marketing activities.

Key financial results are shown in Table 10.1.

Table 10.1   Marks & Spencer plc's key financials 1992–98

	1992	1993	1994	1995	1996	1997	1998
Group turnover (£ million)	5828.7	5949.7	6543.7	6809.9	7233.7	7841.9	8243.3
Group profit before tax (£ million)	588.9	736.5	851.5	924.3	965.8	1102.0	1168.0
Earnings per share (p)	13.5	18.0	20.9	22.4	23.3	26.7	29.1
Dividend per share (p)	7.1	8.1	9.2	10.3	11.4	13.0	14.3

M&S is often seen as a prime example of a company delivering a strategy of superior customer value through excellent customer service and high customer loyalty, a unique brand identity, closely managed relationships with suppliers, employees and customers and continuous innovation in products and trading methods.

'1998 was a year when M&S was in the headlines not for its excellence as a retailer, but for its failing performance and internal upheavals in management'

In addition, M&S is a frequently cited example of a company that has been able to renew itself and grow profitably where many others have failed. M&S has shown outstanding long-term growth performance, profitability and customer satisfaction. The company has grown largely organically, testing new markets with low-risk acquisitions. It accepted social responsibilities to employees and to the community at a far earlier stage than most, and was a forerunner of the now popular 'stakeholder approach' of partnership.

However, 1998 was a year when M&S was in the headlines not for its excellence as a retailer, but for its failing performance and internal upheavals in management. The question is can M&S renew itself again?

The history of M&S – from market stall to public company

The history of M&S is almost folklore. In 1884 Michael Marks, a Russian refugee, settled in the Jewish community in Leeds and scratched a living as a peddler of haberdashery around the villages near Leeds. One of his earliest suppliers was Isaac Dewhirst, from whose factory he bought wool, cotton and knitting patterns. He soon borrowed £5 from Isaac Dewhirst to stock a market stall in the Kirkgate market in Leeds. Purchasing his goods from Dewhirst's, he met Tom Spencer, Dewhirst's cashier. As Marks' business grew, he marked off half his stall for goods sold on the basis: 'Don't Ask The Price. It's a Penny' – this pricing policy was encouraged by Marks' poor grasp of spoken English. When he moved on to covered markets in different towns he traded as 'M. Marks: The Original Penny Bazaar'.

The business continued to grow into a chain of bazaars with Marks responsible for central management and buying. He sought a partner, but was turned down by Isaac Dewhirst who suggested his cashier Tom Spencer. In 1894, Tom Spencer invested his savings of £300 for a half-share in the business. The Marks and Spencer partnership lasted nine successful years, with Marks concentrating on the bazaars and Spencer managing the warehouse and office, and particularly using his experience from Dewhirst's wholesale business to buy direct from manufacturers. In 1998, some companies had been suppliers to M&S for more than 100 years – including Dewhirsts.

'In 1998, some companies had been suppliers to M&S for more than 100 years'

By the end of 1900 Marks and Spencer had thirty-six branches – twenty-four in market halls and twelve in shops – mostly in the North of England, but three shops in London, and with headquarters in Robert Street, Manchester, as well as a warehouse. In 1903 Marks & Spencer became a limited company, with share capital of £30 000 shared equally between Marks and Spencer. In spite of rapid expansion of the business, Spencer retired and died two years later. By 1907, Marks too had died, and there was a fight for control of the business.

Of the founders' sons, Thomas Spencer worked in the business but lacked the ability to run it, and Simon Marks was too young and inexperienced to take an effective role. The two board members appointed to safeguard the families' interests – William Chapman and Bernard Steel – were in constant rivalry. None the less, by 1914 M&S had 140 stores, mostly shops, and additional warehouses in Birmingham and London. Working conditions in the shops were unusually good for the time – rest breaks for staff during the day, holiday entitlements and Christmas bonuses.

Simon Marks and Thomas Spencer joined the board in 1911, at a time when family ownership was threatened by Chapman and Steel, who increased share capital to £100 000. Simon Marks pursued the slow and expensive process of buying up shares as they became available and restored family control. In 1916, Simon Marks became chairman, although only 28 years old. The following year, Thomas Spencer died. Israal Sieff, a school friend of Simon Marks, had also been appointed to the board, and when Simon Marks was called up for military service in 1917, Sieff became chairman. Excepting this interruption, Simon (later Lord) Marks served as chairman for forty-eight years. The Sieff and Marks families had a shared interest in Zionism and the founding of the state of Israel, and Simon and Israal later married each other's sisters. The Sieff family's lasting connection to M&S was established at this time – Marcus Sieff retired as chairman of M&S only in 1984.

In the years following the First World War, M&S bought the freehold of many of its stores and added textiles as an important part of the growing product range. Simon Marks' 1924 visit to the USA brought back many ideas about innovations from the more advanced US retailers such as new accounting machines, a focus on selling space productivity and centralized stock control. Simon Marks is seen as 'the retail prince' who established the enduring M&S philosophy and trading principles. The 1920s significantly also saw the introduction of M&S' own brand – St Michael – named to honour Michael Marks or the archangel Michael, guardian and patron of the Jewish people, depending on who is telling the story.

M&S became a public company in 1926 and moved head-quarters to Baker Street in London in 1931.

The 1930s saw the opening of the flagship M&S Marble Arch store on London's Oxford Street, the formal establishment of a staff welfare department and the introduction of a food department selling produce and canned goods in 1931. During the Second World War, M&S was heavily involved in the government's Utility Scheme designed to bring good quality clothing within reach of the besieged British population. The 1970s brought the opening of the first stores in Europe, in Paris, France and Brussels, Belgium, and in 1975 the national launch of the M&S Chargecard.

In the 1980s, M&S introduced furniture to its stores and the first home furnishings catalogue for direct selling, it acquired Brooks Brothers, the US clothing retailer and Kings Super Markets, a US food chain.

1997 saw M&S win the Queen's Award for Export Achievement for the fifth time.

Leadership in the company has been passed from hand to hand by a succession of chairman developing protegés. Marcus Sieff acted as patron for Derek (later Lord) Rayner, who became the first non-family chairman of the company in 1984. Rayner was responsible for introducing the M&S Chargecard and the controversial 1988 Brooks Brothers purchase (critics suggest results have been disappointing and at £460 million M&S paid too much). Richard Greenbury was Rayner's protegé and successor as chairman.

Many important attributes of M&S' strategy up until the 1990s can be traced to these origins and roots: effective supply chain management; continuous innovation and learning; and a new organizational form – the first 'manufacturer without factories'.

Supply chain management

In several important ways, M&S can be said to have invented supply chain management some fifty years ago. The ability of the company to anticipate and meet customers' needs depends on responsiveness and in turn on the relationships the company has with its suppliers. Those relationships have given M&S an unprecedented degree of control over products at all stages. The supplier base benefits by the high volume throughput created by M&S business. The long-term relationships built by M&S with successful suppliers are close and many business processes are integrated. These partnerships are difficult for competitors to imitate.

'M&S can be said to have invented supply chain management some fifty years ago'

For example, having found consumer demands for more comfort in clothing, M&S worked with its suppliers and Dupont to

'The basis of these partnerships is sharing knowledge and information throughout the supply chain'

pioneer the use of the material Lycra for the mass market. Lycra is now incorporated in three-quarters of M&S clothing, and has been extended to other products such as furniture covers. Partnership also created Tactel Diablo, used to give lingerie softness and 'drape', which has resulted in large sales. The basis of these partnerships is sharing knowledge and information throughout the supply chain.

Continuous innovation and learning

'In spite of its reputation for introspection and conservatism, M&S culture has been one of innovation since its earliest days'

In spite of its reputation for introspection and conservatism, M&S culture has been one of innovation since its earliest days. Technical innovations focus on enhancing products and selling, but management innovations look at working practices, training and education and building a culture that allows new ideas to flourish.

One prime example of the ability of M&S to innovate and learn is its international experience. The company sees the UK as having limited scope for the rate of development M&S wants, and has attempted to take the M&S formula into overseas markets. M&S has lost money in several such ventures. For example, it did not succeed in taking the trading philosophy unchanged into Canada. The company also signed long-term leases with upward rent reviews, and is not only losing money but cannot walk away. Chairman, Sir Richard Greenbury, has, however, taken the level of business down from £230 million to £40 million a year to contain the losses. The company has also learned how to adapt to local culture and trading patterns in moving into Europe and the Far East.

Similarly, an earlier opening of a store in Paris revealed another flaw in the British trading model – unlike their British counterparts, French women will not buy underwear without trying it on, and M&S did not provide changing rooms. The response of French women was to try on the underwear on the shopfloor. The company became aware of the problem when Paris became the requested transfer store for unexpectedly large numbers of male junior managers. Changing rooms were introduced.

The chairman spends two days a week every week in-store talking to managers and salespeople to find out what is selling and where the problems are. The company's culture tries to encourage argument and the expression of new ideas. In spite of his reputation as a forceful autocrat, Greenbury explains, 'you don't get entrepreneurial behaviour and decisions if you give people an ear-bashing every time they make a mistake'. The company has an 'obsession' with its products, high value and customers, and Greenbury claims that a 'total marketing ethos' is the M&S substitute for a marketing department. From the 1920s onwards, M&S has created an intelligence system about consumers, monitoring sales, getting customer reactions to new products, supplemented by informal interpretations from staff in stores who are in direct contact with customers.

> *'Greenbury claims that a "total marketing ethos" is the M&S substitute for a marketing department'*

The first 'manufacturer without factories'

M&S was one of the earliest retail firms in Europe to integrate retailing and wholesaling, by dealing direct with manufacturers instead of through intermediaries. It also understood the concept of the 'virtual company' before that phrase was ever invented. The core is the St Michael brand – so strong a brand that many consumers think it is a company separate to M&S. The brand defines a standard of excellence under which many suppliers can operate and which can be applied to many product areas.

> *'M&S was one of the earliest retail firms in Europe to integrate retailing and wholesaling, by dealing direct with manufacturers instead of through intermediaries'*

M&S suppliers are treated robustly by the company – some trades unions refer to the company as Marks and *Sharks*. Many suppliers operate as subcontract manufacturing facilities for the retailer. In return they get the benefit of M&S' success, marketing expertise and prompt payment of bills. In this relationship, M&S is in control – of design, materials sourcing, production and distribution. Understanding and controlling products from raw materials to finished goods distinguishes M&S from other retailers.

From the 1930s onwards, M&S has moved away from buying ready-made garments from suppliers and has acquired the expertise to design textile products, sometimes in-house and sometimes jointly with suppliers. The goal was to create commercially successful designs based on consumer intelligence, but with external advice about new raw materials.

This led M&S to use its knowledge of new materials to advise and instruct chosen suppliers on modifying equipment and working practices at every stage of production. M&S orders were placed with suppliers as subcontractors with very tight conditions. The supplier increasingly had no problems in product design and distribution and M&S products were closely specified in terms of their manufacturing characteristics and the equipment and raw materials to be used. For example, M&S is famous for defining and monitoring the number of stitches to be used in seaming clothes. The supplier was also told when to produce and to hold specified stock levels in his warehouse until instructed to send them to stores. The costs of stockholding were carried by the supplier. It was this subcontracting approach to buying that developed into supply chain partnerships of the type discussed earlier.

For example, Northern Foods is the biggest single food supplier to M&S and has eight factories dedicated to M&S. The relationship with M&S goes back thirty years and is based on trust – there is no contract. Northern Foods has built particular expertise in chilled food, produced in temperature controlled factories. M&S not only demands traceability in all ingredients throughout the production chain, but also works with Northern Foods on factory standards, down to the detail of wall coverings, flooring and packaging. Northern Foods freely admits that not only does M&S see employees in these factories as working for M&S, but so do the employees in question.

The partnership concept underpins many of the new developments, such as the 1998 entry into selling own-label music CDs in collaboration with PolyGram. The association between M&S and PolyGram includes M&S' chairman sitting on PolyGram's board. As overseas suppliers have built relationships to supply M&S stores with local products, those products have been adopted for the British stores as well.

The traumas of the 1990s

It is reputed that on one occasion the wayward but genius footballer George Best was reclining on a luxury hotel bed with the reigning Miss World, surrounded by thousands of scattered pound notes from his gambling, and when the room service waiter brought champagne, the waiter's comment was 'Oh, Georgie, where did it all go wrong?'

This must be one of the few things that Sir Richard Greenbury, M&S chairman for seven of the forty years he has been with the company, has in common with that particular footballer – although he is a life-long fanatical supporter of Manchester United, for which team Best played. There cannot be many chairmen of major companies who announce record-breaking performance and see share value fall on the same day.

Greenbury is not known for his efforts to court City analysts and says, 'the City doesn't like me, because I don't talk to them'. He is also very impatient with the short-termism of financiers and insists his role is to build the strategy to take the company through the next fifty years. He has paid a price for taking this stand.

Although trading conditions in Christmas 1997 had been difficult, in May 1998, Greenbury announced record sales growth and profits. However, he also announced that trading conditions would become difficult over the following months and his aggressive £2.2 billion long-term expansion programme was likely to depress short-term results.

Greenbury planned to continue heavy investment in staff to underpin the M&S promise of customer service – adding 1700 in 1998 – even at the expense of margins in the short term. Over three years until March 2000, M&S planned to expand selling space by 20 per cent in Britain and 40 per cent overseas (with an 80 per cent increase in Europe). The UK expansion includes rebranding nineteen stores bought from Littlewoods for £192 million; opening new superstores in London, Glasgow and Manchester; regional trials of a clothing catalogue to build on the existing mail-order business for home furnishings, hampers, flowers and wine; and extending product ranges in fresh foods to compete more fully with supermarkets (although Greenbury dismissed with conde-scension the suggestion that M&S should join the supermarkets in offering a customer loyalty programme or compete directly with them). Overseas, Greenbury was planning new stores in France and Germany, and franchise operations in Poland and Australia, as well as franchising Brooks Brothers in Hong Kong and opening Brooks Brothers stores in Europe for the first time.

'Over three years until March 2000, M&S planned to expand selling space by 20 per cent in Britain and 40 per cent overseas'

The strategy was one of becoming the world's first truly global retailer. Deputy chairman, Keith Oates was quoted, 'To some extent we are breaking new ground, I don't think there is another retailer like us, and none attempting to do what we are doing now. We are pioneers . . . I believe that, in the long run, there will not be any part of the globe without a Marks & Spencer store.'

'The strategy was one of becoming the world's first truly global retailer'

However, these plans were not well received in the City. In spite of the record 1998 full-year results, share price slipped 16p on the day.

It slipped again with the November interim results, which revealed declining overseas profits and no growth in food sales, giving overall a 30 per cent fall in half-year profits. M&S' strategy had been undermined by poor UK weather weakening clothing sales, demand in Asia subdued because of the financial crisis there, weakening of the UK furniture market, a fall in tourism to the UK and increased competition in the food market from aggressive supermarket firms. Greenbury described trading conditions as 'a bloodbath on the High Street' and said that the retail business had 'fallen off a cliff'.

'Greenbury described trading conditions as "a bloodbath on the High Street" and said that the retail business had "fallen off a cliff"'

In addition to problems associated with the Asian financial crisis (profits there £40 million less than expected), extra costs had become serious in a number of areas: £150 million to replace ageing tills unable to take the European currency and training staff to use them; £20 million for the new direct mail catalogue operation; new staff for the Warrington, Cheshire call centre.

With this rate of change, concerns began to emerge over management succession. The board asked Greenbury to stay with the company until he was sixty-five (he had been due to retire in July 1998 when he reached sixty-two). City fears included beliefs that Greenbury's UK experience was not adequate to lead an international strategy and that he would choose a successor with similar limitations. Behind the scenes the major contenders for the chairmanship were Keith Oates, deputy chairman, Peter Salsbury, heading the clothing business, Guy McCracken, running operations and Lord Stone, who runs the food business.

By June 1998 it became known that for the first time ever M&S had launched a fundamental review of its entire business to be carried out by external consultants, in an attempt to position the business for the future. The review was to cover such issues as organization and structure, merchandise, international development and store location. The company established a business strategy unit to oversee this review. Part of the review was also to look at whether the company should split Sir Richard Greenbury's role as chairman and chief executive.

The company also began to scale back its Far East operations, reducing the scale of operations in its Hong Kong stores and scaling back franchises in Singapore, Malaysia, Korea and the Philippines as well as closing its Shanghai office. The rate of European expansion was also pulled back and Greenbury settled on a policy of price-cutting in the M&S mid-range products that make up 50 per cent of the total M&S range.

Signs of falling sales and reduced investments by some £380 million a year – halving the earlier plan to spend £2.2 billion in three years – did little to reassure investors. Accusations began to appear that management complacency had allowed costs to rise and market share to fall, along with criticisms of M&S mid-range merchandising and suggestions that M&S had lost its retail flair. However, when the *Investors Chronicle* described the retailer as being 'in a quagmire', Greenbury's response was simply to call this a 'load of old tosh'. However, by the autumn of 1998, Greenbury had seen £6 billion taken off the company's market value that year and falling consumer confidence.

'Accusations began to appear that management complacency had allowed costs to rise and market share to fall'

It was also at this time that M&S began to demand that its clothing suppliers source products from abroad to make them more competitive with overseas manufacturers. This was seen in the textiles industry as an ominous weakening of M&S' traditional pledge to 'Buy British'. Traditional M&S supplier, Dewhirst, plans to source more than 70 per cent of its production overseas as a result. British clothing suppliers lack the strong manufacturer brands of their European counterparts – largely due to the impact of M&S and other strong retailers such as Next – and have little choice but to follow the M&S advice.

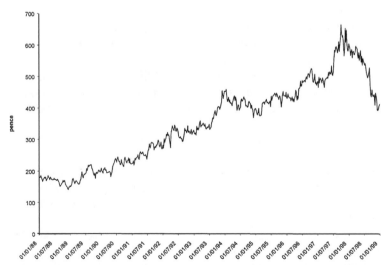

Figure 10.1 Marks & Spencer's share value, 1988–98 (unadjusted prices). Source: Datastream

The overall impact on share values late in 1998 can be seen in Figure 10.1. In the period October 1997 to October 1998, M&S' market value fell by £6.4 billion to £12.5 billion.

The fight for control

Late in 1998, while Greenbury was under continued City pressure to split his CEO and chairman roles and was in open conflict with suppliers angry at 25 per cent cuts in M&S orders and leaking sales information to the press, and while the company was traumatized by its poor trading results, a battle for succession erupted. Greenbury was to survive as chairman in a form, but as one City commentator concluded in November 1998, 'In the past 19 days the company has dissolved from being Britain's most respected retailer to a business that is torn apart by deep divisions'. The underlying question remains the extent to which the fabric of the company has been damaged by this power struggle at the top.

'while the company was traumatized by its poor trading results, a battle for succession erupted'

The battle opened in early November 1998. Rumours circulated that some investors and board members wanted Greenbury to step down earlier than planned as chief executive. In a political move wholly uncharacteristic of the 'M&S way of doing things', deputy chairman, Keith Oates, while Greenbury was visiting suppliers and taking holiday time in India, asked the non-executive directors to consider him for the post of chief executive.

The feeling was that Greenbury's view that he was too busy planning growth to worry about management succession was not acceptable. Oates may also have felt he was being manoeuvred out of a top job, and his age of fifty-six was against him, compared to Greenbury's 'favourite' Peter Salsbury. Although once seen as the 'heir apparent', and loyally supporting Greenbury (turning down jobs with rival retailers J Sainsbury and WH Smith), Oates had fallen out of favour with the chairman. An internal report, leaked to the financial press, had suggested that the new management structure was to be announced in May 1999 and that Peter Salsbury was to be chief executive and had triggered Oates' appeals to the non-executive directors.

Oates supporters promised M&S directors a 'dream ticket' for the management succession: Oates as chairman and Peter Salsbury as chief executive, requiring that Greenbury would as a result leave the company earlier than planned, rather than just splitting his roles as chairman and chief executive. Oates also presented the non-executive directors with his business plan outlining his future strategy for the company.

Furious at what he saw as the unforgivable act of disloyalty to M&S, Greenbury flew back from India early, but on his return failed in an attempt to persuade the board to immediately back Salsbury as chief executive and get rid of Oates. An acrimonious executive director meeting left Greenbury and Salsbury claiming that Oates had briefed the press about the succession battle, and Oates claiming he had been treated shabbily in a political campaign designed to stop him reaching the top job.

The M&S directors said they would not be rushed into making a succession decision and set up a nominations committee chaired by Sir Martin Jacomb (chairman of the Prudential and M&S' senior outside director) to make recommendations to the board on succession. Meanwhile, Greenbury was left with the problem of running the company, while the managing directors were manoeuvring for the chief executive job and lobbying by supporters of the rival camps occupying centre stage. Executives and employees were forbidden to talk to the media, on pain of dismissal.

The players in the succession crisis were thus:

- *'The King'*. Chairman for seven years, Sir Richard Greenbury, aged sixty-two and renowned for his autocratic and intimidating management style, and enjoying near absolute power in the business – known as 'Captain Grumpy' in the City. A lifetime M&S employee, totally committed to the company, City critics of the company are liable to receive lengthy letters in response known as 'Rickocets' or 'Rickograms'. Greenbury followed Lord Rayner as chairman, to consolidate Rayner's international expansion and diversification into financial services, which had shaken up the staid M&S culture of the 1970s and 1980s. The first chief executive appointed from outside the founding families, Greenbury was determined that he would not be succeeded by a 'bean-counter' (such as a finance specialist like Oates), but someone with merchandising and retailing skills.
- *'The Heir Apparent'*. Seen as approachable and easy going, Peter Salsbury, aged forty-nine, joined the company in 1970 as a management trainee after graduating from the London School of Economics. Although little known outside the company, he is regarded as 'M&S through and through'. Less 'verbally forceful' than his mentor, Greenbury, Salsbury graduated to a board job aged forty-one in 1990, and took on personnel where he managed head office redundancies for the first time

in the modern M&S history. Grooming for the top included spells running the stores and the property division before becoming joint managing director in 1994.

- '*The Black Prince*'. Keith Oates, deputy chairman, but still regarded after fourteen years with the company as an 'outsider' by some within M&S, did not follow the traditional M&S route of working up through the ranks. He joined M&S as finance director in 1984, having previously worked at IBM and Black & Decker. He has a high media profile, as deputy chairman, and considerable international and strategic experience, but was seen in the company as lacking retail expertise. He is credited with the success of the financial services operation at M&S.

For two weeks the non-executive directors interviewed all the executive directors to gather their views on who should be chief executive and what Greenbury's role should be.

On Wednesday 25 November the board reached a decision – described as 'overwhelmingly supported' not unanimous – and acted. Greenbury was to be reined in, losing his dual role as chairman and chief executive, and becoming a non-executive chairman for his remaining eighteen months with the company (with a two-page job description telling him what he can and cannot do, and specifically that he cannot 'advise' his chief executive unless asked to do so). The chief executive role was to go to Peter Salsbury. Oates agreed to resign as a director and take early retirement from the company in return for a substantial payoff of £2.4 million. The expectation is that when Greenbury retires he will be replaced by a major player from outside the company. Rumours suggest that former head of Tesco, Lord MacLaurin is a possible candidate.

Oates is being sounded out by furniture retailer MFI and M&S' high street rival, Storehouse, for a top job.

Greenbury announced that, 'The team is in place'. The City, on the other hand, when news of the shake-up broke, wiped £700 million off the value of the company, as analysts expressed their fears that Salsbury having been with the company for twenty-eight years, lacked the vision to steer it out of crisis.

Re-thinking the M&S philosophy?

As new CEO, Peter Salsbury's challenge is seen to be to bring back vitality and zest to a business that has become worthy but predictable. The fear is that the St Michael brand has lost the cachet it once had and that other stores have learned from M&S and caught up, e.g. Tesco in high-quality ready-to-cook meals, Boots in brightly coloured children's clothes and gifts, The Gap in clothes for the young with more street credibility, Next and Principles in the middle of the market. Similarly, Debenhams offers designer names such as Jasper Conran and Pierce Fionda in clothes and a newly launched furniture range from designer Kelly Hoppen. Debenhams' profits have increased at the time when M&S' fell. There are also suggestions that as merchandising and service standards increase in other stores, M&S' somewhat puritanical 'value-first' retailing model of spartan interiors, harsh lighting, crammed clothing racks and 'serve-yourself-if-you-can' may be outdated. However, there are question marks over Salsbury's ability as an M&S insider for twenty-eight years to make fundamental changes.

> *'The fear is that the St Michael brand has lost the cachet it once had and that other stores have learned from M&S and caught up'*

Salsbury's vision for the company is, 'to be as good at marketing and selling as we are at producing', and he says that the company will listen more to its customers, forge better relationships with its suppliers and banish the cult of the personality in favour of a team approach (he is also considering acquisitions for the first time since Brooks Brothers was purchased). Critics suggest this is 'more of the same' rather than an attempt to change the company's strategy.

> *'Salsbury's vision for the company is, "to be as good at marketing and selling as we are at producing"'*

As times have got harder, there have been some signs that the established M&S trading methods have to change, notwithstanding long traditions and management reluctance. Commentators suggested that M&S had lost touch with customers and that in areas like food competitors have caught up with M&S' previously unique offerings.

By the end of 1998, establishing a customer loyalty card programme had become top of the agenda to try to win customers back from competitors. There were signs also that the company was going to make an historic break with its past and allow customers to pay with credit cards. Critics see this as signalling an acceptance that M&S in the 1990s is no longer differentiated in its traditional ways from other high street retailers.

The run-up to Christmas 1998 saw another break with tradition, as M&S substantially increased its advertising expenditure (it relied in the past on reputation and recommendation), as it struggled to clear unsold summer stock at discounted prices. This was followed by the company's first television advertising for fifteen years in December 1998, a radical change in marketing style for M&S to introduce an equally characteristic and massive

New Year sale. By January 1999, M&S had been 'on-sale' for more than five months. Salsbury has long been associated with emphasizing the need for M&S to take a more aggressive approach to its marketing.

The company has also appointed an outside agency for public relations for the first time in its history to explain the business and its plans to the outside world.

The unhappy XM&S of 1998

While Greenbury relaxed in the Caribbean in January 1999, CEO-elect Salsbury was left to announce the worst trading figures in the company's history as a public company – results he described as 'lousy' and to persuade investors that he could build a recovery.

The shock figures of January 1999

Early in January 1999, Salsbury issued a surprise profits warning based on trading up to Christmas 1998 and January 1999 sales period. M&S sales were running around 13 per cent down on the previous years, and in end-year profit forecasts were down to £625 million from the £1.1 billion achieved the previous year. Clothing sales were even worse – 15 per cent down. Stocking and pricing errors involved further discounting at a cost of £150 million. European operations were disappointing, trimming a further £25 million from profit forecasts.

Investor reactions took 13 per cent off the M&S share value, taking it down to 339p from its October 1997 peak of 664p. This one-day fall took £1.5 billion off the value of the company. M&S directors Clare Freeman and Lord Stone extended their shareholdings, providing the City with some reassurance, and by the end of the week the shares were trading at 351p.

Credit analysts downgraded M&S credit rating from triple-A to double-A plus, making future financing more expensive and further embarrassing the company.

M&S' strategic weaknesses are made public

Only a few years earlier, M&S was widely rated as the retailer that most rivals would like to copy. By 1999 it had become a case study of the penalties paid for failing to respond to customer demands for value and encroachment by competitors. M&S had been shocked by consumers paying high prices for clothes in branded fashion retailers, but refusing to pay full prices for M&S products.

It is apparent that M&S had made some serious strategic mistakes. It bought too much stock (around £250 million too much), it priced too high and then was pushed into discounting, it aggressively expanded floorspace domestically and internationally at the wrong time, it lost sight of what consumers wanted and it complacently underestimated the strength of its competitors on the high street.

'M&S had been shocked by consumers paying high prices for clothes in branded fashion retailers, but refusing to pay full prices for M&S products'

The sales results are traced by analysts to a combination of complacency within M&S – where managers still behaved as though M&S could control the market – and much more effective competition in the clothing market from retailers such as Next and Debenhams. Greenbury's autocratic management style was blamed for making the company more risk-averse and leaving it without the ability to innovate.

In terms of selling space – this was extended through the purchase of nineteen Littlewoods stores, just at the time the market for clothing went into downturn. The disruption caused by the refurbishment was far greater than expected.

Value for money rules the new high street

The UK clothing market has changed in important ways. Consumers are buying 'aspirational brand names' or discounted goods. M&S is trapped in the middle of the market offering neither brands nor discounts. The overwhelming pressure is value for money – either in added-value brands or low prices. M&S admits it has lost track of what its customers want and how much they are prepared to pay. Salsbury, himself, admits M&S jeans are 10 per cent overpriced and leisure shirts 15 per cent too expensive.

'The overwhelming pressure is value for money – either in added-value brands or low prices. M&S admits it has lost track of what its customers want'

Predators circle

City investors began in 1999 to consider the unthinkable – that M&S could be ripe for a take-over. Salsbury admitted publicly that a bid could not be ruled out. Possible take-over candidates were rumoured to include the supermarket firms Tesco and Sainsbury,

Kingfisher (owner of Woolworths in the UK), Wal-Mart from the USA and Carrefour in France.

Once protected from predator attention by its permanently high share price, driven by its size, profits record and respected management, in 1999 M&S was seen by analysts as a potential take-over prize. The company's market value had fallen to £10 billion by the beginning of 1999 compared with £18 billion at the start at 1998.

By late-January 1999, active City speculation about likely bids had pushed M&S share price up to 398p.

The plans for recovery

Salsbury has inherited a 'command and control' culture and much bureaucracy, as well as a culture still bruised from the fight over management succession. One of his first moves was a management reshuffle to tackle the problems faced by M&S. However, the changes consisted of moving existing long-serving managers between departments with little outside recruitment. Indeed, a programme of redundancies running into hundreds of jobs is expected as a move towards cost cutting. He is also looking to reduce the costs of dealing with suppliers by £100 million.

Prime among Salsbury's plans for recovery is breaking with M&S tradition to establish a marketing department in the company. The goals of the new marketing department are to take power away from the buying centres and to take a more customer-focused approach. Buyers will no longer be allowed to dictate which ranges a particular store will stock or how they should present the product, since this will be the preserve of the marketing department. By M&S standards this is a big organizational change. However, some disappointment was apparent in the appointment as marketing director of James Benfield, an M&S veteran of twenty-six years standing, rather than an outsider.

'The goals of the new marketing department are to take power away from the buying centres and to take a more customer-focused approach'

Critical to surviving 1999 is the M&S spring/summer clothing ranges. When previewed in January, there was widespread comment that M&S did not have the quality products to hold its position in the market let alone increase it. Shares fell to a five-year low of 335p. Fashion critics said the new collection was disorganized and derivative, with M&S trying too hard to be 'trendy' and win younger customers at the expense of the traditional M&S shopper. Questions were raised also about the quality of the clothes. Critics suggested that M&S was still

'Fashion critics said the new collection was disorganized and derivative'

failing in its attempts to straddle generations of fashion buyers in its new collection – middle-aged customers alienated by M&S pandering to teenage fashion while offering them less choice, while the young were unattracted by the M&S image and name. The new collection was judged a long way from the traditional M&S strength in high-quality staples.

Sources

Alexander, Andrew (1998), 'Oates Takes A Walk As Marks Diverts Its Palace Revolution', *Daily Mail*, 27 November.

Cunliffe, Peter (1998), 'Ad Spend To Spice Up Marks' Christmas', *Daily Mail*, 18 November.

Guthrie, Jonathan (1998), 'M&S Expansions Face Cut Of £380m', *Financial Times*, 12 October.

Hall, Amanda and Richard Newton (1998), 'M&S Links With PolyGram for Own CD Label', *Sunday Telegraph*, 12 October.

Halstead, Richard (1998), '£2.4m For Ousted M&S Chief Oates', *Mail on Sunday*, 6 December.

Halstead, Richard (1998), 'Credit Is On the Cards for Battered M&S', *Mail on Sunday*, 11 November.

Hollinger, Peggy (1998), 'Marks and Spencer Hopes the Man Will Come With a Plan', *Financial Times*, 6 November.

Hollinger, Peggy (1998), 'The Marks and Spencer Succession', *Financial Times*, 27 November.

Jay, John (1997), 'M&S Plans £2 bn Expansion', *Sunday Times*, 2 November.

Jay, John (1998), 'Boardroom Row Erupts Over Top M&S post', *Sunday Times*, 8 November.

Kay, William (1998), 'The Poison That Threatens the Culture of M&S', *Mail on Sunday*, 22 November.

Lyons, Teena (1997), 'More Than Just Comfy Pants', *Sunday Business*, 25 May.

Murphy, Paul (1998), 'M&S Hit By High Street Slump', *Sunday Business*, 4 October.

Olins, Rufus (1997), 'M&S Sets Out Its Stall for World Domination', *Sunday Times*, 7 November.

Olins, Rufus (1998), 'Greenbury Is looking for Growth Not An Heir', *Sunday Times*, 24 May.

Pratley, Nils (1998), 'Marks Searching for Sparks', *Sunday Business*, 1 November.

Pratley, Nils (1998), 'Today's Marksist Realist', *Sunday Business*, 29 November.

Randall, Jeff (1998), 'Top Marksman', *Sunday Business*, 28 June.

Rankine, Kate (1998), 'M&S Asks Outsiders To Review Strategy', *Daily Telegraph*, 4 June.

Rankine, Kate (1998), 'Losing the Way Down Baker Street', *Daily Telegraph*, 7 November.

Rankine, Kate (1998), 'Greenbury Steps Aside To End M&S Board Row', *Daily Telegraph*, 27 November.

Rankine, Kate (1998), 'St Michael's Silent War of Succession', *Daily Telegraph*, 27 November.

Rushe, Dominic (1998), 'Final Cut', *Sunday Times*, 13 September.

Rushe, Dominic (1998), 'Black Marks', *Sunday Times*, 18 October.

Rushe, Dominic (1998), 'On the Rack At Marks', *Sunday Times*, 8 November.

Rushe, Domninic (1998), 'High Noon At M&S', *Sunday Times*, 15 November.

Rushe, Dominic (1998), 'Grey Man Plans To Put Colour In M&S', *Sunday Times*, 29 November.

Rushe, Dominic (1998), 'M&S Plans Loyalty Scheme', *Sunday Times*, 12 December.

Saigol, Lina and Alex Evans (1998), 'Marks Turns On Television', *Sunday Business*, 12 December.

Simms, Jane (1998), 'Top Marks', *Marketing Business*, July/August.

South, Gill (1998), 'Brooks Brothers Set To Open Up in Britain', *Sunday Business*, 24 May.

Terazono, Emiko (1997), 'M&S Goes On £192m Spree in Littlewoods', *Financial Times*, 18 July.

CHAPTER 11

Skoda Cars*

So, who's the joke on now?

A quite remarkable story of decline, reinvention and renewal is that of Skoda Cars of Czechoslovakia. From a position of international prestige (which many have forgotten about), this brand declined to become the butt of numerous derogatory jokes (especially in the British marketplace), but has rebuilt its brand value and achieved outstanding success across Europe, as the leading Central European car producer by the late 1990s, including huge successes in that same British marketplace that produced the derogatory jokes about its cars.

'A quite remarkable story of decline, reinvention and renewal is that of Skoda Cars of Czechoslovakia'

There are important lessons in examining how this company has been turned around, because the same may happen anywhere in any industry where a determined competitor has a vision of how to build value for customers and is prepared to make a fight of it. The Skoda story also raises some major issues about continuing the processes of renewal after a turn-around.

---

* This material has been produced by Nigel F. Piercy, Cardiff Business School, Cardiff University from published sources and discussions with motor industry executives. © Nigel F. Piercy, 1999.

The history of Skoda Cars

It is not widely known in Britain that Skoda was one of the earliest European car producers. Its origins trace back to 1895, when Vaclav Klement and Vaclav Laurin started a bicycle assembly and repair shop in Mlada Bloesalv, because German bicycle manufacturers would offer after-sales service only to those who wrote to them in German rather than Czech. Within twenty years L&K had progressed from bicycles to motorcycles and produced a passenger car – the Voiturette – in 1905. By the 1920s, L&K cars were sold throughout the world and the company had subsidiaries in Moscow, St Petersburg, Kiev, Warsaw, Amsterdam and Rio de Janeiro. This business was the largest carmaker in the Austro-Hungarian empire and was taken into the Skoda industrial group in 1925.

Prior to this acquisition, Skoda had produced Hispano Suiza cars, under licence, at its Pilsen factory. Skoda has also produced wheeled and tracked military tractors, steam locomotives, the Tillings-Stevens gas/electric vehicle, airplanes and *'Skoda claims to be* trucks and buses. As a result of this history, Skoda *the third oldest* claims to be the third oldest carmaker in the world. *carmaker in the* Indeed, the Skoda winged arrow motif, carried on its *world'* current vehicles, was first registered in 1923. The winged arrow is said to derive from a wall-mounted relief of an Indian's head, which originally hung in Emil Skoda's study.

Before the Second World War, Czechoslovakia was the fifth richest country in the world, in terms of per capita wealth, and Skoda cars had the image and cachet that BMW enjoys today. Indeed, at the 1998 International Motor Show, when an 1100 cc 1958 racing car changed hands for £47 150 – it was a Skoda. With a top speed of 130 mph, which was outstanding in the 1950s, this Skoda won the 1959 Leningrad Grand Prix. In fact, the Skoda rally and racing team is one of the most successful in the world – it won the Monte Carlo rally in the 1920s, the European Touring Car Championship in the 1980s, has achieved twenty-five RAC class wins in twenty-six years of competition, and in 1994 won the Formula 2 World Championship.

Following the Second World War, Czechoslovakia was under communist rule for some forty years. After the 'Velvet Revolution' of the late-1980s, Czechoslovakia emerged from communism in 1989 and the decision was made to privatize Skoda. There were around twenty-four potential purchasers, short-listed to Renault and Volkswagen. Skoda became part of the German Volkswagen group in the early 1990s, and VW now owns 70 per cent of Skoda and has management control.

The Skoda acquisition was part of VW's multi-brand strategy in Europe, which by the end of the 1990s has broken the company free of a long-standing static oligopoly with VW, Fiat, Ford, GM, Peugeot and Renault all holding similar shares of the market, to gain increasing dominance over the European car market. By 1998, the VW group held more than 18 per cent of the European market – six points clear of the nearest rival, Fiat. VW has shown interest in acquiring further brands such as Rolls-Royce, Lamborghini and Bugatti to gain even broader market coverage as well as the 'halo effect' of owning some of the most prestigious names in the global motor industry.

'The Skoda acquisition was part of VW's multi-brand strategy in Europe'

Skoda is the biggest Czech industrial company and is the biggest employer in the country. It employs around 30 per cent of the Czech labour force either directly, or indirectly through its suppliers, it pays the highest wage rates and accounts for 9 per cent of all Czech exports. Czechoslovakia has a high rate of car ownership and Skoda currently takes 57 per cent of its home market.

The decline to a bad joke

Skoda's mission is 'Quality is our aim in everything we do – products, services, workforce, financial results', which reflects its distinguished history. However, during the 1970s and 1980s, this statement would have been liable to reduce British car buyers to helpless laughter. The perception of Skoda quality and design was so negative that it generated and in turn was fuelled by a huge number of popular jokes in Britain:

Question: How do you double the price of a Skoda?
Answer: Fill it with petrol.

Question: What do you call a convertible Skoda?
Answer: A skip.

Question: What do you call a Skoda with twin exhaust pipes?
Answer: A wheelbarrow.

Question: Why do Skodas have heated rear windows?
Answer: To keep your hands warm when you are pushing it.

Question: What do you call a Skoda driver with two brain cells?
Answer: Pregnant.

Question: Why do Skodas have rear screen wipers?
Answer: To clean off the flies that crash into them.

Question: What do you call a Skoda at the top of a hill?
Answer: A miracle.

These are not very good jokes. They are, however, illustrative of the depths to which Skoda had fallen in the eyes of the car purchaser and the industry in Britain.

The real impact of customer scorn and derision is underlined by a 1996 survey for Motor Research Ltd of Britain's ten most worthless cars, in terms of second-hand value to a dealer. The list was topped by the Hyundai Pony – a D-registration model with 100 000 miles on the clock had a dealer value of £10 – and second place went to Skoda, where an E-registration Favorit with 95 000 miles was worth only £20 in trade-in value to a dealer. Even the Russian-made Lada had slightly better trade-in values and eventually Lada had to withdraw from the UK market altogether.

The Skoda Favorit was the model marketed in Britain until the early 1990s and it had a severely dated design and 'utilitarian' appearance, with a reputation for very poor reliability.

The decline of Skoda in the automotive market during the 1970s and 1980s is associated with the period of communist rule in Czechoslovakia and state-ownership of the company, with shortage of capital investment, limited technical expertise and a lack of quality control. Indeed, at this time Skoda cars were assembled in part by prison labour.

'Skoda became the classic example of negative brand value ... the Skoda badges actually reduced the value of the vehicle in the customer's eyes'

In famous 'blind and seen' testing of new models for the British market in the early 1990s, Skoda became the classic example of negative brand value. Consumer evaluations of value and likelihood of purchase were substantially lower when they knew the car was a Skoda, than when they did not know the brand identity, i.e. the Skoda badges actually reduced the value of the vehicle in the customer's eyes.

Renewal of the company and the brand

Heard the one about the Skoda that's a great car?

In 1998 Skoda came top in the J D Powers/Top Gear UK customer satisfaction survey, ahead of Subaru, Mazda, Jaguar, Nissan and

BMW. This was the first time since the survey started five years earlier that a European manufacturer had finished top, as opposed to a Japanese firm. In fact, Skoda had been climbing the J D Powers European ratings for some years. In 1994 it was twenty-first, in 1995 it rose to thirteenth, it was seventh in 1996 and

'In 1998 Skoda came top in the J D Powers/Top Gear UK customer satisfaction survey'

sixth in 1997. In 1998 the Skoda Felicia featured as equal-third in the survey list of top ten cars, ahead of the Nissan Micra, the Jaguar XJS, the Mazda Xedos, the Nissan QX and the Toyota Celica.

The success of the Felicia was followed by the introduction of the Octavia in 1998. Following the UK launch in the summer of 1998 with a bold advertising campaign but a modest budget of £5.6 million, motoring correspondents' comments about the Octavia are illustrative:

> The Skoda Octavia . . . is an excellent car. If I had been once told that I would write those words about Skoda, I would have laughed out loud. (Stuart Birch, *The Times*)

> The Octavia is a class act . . . I am a convert to the new Skoda. (Ken Gibson, *The Sun*)

> There has never been a better quality budget hatchback on sale. (*Autocar*)

> Skoda shows what can be done with a good honest family car and decent dealers. (Kevin Blick, *Top Gear*)

> These results demonstrate just what can be achieved when a company sets its mind to exceeding customer expectations. In Skoda's case, a preconceived myth is now well and truly dispelled. (Dave Sargent, *J D Powers*)

The Octavia has been accepted as a stylish, comfortable, reliable and safe family car – twin airbags and special safety seat belts are standard, most models have ABS, and the car comes with ten-year guarantees, at a starting price of £11 499. An estate version followed later in 1998. The Skoda Octavia competes effectively against the Ford Mondeo and the Vauxhall Astras and Vectras. In fact, on price the Octavia undercuts the mainstream suppliers such as Ford and Vauxhall and is very competitive with other imports such as Daewoo, Proton, Hyundai and Kia.

Although the Skoda Felicia launched in 1994 was highly successful, the Octavia is the first Skoda to be built on a VW group platform, shared with the VW Golf, the new Beetle and the

Audi A3. The Octavia's sales success exceeded even Skoda's expectations and planned production of 90 000 vehicles a year has been increased to 110 000 in 1998 and projected to 140 000 to meet demand for the new estate version. However, contrary to fears that the Octavia would sell as a rebadged VW and cannibalize VW's customer base, in the UK, 52 per cent of the new customers gained in 1998 switched from Ford, Vauxhall and Rover.

The remarkable fact is that only a few years earlier, the idea of paying £11 500 for a Skoda, let alone trusting its 'total care' package of warranties, roadside assistance and free servicing for three years, would have been laughable. However, by 1998 Skoda was recognized as a producer of solid, sensible family cars that are good value for money. This success has not been restricted to Britain, as shown in recent sales and market share figures in Table 11.1.

Table 11.1   Skoda's sales and market share, 1996–98

		UK			Europe		
		1996	1997	1998 (Jan–Oct)	1996	1997	1998 (Jan–Oct)
Total market	Volume		2,170,725	1,988,742		13,410,200	12,276,164
	% change		7.2	3.4		4.8	6.0
Skoda	Volume		15,750	17,242		114,866	133,574
	% change		21.0	22.1		41.1	41.2
	% share	0.6	0.7	0.9	0.6	0.9	1.1

Source: Society of Motor Manufacturers (UK) and ACEA (European Auto Manufacturers Association) (Europe).

Volume growth of more than 20 per cent a year in the UK and more than 40 per cent a year across Europe in a relatively low growth market is outstanding. Skoda exports to more than seventy markets worldwide – more than half of Skoda sales come from the emerging east European markets and Skoda holds key shares in Germany, Slovakia, Poland, Italy and the UK.

In 1998 Skoda overtook the Polish operations of Fiat of Italy to become the leading car producer in Central Europe and has moved strongly into profit. Net profits announced in March 1998 were Kc1.17 billion on turnover of Kc90.1 billion, compared to Kc163 million profit on Kc59 billion in 1996, when Skoda ended several years of losses. Skoda production is planned to reach 500 000 vehicles in 2000.

The turn-around at Skoda

Much of the renewal of Skoda can be traced to the ownership share taken by Volkswagen in 1991 – a 30 per cent stake in 1991 rising to 70 per cent in 1995. In effect, Skoda has become the fourth brand in the VW group, alongside VW, Audi and SEAT. Volkswagen brought a £1.4 billion investment in a new manufacturing plant at Mlada Boleslav, outside Prague, and provided access to its leading-edge manufacturing technology, quality management and technical personnel. The impact was dramatic throughout – Skoda marketing director Alfred Rieck says that in eight years 'the entire company has been turned upside down'. The integration of Skoda into the VW group has not been wholly straightforward and there have been periods of friction between the determined regime of Ferdinand Piëch, VW CEO, and the Czech government, which remains suspicious about VW's motives.

However, the impact of VW on Skoda production and quality has been dramatic. The new manufacturing plant outside Prague is the first 'fractal factory' in Europe. Pre-assembled components feed into the central spine from ribs, supported by component manufacturers who have their own production facilities and staff within the Skoda factory (for example, Johnson Controls for seats, seat belts and runners; Rockwell for doors, sunroofs, trim and speakers; Expert for the front-end components; Siemens for the cockpit equipment; and Lener for the wheels). These components and outside supplies are co-ordinated by a sophisticated 'just-in-time' production control programme. Work is designed around small teams and management and production employees work in close proximity to promote harmony and effectiveness. Automation is low – about 30 per cent – reflecting the fractal philosophy of teams and individual initiative, but also the very low labour costs in Czechoslovakia. Factory employment increased from 18 000 to 20 000 in 1998 and labour shortages have forced Skoda to import workers from Poland. It has been estimated that labour costs at Skoda's factory are as low as one-eighth of those in VW's German operations. At the end of 1998, VW was negotiating with the Czech government for an incentive package to build a $450 million new engine plant, to supply not just Skoda but other VW companies.

'the impact of VW on Skoda production and quality has been dramatic'

Re-positioning Skoda in the UK market

In fact, the re-positioning of Skoda in the UK substantially pre-dates the Octavia success of 1998. In the early 1990s, the British

Skoda operation was working to change the popular perception of Skoda as a low quality, 'joke' supplier. An enhanced Favorit model was supported with what Dermot Kelly, UK managing director, calls 'exposure marketing'. He says of the challenges faced then that 'we had to let people "see, feel and touch" the car, we even paid them £10 to test drive it'. This approach was used again in 1998 – the 'Skoda Challenge' pays £10 to car buyers if they road test a Nissan, Daewoo, Ford, Vauxhall or Rover, and then road test a Skoda Felicia or Octavia.

'We've changed our cars; can you change your mind?'

The UK launch of the Felicia in 1995 used the brand appeal: 'We've changed our cars; can you change your mind?', and stressed the link between Skoda and VW, to counter negative images of poor reliability and quality. Even at this stage in the turn-around, the achievements of Kelly's operation in building high customer loyalty and retention were remarkable, as evidenced by some of the highest re-purchase rates in the industry by loyal Skoda customers. The company estimated in 1996 that 72 per cent of first-time Skoda buyers returned for a second purchase, and were willing to join a six-week waiting list for a new Skoda. However, Kelly cautions that brand image and customer perceptions are slow to change, in spite of the superior technology VW has given Skoda. His problem is that the new Skoda models compete in a different marketplace to earlier models – the days of the £6000 car have gone. This is a major challenge to the distributors.

However, by 1998, Skoda was even confident enough to make jokes at its own expense – a special edition all-yellow Felicia pick-up truck was launched with a crowned frog on the bonnet as a symbol of what happens when a princess kisses a frog (actually, the back of the cab swings to transform the 2-seat pick-up into a 4-seat truck, but the message is about the wider transformation of Skoda). The yellow vehicle is called the Felicia Fun.

The Skoda brand identity

'One criticism of the new Skoda vehicles has been that they are no more than Volkswagen cars with a different badge on the front'

One criticism of the new Skoda vehicles has been that they are no more than Volkswagen cars with a different badge on the front. One commentator at the Octavia launch suggested that without the badges, the Octavia could be a Toyota, Nissan or a VW. In fact, much effort has gone into retaining a unique central European identity for Skoda that reflects its heritage, of which Skoda is fiercely proud.

The Octavia, for example, is based on a VW group platform, but the design incorporates many features from past Skoda models – upright lights, Cubist lettering, the distinctive radiator grille with upright ribs and prominent badge, based on Skodas from the 1930s and 1940s. Indeed, Skoda makes its own engines (for the Felicia) and gearboxes.

The VW 'platform strategy' leads to a certain level of components across the brands in the group, but the VW goal is that each brand should be independent, and each part of the operation has responsibility for its own brand development and profitability as an autonomous business within the group.

Technical director at Skoda, Wilfried Bockelman, distinguishes Skoda from the other VW group marques when he says:

> Skoda is the value for money brand. It's not good enough to be the price leader, like the Koreans. We can't sell cheap cars; we have to offer a good buy and convince customers of the quality of a Skoda.

However, concerns remain about the Skoda image, and the danger it will simply sell as a generic product in the 'family car' market, in the position currently held by VW.

The future for Skoda?

VW's long-term strategy requires that Skoda should challenge Volvo and Rover in the European marketplace, and this underlines the new goals to be attacked from the foundation that has been built with the Octavia. A third range of larger Skoda cars, aimed at taking the brand further upmarket is under development for launch in 2001/2 (these will be based on the VW B-chassis platform, which currently supports the Audi A4 and the VW Passat executive cars). In the small car market the Felicia is to be replaced in 1999/2000 with a new model based on a common chassis platform with the VW Polo. Trade rumours also point to plans for a four-wheel drive Skoda within the same time period.

Czechoslovakia is likely to join the European Union in 2002 or 2003, and if this happens its wage rates are likely to move upwards to European levels. In January 1999, the company agreed to 9 per cent wage increases for 1999. VW is looking to extend the assembly operations of its Czech subsidiary to other countries and has been conducting feasibility studies in Russia, India, Egypt and Bosnia, while Skoda is upgrading the VW plant in Poznan in Poland to full assembly capability.

In the UK, Dermot Kelly, managing director of Skoda's British operation, stresses his goal for the brand:

> We have to exceed people's expectations. We have to make the Skoda not just as good as Ford, but better, if we're going to get our message across.

From a global perspective, Skoda marketing director, Alfred Rieck, summarizes the company's view of what it has achieved and where it aims to go:

> There are three pillars to the transformation of Skoda. There's the production process; the product strategy and philosophy – including the quality and technical standards and attractive prices; and the image. And we have yet to build the image.

Rieck describes success to date as a result of the product itself, a dealer network offering the highest levels of personal service, and the competitive price, but the new challenge is to use the Octavia launch to build a 'one-face brand' across Europe with the same message, brand values, and positioning in each market. He has introduced monthly meetings of importers, dealers and customers to build a common understanding of the brand strategy and he is moving towards a common communication strategy across the world.

Rieck also believes strongly in the value of the 2500-strong dealer network as a source of competitive differentiation through offering a high level of personal service. In the UK, Skoda had 208 dealers, 94 per cent selling only Skoda, mainly small, family-owned garages, and the company is committed to maintaining existing dealerships as the brand moves upmarket. However, Skoda also sells direct from its Internet site.

'the company is committed to maintaining existing dealerships as the brand moves upmarket'

Sources

Anderson, Robert (1998), 'Exports Drive Skoda Advance', *Financial Times*, 20 March.

Anderson, Robert (1998), 'Skoda in Talks Over $450 Million Engine Plant', *Financial Times*, 11 September.

'Britain's Ten Most Worthless Cars', *Guardian*, 5 December 1996.

Done, Kevin (1998), 'Skoda Overtakes Fiat in Eastern Europe', *Financial Times*, 3 February.

English, Andrew (1998), '£46 000 For A Third-Hand Skoda Without A Roof', *Daily Telegraph*, 30 October.

Griffiths, John (1998), 'Car Sales Fall But Trade Rejects Recession Fears, *Financial Times*, 11 November.

Griffiths, John (1998), 'New Car Market Falters', *Financial Times*, 11 November.

Griffiths, John (1998), 'Skoda Powers To Satisfaction Award', *Financial Times*, 9 April.

Griffiths, John (1998), 'VW Multi-Brand Strategy in Europe Pays Off', *Financial Times*, 17 June.

Hutton, Ray (1998), 'Quality Time With Skoda', *Sunday Times*, 26 June.

Lewin, Tony (1998), 'Heard The One About The Skoda That's A Great Car?', *Sunday Business*, 18 October.

Massey, Ray (1998), 'The Cream Skoda', *Daily Mail*, 9 April.

Simms, Jane (1998), 'Time To Get Serious', *Marketing Business*, November.

Vivian, David (1998), 'What's The Difference Between A Skoda and a Volkswagen?', *Daily Telegraph*, 25 April.

CHAPTER 12

The Body Shop*

A case for burial or rising from the grave?

'The Body Shop created a new retail sector for a particular mix of natural cosmetic and personal care products'

The Body Shop is a global business originating in the UK, with worldwide sales of around £300 million. It is one of Britain's best-known businesses and one of the most unconventional. The core of The Body Shop business is the sourcing and retailing of very distinctive toiletries and cosmetics, particularly associated with environmental friendliness and the avoidance of animal testing in product development. The Body Shop created a new retail sector for a particular mix of natural cosmetic and personal care products. From its outset, The Body Shop has been strongly associated with the ethical, political and environmental beliefs of its founder, Anita Roddick, and many have argued that this focus on social responsibility in harmony with commercial distinctiveness is a prototype for new types of business. Certainly, there have been many attempts by others to imitate at least some of the characteristics of The Body Shop. Following spectacular successes in the 1980s, more recently The Body Shop has run into serious commercial difficulties. The critical question is whether The Body Shop's business design has become outdated or whether the company can renew itself.

'The critical question is whether The Body Shop's business design has become outdated or whether the company can renew itself'

---

* This material has been prepared from secondary sources by Nigel F. Piercy, Cardiff Business School, Cardiff University. © Nigel F. Piercy, 1999.

From humble origins . . .

The story of The Body Shop is in many ways the story of Anita Roddick. She came from an Italian family that ran a small cafe in Littlehampton and later a nightclub over a butcher's shop. Littlehampton remains the somewhat unlikely location of The Body Shop's head office.

Roddick's background was not poor, but she experienced poverty at school – on one occasion giving her new school uniform to a fellow pupil in tattered clothes. Having failed to get into drama school, she trained as a teacher in Bath, and for a time lived on a kibbutz in Israel, before spending time in Paris and working for the International Labour Organization in the Department of Women's Rights in Geneva. On return to Britain she met Gordon Roddick, with whom she shared interests in the Campaign for Nuclear Disarmament and raising money for charities like War on Want and Freedom from Hunger. Children and marriage in Reno, Nevada in 1970 were followed by a tour of the hippie trail. When they returned to Britain they established a hotel and Italian restaurant business – early signs of the Roddicks' non-conventional approach to business were loud music and a blackboard for political messages attacking the local council.

Roddick describes the impact of her upbringing, Third World travel and campaigning for social causes:

> I feel good on the streets . . . Marching and shouting is part of my DNA. I've been doing that kind of thing since I was 10, when I went on a CND march. That came from my background. I came from a very dissenting family. We were Italian immigrants and my mother hated and protested against the Catholic Church. They would not give my father a Catholic burial because he was an atheist. That attitude kick-started the protester in me.

Indeed, in 1996 this fifty-something grandmother and corporate CEO was pounding the streets dressed as a rabbit, as part of her anti-animal testing campaign.

Following the sale of the restaurant business, Gordon Roddick left Anita for two years with two small children to fulfil a life ambition of riding a horse the 5700 miles from Buenos Aires to New York. It was at this time that she decided to pursue the idea of opening a shop selling cosmetic products packaged in unconventional sizes and cheap containers. She had

'in 1996 this fifty-something grandmother and corporate CEO was pounding the streets dressed as a rabbit, as part of her anti-animal testing campaign'

in mind the practices of Tahitian women and others in the Polynesian islands who based cosmetics on local, natural products. The name 'The Body Shop' was taken from a car body repair shop she had seen in the USA (although the same name had also been adopted by a cosmetics company in California). Many of The Body Shop's enduring characteristics were created at this time – packaging, retail design and identity.

The necessary £4000 loan was initially denied the Anita Roddick approaching a bank manager in jeans and a Bob Dylan T-shirt. However, on Gordon's advice, the Anita Roddick dressed in a smart business suit with a business plan drawn up by an accountant friend had no trouble raising the loan needed.

Initially, Roddick made the products in her own kitchen, but then found a small manufacturing chemist to help. She bought small plastic bottles, designed for collecting urine samples, because they were cheap. To overcome supply shortages, she also offered to fill customers' own bottles – recycling started out of necessity. Friends helped filling the bottles and writing the labels.

'She painted the walls dark green to hide the damp patches and hung the walls with wooden larchlap fencing to cover the running water'

The first store was located in Brighton because that town had a large student population. Roddick found a run-down shop in a pedestrian precinct called Kensington Gardens. She painted the walls dark green to hide the damp patches and hung the walls with wooden larchlap fencing to cover the running water. A designer created the logo for £25.

Interestingly, Kensington Gardens was shared by the premises of two undertakers who, for obvious reasons, were not enthused about having 'The Body Shop' next door to their funeral parlours. They attempted legal threats and found the response was a centre-page spread in the local paper concerning their harassment of a 'defenceless woman'. The problem for Roddick desisted and the lessons about the value of free publicity were not missed – until very recently The Body Shop did little media advertising.

The Body Shop opened on 27 March 1976, taking £130 on the first day. After Gordon's departure for Buenos Aires, Roddick needed finance for a second shop, which was denied by the bank. An assistant in the shop introduced her boyfriend, Ian McGlinn, a local garage owner, who was willing to lend the £4000 in return for a half share in the business. When The Body Shop floated, McGlinn's share was worth £4 million and by 1991 it was worth in excess of £140 million. McGlinn still owns about 24 per cent of the business, compared to the 25 per cent held by the Roddicks. Roddick claims she has no regrets about this deal – McGlinn's money was there when she needed it and the bank had turned her down. On the other hand, Gordon apparently was very unhappy about this deal.

The second and larger shop was opened in Chichester, now with staff in Body Shop uniform. Further expansion plans following Gordon's return were stalled by continued lack of access to bank loans. As a result, other branches were opened via an informal arrangement under which the Roddicks supplied the products to be sold in shops owned by others. Roddick called this 'self-financing' and it was the forerunner to the franchising strategy adopted later. By 1980, shops were opening in mainland Europe using this approach, but with tighter arrangements for the use of the corporate identity. Even in the 1990s most of The Body Shop's income is from wholesaling its products, not retailing – all but twelve of the 840 shops outside the USA and Britain are franchises.

'Even in the 1990s most of The Body Shop's income is from wholesaling its products, not retailing'

The Body Shop was successfully floated in 1984, making the Roddicks millionaires, and when the shares reached 350p in 1990 Anita Roddick's stake made her the fourth richest woman in Britain. The business has expanded globally, most importantly into the USA and by 1997, The Body Shop had around 1510 owned or franchised stores in forty-seven countries throughout the world. The Body Shop has a larger foreign presence than almost any other British retail name. International expansion has continued throughout the life of the business. In 1996 The Body Shop was putting its first stores into Africa, while also opening in Korea and the Philippines.

'The Body Shop has a larger foreign presence than almost any other British retail name'

The business has continued to be used by Anita Roddick to lobby for environmental and human rights issues, and she has done much work to attempt to help remote tribes in the Third World, and to offer assistance in specific areas where environmental or economic problems blight people's lives. It is not widely known, for example, that the Roddicks introduced and financially supported *The Big Issue* in the UK – the magazine sold by homeless people on the streets of Britain to raise income. Staff in the shops are expected to share in such concerns and to participate in campaigns to raise public awareness and to find solutions to societal problems. Roddick herself has become a prominent spokesperson for these issues and has championed the incorporation of social responsibility issues into management education. She has been quoted as saying, 'I'd like the stores to be embassies with safe areas where people can come and feel protected; where they can pass on information'.

'the company's Articles of Association explicitly states that it exists to institute and support campaigns for human and civil rights; to protect the environment and campaign against animal testing'

Indeed, the company's Articles of Association explicitly state that it exists to institute and support campaigns for human and civil rights; to protect the environment and campaign against animal testing.

In commercial terms, the unique 'enviro-activism' practised by The Body Shop gave an advantage in linking cosmetic purchases to a 'feel-good' factor of social responsibility.

. . . To worldwide success . . .

'The Body Shop has been disparaged by conventional analysts as selling "externally applied fruit and vegetables"'

The Body Shop has been disparaged by conventional analysts as selling 'externally applied fruit and vegetables', and Roddick has been derogatorily labelled the 'Queen of Green', who has tried to operate 'retailing as new age democracy'.

None the less, the Roddick partnership was spectacularly successful in making The Body Shop one of the great retailing success stories of the 1980s, growing in twelve years from seventy UK staff to 5000, employed by a company worth £350 million at its peak. A truly global presence has been built through a network of franchisees operating as smaller companies. Financials for recent years are summarized in Table 12.1.

In this partnership Anita Roddick's role has been to provide a 'torrent of wild ideas', while Gordon sifted and selected which to pursue. He says, 'She dreams and I try to make her dreams come true'. Less well known but also important was the role of Stuart Rose who has been responsible for day-to-day management of The Body Shop.

However, The Body Shop's share value has ridden a rollercoaster (see Figure 12.1). From a share value of £3.70 in 1992,

Table 12.1 The Body Shop's key financials, 1994–98

	1994	1995	1996	1997	1998
Turnover (£ million)					
UK	91.1	96.5	104.8	106.1	116.2
USA	50.4	58.8	70.8	73.1	78.0
International	53.9	64.4	80.9	91.6	98.9
Total	195.4	219.7	256.5	270.8	293.1
Operating profit (£ million)	30.1	34.5	33.7	31.9	38.1
Earnings per share (p)	10.3	11.5	9.8	9.2	11.8

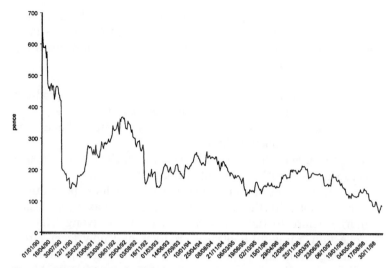

Figure 12.1 The Body Shop's share value, 1990–98 (unadjusted prices). Source: Datastream

by mid-1995 the price had fallen to just over £1, rising to £1.20 in 1998, giving a group valuation of £232 million. By the mid-1990s profits reached a plateau and major losses had started in the US shops.

... To a not quite so humble ending?

In 1992 The Body Shop issued its first profit warning to the City and shares fell by 40 per cent. Four years later the shares fell again when the company warned it could not meet its profit forecasts. The company was worth around half its peak valuation.

By the middle of the 1990s, the first serious suggestions began to emerge that like other niche retailing concepts, The Body Shop formula was stale. It seemed that even the campaigning stance was no longer so important to the twenty-something young mother, who seven years earlier could not seem to get enough banana shampoos, soaps made from Amazonian oil extracts or Polynesian cocoa butter, or peppermint foot lotion.

In fact, although The Body Shop is normally seen as a retailer, in reality it has grown to a complex manufacturing, *'it has grown to a complex manufacturing, wholesaling, retailing, franchising and direct selling organization'*

wholesaling, retailing, franchising and direct selling organization. This growth into complexity has been accompanied by a number of fundamental operating problems:

- the company has failed to produce new products and to get them to market *quickly*
- the stores have generally not been updated, and are looking tired
- it has struggled to compete effectively against new cheaper competitors who have imitated Body Shop products, without bearing the costs of its expensive ethical business procedures. For example, in the UK The Body Shop has been losing market share to the Boots chain with their strong 'Natural Collection' range of bodycare products and now faces direct challenge from the Virgin Vie launch and even supermarkets selling imitative products under their own labels. Major competitive challenges include straight imitation of the shops, like 'Body Reform' in the UK and aggressive international chains targeting The Body Shop's market niche. For example, Red Earth, an Australian natural cosmetics chain founded in 1991 with a similar environmental stance to The Body Shop, is looking to enter the UK and other European markets for expansion. Similarly, US clothing retailer The Limited is targeting The Body Shop in the USA and Europe with its Bath and Body Works personal care chain. The Body Shop has been losing market share rapidly in the USA.

Why do people hate The Body Shop?

'they are either seen as brilliant visionaries or they are loathed as "tree-hugging hippies"'

Popular opinion about the Roddicks seems to polarize – they are either seen as brilliant visionaries or they are loathed as 'tree-hugging hippies'. For honourable and caring people who have created a major new type of enterprise and supported many important causes, the Roddicks have attracted many vitriolic attacks in the media – accusations of 'stealing' The Body Shop concept from others, of operating double standards to make money and so on. The Roddicks are, however, well able to defend themselves in this arena, as several court actions have demonstrated. There is a more troublesome aspect of this relationship.

Anita Roddick and The Body Shop have achieved unusual degrees of unpopularity in the City and the business community. Indeed, Roddick herself has said:

I know it sounds arrogant, but I've never understood why I'm so effing deeply unpopular. My daughter is always saying 'you're too po, you're too pious. Just lighten up'.

However, in case this sounds uncharacteristically conciliatory, she adds:

... having a great relationship with the City is not the most important thing I do. I put my energy into creating new products and that's the life blood of their profits.

Lack of enthusiasm for The Body Shop in the City may also be related to Roddick's very public attacks on financiers as 'those pin-striped dinosaurs in Throgmorton Street', and on at least one occasion as 'wankers'. In 1996, the Roddicks failed in an attempt to take The Body Shop back into private ownership, as a charitable trust, when US financing for the share buyback fell through. This venture attracted a formal Stock Exchange inquiry, after news leaked out.

The standing of The Body Shop in the City remains problematic, and this is particularly important when performance is lower than in earlier stages when the company was growing fast.

Are the fruit and vegetables stale?

There have been a number of suggestions that the underlying Body Shop formula has become stale and that it was no more than a short-term niche retailing concept, which has reached the end of its life cycle.

Even the distinctive campaigning stance of the company has attracted problems. A 1992 television documentary charged that The Body Shop made false claims about its stand against animal testing – the Roddicks sued for libel and won. A highly publicized campaign by a US journalist attacked The Body Shop's ethical stance and accused the company of operating double standards and misleading its customers. These claims were refuted in a successful libel action, but not before stock value had fallen.

By 1998, the company was facing campaigning by London Greenpeace (the lobby group behind the 'McLibel' case against McDonald's), involving attacks on The Body Shop's green image in a leaflet called 'What's Wrong With The Body Shop?'.

By contrast, there have been suggestions that one of the company's problems was actually that Gordon Roddick and company executives have been spending too much time launching environmental projects rather than running the business. For example, in the difficult early 1990s, the head of finance was detailed to help set up a windmill farm in Wales, designed to ecologically replace the electricity used by The Body Shop's head office.

Franchise problems

'Serious problems have emerged in relationships between the company and its international franchisees'

Serious problems have emerged in relationships between the company and its international franchisees. In particular, as The Body Shop has become involved in direct marketing, it has moved into direct competition with its own franchisees. This came to a head in 1996 with the launch of Body Shop Direct with agents to sell in the consumer's home and in 1998 with the start of Internet-based direct sales to customers in the USA.

Roddick is committed to this direct strategy: 'I think the importance of the shop is lessening and that companies in this market have really got to go out and find the customer.' Roddick's thinking about non-conventional outlets for Body Shop products includes locating new services in hotels and leisure complexes, products in petrol station forecourt shops and selling to air travellers en route. Commitment to direct marketing pushes The Body Shop further down the road of competing with the conventional outlets of its own franchisees.

An example of the problems faced in The Body Shop franchise network is the experience of Anya Robson in franchising The Body Shop in France. Robson looked like the ideal Body Shop franchisee – young, energetic, idealistic and happy to endorse The Body Shop Charter that 'Honesty, integrity and caring form the foundations of the company, and should flow through everything we do.' A British graduate settled in France, Robson put up £100 000 raised through her husband's motor-cycle business and borrowed a further £170 000 from a bank. The Robson's opened their franchise for business in August 1991, occupying smart premises in the Polygone shopping centre near Montpellier. The first year's trading was acceptable, but demand was not great for The Body Shop's environmentally friendly soaps and shampoos. Animal testing and animal rights are not major issues to the French consumer, and in the land of classic design, Chanel and Yves St Laurent, The Body Shop's formula of plastic bottles, recycled packaging and green store design were not well received. The Robsons now accuse The Body Shop of 'colonial arrogance' and not keeping financial promises about margins and promotional support. By 1997, the French Body Shop operation fell into a round of lawsuits, writs and counter-claims. A number of Body Shops in major French cities had closed – some filing for bankruptcy. The Robsons now own the top-performing Body Shop in France, outside Paris, and it does not make money.

The Body Shop admits its failure in France. It made the mistake of having no French directors on the French holding company, and having a head franchisee who was not French. The company is trying to find a French company to buy out the French operation.

By early 1998, The Body Shop had bought back more than 100 franchises, but was facing lawsuits brought by franchisees in the USA, Canada, France and Spain, as well as Britain. Publicity has been minimized by confidentiality agreements in franchise buy-backs – but it is clear that some US franchisees have settled for 5–20 cents on the dollar for their $500 000 investments to get out of their loss-making franchises.

However, getting out of franchising problems is unlikely to be cheap. Late in 1998 The Body Shop settled two legal battles with franchisees – one in the UK and one in the USA – who claimed that The Body Shop misled them. Estimates suggest that the total cost of the two settlements will exceed £2 million.

International problems

Strained relations with franchisees are symptomatic of much bigger problems underlying the company's international operations.

Probably the most important area has been The Body Shop operation in the USA, and some have suggested that the US problem illustrates all that is wrong with The Body Shop.

'the US problem illustrates all that is wrong with The Body Shop'

In what has turned out to be an over-ambitious attempt to expand in the highly competitive US market, substantial problems have been encountered. From the outset, some products have proved badly named or designed for US consumers. Indeed, for an international cosmetics company, The Body Shop has been slow to adapt its products to local preferences and needs in overseas markets. It failed, for example, to understand that shampoo formulation has to be different for Japan simply because Japanese hair is coarser than Caucasian hair.

The US market was already crowded when The Body Shop entered and the company made no allowance for the fact that US consumers care more about discounting than about novel retail environment or social causes. Competition in consumer markets of this kind in the USA is ferocious and initial Body Shop sales fell in the face of aggressive discounting by rivals, as well as the emergence of cheaper 'copy-cat' operators with shops painted green and 'look-alike' products. In Christmas 1997 The Body Shop's main US competitors were cutting prices on gift ranges by 50 per cent, forcing The Body Shop to follow suit.

As well as lack of adaptation, one analyst has said of The Body Shop's US operation: *'the strategy it has followed in the US is tantamount to commercial suicide*. Body Shop's strength is in manufacture and wholesale. It is not a strong retailer. But it has been getting more and more involved in US retailing.'

The Body Shop has not made a profit in the USA since 1994. In 1997 The Body Shop's 290 US shops made operating losses of $1.7 million on sales of $290 million, following a loss of $3 million the previous year. In February 1998, Steen Kanter, heading the US operation, announced his sudden departure from the company after just seventeen months in post – believed to have been at the personal suggestion of Anita Roddick. Kanter had joined The Body Shop from IKEA, the highly successful Swedish furnishings retailing group. This is one of several senior appointments from outside the company, which Roddick admits failed to work.

Financial crisis in the Far East underlines further international problems emerging for The Body Shop. The Body Shop has around 300 shops in Asia and sales have been falling. Much of the fall in business has been accounted for by Japan where financial crisis was accompanied by regulatory problems in getting new Body Shop products to market.

The end of the dream?

By October 1998, the Roddicks' stake in The Body Shop had fallen in value from £81 million to £36 million, sales were falling throughout the world, profits had slumped by a further 27 per cent and shares sank to a new all-time low of $77\frac{1}{2}$p (see Figure 12.1). Stuart Rose identified the challenge as transforming The Body Shop from an innovative and entrepreneurial business into a company with the enduring appeal of retailers such as Marks & Spencer or Boots. While once a genuinely new type of business, The Body Shop was forced to confront the fact that competitors have now caught up with the imaginative combination of ingredients which formerly differentiated The Body Shop. Most competitors on the high street have their own 'green ranges'. The pressure was on to reinvent The Body Shop brand. This was not lost on Anita Roddick who underlines her determination to continue in 1998:

> There has to be a reinvention now. The employees just hope to God this is going to work. There have been black times. But the idea that I can cash in my chips and put my bum on the sofa is nonsense. The business is my family, my university without walls.

The years 1997 and 1998 have seen major changes in the company's structure, plans and leadership, though many of Roddick's 'friends' in the City remain very vocally sceptical about the chances of success.

The search for renewal

Notwithstanding criticisms of its skills as a retailer, 1997 saw The Body Shop announcing that it was to refocus on retailing, alongside its direct marketing operations. This initially involved selling the business which makes its trademark opaque plastic bottles, to be able to buy a wider range of bottles. The company is also exploring proposals to sell off its manufacturing division, following advice from the management consultants OC&C in 1998.

The refocus on retail also involved the launch of a new store design. The new-look stores abandon the green-stained wood that has characterized The Body Shop for twenty years. The new stores have semi-private areas where customers can pay for massages and other beauty and health treatments, such as aromatherapy. Early results suggested that customers using the £12 massage service subsequently bought substantially more products on the same visit. The new services package will also include 'makeovers' and other treatments. New retail director, Ivan Levy, announces that, 'The front will look the same, but once you enter the store, you will feel you're in a different world'. The new stores also have upgraded displays and presentation, to identify product categories more clearly, and EPOS, while product lines and distribution channels are to be rationalized.

The success of the new shop design and massage and facial services – the 'Doorway' concept – on its trial in 1997, led to plans to take the new concept into new locations such as hotels and leisure complexes as well as conventional retail outlets.

In May 1997, The Body Shop recruited David Arnold, formerly chief executive with Avon cosmetics, to run its big expansion in direct selling. Already introduced in Britain, trialled in Switzerland and planned for Australia, the Body Shop Direct strategy is to be used in new international markets such as South America, where it has proved difficult to establish franchises. The direct strategy is based around home parties organized by the homeowner, with consultations provided by Body Shop personnel.

Also, as well as pursuing alternative selling methods, the company is exploring ways of extending its brand into areas sympathetic to the values of the core business, such as publishing. Anita Roddick enthuses about her plans for a Body Shop Human Rights Commission, two new books, strategic alliances, a publishing company and saving the endangered bergamot.* A slightly panicked Gordon Roddick has since assured the City that The Body Shop is not aiming to emulate Virgin in entering large numbers of unrelated markets and that the new areas may involve joint ventures with partners. A link has also been established with British Airways, to supply Body Shop products to passengers.

The company is attempting to confront its 'colonial' approach to international markets. Gordon Roddick has said that if overseas markets need different products The Body Shop will attempt to meet that demand, even if the products have to be outsourced.

The board has been strengthened by new non-executive directors and the business has been restructured into retail and product marketing. An executive from Benetton has been recruited to handle communications, including Roddick's public relations and the company's first major advertising campaign ('which doesn't involve us selling out', Stuart Rose hastens to add).

Sorting out the USA

By the early part of 1998, the loss in the critical US operation was estimated to have risen from $3 million to $5 million for the year. The Body Shop continued to search for a US partner to revitalize the American chain.

In May 1998, the company announced its rescue strategy to turn the US problems around. The strategy involves Adrian Bellamy, a non-executive director of The Body Shop since August 1997 and former chairman and CEO of US-based duty-free group

---

* Strangely, the bergamot is not a small furry animal, or a lost South American tribe, but is in fact a type of Italian grapefruit, which has inspired a new range of Body Shop products.

DFS. He is also a non-executive director of The Gap and Gucci. Bellamy paid $1 million to acquire an option to buy 51 per cent of The Body Shop's US operating company (Buth-Na-Bodhaige), if the subsidiary breaks even in the year to February 2000, and either makes aggregate profits of $5 million in the two years to February 2002 or makes $7 million in the year to February 2002. Bellamy has taken over management of BNB, which is to operate as a joint venture.

By October that year the first signs of needed change were apparent – the closure of warehouses and twenty-five of the US Body Shop stores.

An 'unthinkable' change in leadership?

Even the dramatic strategy for the USA was overshadowed by the dramatic restructuring of management at The Body Shop in July 1998. At this time, Anita and Gordon Roddick became co-chairs of the company and Anita vacated the CEO post in favour of Patrick Gournay, partly in response to pressure from City investors.

Fifty-year-old Frenchman Patrick Gournay was approached regarding the CEO post early in 1998 by Body Shop head hunters. He had spent twenty-six years working for Danone, France's biggest food group, latterly in the USA where he helped turn round Danone's struggling operations there. When approached by The Body Shop, the name meant little to him – he says, 'My consumption of cosmetics was more limited than my consumption of yogurt.'

In early March he met a group of The Body Shop's non-executive directors and then flew to London to meet the Roddicks. His goal was to establish if the Roddicks, and Anita in particular, really wanted change, and were prepared to accept a professional manager taking responsibility for running the business. Satisfied on this point and having won the approval of the Roddicks, Gournay accepted the job.

Gournay intends not to interfere in the ethical and campaigning side of the operation because he sees this as a defining part of the business. This issue had ruled out a number of other potential candidates for the CEO post. On joining the company, he described his role in the following way:

I see my primary role as to bring clarity to what we want to be and how we want to do it . . . A lot of things have been imitated. The question is how do you find the uniqueness that makes us different and better.

'I see my primary role as to bring clarity to what we want to be and how we want to do it'

However, by October 1998 after his speedy tour of Body Shop stores Gournay was promising a sweeping shake-up of the company. His plans include cutting the number of products by 25 per cent, further changes to store design and cutting the time taken to bring products to market. The goal is to take the eighteen months lag between new ideas and products on shelves to less than a year, with less stockholding in the channel. He was concerned that the stores were too cluttered with too many products that looked generic. He wants to focus on 'heritage' products such as the hemp and tea tree ranges and to differentiate products more. He is looking for 'radical change in the way we run the business'.

His first acquisition was the £7 million purchase of Cosmo Trading, which runs The Body Shop franchise in Germany, to take tighter control over European operations.

Stuart Rose, long-time advocate of the need for change at The Body Shop, moved at the same time from Managing Director to Deputy Chairman, giving up his day-to-day management responsibility.

Roddick's public reaction has been that she never wanted to be CEO – 'Chief Environmental Officer is more like it' she says and sees her contribution as creative rather than administrative. Her public approval of Gournay was seen by some as less than helpful to his credibility, when she said:

> I've spent time with him. I've gone out to dinner with him. He's a delightful conversationalist. He's not dictatorial. He's not arrogant. I like the way he treats his wife.

She was, however, severely irritated by those who saw this as her taking a 'back seat' or retiring. Her role is to focus on the creative side of the business – shop design, product development and campaigning. She sees the new structure as a way to improve the company's speed of innovation and the implementation of new ideas. She promised that Gournay's appointment will be more successful than other external appointees: 'It will have to work. There is no option.'

Indeed, the launch of a unique range of products, named Hemp and made from a non-narcotic marijuana substance, has been seen by some as a stylish joke by Roddick, likely to appeal to Body Shop consumers and irritate others. The slogan on these products reads 'Hemp is hope not dope'. Interventions by suspicious policemen provided suitable testimony to the continuing powers of mischief and creativity of the 'Queen of Green'.

However, City analysts remain sceptical and cynical about The Body Shop's US strategy and management restructuring:

I don't think this is going to improve the company. We've heard it all before about how they plan to improve profits in America by being better retailers, but it hasn't worked. As for Anita stepping down as chief executive, it doesn't really change anything. She is sitting there with a quarter of the company.

The new management structure looks rather odd. What will Stuart Rose do as the company's deputy chairman? That hasn't been made clear.

Nobody would accuse Anita Roddick of being like other chief executives. Her views on the City suits who control most of the shares in Body Shop have, for most part, been hardly fit for publication ... but yesterday she said she 'adored' the City. She also launched a new range of products made from a relative of marijuana. Has she been testing them too vigorously? ... In her place comes Patrick Gournay, fresh from running a yogurt company, and who clinched the job because Mrs Roddick decided he was nice to his wife. This is not a quality held in high regard by her new friends the City suits, but they can hardly have expected a conventional boss for this unconventional business.

At the end of 1998, The Body Shop signalled more than £14 million of exceptional costs in restructuring the business, as well as a sharp drop in profitability in the UK operation. These costs included charges for the closure of twenty-five stores in the USA and redundancy costs for fifty-five managers at the Sussex headquarters.

The plans for 1999 and beyond

Christmas 1998 led to further disappointments for The Body Shop. In January 1999, Patrick Gournay had to warn investors that profits would be lower than expected because of weak Christmas sales. UK sales in the ten weeks to 2 January were down 2 per cent, with even worse results in the USA – sales down 8 per cent in the same period. Without growth in the figures for Body Shop Direct, the home shopping business, UK performance would have looked even worse – the traditional shops were 6 per cent down. There was some improvement in sales in the Far East, Canada and Europe, but profit expectations for the full year of

£30.5 million were scaled down to around £25 million. Body Shop shares fell to 77p on this news but recovered to 88p.

Explanations for the poor figures included buying mistakes, poor product choices and presentation in the US market missing out on seasonal sales, understocking of fast-selling items in stores and lower wholesale sales to franchisees.

A plan for recovery

Expectations rose that there would be dramatic changes at The Body Shop to attempt to stop the slide in sales and profits and revitalize the operation. Store closures and management changes were forecast, as well as factory closures and significant job losses. Gournay admitted that continued poor performance in the USA called for cost reduction, including store closures.

On 26 January Gournay announced his plans for a structural makeover to streamline manufacturing operations and product lines at an exceptional cost of £23.5 million. His conclusion after his strategic review of the business is that:

'We had to decide what we wanted to be – manufacturer, wholesaler or a retailer. We have decided to be a retailer'

Body Shop has very strong fundamentals, but the problem is we haven't delivered in the past. We had to decide what we wanted to be – manufacturer, wholesaler or a retailer. We have decided to be a retailer.

The goal of Gournay's plan is entirely to position The Body Shop as a more powerful retail player. His plan comprises actions to improve the presentation of the shops, to outsource manufacturing, to cut administration costs, to move some creative jobs from Littlehampton to London and to change the franchise structure. The key elements of his 1999 strategy are:

- Decentralizing the management of The Body Shop through the creation of four regional business units – the UK, Europe, the Americas and Asia – each with its own profit-responsible management team, to streamline the supply chain.
- Looking for manufacturing partners in each region (the Body Shop factories are running at 30 per cent capacity and currently supply only half the products sold) to produce Body Shop products closer to the market and more appropriate for local market requirements. Anita Roddick insists partners will have to meet Body Shop ethical standards particularly

regarding no animal testing, and submit to 'social and environmental' audits.

- This reorganization of the supply chain is to reduce manufacturing costs, but will lead to the closure of factories – including sale of the two manufacturing operations at the Littlehampton base in West Sussex (currently running at 25 per cent capacity). The new manufacturing partner is expected to be American or Japanese, and the sales are expected to be completed by June 1999. US production has already been sold.
- Reappraising the franchising relationship – increasing the number of company-owned shops rather than franchised outlets, particularly in the UK.
- Continuing to redesign the stores to give them a 'more vibrant' feel, with less cluttered shelves, top selling lines displayed more prominently and more customer information provided. Franchisees not willing to invest in the upgrading of the stores are to be bought out.
- New store openings are expected at the rate of fifty or sixty a year, but owned not franchised.

City analysts approved of Gournay's plans to make The Body Shop 'a really good retailer' instead of a vertically integrated manufacturing and wholesaling business. Shares rose to 89p.

Gournay plans that Anita Roddick will continue to work on new product and shop development in a handful of 'founders' stores' but is noncommittal on her final veto over new products, he is also recruiting a new product director from outside the company. Gordon Roddick and Stuart Rose are to focus on the franchise part of the operation. In fact, some question marks exist regarding the Roddicks' involvement. In January 1999, they invested £5 million for a 29 per cent stake in the Alternative Hotel Company, which runs Hotel du Vin, with Gordon Roddick joining the hotel chain's board. A sleeping partner is Ian McGlinn, the original investor in The Body Shop.

Sources

Clark, Andrew (1998), 'Ailing Body Shop Gets A Makeover', *Daily Telegraph*, 23 October.

Cousins, Robin (1997), 'Retailing As New Age Diplomacy', *Sunday Business*, 4 May.

Entine, Jon (1998), '"McLibel" Campaign Turns on Body Shop', *Sunday Times*, March.

Feltham, Cliff (1998), 'Profit Plunge of 27pc Is A Body Blow for Body Shop', *Daily Mail*, 23 October.

Fletcher, Richard (1998), 'Body Shop Seeks Balm for Cynics', *Sunday Business*, 18 October.

Fluendy, Simon (1998), 'Anger Over Body Shop on the Web', *Mail on Sunday*, 14 June.

Fluendy, Simon (1998), '£2m Bill As Body Shop Quits Battle', *Mail on Sunday*, 22 November.

Hollinger, Peggy (1998), 'Body Shop Charges to Exceed £14m', *Financial Times*, 23 October.

Josephs, Jeremy (1998), 'When the Greenness of England Doesn't Translate Into French', *Daily Telegraph*, 22 September.

Olins, Rufus (1997), 'Avon Man To Direct Body Shop', *Sunday Times*, 1 June.

Olins, Rufus (1997), 'Body Shop Goes for a New Shape', *Sunday Times*, 1 June.

Olins, Rufus (1998), 'Body Shop Calls In Corporate Man', *Sunday Times*, 17 May.

Rankine, Kate (1998), 'Body Shop's US Chief Quits', *Daily Telegraph*, 2 February.

Rankine, Kate (1998), 'A Body Blow As Roddick Hands Over the Reins', *Daily Telegraph*, 13 May.

Rankine, Kate (1998), 'Body Shop Goes for New Blood', *Daily Telegraph*, 13 May.

Rivlin, Richard (1998), 'Body Shop Holds Production Review', *Sunday Telegraph*, 17 May.

Wright, Robert (1998), 'Body Shop Tries Out Another Facelift', *Financial Times*, 13 May.

Wright, Robert (1997), 'Make-Over To Create New Look Body Shop', *Financial Times*, 30 October.

CHAPTER 13

Kellogg's Cornflakes*

Brand versus value?

There can be few better known brands in the world than Kellogg's, and most particularly its branded breakfast cereals, led by Cornflakes. However, at the end of 1998 the world saw the unthinkable spectacle of Kellogg's losing market share and profitability; and share value suffering accordingly. The company is struggling to find a way to revive the brand and its experiences suggest that the underlying problem may be more serious than can be overcome with conventional marketing responses such as price cuts and increased promotion, or through management restructuring.

'at the end of 1998 the world saw the unthinkable spectacle of Kellogg's losing market share and profitability'

The strength of the Kellogg's brand

Kellogg's is one of the best known brands in the world. A 1998 survey – Brandz – commissioned by WPP, concerned with how closely consumers bond with a brand and 'brand voltage' (the

* This material has been prepared by Nigel F. Piercy, Cardiff Business School, Cardiff University from published sources. © Nigel F. Piercy, 1999.

'British consumers would put more trust in a packet of Kellogg's Cornflakes than the church, the police, the armed forces'

degree to which the brand meets customer needs better than competitors), rated Kellogg's on a par with McDonald's, Nescafé and Heinz as leading global brands. Indeed, a Henley Centre research study in the same year found that British consumers would put more trust in a packet of Kellogg's Cornflakes than the church, the police, the armed forces, or leading retailers such as Boots, M&S and Sainsbury's!

The history of the brand

Dr John Kellogg was the chief physician of the Western Health Reform Institute, founded in Battle Creek, Michigan in 1866 to propound the belief that a diet based on grains, nuts and vegetable-based foods was essential to 'right living'.

Dr Kellogg, and his brother William Keith Kellogg, were the inventors of the first pre-cooked breakfast cereal in 1894, while attempting to locate a digestible substitute for bread through experiments with grains for patients' diets, rather than develop a breakfast food. Grain was boiled for varying amounts of time to see what would happen and the sticky mess was pushed through rollers. One batch produced large, thin flakes: each grain producing a flake. The final result was a paper-thin malt-flavoured toasted flake of maize. The flakes were so popular that Kellogg received many requests from ex-patients for regular supplies to be sent to them. Demand continued to grow between 1902 and 1904.

In 1906 W. K. Kellogg established the Battle Creek Toasted Corn Flake Company in a small wooden building in the town, the forerunner to the Kellogg Company. The original building burned down in 1907, but was quickly replaced with a larger plant.

Kellogg emphasized rigid quality controls and to avoid confusion with competitors had his signature printed on the packaging. For many years the pack also had the slogan 'The original bears this signature'.

Kellogg advertised the product extensively and output rose from an initial thirty-three cases a day to over a million cases a day by 1909. The advertising budget in 1911 was $1 million and by 1912 the company had the biggest advertising sign in the world in New York's Time Square.

The company added Bran Flakes in 1915 and All-Bran a year later, with Rice Krispies launched in 1928. Kellogg pioneered nutritional labelling in the 1930s and produced an increased-protein cereal, Special K, in 1955.

By the 1980s, Kellogg had twenty-two plants operating in seventeen countries and global sales in excess of $6 billion.

The Kellogg's group, still based in Battle Creek, Michigan, makes twelve of the world's top-selling cereal brands. The company has not diversified far from the expanded range of breakfast cereals, although now around 20 per cent of global sales come from Pop-Tarts toaster pastries, frozen waffles, pancakes, bagels and Nutri-Grain cereal bars. It bought Sanka decaffeinated coffee in 1927 but later sold it to General Foods.

Kellogg Company has a mission in the following terms:

> Kellogg is a global company committed to building long-term growth in volume and profit and to enhancing its worldwide leadership position by providing nutritious food products of superior value.

Indeed, Kellogg's products have always stressed nutritional value and healthy eating. However, by the end of the 1980s, things had started to go wrong for Kellogg and the mission of global leadership and superior value looked to be crumbling. Much of the story is told by the share value shown in Figure 13.1.

Figure 13.1 Kellogg's share value, 1988–98 (unadjusted prices).
Source: Datastream

The cosy world of breakfast cereals

The turning point for the breakfast cereals industry was in 1993–94. Until this time the industry had been dominated by the big three producers: Kellogg, General Mills and Philip Morris. The sector had been characterized by competitive stability and above-average profitability. The big three cereal manufacturers had traditionally avoided destructive, head-to-head competition with each other and had moved their prices and promotional spends in line with each other. This high degree of concentration had allowed the large cereal manufacturers to frequently achieve rates of return on assets of 30 per cent for their cereal operations.

'concentration had allowed the large cereal manufacturers to frequently achieve rates of return on assets of 30 per cent for their cereal operations'

Interestingly, these high profit potentials did not attract significant competitive entries that would have destroyed the stability of the market and driven prices down. A Federal Trade Commission anti-monopoly case in 1972 suggested some of the reasons that might explain the continued domination of the three big brand owners in breakfast cereals and the deterrence of entry by new firms:

- one form of restraining competition was the 'unwritten agreements' between the firms that they would limit promotions (such as free gifts) to one brand at a time for each company
- the same informal understanding led the dominant firms to refrain from adding fortification to their brands in case the new products disrupted the competitive status quo
- the code of conduct extended to avoiding trade dealing – offering discounts to retailers for special treatment or special promotions – since the temporary increase in market share would lead to imitation by the other brands and the escalation of costs and reduction of profitability for all firms
- the big three encouraged supermarkets to adopt a shelf space plan that gave them the best position and allocated space on the basis of historical sales volume – while a fair system for the big three, it excluded newer, smaller companies with no historical sales base (which could only get shelf space by offering the retailer an enhanced discount off the wholesale price)
- the proliferation of new products was suggested by the FTC to have allowed the big three to dominate all the profitable niches in the cereals market, blocking the entry of new competitors.

For example, the popularity of natural cereals in the 1970s caught the big three unawares and they had no natural cereals brands in position. This opportunity attracted the entry of small firms and large food manufacturers, such as Pillsbury. The big three launched their own brands and within five years virtually all the new competition had withdrawn

In addition, the advertising expenditures by the big three were massive. In 1993, in the USA their spending exceeded $800 million, and constituted over a quarter of all food industry advertising. In the same year, the US producers issued over 25 billion coupons and over a quarter of all cereal purchases were made with coupons.

The industry was characterized by regular rounds of price increases, usually initiated by Kellogg and followed by the others. For example, in the USA cereal prices went up 16 per cent between 1990 and 1993, compared to a 6 per cent increase in overall food prices. These price increases were explained as necessary to generate funds for the promotions and advertising – the 'price up and spend back' strategy (see below).

The major firms also continually introduced new products, either in new brands or extension of existing ones. Of the big three, Kellogg had the greatest dependence on cereals sales – in 1994 they accounted for over 80 per cent of total sales. The other players were General Mills, a diversified consumer goods company and Philip Morris, a consumer packaged goods company with major interests in drinks and tobacco.

The only major intrusion into this marketplace had been the growth of private label breakfast cereals – from 1991 to 1994 in the USA they grew 50 per cent to reach a 9 per cent market share. The private labels offered consumers lower prices and retailers higher margins and quality was increasing rapidly.

The first sign that the end might be coming came in summer 1993, when Kellogg announced its third price increase of the year – a further 2.1 per cent, bringing the total for the year to 6.2 per cent. The competitors did not follow.

The creeping decline of the Kellogg's brand

Since 1988, Kellogg's market share has fallen from 40.5 per cent in the US market to 32 per cent and slipped 5 per cent across the rest of the world. Its US profit margins were once the envy of the food industry, but between 1995 and 1998 margins fell from 19

Table 13.1 US breakfast cereals market 1997–98

Brands	Market share (%)
Kellogg	32.0
General Mills	28.9
Post	16.3
Quaker Oats	8.6
Own label	7.8
Others	6.4

Source: *Financial Times*, 23 September 1998.

per cent to 15 per cent. In 1998 share price fell to the $33 level of 1993, after reaching more than $50. Revenues of $7 billion in 1994 had fallen to around $6 billion by 1997. Kellogg's 1997 net profits were down 2.8 per cent on the previous year, barely above the levels achieved at the start of the decade. The new structure of the US cereals market is indicative of the inroads made by competitors during the 1990s (Table 13.1).

At the beginning of 1999, Kellogg's lost US market leadership to General Mills, the maker of rival breakfast products Cheerios, Golden Grahams, Wheaties, Cinnamon Toast Crunch and Raisin Nut Bran. General Mills edged ahead of Kellogg with 32.5 per cent of the market in revenue terms (boosted by Thanksgiving sales of Chex cereals), compared to Kellogg's 31.6 per cent. (Kellogg still leads in volume terms.)

The sources of the problem

'Many of the roots of the problems of the 1990s can be traced back to the strategies of the 1980s'

Many of the roots of the problems of the 1990s can be traced back to the strategies of the 1980s. At this time, Kellogg pursued the policy of 'price up and spend back', described earlier. In other words, assuming that the consumer would remain loyal to the Kellogg's brand, Kellogg raised prices as often as twice a year and invested the profits in advertising, coupon promotions and the launch of one or two new products every twelve months. Ultimately those high prices, driven by Kellogg as market leader, made the company highly vulnerable to competition. High margins gave competitors the incentive and ability to invest and build a position in the market.

In effect, once established, Kellogg's competitors declared what escalated into a vicious price war. General Mills – manufacturers of Cheerios and Wheaties – started to cut prices in 1994. Two years later, Post (owned by Philip Morris) and maker of Shredded Wheat and Quaker Oats slashed prices by a full 20 per cent, forcing Kellogg to follow – in response to losing 3 per cent of the US market. Kellogg slashed prices on sixteen brands by around 19 per cent. Competitors have also been more innovative than Kellogg, e.g. General Mills introducing higher-value products such as Cheerios and Cinnamon Toast Crunch, requiring elaborate manufacturing processes that Kellogg and other competitors such as own labels cannot duplicate, with the effect that General Mills' average revenue per box is $3.29 compared to Kellogg's $2.95.

'Kellogg raised prices as often as twice a year and invested the profits in advertising, coupon promotions and the launch of one or two new products every twelve months'

In a parallel attack on the market leader, it was also at this time that low-cost, big-bag own-brand products started to appear on supermarket shelves. For example, in the UK, Cereal Partners Worldwide, a joint venture between Nestlé and General Mills, provides Tesco and Sainsbury with inexpensive, high-quality own-label breakfast cereals.

Kellogg's position was also undermined in part by changes in the consumer marketplace – busy people eating breakfast on the run instead of sitting down to eat cereal, switching to muffins, doughnuts and bagels. From 1994 to 1998, the US cereal market shrank from $8 billion to $7.2 billion.

The company believes that the problem is that by being drawn into a price war by competitors, it made the mistake of losing its focus on brand building and advertising. Outsiders suggest that the real problem is management isolation and inertia. Isolated from change at the Battle Creek headquarters, most senior staff, including new president Carlos Gutierrez, have risen up through the Kellogg's ranks and lack external experience or perspective.

By the start of 1999, analysts were suggesting that Kellogg was losing market share so rapidly – and market leadership along with it – that it will quickly become a candidate for take-over unless the situation is remedied rapidly. Analysts suggest that Nabisco, Unilever, Proctor & Gamble and even PepsiCo could be interested in buying Kellogg. (A hostile bid is unlikely to succeed because 34 per cent of the shares are held by the W. K. Kellogg Foundation, one of the world's biggest private charities.)

Management responses

Aggressive promotion

At the end of 1998, Kellogg warned that earnings per share would fall by 15 per cent because of the actions it needed to take to restore market share. Those policies centre on boosting sales *'policies centre on boosting sales with heavy spending on promotions, such as coupons, price cuts and "buy one get one free" offers'* with heavy spending on promotions, such as coupons, price cuts and 'buy one get one free' offers. Some impact on volume has been achieved, but analysts are concerned that this is wholly at the expense of profits.

For example, in January 1999, in response to continued loss of market share to supermarket own-label brands, Kellogg was unleashing a double assault on the £1 billion UK cereals market, simultaneously cutting prices across its major brands by 12 per cent and increasing its advertising budget by 40 per cent to around £75 million for the year. Historically in the UK market as in most others, Kellogg used its big advertising spend to support its premium price and reinforce consumer loyalty – the image of the healthy, wholesome family and catchy jingles. The new campaign will attempt to use advertising to stress lower prices but without damaging the brand – it has to retain the high ground when faced with retailer own-label products 30–40 per cent cheaper than the Kellogg's equivalents.

Retrenchment and new products

In the mid-1990s, the company began to cut costs: closing plants and shedding 1000 jobs. A review of the work of Kellogg's 2000 salaried employees in North America led to white-collar job losses to the level of 20 per cent in December 1998. This was mirrored by elimination of 20 per cent of Kellogg's European salaried staff announced in January 1999. These headcount cuts are expected to save around $10 million a year.

The company is also diverting advertising spend into the Kellogg brand name and away from individual products. The company is also looking to raise prices of two-thirds of its cereals in 1999.

It has also significantly attacked the convenience food market by acquiring the US bagel maker Lenders, introducing Breakfast Mates cereal and milk packets and Snak Pak pouches of several of the biggest brands – Kellogg's fastest selling new products. In 1997, Kellogg launched a $75 million research and development facility in Battle Creek.

A management shake-out

Carlos Gutierrez was appointed president and chief operating officer in June 1997, as heir apparent to chairman and chief executive Arnold Langbo, and with a brief to restore Kellogg's fortunes. Gutierrez has the goal of growing earnings by using the company's brand name to promote innovative new products. The following year, two top regional executives – North American president Thomas Knowlton and European chief Donald Fritz – departed from the company, believed to be at Gutierrez's suggestion. Kellogg has announced a total of eight restructuring programmes in the space of three years and Gutierrez says he will continue to reorganize it.

A new strategy for 1999

In December 1998, chairman and chief executive Arnold Langbo unveiled Kellogg's strategy for 1999 and beyond to achieve new growth. Kellogg's strategy includes:

- leadership in product innovation – launching a new premium price line of cereals and a new fortification programme for cereals to improve nutritional value
- strengthening the company's seven largest cereal markets (the USA, Mexico, Canada, Australia, Germany, France and the UK), which account for 80 per cent of Kellogg's global business
- accelerating the growth of convenience foods with expansion of markets and distribution channels, such as petrol stations, vending machines and convenience stores
- developing a more focused organization to support the growth strategy
- continuing to reduce costs

In January 1999, chief executive for seven years, Arnold Langbo, announced his early retirement as chief executive (remaining as chairman), to be replaced by Carlos Gutierrez in April 1999. Overseeing Kellogg's fall in market share from 38 per cent in 1991 to 32 per cent, Langbo was nicknamed the 'Cereal Killer' by some investors.

'Overseeing Kellogg's fall in market share from 38 per cent in 1991 to 32 per cent, Langbo was nicknamed the "Cereal Killer" by some investors'

Bowing to the inevitable?

Critics suggest that management changes have come far too late to put the magic back in the Kellogg's brand and that the company has squandered its outstanding brand assets.

There is also the question of whether the brand is the real issue in a market such as this one. Kellogg has been outmanoeuvred by competitors such as General Mills producing differentiated high-quality brands such as Cheerios on the one hand, and low-cost own-label retailer products attacking the market with value products on the other hand. This leaves the company trapped in the middle ground and looking for a future for its brand-based strategy.

Sources

Alexander, Garth (1999), 'Kellogg Faces Crunch As Rival Overtakes It', *Sunday Times*, 10 January.

Cave, Andrew (1999), 'Cheerio to Kellogg's Table-Topping Position', *Daily Telegraph*, 4 January.

Corts, Kenneth S. (1995), *The Ready-To-Eat Breakfast Cereal Industry in 1994*, Boston, MA: Harvard Business School.

Mills, Dominic (1998), 'Battle Lines Drawn Down Cereal Aisle', *Daily Telegraph*, 22 December.

Norris, David (1997), 'MPs? We'd Rather Trust Cornflakes', *Daily Mail*, 14 October.

Rees, Jon (1998), 'US Goods Inspire Greatest Loyalty', *Sunday Business*, 6 December.

Tomkins, Richard (1998), 'Putting the Snap, Crackle and Pop Back Into Kellogg', *Financial Times*, 23 September.

Wheatley, Catherine (1998), 'Creeping Brand Decline Catches Up On Kellogg', *Sunday Business*, 27 September.

CHAPTER 14

Laura Ashley*

The Frocky Horror Picture Show

Laura Ashley Holdings is famous for its frilly floral fashions. It currently operates more than 400 retail stores worldwide, selling women's and children's clothing and home furnishings. Clothing makes up around half of total sales and furnishings 44 per cent, including fabrics, curtains, blinds, wallpaper, paint, lighting products, carpets, furniture and bathroom accessories. The Laura Ashley brand is also franchised to other products such as sunglasses and fragrances.

Spectacular success by Laura Ashley has been followed by the collapse of sales, profits and share value in the 1990s, and by 1999 the company was on its sixth CEO since 1994. The story of Laura Ashley raises major questions about the obsolescence of a business design and the search for renewal. Some major strategic issues come from tracking the history of the company and its current decline.

'Spectacular success by Laura Ashley has been followed by the collapse of sales, profits and share value in the 1990s'

The key financial results of the late 1990s are shown in Table 14.1.

---

* This material has been prepared by Nigel F. Piercy, Cardiff Business School, Cardiff University from published sources. © Nigel F. Piercy, 1999.

Table 14.1 Laura Ashley's key financials 1994–98

Year ending January:	1994	1995	1996	1997	1998
Turnover (£ million)	300	323	337	328	345
Pre-tax profit (loss) (£ million)	3.0	(30.6)	10.3	16.2	(49.3)
Earnings per share (p)	0.43	(12.9)	2.86	4.13	(20.1)
Dividend per share (p)	0.10	0	0.48	0.96	0
Market capitalization (£ million)	221	179	318	376	87.1

The origins of the Laura Ashley business

The history of the company mainly reflects the story of the lives of its founders – Laura Ashley and her husband Bernard. Laura was born in 1925 in Wales but was brought up in London by her Welsh parents until she was evacuated to Wales during the Second World War. She had a life-long goal of benefiting the land of her birth by locating her business there and providing local employment. In 1943 she joined the WRNS and met Bernard, son of a South London grocer, who she married in 1949.

At this time, Laura worked with the National Federation of Women's Institutes, with a growing interest in their traditional handicrafts – high-quality embroidery, patchwork and hand-printed fabrics in particular. When pregnant for the first time in 1953, Laura turned to sewing as a pastime, and unable to find the fabrics she wanted, she and Bernard borrowed books to construct their first textile printing screen stencil. Working evenings and weekends in their Pimlico flat, they produced fabrics with polka dot and striped designs (since neither could draw) and hung them on wires in their attic dining room to dry.

A week after they started production, Bernard sold six linen tablemats, with an African two-colour design, to a London handicraft shop for £1. This income funded the purchase of silk fabrics to make women's headscarves. Laura hemmed the squares by hand, attached small Ashley labels and packed the goods herself. She then caught a bus to the John Lewis store on Oxford Street and persuaded them to take two dozen scarves on a sale-or-return basis. This was followed quickly by an order for six dozen more, which the Ashleys produced in their flat and Bernard delivered by motor bike the next morning on his way to work. The following day, the John Lewis order was repeated. Other customers included up-market stores such as Liberty. The headscarves had sold out on the back of the film *Roman Holiday* featuring Audrey Hepburn in a silk headscarf.

By September 1953, Bernard began working full-time in the new business to increase production and by Christmas sales had reached £1500 for the year. In 1954 the Ashleys formed the Ashley Mountney Company with capital of £500 (Mountney was Laura's maiden name).

Now with two small children, Laura took a less active role in the business. Bernard began designing his own furnishing fabrics, sold as Bernard Ashley Fabrics to hotels and others. The furnishing designs were brash, modern abstracts, but tellingly another success was tea towels printed with Victorian subjects. Helped by publicity in *Home and Gardens* magazine and orders from Harrods and Fortnum & Mason, by the end of 1955 they had 200 accounts and enquiries from overseas, and opened a showroom in the heart of London's wholesale textile trade area, expanding their range to include cotton aprons and oven gloves. Because Bernard thought that domestic products should carry a woman's signature, Laura Ashley's signature became part of the design. This signalled an important change in the identity of the company's products.

> '*Because Bernard thought that domestic products should carry a woman's signature*'

A move to Machynlleth in mid-Wales followed, and they employed a dress designer to create a range of garments. Early products were a shirt-dress and a Victorian nightdress, followed by the characteristic full-length Laura Ashley dresses. The long flowing skirt design was launched in the era of the mini-skirt and sold little at first, but within two years fashion had changed to favour the maxi-skirt and the Ashley design became a 'must have' fashion item.

In 1968 Ashley Shops Ltd was formed, and the first shop trading as Laura Ashley, opened in Kensington in London. The popularity of the store was such that they had, on occasion, to lock customers out. Expansion of the shops in Britain and abroad led to media talk of the 'Laura Ashley look', as furnishing materials, co-ordinated wallpapers and patchwork pieces were added to the range. By 1975, the company had a turnover of £5 million, three factories, 5000 employees worldwide and its own jet. By this time, the company had expanded into Australia, Canada and Switzerland, and had added home furnishings to the clothes ranges. Laura Ashley won the Queen's Award for Exporting in 1977.

However, the first venture into the USA was not a success – a San Francisco location was not appropriate. The 1980s saw greater success there, with a

> '*the first venture into the USA was not a success*'

move to New York as a base, and David Ashley's involvement in the US business. The product range was extended to include soaps and perfumes marketed in boxes designed by Nicholas Ashley, and the *Laura Ashley Book of Home Decorating* was published, selling 60 000 copies in its first edition.

In 1985, Laura Ashley died, aged only sixty, as a result of falling down a flight of stairs at home. The company was floated two months after her death with a valuation of £270 million, 5400 staff and anticipated profits of £20 million for the year. Bernard Ashley was knighted in 1987.

The rise and fall of the Laura Ashley empire

It is difficult to exaggerate the impact that Laura Ashley had on a generation of, mainly female, shoppers for fashion and fabrics for the home. In the 1960s and 1970s, Laura Ashley's designs and Victorian and Edwardian-style products came to represent all that was 'quintessentially British'. Laura Ashley fabrics decorated the walls of the British embassy in Washington, its fabrics were to be found in Highgrove, home of the Prince of Wales and its floral smocks and chintzes were favoured by a young Princess Diana, Princess of Wales. Laura Ashley design blossomed, characterized by long, flowing dresses invariably covered with floral patterns. With romantic prints, long billowy skirts and puffy sleeves, the clothes appealed to women with conservative tastes and an appetite for Victorian design. With a demure and feminine image, the Laura Ashley 'look' became a classic, which continued to win support from younger women too (the clothes typified the 'Sloane Ranger' look, associated with Princess Diana and her London contemporaries).

'Laura Ashley's designs and Victorian and Edwardian-style products came to represent all that was "quintessentially British"'

'the clothes typified the "Sloane Ranger" look, associated with Princess Diana and her London contemporaries'

Laura Ashley had become a fashion force with almost universal recognition for its unique and readily identified style. Laura Ashley was synonymous with a romantic design vision of tiered dresses in floral prints, dirdl skirts and needlecord pinafores – referencing fashion ideas of earlier eras. One fashion commentator notes, 'The Laura Ashley devotee, in long, lace-trimmed cotton-print frock (teamed with dainty lace gloves and a straw cloche hat) became a fixture at weddings, race meetings, garden parties and all other formalized social occasions of the British summer season.'

The growth of the business up to its floatation into a global retail chain supported by its own factories in Wales and elsewhere was truly spectacular.

However, a major change in the company's fortunes followed the death of its founder, Laura Ashley, in 1985. Momentum kept the business successful for several years, but by 1989 the company was losing money and continued to do so for four years, with a brief return to profit in 1993, followed by further losses. By 1989 Laura Ashley had run up debts of £107 million, and the company was rescued from near bankruptcy in 1990 with an investment of £30 million by the Japanese group Jusco, and the loss of 4000 jobs. It was at this point that Bernard Ashley stepped down as chairman to become life president of the company. From a peak value of more than 220p, Laura Ashley shares were worth around 60p by the end of 1997, having lost three-quarters of their value in that year alone. By the later 1990s, Laura Ashley was selling and closing factories in Europe and closing retail stores in the USA.

By the beginning of the 1990s, tastes in design and fashion had changed, and to many consumers the stores looked dowdy and dated. One British commentator concluded disparagingly that, 'There's a difference between being timeless and being out of date', and in the USA a leading analyst suggested, 'Laura Ashley really isn't with-it any more'. Laura Ashley had been squeezed out of the younger women's clothing market by brands such as Next, Monsoon and Oasis, and in the older women's market by stores selling classic brands such as Gucci, Ralph Lauren and Chanel. In the home furnishings market they were facing successful entry by Marks & Spencer as well as traditional competitors.

'There's a difference between being timeless and being out of date'

In addition, many of the stores were too small to display the full range of fashion and home furnishings. The ten years following Laura Ashley's death saw four chief executives come and go, debt problems grow as a result of rapid expansion and distribution systems begin to fail, for example, taking supplies from Asian factories destined for Japan on a tour through Wales.

Jim Maxmin was appointed in 1991, moving from a successful period with Thorn-EMI's rentals business, enthusing that 'Laura Ashley is an expression of England. It represents a way of life'. He brought some modernization, but created problems in the US distribution network and was removed in 1994 by the chairman, who succeeded him as CEO.

'Laura Ashley is an expression of England. It represents a way of life'

The company struggled to maintain Laura Ashley's self-imposed mission to cut unemployment in Wales by not reducing

'Bernard Ashley's management style was deeply unpopular'

employment in its Welsh factories. However, Bernard Ashley's management style was deeply unpopular. Described as 'irascible', many saw the penalty for non-conformity with his views as the sack, and he is seen as one major reason for the high turnover of senior management in the company.

The search by the company for a new strategy and for the rejuvenation of its brand can be seen in the events of 1996, 1997 and 1998.

The search for a turnaround

In 1996, Laura Ashley was back in profit with pre-tax earning of £10.3 million, following the losses of £30.6 million in 1995. It was also the first full year with Ann Iverson, a US executive, as CEO.

The Iverson strategy

Ann Iverson became Laura Ashley's CEO in 1995, with a reputation as a one-time rodeo rider with four marriages behind her and a successful record at Mothercare. When she appeared on the cover of Vogue magazine in provocative pose

'All those City guys love to think of me in black leather, so I may as well live up to expectations'

and little more than a leather coat, she joked, 'All those City guys love to think of me in black leather, so I may as well live up to expectations'.

Iverson is a retailing specialist and developed her approach in working with companies in trouble. She returned to Britain from running the Kay-Bee Toys and Hobbies retail chain in the USA, and had earlier worked for Bloomingdales, the US department store, and had thirty years' retail experience. In the UK she had boosted profits at British Home Stores, a division of Storehouse plc, and was rewarded with the CEO position at Storehouse's Mothercare chain. At Mother-care she introduced novelty attractions such as talking trees and singing clocks to get mothers and children back into the stores that they had deserted.

As the incoming CEO at Laura Ashley, she inherited a company that had lost £31 million in 1995, and had been through a series of restructuring programmes, management changes and job losses. She also inherited Bernard Ashley as a major shareholder still active in the company.

Her vision for Laura Ashley was to recapture the imagination of 35–50-year-old women clothes shoppers. Her reasoning was that everybody wants to dress the 18–25 year old, but this group represents only 35 per cent of shoppers, who get nearly half the retail shop space. By contrast, the woman of 35–50 age represents a larger proportion of the population, but has nowhere to shop. This was the battleground for the renewal of Laura Ashley. She believed that this gave her a market for the Laura Ashley 'Victorian look', of around 19 million women in the UK and the USA, and she hired a new designer to freshen the product line, while retaining the flowing, romantic look. She was frustrated that there was a lack of a common product – shops in different locations offered different clothes – and a global brand identity. She was also planning that home furnishings should become 65 per cent of the business (up from the existing 40–45 per cent). She announced from the outset that although it was 'fixable', turning Laura Ashley around would take three or four years.

'Her vision for Laura Ashley was to recapture the imagination of 35–50-year-old women clothes shoppers'

Iverson brought some tough policies to Laura Ashley. In her first year with the company, she replaced most of the top management team, cut the payroll substantially, abandoned profit-related pay, made deep cuts in other costs, took back control of the company's distribution from Federal Express (at a cost of £1 million) and announced an aggressive expansion plan in the USA.

With Bernard Ashley (whose family interests continued to own 35 per cent of the shares) agreeing to take a back seat, Iverson made significant progress in her first year: restoring dividends for the first time since 1989, pulling the company back into profit, and impressing City investors with her cost-cutting and expansion plans. By May 1996, Laura Ashley shares had reached 210p from the 80p when Iverson joined the company. Iverson's pay package was worth £1 million in 1996.

Iverson's new director of design, Basha Cohen, was developing new clothing lines that were designed to regain lost customers, even at the risk of losing some long-standing existing customers. Her goal was to overcome the 'frumpy' and 'twee' image with clothes that were 'feminine, but not in a delicate, flowery sort of way ... fashionable without being on the cutting edge of fashion'. The floral prints and long dresses were discarded as deeply unfashionable in the 1990s. Iverson's US advertising campaign illustrates her goal with the slogan 'Laura Ashley – say it without flowers'.

'Laura Ashley – say it without flowers'

The Iverson strategy unravels

In March 1997, Laura Ashley issued the first of what was to be a series of profits warnings and announced that it was selling its spring and summer collections at discounts costing £4 million – blaming over-buying and overoptimistic sales forecasts. By May, Iverson had to announce that trading had deteriorated further and that key members of the top management team were leaving the company, including the buying director who had been responsible for the critical strategy of sourcing more up-to-date designs from the Far East.

The US expansion had proved problematic. The USA was Iverson's key growth market and she had planned to take selling space up to more than 40 per cent of the company's total worldwide merchandising area. The US chain had grown to 155 stores out of the total of 418 worldwide. By mid-1997, the US stores were slashing retail prices by up to 75 per cent to move the stockpiles in its warehouses, but the company remained committed to further store openings.

'By mid-1997, the US stores were slashing retail prices by up to 75 per cent to move the stockpiles'

Disappointing trading and low public awareness of Laura Ashley in the USA had been underpinned by supply chain problems that prevented the company getting its best selling items to market, while providing excess supplies of the slow selling products. The shift in emphasis from clothes to selling more home furnishings in larger stores did not seem to be working.

By July 1997, Iverson faced the problem of explaining even more disappointing results to the City and in August the company declared a half-year trading loss of £4.5 million. The company moved into a further round of job cutting at its garment factories in Wales (40 per cent of the staff were to be shed as redundant) and announced a slowing of its aggressive expansion programme in the USA. Share value settled in at around 61p. Ominously, chairman, John Thornton, reiterated his support for Iverson, saying, 'Ann is pursuing the right strategy . . . and will be able to turn the company around – although it will take time.' However, Iverson was looking at her third year as CEO being marred by a return to loss by the company. Meanwhile her relationship with the vocal and aggressive Sir Bernard Ashley became increasingly tense.

The newly restructured Board was chaired by 45-year-old John Thornton replacing Sir Bernard Ashley in this role, a member of the executive committee of Goldman Sachs and chairman of its Asian operations. He was also on the US boards of Ford Motor Company and Pacific Century Group, and British Sky

Broadcasting and Diamond Cable Communications in the UK. The ownership of the company by 1997 had three main constituents: Sir Bernard Ashley's family interest, the holding by the Japanese investors group, and the remaining half held by institutional shareholders. The company results in 1997 caused several shareholder groups to demand Thornton's replacement and the appointment of independent non-executive directors.

Predators began to circle at this time, most notably Georgette Mosbacher, who revived the cosmetics company La Prairie, and had made an unsuccessful offer for Laura Ashley in 1995, but remained interested in the possible acquisition of the company.

By September 1997, Laura Ashley confirmed that it would fail to break-even for the year; some five weeks after making a trading statement suggesting that it would do so. The company blamed poor trading in its home furnishings business, particularly in the USA, and excess stock and supply problems. City reports referred to Iverson's position as 'untenable', but she declared she had no intention of resigning and that she had the 'full support' of the board. She admitted the company had tried to move too fast without the proper infrastructure, but that excess stock had been sold off and greater controls introduced.

The company also undertook yet another restructuring: David Hoare was appointed chief operating officer, the furnishings and garments businesses were to be split and managed separately and further cost cutting was underway. Declining sales in the USA, particularly from the newer stores, prompted a halt to further store openings. Hoare, a management consultant and finance specialist, was appointed to allow Iverson to concentrate on the retailing side of the business.

While the first half-year results showed a 12 per cent rise in sales, current trading in the weeks up to the September 1997 statement was a cause for alarm. Group sales in the first eight weeks of the second half grew only 1 per cent, mainly because of a 14 per cent fall in US furnishings sales. The company blamed the US problems on supply chain failures – taking four weeks to get ordered goods to the stores – and opened its own US warehouse. Laura Ashley shares fell to 59p and a leading City analyst commented, 'The management are admitting that they have lost control of the business.'

'The management are admitting that they have lost control of the business'

The departure of Iverson

Seven weeks after saying she had the full support of the board, in November 1997, Ann Iverson parted company with Laura

Ashley, and finance director, James Walsh, an Iverson appointee also resigned, both departures being at the request of the non-executive directors (with Sir Bernard Ashley as main instigator). The payoffs were £450 000 and £300 000, respectively. Rumours were that these departures were triggered by a need to reassure the company's bankers that banking covenants would not be breached. Iverson's total earnings from the company during her tenure as CEO amounted to £3 million. Control passed to chief operating officer, David Hoare. The following month, Patricia Manning, marketing director and a close ally of Iverson, also resigned from Laura Ashley, following Hoare's 'reorganization' of the marketing department to improve the marketing of the Laura Ashley brand. The designer, Basha Cohen had already departed, along with Julie Renshaw, head of merchandising.

Iverson's initial successes in restoring profitability and share-holder dividends, increasing the stock price and aggressively expanding sales had come to nothing. When she left the company was predicting pre-tax losses for the year of £10 million and share price fell to 45p.

Overstocking to hold £93 million of stock in a £300 million turnover business, while customers were waiting up to four months for the delivery of sofas, and the company being out of stock of its best-selling bed linen ranges in the USA for up to ten weeks in the summer of 1997, had undermined the company's profit recovery.

Failure to achieve goals in the USA was underlined by the company having too many shops in the wrong locations and the mistake of emphasizing home furnishings instead of the more popular clothes. Some feared that the company was close to collapse at this point.

One City analyst commented that, 'It is hard to see a future for Laura Ashley now' because the company had 'tried to be a global retailer without a global brand, and the danger is that they have lost the core business in the process.'

'the company had "tried to be a global retailer without a global brand, and the danger is that they have lost the core business in the process."'

The immediate tasks confronting David Hoare, brought to the company to counter Iverson's excess optimism, were cutting costs, eliminating loss-making operations and stabilizing cash flow. If Iverson's experience was typical, he also had to learn to work with the elderly Bernard Ashley shouting in his ear at every turn.

Sir Bernard was determined to play a key role in purging Laura Ashley of fashion-following Iverson's bequest. As old-style dresses appeared in the shops again, he declared, 'I'm back!' – as was his son, Nicholas, heading the design department.

Is the money running out again?

In the autumn of 1997 the effects of the negative cash outflow and lack of the profitability became apparent. From September to Christmas 1997 Laura Ashley management was preoccupied with emergency talks with the company's bankers. As trading had deteriorated, the company had been forced to contact its six banks as it came close to breaching its interest cover covenants on a £50 million loan. By Christmas the banking syndicate had extended its loans until April 1999, giving the group a total of £70 million committed borrowing facilities, but on more onerous terms. Thornton was in talks with venture capital investors to gain an injection of cash. Laura Ashley shares reached a then all-time low of 26p. Richard Pennycook joined the company as the new finance director.

Emergency action

Following refinancing, Hoare and Thornton undertook a number of measures in an attempt to address the company's main problems.

In January 1998, they attempted to cut Laura Ashley's last ties with manufacturing by selling its four factories in Wales and production facilities elsewhere. At the same time they announced that annual losses were likely to reach £26 million before restructuring charges (compared to City expectations of £15 million), as a result of declining sales in the UK and USA and heavy discounting to move stock. The total loss for the year reached £49 million, including restructuring costs.

They named a new chief executive for the US operation: Michael Appel, a former merchandising director with Bloomingdales. Appel's first task was to arrange the closure of some of the thirty-two large stores in the USA opened by Iverson, by negotiating with landlords to find new tenants to take over the ten-year leases signed by Iverson. (Putting the US business into Chapter 11 bankruptcy was unattractive because the main creditor was Laura Ashley's UK business.) Restructuring costs for closing ten of the large-format US stores and covering stock losses was estimated at £10 million. One estimate was that complete withdrawal from the USA would require a write-down of £100 million.

'One estimate was that complete withdrawal from the USA would require a write-down of £100 million'

They also sold a 13 per cent stake in Laura Ashley Japan to Jusco, Laura Ashley's Japanese joint venture partner, for £8 million, as part of the disposal of non-core assets.

A rescue package

As the company moved towards collapse with sales a further 15 per cent down overall and 28 per cent in the USA, a lifeline was thrown by Malayan United Industries (MUI) in April 1998 – taking a 40 per cent stake by buying new shares at 28p each at a cost of £44 million (less than the market price of 35p a share). The Malaysian stake does not give MUI complete control but dilutes Sir Bernard Ashley's stake to 20 per cent and the Japanese AEON holding to 9 per cent. Four Malaysians were to join the board, with Victoria Egan becoming deputy chief executive and Paul Ng president of the US business. Around £20 million of the MUI money was destined for the US operation to cover losses (running at more than £13 million the previous year).

In June 1998, Sir Bernard Ashley stepped down from the board of directors (leaving family interests to be represented by his son, Nicholas Ashley) to concentrate on his award-winning luxury hotel business.

Another chief executive?

'By August 1998, the company was in the midst of yet another major management reshuffle'

By August 1998, the company was in the midst of yet another major management reshuffle – the fifth in seven years. David Hoare was replaced as chief executive by Victoria Egan. Richard Pennycook, the new finance director also left. Both had held their jobs for less than a year. This was part of a 20 per cent reduction in head office jobs at the company, which the company defended as 'phase two of its recovery plan'.

Egan is a director of MUI, and formerly president of Shangri-La Plaza Corporation, which owns an up-market shopping mall in Manila, part-owned by MUI. Her strategy involves transforming the company into a wholly retailing operation, with an emphasis on brand management instead of manufacturing (in-house manufactures constituted only 20 per cent of total sales at this time).

In November 1998, Egan prepared to close two factories, in Holland and Wales, since in ten months no buyer had been found, with the remainder still on the market for the time being. She also announced her intention to close, reduce in size or move nineteen of the thirty-two loss-making US stores.

And another . . .

In January 1999, after only six months in post, Victoria Egan resigned from the company for 'personal reasons', at the time of the announcement of the disappointing results for Laura Ashley in the trading quarter up to January. She was replaced as CEO by Ng Kwan Cheong, managing director of MUI. Cheong becomes the seventh CEO at Laura Ashley in the space of eight years. Cheong is expected to stay with the strategies introduced since the Malaysian investment in 1998. Following Iverson's failure to change the dowdy image, a new designer has been recruited from Ralph Lauren, costs are being cut, manufacturing is being run down, ways are being found out of the over-ambitious US expansion, and the company is trying to operate as a full-price retailer.

Sales results in the eight weeks up to mid-January 1999 had fallen by 14 per cent and for the half-year they were down 16 per cent. The company's share value fell to a record low of 12p, and its market value was around £45 million. Morale among staff was reported to be at its lowest ever.

Seven chief executives – still no strategy?

The company's response has been to weaken its resolve to be a full-price retailer and to frantically advertise a 'Blue Cross' sales with an additional 20 per cent off clothing and furnishings already reduced by 50 per cent for the 1999 New Year sales. The store windows are covered with signs reading 'Sale! Sale! Sale!'. Investors have suggested that bargains for customers signal a business in crisis.

'The store windows are covered with signs reading "Sale! Sale! Sale!"'

Questions have been raised about the retail concept of attempting to sell women's wear, children's wear, and home furnishings and accessories all out of the same store. Further, many of the stores are very small and are flung far and wide.

The search for divine intervention?

January 1999 also saw the appointment of bible-thumping US television preacher, Pat Robertson, as a non-executive director, holding two million shares (a stake of around 1 per cent of the business). Robertson is an acquaintance of chairman, John Thornton. Described by the company as 'a noted media pioneer, educator, philanthropist and religious broadcaster', Robertson has been a strong voice of ultra-conservatism in the USA, with wide-ranging business interests.

When asked by the *Financial Times* if the company was turning to the power of prayer, a senior Laura Ashley manager said, 'If that's what it takes . . . and don't quote me on that.'

Is it curtains for Laura Ashley?

By the early part of 1999, it looked as though Laura Ashley would soon be worth less than the £44 million of MUI money invested in April 1998, with shares sitting at 12p and market value at around £45 million. While Victoria Egan had talked about the need to 'move from improved financial stability to profitability', there were few signs that this was happening. Announcements in October 1998, showed that the half-year loss had doubled on sales down by 20 per cent and the forecast in January 1999 was for a full-year loss of £20 million. The value of Laura Ashley shares over the decade is shown in Figure 14.1.

'the old look is outmoded and the new one has not sold, while old customers have been alienated by style changes that have failed to win new ones'

The underlying question is whether the Laura Ashley formula is simply tired and out of date, or whether the company has a future as a niche retailer

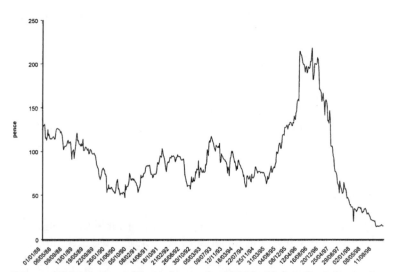

Figure 14.1 Laura Ashley's share value, 1988–98 (unadjusted prices).
Source: Datastream

for women in the 30–50 age group. At its simplest, the old look is outmoded and the new one has not sold, while old customers have been alienated by style changes that have failed to win new ones.

However, Ng Kwan Cheong reports some more favourable metrics in the business as a result of the operational changes introduced by the Malaysians. Although there have been declines in sales volume in recent trading, this has been accompanied by a 3 per cent increase in margins, reflecting the Malaysian policy of returning to full-price retailing instead of discounting. The business is free of most debt burden and has the support of its bankers. Also tighter buying policy had produced a 10 per cent reduction in stocks. Losses in the 1999 financial year are expected to be held to around £20 million. Cheong believes that he can get the company back into profit within two years. He is committed to a return to more traditional Laura Ashley styles, since the more contemporary designs failed to attract customers.

Laura Dunn, deputy editor of the fashionable interiors magazine *Living Etc* comments, 'Laura Ashley has a reputation for chintzy swags. It's a shame because it has some great modern stuff. But who's to say their old look won't be fashionable in five years' time?'.

'Laura Ashley has a reputation for chintzy swags. It's a shame because it has some great modern stuff'

Sources

Alexander, Andrew (1997), 'Ashley Loss Raises New Doubts About Iverson', *Daily Mail*, 26 September.

Alexander, Andrew (1997), 'Iverson Sacking Still Leaves An Uphill Struggle for Laura Ashley', *Daily Mail*, 19 November.

Clark, Andrew (1998), 'Boardroom Reshuffles Again At Laura Ashley', *Daily Telegraph*, 13 August.

Grose, Thomas K. (1997), 'Don't Say It With Flowers', *Time*, 14 April.

Hollinger, Peggy (1997), An English Rose Loses Some of Its Glamour', *Financial Times*, 19 November.

Hollinger, Peggy (1998), 'Laura Ashley Drops 25 per cent', *Financial Times*, 16 January.

Hollinger, Peggy (1998), 'Laura Ashley Announces Its Fifth Reshuffle', *Financial Times*, 13 August.

Kay, William (1997), 'Challenge to the Queen of Chintz', *Financial Mail on Sunday*, 24 August.

Lynn, Matthew (1997), 'Laura Ashley Wakes Up To A Nightmare', *Sunday Times*, 23 November.

Norris, David (1997), 'Laura Ashley Axes Wonderwoman Who Failed Rescue Mission', *Daily Mail*, 19 November.

Olins, Rufus (1997), 'Wilting', *Sunday Times*, 24 August.

Olins, Rufus (1997), 'Iverson In More Trouble On Laura Ashley Figures', *Sunday Times*, 24 August.

Price, Christopher (1997), 'A Retailer Out of Fashion in the 1990s', *Financial Times*, 20 August.

Rankine, Kate (1997), 'Laura Ashley Meets Bankers As Losses Rise', *Daily Telegraph*, 26 September.

Rankine, Kate (1997), 'It's Curtains for Laura Ashley Chief', *Daily Telegraph*, 19 November.

Rankine, Kate (1997), 'Banks Agree Rescue Package for Troubled Laura Ashley', *Daily Telegraph*, 20 December.

Rankine, Kate (1998), 'Laura Ashley To Announce Major US Restructuring', *Daily Telegraph*, 11 April.

Rankine, Kate (1998), 'Lifeline Thrown to Laura Ashley', *Daily Telegraph*, 18 April.

Walters, Michael (1998), 'Troubled Laura Ashley Finds Far Eastern Friend', *Daily Mail*, 18 April.

Wright, Robert (1998), 'Laura Ashley Joint Founder Steps Down', *Financial Times*, 10 June.

Wright, Robert (1998), 'Laura Ashley To Maintain Welsh Factories', *Financial Times*, 27 November.

CHAPTER 15

Boots the Chemists*

Vanity, value and vision

Boots is best known as the UK's leading pharmacy or drugstore chain, with more than 1300 outlets in the UK and Ireland. In fact, there are six separate businesses making up The Boots Company, each operating largely independently, with a total sales revenue of just under £5 billion in 1998 and more than 85 000 employees. The market value of the company is just under £9 billion. Table 15.1 shows the company's financial highlights in the later 1990s.

The six businesses operating in the Boots Company by the end of the 1990s are described briefly below.

Boots the Chemists (BTC) positions itself as Britain's leading retailer of health and beauty products with a heritage going back 120 years, and operating stores ranging from small community pharmacies to large city centre department stores, as well as health centres.

BTC employs 55 000 staff and has a massive customer base – 14.5 million people shop at BTC every week (32 per cent of the population) and 27 million people shop at BTC every month (59

---

* This material has been prepared by Nigel F. Piercy, Cardiff Business School, Cardiff University from published sources and discussions with executives. © Nigel F. Piercy, 1999.

Table 15.1   **Financial highlights of The Boots Company, 1994–99**

Year to March	1995	1996	1997	1998	1999 (estimate)
Turnover (£ billion)	4.31	4.12	4.58	4.97	4.50
Pre-tax profit (£ million)	850	508	571	553	555
Earnings per share (p)	65.7	35.8	42.9	42.6	42.0
Dividend per share (p)	17.0	18.5	64.7	22.3	24.0

per cent of the population). The product range extends from dispensing medicines in the pharmacies, to selling over-the-counter medicines, to market leadership in baby food and toiletry products, to beauty products (selling around £1.7 billion of cosmetics and personal care products) to gift merchandise and greetings cards, to photographic supplies, to food (mainly lunchtime sandwiches and chilled foods). Large BTC stores stock up to 27 000 product lines.

Boots Opticians is one of the major opticians in the UK with 280 practices, located either in BTC stores, or in free-standing premises in city centre shopping sites, many with on-site optical laboratories; it conducts around 25 000 eye examinations a week.

Boots Opticians supplies spectacle frames and prescription lenses, as well as non-prescription eyewear such as sunglasses and sports glasses. It is also a major supplier of contact lenses. A large proportion of the lenses, frames and contact lenses are Boots own-brand products.

Boots Contract Manufacturing is the largest European contract manufacturer in the field of high quality healthcare, cosmetics and toiletry products, for the private label and contract markets. The majority of its sales are within the Boots group, but over 25 per cent of sales are to third-party customers outside the Boots group. Contract Manufacturing has eight factories in the UK and Europe and one major development laboratory.

Boots Healthcare International (BHI) is a leading developer of consumer healthcare products, in the global self-medication market. BHI has twenty operating businesses based in Europe, Asia/Pacific and Australasia, as well as an extensive export sales operation from its Nottingham headquarters. Around three-quarters of BHI's business is done outside the UK.

BHI's product range spans three core categories with major brands in each, as well as a number of local product ranges:

- analgesics – the major brand is Nurofen
- cough/throat medicines – the leading brand is Strepsils
- dermatology/skincare – E45, Lutsine, Onagine, Balneum, Curatoderm
- other leading brands include Optrex and Sweetex, and the Crookes Healthcare over-the-counter medicines in the UK

Boots Health & Beauty is responsible for the development and management of Boots retail stores outside the UK. These stores stock international and local brands, including the leading Boots brands – No7, No17, Natural Collection and Botanics – and a pharmacy (where allowed by local law). 1997 saw the opening of five trial stores in Thailand and three in the Netherlands.

Boots Properties is responsible for managing the property needs of The Boots Company's businesses, and has been involved in developing major shopping centres and multi-tenant retail parks. Its disposal programme has been a major contributor to increased returns to shareholders.

Halfords, the UK's leading retailer of car parts and accessories, cycles and cycle accessories, and with a growing business in car servicing and repair, is also a Boots Company business.

Halfords operates more than 400 retail stores – 276 super-stores (135 of which have garages) and 134 high street stores. The core product ranges are car parts and accessories including audio, cycles and accessories – the Bike Shop, oil and car bodycare products, as well as garage servicing. Halfords was acquired in Boots' £900 million purchase of the Ward White group in 1989, together with a number of home decorating and do-it-yourself businesses comprising the Ward White group.

Boots' performance in the 1990s

The early 1990s saw a marked erosion in the share performance of The Boots Company (see Figure 15.1), although it has been sustained by remarkably high returns to shareholders. Shares hovered around the £4 level in 1993 and 1994, but had recovered to around the £9–10 level by 1998. This mirrors a failing strategy in the late 1980s and early 1990s, a vision of maximizing shareholder value and a strategy to redefine and renew this large and complex business.

'The early 1990s saw a marked erosion in the share performance of The Boots Company'

The history of the Boots Company

Part of the context for the Boots' story during the 1990s is the lengthy history of the organization and the heritage it carries from its origins.

The Boots Company has its roots in the middle of the nineteenth century, in a small herbalist's shop opened by John Boot in Nottingham (still the location of Boots headquarters and its primary manufacturing site). In 1877 this business was taken over by Jesse Boot, whose business approach was to buy in bulk and sell cheaply in cash – 'Drugs and Proprietary Articles at Reduced Prices' – making herbal remedies, medicines and household toiletries affordable for the first time to many working-class people. He advertised his low prices in the local newspaper and through bell-ringers touring the streets of Nottingham. This strategy was designed to counter the power of 'proper' chemists who practised a price-fixing monopoly in medicines and provoked violent opposition from them.

'The Boots Company has its roots in the middle of the nineteenth century, in a small herbalist's shop opened by John Boot'

Jesse Boot's business approach was driven by his concern for the poor, reflecting his Methodist and Wesleyan upbringing. He later renamed the shop 'The People's Store' and later again 'Boots Cash Chemist'. By 1884, Boot and the chemist E. S. Waring, had won the fight against the doctors' and established chemists' monopoly to handle over a million prescriptions a year, charging only half what other chemists were demanding. By 1896, the company had sixty shops spread over twenty-eight towns, and survived further opposition in the form of a parliamentary decree in 1908 stating that a qualified pharmacist had to be in attendance in each branch.

Jesse Boot's wife, Florence, established new lines in the rapidly growing business – fancy goods, stationery, books, silverware and picture framing, as well as introducing cheap cafés and Booklovers Libraries in major stores.

In 1909, the chain had 600 shops, and the elderly, ailing Jesse Boot sold his controlling interest to an American, Louis K. Liggett, and the United Drug Company.

Jesse and Florence were remarkably enlightened employers for their time and their workforce benefited from innovatory welfare policies, such as pensions, education, sports and social facilities provided by the company. Boot's gifts to Nottingham had exceeded £2 million by the time of his death in 1931.

By the time of Jesse Boot's death in 1931, Boots had a chain of around 1000 stores and a 300-acre site on the outskirts of

Nottingham for manufacturing. In 1931, Jesse's son John Boot led a consortium of British financiers to buy Boots back.

Milestones in the 1930s and 1940s were the opening of the thousandth shop in 1933, the launch of No7 cosmetics in 1935, and a major involvement in chemicals and pharmaceuticals production for the Second World War effort, as well as the start of international expansion with a factory in Kenya in 1942. The 1950s and 1960s saw the death of John Boot and the end of family participation in the business and the acquisition of other chemists' chains (Timothy Whites, Taylors) and pharmaceutical brands and producers.

This history of the company underlines many of the characteristics that remain in the 1990s: a non-conformist and tradition of enlightenment; a focus on health and accessibility to remedies for all; for many years a 'pharmacist-led' culture, even as late as the 1970s most Boots retail managers had started their careers as pharmacists.

'This history of the company underlines many of the characteristics that remain in the 1990s'

Vanity and the urge to merge

Boots in the 1980s was a major feature of every British high street, and was pursuing the path of becoming a departmental store by expanding from medicines and cosmetics/toiletries into a wide range of household products – for example the 'Children's World' stores, household electrical products, newspapers and magazines, and so on.

This strategy was brought to a climax in 1989 with the acquisition by Boots of Ward White for £896 million, by the new chairman and chief executive Lord Blyth. The purchase price was equal to a third of Boots' own market value at the time. This acquisition brought into the Boots group: Payless, a DIY group; AG Stanley, owning FADS and Homestyle home decorating chains; and Halfords, the car and cycle accessories chain. The take-over involved a fiercely contested battle in the summer of 1989 and enabled Lord Blyth as a relatively new chief executive to make his first mark on Boots.

'The take-over involved a fiercely contested battle in the summer of 1989 and enabled Lord Blyth as a relatively new chief executive to make his first mark on Boots'

The logic underlying this strategy was that as a high street retailer and drugs group, Boots had reached maturity. Conventional portfolio modelling suggested that Boots could move into a new era by using the cash generated from its core drugs and retail businesses to make an acquisition in a rapidly growing sector. Extending its reach into home decorating, home improvement and the automotive field looked an ideal way of leveraging Boots' growth and earnings potential, and establishing the business as more than simply a high street chemist, but staying close to the existing customer base and building synergy in this way. Indeed, the DIY sector had been growing consistently at 20 per cent a year during the 1980s.

The nightmare begins

It turned out that Boots had bought into the home decorating business at the top of the market and the collapse of property prices in the early 1990s devastated the home decorating and DIY markets. For example, the AG Stanley Group home decorating businesses (FADS and Homestyle) were showing in excess of annual £2 million pre-tax profits in 1993, but by 1996 and 1997 had settled in to pre-tax losses of £12 million a year.

The Payless DIY business also began to falter a year after the take-over. Boots responded by a joint venture which merged Payless with another DIY chain – Do-It-All (then owned by WH Smith, the newspaper retailer, as part of its own diversification strategy). The joint venture continued to make substantial losses in a time of depressed DIY demand caused by a continuing housing market crash. In 1996, WH Smith paid Boots £50 million to take away its half of the DIY business, which Smith's then chief executive Bill Cockburn called a 'financial disaster'. By that stage, the venture had cost both businesses around £150 million in losses and restructuring costs. Even with some subsequent recovery in the housing market, the Do-It-All business showed low growth – around 2 per cent a year by the later 1990s, although by 1997 the business showed a small £2.5 million profit on sales of £337 million.

'The only Ward White business which has consistently turned in profits and reasonable growth has been Halfords'

The only Ward White business which has consistently turned in profits and reasonable growth has been Halfords – though generating only £27 million in annual profits after nearly a decade of Boots' ownership. City analysts have suggested that £896 million was a high price to pay for a business generating this level of earnings.

Recovering from Ward White

To begin unwinding from a disastrous strategy, in 1997 the loss-making AG Stanley home decorating businesses was sold for a nominal sum of £1 to Alchemy Partners, a private venture-capital group. AG Stanley was transferred to the new owners with cash balances of £7.5 million. Boots took a resulting £180 million write-off against shareholder funds to rid itself of AG Stanley – though share value rose 14p in a depressed market when the news was released.

In 1998, Boots sold the 139-store Do-It-All chain to private DIY retailer Focus Group for £68 million in cash. This gave Boots a £312 million exceptional loss (as a 'non-cash' write-off of goodwill), on top of the £80 million investment in restructuring and trading losses. Focus Group's chief executive plans to inject his Petworld format into the Do-It-All stores and believed that the disasters of the 1990s were because Do-It-All 'suffered from being at the bottom end of both Smith's and Boots' attention span.' The bargain-price purchase makes Focus the UK's third largest DIY group.

Some commentators suggest that Lord Blyth must have got over-excited during the fiercely contested take-over battle for Ward White and forgot to look closely at the accounts. There is now little doubt that the price paid was dramatically too high. It has also become apparent that in spite of the conventional logic, any supposed synergy with the core Boots' businesses and management competencies was an illusion. In spite of the attraction of the apparent 'strategic fit', Boots entered a market which was entering a downturn, and badly underestimated the ability of the market leaders in DIY to defend themselves against competition – B&Q and Sainsbury's Homebase turned out to be formidable and skilful competitors.

'Lord Blyth must have got over-excited during the fiercely contested take-over battle for Ward White and forgot to look closely at the accounts'

However, Blyth admits the mistake. He has found a way out of the disaster. However, he has also maintained impressive share-holder value and overseen the renewal and reinvention of the business around its real core – the worldwide health and personal care business.

Value and paying penance

Blyth has made amends to shareholders who might have been unhappy about his strategy by returning £1.7 billion to shareholders through special dividends and share buy-backs. This is an impressive way of saying 'sorry' to your owners!

In fact, since the Ward White experience Blyth has become a strong advocate of the management of a business for shareholder

'Blyth has become a strong advocate of the management of a business for shareholder value'

value – so-called 'value-based management'. The guiding principle is to maximize over time the cashflow value of each of the businesses, i.e. the excess of cashflow over the cost of capital.

Blyth has attempted to move his managers from thinking about market share and sales per square foot to thinking about value-based strategic planning on a longer time horizon than conventional budgeting. The approach rests on identifying the five or six things which really make a difference to the business, and which of those are most capable of being levered by management. Out of that come alternative courses of action. The overriding principle is that all uses of cash require a return. The results are sometimes surprising – Boots Nottingham site has its own electricity plant built two years ago for £19 million. The alternatives were to refit an older power station for £11 million or take power from outside. The most expensive option shows by far the highest discounted cashflow.

Blyth is also convinced that the key to building shareholder value lies simply in giving investors pleasant surprises. Between 1994 and 1997, Blyth returned £1.7 billion to shareholders and said, 'If we don't have a sensible use for the money, we should return it to the shareholders. They can use it better than we can.' Boots has outperformed all its retailer peers in total shareholder value in this period and in most cases dramatically so – this includes Marks & Spencer, Kingfisher, WH Smith, and Sainsbury. This has included the proceeds from the sales of Boots Pharmaceutical to BASF in 1995, the sales of the Children's World retail venture to Storehouse in 1996 and property disposals of £100 million in 1997.

'If we don't have a sensible use for the money, we should return it to the shareholders. They can use it better than we can'

Returns to shareholders are important for numerous reasons. At the end of 1998, Blyth declared slightly lower profits for the group and a loss after write-offs, yet saw share value soar 82p on the day to 948p.

Vision and renewal

While Lord Blyth has overseen a damaging and unproductive strategy – the Ward White foray – he has also been instrumental in subsequently rebuilding Boots around its key competencies and capabilities and building a new vision of how to position and develop the business. This new vision has a number of critical elements. It is also vital for the future. By the end of 1998, Boots had reached the point where new store openings were 'cannibalizing' sales of existing stores at significant levels. The search is for growth from the brand in new areas, but without the trauma of further attempts at diversification.

Levering the customer relationship

In mid-1997, Boots the Chemists announced the launch of its Advantage loyalty card. Similar in concept to the supermarket loyalty schemes, the Boots card promised to be four times more generous – a point for every 25p spent redeemable against everything except medical prescriptions and gift vouchers – and was expected to lift sales by 4 per cent. This was a £52 million investment.

The card was aimed mainly at female Boots shoppers (who make up two-thirds of the customer base) with most of the free offers available on women's products. One of the first outcomes, for example, was the launch of a Boots catalogue for 'mothers and babies'. One potential benefit is direct contact with customers, for example, to jog someone's memory about when they should get a new toothbrush or pointing out special offers on their favourite dental products.

At one level, the card was important to defending Boots pharmacy sales against the supermarkets who are developing in this field. However, the underlying significance of the scheme lies in the information collected through the card system – Boots cards contain a microchip instead of a magnetic stripe. Unlike the conventional magnetic strip card, the microchip card allows instant collection and redemption of points against purchases. Boots outsourced the loyalty scheme operations to AT&T.

In particular, the Boots' customer database tracks customers' medical prescriptions as well as over-the-counter purchases in the focused area of health and personal care. For example, there are possibilities for the microchip card to include the consumer's medical records and drug purchase records by combining the Advantage card with the existing 14 million Medilink cards, which already hold that information. The card may also be converted to a debit or credit card.

The card scheme was more expensive than expected, but was judged by the company to be profitable after the first nine months of operation. By the end of 1998, three and a half million cards had been issued, 20 per cent of sales were linked to the card, and Boots had thirty analysts working on the card data in its marketing department.

'The first impact of the customer relationship leverage is in Boots' "look good, feel good" strategy in its core personal care business'

Health and personal care

The first impact of the customer relationship leverage is in Boots' 'look good, feel good' strategy in its core personal care business. Given the customer relationship, the information resources from the card and its traditional competencies in this area, Boots is transforming into a healthcare business. The signs of this are many:

- *'Positive staffing'* – consumer concerns and interests are leading to the introduction of healthcare specialists to stores, to advise customers, focusing on people's growing interests in 'well-being, self-esteem and healthy living'. A company spokeperson says, 'It's our territory'. Possibilities include skin and haircare specialists and aromatherapy centres, depending on customer reactions. For example, January 1999 saw the announcement of the recruitment of 100 staff to train as specialized consultants in preparation for the launch in February of three ranges of French skincare products, positioned to bridge the gap between medicinal and cosmetic products.
- *Medical and dentistry services* – in 1998 Boots paved the way for 'Boots the Dentist' by paying £250 000 for Wilson's Dentistry in Birmingham. Wilson has the necessary 'dental body corporate' licence allowing Boots to practise dentistry and open new practices. Boots is looking at a £10 million spend to trial six dental practices in-store as Boots Dental Care. Emphasis will be on preventative and cosmetic dentistry. Also in 1998, Boots announced it would open drop-in doctor's surgeries in co-operation with Sinclair Montrose. The availability of treatment and advice from qualified nurses in-store is also possible.
- *Health insurance* – in 1997 Boots was planning a move into offering private medical insurance, sold under its own name but underwritten by an insurance company partner. It also provides a dental cover insurance plan. The launch of its first insurance products in 1998 was a portfolio of health and travel plans, sold over the counter with the till receipt acting as the cover note.
- *Nursing homes* – Boots has also been looking at the nursing home market in talks with Westminster Healthcare about a joint venture. Boots nursing homes would provide specialist treatment for allergy sufferers, those recovering from operations and the elderly.

A City analyst comments on these moves: 'Boots has a brand name synonymous with healthcare and this is a natural extension. It makes perfect sense and will be welcomed by the market.' Even the slightly disappointing sales figures after Christmas 1998 saw strong results in healthcare compared to weaker performance in leisure products and giftware.

'Boots has a brand name synonymous with healthcare and this is a natural extension'

Globalizing the healthcare business

Major emphasis has also been placed on Boots Healthcare International, the over-the-counter (OTC) business set up to market Boots' own-brand products such as Strepsils and Nurofen. Heavy marketing spends have kept profits low, but margins of 20 per cent on mature OTC products are attractive. A programme of acquisitions culminated in 1997 with the purchase of Hermal, the German skincare products group, for £174 million. In a European market dominated by independent pharmacies (most countries ban multiple ownership), Hermal brings a salesforce with strong links to independent retail outlets, who can sell the Boots skincare ranges from the UK and France.

There have also been major moves to internationalize the retail operation. Regulatory restrictions on the ownership of pharmacies rule out expansion into most of Europe (except Holland). 1997 saw the opening of Boots stores in Rotterdam offering Boots' products but also local and international brands. (Boots has learned from its experiences in Canada in the 1980s when it opened British shops with no local concessions and had to close them down because of losses.) Then in 1998, plans unfolded for forty pharmacy stores in Thailand, following a year's operation of six pilot health-and-beauty format stores. The same year saw the formation of a joint venture with Mitsubishi Corporation to open a chain of stores in Japan. The goal in Japan is to position in the health and beauty market in the gap between the expensive department stores and the budget outlets. Closer to home, the retail business has also acquired Connors Pharmacy Chain in Northern Ireland and Hayes, Conygham and Robinson in the Republic of Ireland, gaining market leadership in the whole country.

Even in the hard trading conditions of 1998, BHI doubled its profit contribution and increased sales by over a quarter compared to 1997.

The moral of the story?

Boots' performance during the 1990s has been characterized by three issues: the *'vanity'* of becoming a general household trader through the disastrous Ward White acquisition driven by conventional portfolio thinking; the rediscovery of *value* for shareholders as the driving force for management and a remarkable level of achievement in return to shareholders; and the development of a *vision* for the future of a global healthcare business in manufacturing, retailing and services.

None the less, the company's underlying resilience is underlined by the company's share performance shown in Figure 15.1.

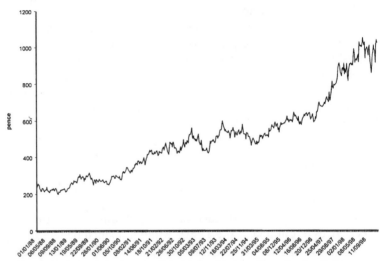

Figure 15.1 Boot's share value, 1988–98 (unadjusted prices). Source: Datastream

'the trick of managers such as Lord Blyth and companies such as Boots is to learn, recover and rebuild to evolve'

If there is a moral from this story it must be that everyone makes mistakes – sometimes big ones – but the trick of managers such as Lord Blyth and companies such as Boots is to learn, recover and rebuild to evolve and implement more robust strategies and to deliver superior shareholder value. Richard Perks of the Verdict consultancy concluded in 1998:

> Over the last 10 years the improvement of this business has been staggering. Slowly and surely it's worked its way out of the fringe businesses to concentrate on health and beauty. If there is a serious downturn, Boots is pretty resilient.

Sources

Brown-Humes, Christopher (1998), 'Boots Sells DIY Chain for £68m', *Financial Times*, 20 August.

Cunliffe, Peter (1998), 'Healthy Glow At Boots In Spite of High Street Chill', *Daily Mail*, 6 November.

Day, Timon (1998), 'Boots' Loyalty Card Is the Right Prescription', *Daily Mail*, 5 June.

Fletcher, Richard (1998), 'Boots gets Set To Trot Out Excuses', *Sunday Business*, 1 November.

Hindell, Juliet (1998), 'Boots targets Tokyo In Tie-Up With Mitsubishi', *Daily Telegraph*, 29 July.

Hollinger, Peggy (1997), 'Boots Sells Decorating Group for Nominal Amount', *Financial Times*, 28 August.

Hollinger, Peggy (1997), 'Slow Waking From A Nightmare', *Financial Times*, 29 August.

Jackson, Tony, 'Registering the Value of Cash', Financial Times, January 19 1998.

Hollinger, Peggy and William Barnes (1998), 'Boots To Launch £9m Expansion in the Far East', *Financial Times*, 14 May.

Hollinger, Peggy and Graham Bowley (1997), 'Boots Expands Into Germany', *Financial Times*, 11 September.

Osborne, Alistair (1998), 'Boots Counts the Cost of DIY Venture', *Daily Telegraph*, 20 August.

Osborne, Alistair (1998), 'Boots To Drill Into the Dentistry Market', *Daily Telegraph*, 9 September.

Parsley, David (1997), 'Boots Glows From Sales of Property', *Sunday Times*, 2 November.

Potter, Ben (1998), 'These Boots Were made For Buying', *Daily Telegraph*, 6 November.

Pratley, Nils (1998), 'Boots looks To Health As Advantage Pays Off', *Daily Telegraph*, 7 November.

Pratley, Nils (1998), 'Check-Up Finds Boots In Best of Health', *Daily Telegraph*, 7 November.

Rankine, Kate (1998), 'Boots Chairman Ready To Toast Christmas', *Daily Telegraph*, 6 November.

Spero, Rosanna (1998), 'Now Boots Is Selling Insurance', *Daily Mail*, 25 March.

Taylor, Roger (1998), 'Boots Pays £18m To Buy Pharmacies in N Ireland', *Financial Times*, 8 April.

Wall, Matthew (1997), 'Boots To Offer Health Cover', *Sunday Times*, 1 June.

Wright, Robert (1998), 'Boots Beats Expectations and Dispels Card Doubts', *Financial Times*, 6 June.

CHAPTER 16

WH Smith and John Menzies*

Revolution and renewal on the high street

'These are old-established firms whose market has crumbled underneath them'

'resilient companies with differentiated capabilities can survive and rebuild after near catastrophe'

A quiet revolution has taken place on the British high street in the 1990s, and a process of company and brand renewal. It has involved the way in which people buy their newspapers, cigarettes, books and music. It is the story of WH Smith (WHS) and John Menzies. These are old-established firms whose market has crumbled underneath them in the revolution in the distribution channels for their traditional products. They have pursued different approaches to renewal. Their example instructs us that resilient companies with differentiated capabilities can survive and rebuild after near catastrophe.

---

* This material has been compiled by Niall C. Piercy and Nigel F. Piercy, Cardiff Business School, Cardiff University from secondary sources and interviews with managers and employees in the companies discussed. © Nigel F. Piercy, 1999.

The 'CTN' marketplace

The CTN marketplace (confectionery, tobacco and news) was for generations a stable and static sector, with channels fragmented into many small independent retailers, some national or regional chains of small outlets and the dominant large national players: WHS and Menzies (WHS strong in the south and Menzies stronger in the north and Scotland). While maintaining many small outlets for many years, WHS and to a lesser extent Menzies developed larger outlets on British high street by selling a range of products such as books and music, videos and stationery. The underlying model was one of selling convenience products through an extensive distribution network to locate the products close to the consumers: on high streets, in local convenience stores and at railway stations, bus stations and airports.

'The underlying model was one of selling convenience products through an extensive distribution network'

The history and present position of WH Smith

Henry Walton Smith and his wife Anna opened a tiny retail newsagents shop in Mayfair, London in 1792, and after their deaths the business passed to their sons Henry Edward and William Henry in 1816. They moved the business first to Duke Street and then to 192 The Strand: an association commemorated in the name of WHS head office, Strand House.

When Henry Edward retired in 1826, the business changed from H & W Smith to WH Smith. William Henry exploited the growth of newspaper publishing in London's nearby Fleet Street to build his business as a newspaper distributor, using a fleet of small horse-drawn carts to collect daily newspapers from Fleet Street and then distribute them to stagecoach collection points. The effect was to get newspapers to readers twelve hours earlier than traditional overnight mail coach delivery. In 1830, WH Smith chartered a special boat to get the news of the death of King George IV to Dublin a day before the King's Messenger.

The business became known as WH Smith & Son, with the involvement of his son, also named William Henry. William Henry Junior was responsible for promoting the first WH Smith railway bookstall in 1848 at Euston station in London. The expansion of the railway bookstalls was huge: at one point in

1901 WHS operated more than 1200, some of which became wholesale distribution points at railway stations for local retail newsagents. In 1888, the novelist Henry James wrote about: 'The fine flare of Mr WH Smith's bookstalls – a feature not to be omitted in any enumeration of the charms of Paddington and Euston ... A glamour hangs over the glittering booth, and a tantalising air of clever new things' (Henry James, *Essay of London*, 1888). WHS even offered rail travellers a lending service, so the passenger could borrow a book at the start of the journey and return it at the end.

In the early 1900s, the company chose to avoid the high rents of railway station sites and to open shops on the approaches to stations, and by 1906 had 150 such WH Smith bookshops. The pruning of the British railway system drastically reduced the number of bookstalls – by the 1990s WHS had only eighty railway and airport bookstalls, but more than 400 shops in town and city centres. The merchandise range expanded at the same time from newspapers and magazines to books, music and stationery, although in the 1980s the company took the then controversial decision not to continue selling tobacco products.

Recent decades have seen WHS involved in the Our Price music and video stores, Waterstone's bookshops, Paperchase and the Do-It-All home maintenance and decorating retailers (owned jointly with Boots). In the 1990s, WHS employment peaked at around 30 000 people in the UK. Until 1964, WHS traded as a private partnership, floating on the stock market only in that year.

For seven generations of shoppers, WHS was a national institution – the natural destination for the purchase of newspapers, magazines, the latest best-selling books, Mother's Day cards and fountain pens.

'For seven generations of shoppers, WHS was a national institution'

WHS was so powerful as a bookseller, it could make best-sellers or condemn books to obscurity by its stocking decisions. It could dictate the design of book covers on the basis of merchandising requirements. It could dictate what was fit to be sold – for years refusing to distribute or display the satirical magazine *Private Eye*. With some prescience the *Eye* nicknamed WHS 'WH Smug'.

'With some prescience the Eye *nicknamed WHS "WH Smug"'*

However, by the 1990s the company had hit some major problems, which are reflected in its share price, shown in Figure 16.1, with major downturns in 1995 and 1997.

The company's performance problems in the mid-1990s are reflected in its financials, shown in Table 16.1.

Figure 16.1 WH Smith's share value, 1990–98 (unadjusted prices).
Source: Datastream

Table 16.1 WH Smith key financials, 1994–98

	1994	1995	1996	1997	1998 (15 months to August)
Turnover (£ million)	2423	2689	2828	2763	3456
Pre-tax profit (loss) (£ million)	83	101	(194)	60	251
Earnings per share (p)	19.90	23.30	(71.40)	8.60	77.00
Dividends per share (p)	19.40	15.70	15.70	15.70	20.75
Market capitalization (£ million)	1327	984	1287	1190	1169

The history and present position of the John Menzies Group

Menzies comes from somewhat different origins to WHS, but it is also a long-established business. John Menzies was born in Edinburgh in 1808. The Edinburgh of this time had as many as ninety-three booksellers to serve a population of 130 000, in spite of widespread illiteracy and poverty. At this time, booksellers actually published many of the books they sold, acting as a broker between author and printer.

Menzies was apprenticed to a bookseller when he left school and on completion of his apprenticeship went to work for a bookseller in Fleet Street, London. On the death of his father in 1833, Menzies returned north to establish a business of his own. He opened a bookstore on Princes Street, Edinburgh, and shortly afterwards became agent for the publishers Chapman & Hall, providing him with the rights to sell Charles Dickens' works in the east of Scotland. The retail shop added products such as inks, pens, magazines, account books and office equipment. He also developed wholesale activities, for example acting as Scottish agent for the new *Punch* magazine. He also started selling the *Scotsman* newspaper, which had previously been available only on subscription from the publisher, and published monthly book lists for book retailers.

The 1840s and 1850s was the era when long-distance railway services began to span the UK. Railway bookstalls were 'invented' by Horace Marshall in London (whose firm was later *'the name of* acquired by Menzies), but the name of Menzies became *Menzies became* synonymous with railway bookstalls in Scotland. By *synonymous with* 1857 Menzies had sole rights on all rail services in *railway bookstalls* northeast Scotland, as well as on the first train-ferry in *in Scotland'* the world. Another development was 'basket boys' with trays strapped to their shoulders, who sold to passengers on trains stopping only briefly at a station, and who worked on the Clyde ferry steamers, until bookstalls were established on them. Over time, managers were allowed to choose their own stock from Menzies' wholesale catalogue, including tourist guides and the famous 'yellow-back' novels (cheap editions of books produced specially for travellers).

As duties on newspapers were abolished, cheap daily newspapers began to appear on bookstalls – notably the *Daily Mail* and the *Daily Express*. The proprietors of these newspapers needed agents throughout the country, who would receive newspapers in bundles, split them up and distribute them quickly to small newsagents, who might be located hundreds of miles from the wholesaler. From an early stage, Menzies took a dominant position in the newspaper distribution trade in Scotland.

Menzies incorporated his business in 1867, celebrated by opening a branch in Glasgow, to trade as John Menzies & Co, Edinburgh and Glasgow. He died in 1879, to be succeeded by John Ross Menzies and after his brother's death by Charles Thompson Menzies. The family involvement has continued until recent times growing the business into a public company registered in Scotland, operating as one of the two leading UK wholesalers of newspapers, magazines, books, video and audio products and commercial stationery products, and a retail division with over 200 John Menzies outlets and 200 Early Learning Centres. The founder's great-grandson retired as chairman in 1997 after forty-six years in the business and remains as life president of the company.

The company remains proudly Scottish – right down to the tartan carpet in its store design – and more than half the 232 unit retail chain is located in Scotland. The position of the Scottish business was protected against the intrusion of WH Smith from the south by heavy press and television advertising, which Menzies does not do in England and Wales.

'The company remains proudly Scottish – right down to the tartan carpet in its store design'

However, by the 1990s all was not well at Menzies. The later 1990s in particular showed a steady erosion in the share price,

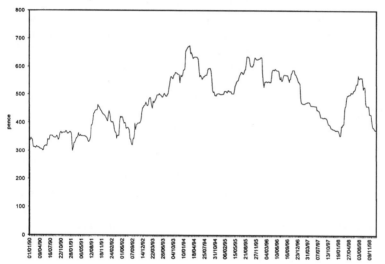

Figure 16.2 Menzies' share value, 1990–98 (unadjusted prices).
Source: Datastream

Table 16.2 Menzies group key financials, 1994–98

	1994	1995	1996	1997	1998
Turnover (£ million)	1231.6	1258.0	1413.4	1417.4	1543.0
Pre-tax profit (£ million)	34.1	38.1	35.9	30.6	34.0
Earnings per share (p)	40.7	44.6	40.1	33.6	40.0
Dividends per share (p)	11.8	13.2	13.8	13.8	15.2

shown in Figure 16.2, with unexpected profit warnings in 1995 and 1996.

The lacklustre profit performance of the late 1990s is seen in the key financial results shown in Table 16.2.

WH Smith – the shop that time forgot

The crisis of 1995

The position in which WHS found itself in the 1995–97 period underlines the impact of fundamental changes in the traditional marketplace, which it shared with Menzies. It was at this time that the strong, traditional – and somewhat introverted, some would say, smug – culture of WHS, linked to the Smith family dynasty began to be seen as negative and outdated. Many judged that WHS had simply failed to keep up with the changes in its core marketplace – it was simply left behind by the changing consumer. One commentator at the time noted that WHS senior managers, 'exuded the beaming self-confidence of those who believe that their market position is unassailable'.

'WHS senior managers, "exuded the beaming self-confidence of those who believe that their market position is unassailable"'

'the company's historical strength and its own culture blinded it to competitive encroachments'

It seemed inconceivable that a company with around £3 billion turnover, 10 million customers a week and dominant market shares in its core business (see Table 16.3) could lose its way, but as its commercial position deteriorated, the company seemed to lack the flair or imagination to recover. If anything the company's historical strength and its own culture blinded it to competitive encroachments.

None the less, by mid-1995 WHS had become so weak that predators were circling with hostile take-over bids in mind. In May 1995, a profits warning drove a 15 per cent fall in share value, taking £180 million off WHS' market value, and the full-year results for 1996 ended a 203-year run of profitability. Sir Malcolm Field, WHS CEO blamed the poor results on weak market conditions with fewer shoppers on the high street and a shift in demand away from high margin products such as magazines, but he had to admit also that sales of newspapers, stationery, cards and videos were also coming under pressure. The crisis was not helped by John Menzies announcing on the same day that it was experiencing the same

Table 16.3 WHS market shares in UK core businesses in 1995

	Books	Music	Video	Stationery
Total market	£1.7 bn	£1.2 bn	£500 mn	£520 mn
WH Smith: total share	23%	31%	28%	17%
	(Waterstone's 9%, WHS Retail, 14%)	(Virgin Megastores 6%, WHS Retail 7%, Our Price 18%)	(Our Price 3%, Playhouse 4%, Virgin Megastores 5%, WHS Retail 16%)	(all WHS Retail)

factors, but its sales and profits were holding up (this turned out to be tempting fate, as we will see below).

The WHS revival programme of 1995 – Project Enliven – was a collection of new department openings (e.g. multimedia and children's departments), new store designs and promotions for the WHS retail chain, with a new logo and staff uniforms.

The strategic floundering of the 1980s and 1990s

The first sign of WHS' problems began in the 1980s, when imaginative new-style specialist retailers had come into the market, for example, Tim Waterstone building up his specialist bookstores chain and Richard Branson establishing retail outlets as home entertainment centres, offering everything from computer games to huge ranges of music and videos as Virgin Megastores.

On the other side of the market, the powerful large supermarkets had moved into selling newspapers, books and videos – in high volume and often at discounted prices (even on books with the end of the restrictions of the Net Book Agreement). Much of the newspaper retail business had also passed from the high street to the local convenience store and petrol station. The specialist retailers offered superiority in choice, while the supermarkets offered convenience and low prices. In the process, WHS had lost its status as a 'destination store'. High consumer traffic continued to pass through WHS retail outlets, but one mid-1990s' survey suggested that 38 per cent of them bought nothing and average purchase size was plummeting.

'WHS had lost its status as a "destination store"'

Even before the crisis of 1995, Field and his top management team had been aware of the need to find new sources of profit beyond their two core businesses – news distribution and the WHS retail chain. The 1980s saw WHS spend several hundred million pounds on unsuccessful and unrelated diversifications. The group launched travel shops, moved into satellite television and tried to build a stationery business called Paperchase. These all failed and led to a £148 million rights issue in 1991.

The biggest catastrophe had been a joint venture with Boots in the do-it-yourself chain Do-It-All. By 1996, the losses of this business had reached the point where WHS paid Boots £50 million to buy its way out of the joint venture.

Two investments remained with WHS at this point: the music retailer Our Price, acquired from its founder Gary Nesbitt for £48 million in 1986 and Waterstone's, the bookstore chain built by Tim Waterstone bought for £45 million in 1989, offering book buyers wider choice in more elegant surroundings than WH Smith shops. However, neither founder had stayed with WHS for long. Nesbitt left to work with Kingfisher to launch MVC, a discount music and video store in competition with Our Price. Waterstone became an adviser to Thorn EMI in its acquisition of Dillons, a specialist bookstore chain in competition with Water-stones, and was to play an even more dramatic role in WHS' history later.

None the less, the Waterstone's chain was performing well, although Our Price moved into losses in 1993, when Virgin management was brought in to rescue the business. WHS had spent £23 million in 1988 to acquire sixty-seven of Virgin's small stores and had bought half the Virgin Megastores in 1991, and then looked to Virgin for a joint venture. Virgin Our Price became 75 per cent owned by WHS but was run by Simon Burke from Virgin. However, the growth of both these businesses has been partly by cannibalizing trade from the core WH Smith retail stores.

In addition, WHS had acquired newstand concessions in US airports and hotels which were paying off.

New leadership

As the search for a new role became more urgent, in January 1996, WHS appointed Bill Cockburn, former head of the Post Office as CEO, succeeding thirty-three-year WHS veteran, Sir Malcolm Field. Described by a former colleague as 'a human tank', Cockburn launched a comprehensive strategic review and found 'rotten margins, too much stock and customer service that is not good enough; apart from that it's really terrific.' He also discovered that WHS sold ten types of elastic band and dealt with fifty different suppliers of Christmas wrapping paper.

'rotten margins, too much stock and customer service that is not good enough; apart from that it's really terrific'

Cockburn took 14 000 product lines out of the WHS retail operation and 1000 jobs, including those of many long-serving WHS managers. The last active member of the Smith family was one of several directors to leave the board.

Cockburn bought WHS out of the loss-making Do-It-All chain and sold peripheral companies, including Business Supplies and Paperchase. Restructuring contributed much to the 1996 £194 million loss.

He was also responsible for focusing the business into six divisions: WH Smith Retail; Virgin Our Price; Waterstones, WH Smith USA; WH Smith News; and The Wall (a US music chain). This grouping made it clearer that the real problem was the retail business, which still lacked a clear customer proposition. Beverley Dobson was recruited from Sears as a retail specialist to try to revive the stores.

Jeremy Hardie, chairman of WHS, claimed, 'People go to WH Smith because they like a middle-of-the-road store where you can buy music, books, videos, magazines and stationery. They like the fact that it is a variety store. They are not Dillons customers or Tesco customers.' Meanwhile average purchase in the stores continued to shrink.

'Meanwhile average purchase in the stores continued to shrink'

After only eighteen months, Cockburn left WHS, in June 1997, to join British Telecom. A search for a replacement dragged on, leaving chairman Jeremy Hardie to present the year's results to stockholders with no CEO in position. Those results included wafer-thin growth of only 1.5 per cent in the core retail business. With no CEO, reports from the company were of plummeting morale and in-fighting among internal candidates for the job. After a damaging four-month gap, in October 1997, the CEO job went to Richard Handover, head of the newspaper distribution operation.

New ownership?

In the absence of any clear strategy at WHS to rebuild its core business and growing conviction that the retail format was obsolete, investor pressure led to talks starting about the possibilities of breaking up the group – splitting off the newspaper distribution division, selling Waterstones back to Tim Waterstone

'the absence of any clear strategy at WHS to rebuild its core business and growing conviction that the retail format was obsolete'

Table 16.4 WHS 1996 performance and break-up values

	WHS Retail	WHS News	US Retail	Waterstones	Virgin Our Price	Total
Turnover (£ million)	927	895	249	169	444	2684
Operating profit (£ million)	48	28	11	13	16	116
Estimated break-up value (£ million)	277–390	415–530	124–175	275–280	104–165	1.3–1.5 bn
Comments	Low growth and falling profitability	Steady wholesale business	Good growth potential	The 'jewel in the crown' with a premium rating and profit growth	Struggling in tough music market conditions	

Source: *Financial Times*, 19 August 1997.

and selling Virgin Our Price to Richard Branson. Analysts calculated that breaking up the group would unlock substantial value – valuing the separate parts at £1.5 billion compared to the current market value of £1.1 billion (see Table 16.4).

The constraint on break up was that there were no likely takers for the rump of the business – the WH Smith retail stores. Of 1996 group operating profits of £116 million, the Waterstones and Virgin Our Price operations contributed £30 million and Waterstone's profit grew 33 per cent by 1997. The WHS board also discussed the possibility of closing the retail business. In August 1997, WHS dismissed rumours of an imminent break-up.

WHS was also increasingly talked of as a take-over target – rumoured potential buyers included Boots, Dixons, Kingfisher and Asda, the supermarket chain. In July 1997, WHS and its financial advisers were on full 'bid alert'.

The problems at John Menzies

Although the crisis came slightly later, the impact of an introverted and traditional culture in the midst of competitive and cultural change caught up with John Menzies by 1997. The Menzies retail operation in particular was looking dated and cumbersome.

'The Menzies retail operation in particular was looking dated and cumbersome'

The signs of obsolescence

Major problems existed at John Menzies at every level of the retail operation, from lack of training of shop floor personnel to confused senior management.

Menzies' director of operations was a man who had worked his way up through the company, starting out as a store manager. While this gave him insight into front-line operations, by the 1990s this experience was about twenty years out of date, in a marketplace that had changed dramatically. Senior management throughout the company had little formal business training, although attempts were made in 1996 to remedy this by sponsoring head office staff on MBA programmes. This was, however, only available in Scotland and then only to a small number of staff.

Across the company there were problems of co-ordination between shop floor employees and head office. The company was run by dictatorial weekly updates from the Scottish head

'The company was run by dictatorial weekly updates from the Scottish head office to shops covering all areas of operations'

office to shops covering all areas of operations. The main interaction between managers and store employees was in formal visits, primarily by area managers (every couple of months) and senior head office personnel such as directors (once every couple of years). This proved to be inadequate to gain any useful, consistent picture of front-line operations or to try to adopt policy to suit changing situations. The problem of infrequent head office visits (not helped by the remoteness of head office in Scotland) was compounded by the fact that visits were always announced long in advance, enabling problems to be concealed and an unrealistically positive picture of shop floor operations to be painted. This artificial view prevented any real insight being gained from these store visits.

Menzies stores operated around a yearly plan, trying to focus sales on peak times to make up for shortcomings the rest of the year. These sales peaks are Christmas and the January sale (all shop areas); Valentine's Day (cards and chocolates); Easter (chocolate eggs); summer/autumn Back to School (stationery); Halloween and Bonfire Night (fireworks); and, Mother's and Father's Day (cards, chocolates and gifts).

These sales focuses have two-month build-up periods. For example, Valentine's Day cards for 14 February were first put on sale on Christmas Eve as Christmas stock was sold through, while Back to School stock first appears at the end of term before the long summer break in June. All these focuses were backed by reductions on normal prices and wide-scale promotions such as 'three for the price of two' on key lines. However, success was very varied, with wildly inaccurate sales predictions leading to poor buying decisions and severe overstocking and under-stocking problems. For example, in 1998 the Back to School core products (pads and folders) sold 40 per cent less than forecast leading to huge overstocking, while sales of product ranges based on the popular 'Friends' television series were nearly 300 per cent greater than expected company-wide. The creaking supply chain also led to stock problems with promotions, where stock often arrived in the stores long after the promotion had started.

'success was very varied, with wildly inaccurate sales predictions leading to poor buying decisions and severe overstocking and understocking problems'

Stocking failures also surrounded the 'crazes' which lead to high demand for certain products and which are typical of this market. For example, with the release of videos such as *Titanic*, *The Full Monty*, the re-release of the *Star Wars Trilogy* and *Pride and Prejudice*, and the merchandise associated with them, in most cases there was a huge shortage of supply in Menzies stores – customers asking for the products for weeks and stock not arriving till after the 'craze' had finished. The results were dissatisfied customers and huge over-stocking of lines that were no longer in demand. Such problems were not helped by an inefficient and outdated store computer system. Stock inefficiencies also led to high wastage in merchandising support materials for stores. In 1997, Menzies' central administration costs were £10 million compared to a profit in retailing of less than £5 million.

Other idiosyncrasies existed in the product range. For example, all Menzies stores (wherever located) carry a large selection of Scottish maps, with many different styles and sizes of maps for Glasgow and Edinburgh, while these same stores carry only a limited range of maps of local cities and other places of interest.

The location and size of Menzies stores was also problematic. In cities with both Menzies and WH Smith shops on the high street, size and turnover of WH Smith stores is typically many times greater. In addition, the appearance of many Menzies stores had become very outdated. Many older stores (10–20 years old) had never been refitted since their openings, retaining old-fashioned cream and orange fixings and a muddy-brown carpet, often with shelves rusty and bent out of shape from constant mishandling. In contrast the modern Menzies stores (those built within the last two years) are very attractive and share WH Smith's preference for black fittings, darkened ceilings and mock wooden polished floorings.

Further inefficiencies came from the division of the Menzies retail chain into the high street stores and what are known as 'travel point' shops, which are found in railway stations and hospitals. When he became retail managing director in 1997, Steve Robinson was astonished to find that these two separate divisions, which were for all intents and purposes identical (same store layout, same product ranges, same suppliers and deliveries) had separate area managers.

Through the 1990s, retail store sales performance weakened, and by 1997 some stores were experiencing up to a 40 per cent fall in turnover week on week. Over the 1997 to 1998 Christmas period all stores nation-wide were given an ultimatum that if they failed to achieve a 4 per cent increase over the same period the previous year then they would be closed. Most failed to achieve this target, even though in real terms it only meant sustaining sales at the same level. No direct action was taken as a result of this.

'Through the 1990s, retail store sales performance weakened'

The attempts to 'modernize' Menzies

Menzies made numerous attempts to modernize the retail business and its management, for instance sending supervisors on highly unpopular team-building exercises. Supervisors were renamed team leaders, in the hope that 'teams' would enhance productivity.

In 1996 a new internal campaign started to increase customer focus. This was centred around the concept of 'The Customer is Queen'. This was backed-up by a campaign calling for each staff member to 'Be a Roman' (this meant that staff should act like Romans because Romans built straight roads letting nothing get in their way, because they had a 'can do' mentality). This campaign too did little to improve falling morale in the business. Shop staff were also issued with bright red badges proclaiming 'I am here to help you', a message regarded by many customers as lacking credibility or value.

In 1995, Menzies, in a further attempt to win customers back to the stores, launched its loyalty card – the 'Smart Card' – in conjunction with Shell. It was the first card of its kind seen on the high street. At the outset customers collected about 1.5 points for every pound spent over £20 and 1 point per pound for everything over £50. Redemption was set at fourteen per pound. This meant if a customer spent £20 she or he got a pound back on the next shopping trip. Unfortunately for Menzies, while Shell carried out extensive promotion of the card, little mention was made of its association with Menzies.

The 'Smart Card' never worked to Menzies' advantage. As well as a lack of advertising, the idea itself was fundamentally flawed from the outset – low average customer spend and no value for Menzies in the customer data collected. This was compounded by customers who travelled a great deal and used a lot of petrol, spent money in Shell garages and came to Menzies stores to get free goods. Menzies bore the loss as there was no way of tracking where points had been awarded. Throughout the following two years, changes were made to collection rates, lowering the minimum spend to £5 whilst keeping the award rates the same.

In 1998 the 'Smart Card' was quietly relaunched, awarding one point for every pound spent over £2, whilst redemption moved all the way up to 100 points to get a pound. This brought the Smart Card a little closer in line with the WH Smith Clubcard.

Critics suggest that Menzies spent several years ignoring the underlying reasons for its decline – increased competition from specialists and supermarkets and massive supply chain inefficiencies –

'Critics suggest that Menzies spent several years ignoring the underlying reasons for its decline'

instead picking out aspects of successful companies and blindly imitating them (for example loyalty cards from supermarkets and customer focus campaigns from companies like the Disney Store).

While, similar to WHS, Menzies thought of the business as a mini-department store, vying for customers who did not go to specialist stores (e.g. Waterstones or Blackwell for books, Virgin or HMV for music). The result was that it carried a small stock of many items, but nothing stocked in depth to offer customer choice. Customers viewed Menzies as a big newsagent (a place to go to for the occasional purchase, not as a shop identified with any specific product line). Like WHS, Menzies has ceased to be a 'destination shop'. After all the campaigns, confectionery, news and tobacco lines with wafer-thin profit margins still accounted for 70 per cent of Menzies' retail turnover. The high street stores struggled to make a profit, while the travel point stores were prospering.

The end is in sight

In 1997, Menzies made further efforts to improve store layouts, refit older stores and centralize promotions for greater control. However, from the start of 1998 there were suspicions about the future of Menzies retail, as part of the wider group. David Mackay (the new group chief executive) had the company reclassified on the stock exchange as a distributor rather than a retailer. Menzies' first and flagship store in Princes Street, Edinburgh was closed at the start of the year.

The 1998 January sale at Menzies saw a huge sell off of stock with up to 80 per cent off prices of some lines, with most selling well below cost. Previously slow-moving lines had been stripped from shelves and managers issued with instructions to 'dispose of them any way they saw fit'.

On 7 March 1998, a statement was issued saying that there were 'no plans for any significant store closures or redundancies'. On 9 March 1998 the Menzies group announced the sale of its retail arm after 165 years of trading, because the group board could no longer see a future in pursuing a loss-making division.

'the Menzies group announced the sale of its retail arm after 165 years of trading'

Renewal at WH Smith

New WHS CEO, Richard Handover and chairman Jeremy Hardie faced an exceptionally hostile shareholders' meeting in October

1997. Unhappy employees were looking at the prospect of a 27 per cent pay cut the week after Christmas, the WHS distribution centre had been raided by police looking for illegal immigrant workers and shareholders were hungry for resignations. Handover declared his approach to be focused on three issues: setting a sound commercial strategy for the business; ensuring focus on the retail business; and creating value for the shareholders. His restructuring identified three core businesses: WH Smith Retail; WH Smith News; and the travel business.

'an unexpected bid for the company from Tim Waterstone, founder of the Waterstones bookstore chain'

Handover's move into the CEO role had been accompanied by another shock: an unexpected bid for the company from Tim Waterstone, founder of the Waterstones bookstore chain.

The Waterstone shock

Tim Waterstone had run the WHS US business in the 1970s, but was sacked by the company in 1981 after incurring heavy losses. He used his pay-off from WHS to establish the bookstores bearing his name, which he sold to WHS in 1989 for about £45 million (he later confessed WHS had paid too much).

Waterstone's bid was only technically a take-over (although interpreted as such by WHS). It was a 1980s' style leveraged bid. Waterstone's proposals were: 200p for each WHS share and shares in a new company, WH Smith Newco, raising up to £1 billion of debt to finance it; Waterstone's appointment as CEO; the acquisition of his new Daisy and Tom shop on the King's Road for £35 million; and the issue of warrants to the promoters of the bid (Waterstone and banker SBC Warburg Dillon Reid). Waterstone described this as a 'proposal to enhance shareholder value' not a take-over. His strategy would be to make the core news and book business concentrate on middle-market books and stationery; to expand the stock to include foreign newspapers and specialist magazines, but to remove the music and videos from the stores. This would reverse many of the company's cost-cutting policies, to carry ranges that the supermarkets could not equal. He planned to sell the US business and Virgin Our Price and move his children's retailer, Daisy and Tom, into some existing WHS sites.

The WHS board rejected the bid out of hand as 'opportunistic' and refused to meet Waterstone unless he changed his plans. Meanwhile, Waterstone pressed on with investor meetings. Institutional reactions were muted; there was some lack of enthusiasm for the level of debt and the inclusion of Daisy and

Tom's in the deal, but also pressure on WHS to adopt some of Waterstone's suggestions.

Waterstone's next step was to revise his plans reducing the debt incurred and revising the value of Daisy and Tom's to £9 million, as well as leaving Handover in the CEO position. This led to a meeting with WHS top management. Investor pressure on WHS management began to grow. At this point, the City Takeover Panel intervened, in what was becoming an increasingly bitter fight, requiring WHS to make Waterstone's proposals fully public and Waterstone not to make a full bid by going direct to WHS shareholders. The company rejected Waterstone's bid.

The WHS restructuring response

Following the shock of the Waterstone approach, Handover began to meet investors to put forward his own restructuring plans, in late October 1997, including the de-merger of the Waterstone's chain, the sale of Virgin Our Price and The Wall, and a share buyback to return cash to shareholders. His goal was to pare the operation back to activities carrying the WH Smith brand – the main WH Smith retail chain, WH Smith News and WH Smith International and Travel Retail. City fears emerged that the de-merger of Waterstone's would spark a massive sell-off by institutional investors (not wanting to hold shares in the less profitable rump of the business), and that there was still no strategy for turning around the retail business.

Doing the splits

- *The Wall* – early in November 1997, WHS agreed the sale of The Wall, its struggling US music business with 153 outlets in north-east USA, to Camelot Music for £28 million.
- *Waterstone* – Tim Waterstone emerged again as a bidder, in a deal with EMI and a joint venture partner. Interest was also shown by Barnes & Nobles and Borders from the USA, using a possible Waterstone's purchase to leverage entry into the UK. In February 1998, terms were agreed for sale of Waterstone to HMV Media for £300 million. HMV Media puts Waterstone into the same business as Dillons, its chief rival, and the HMV music stores, in a joint venture between EMI, the music group, and Advent International, the US venture capitalist. HMV Media is chaired by Tim Waterstone. In March WHS announced it would be handing back £150 million to shareholders from the sale.

- *Virgin Our Price* – the deal with Virgin gave WHS until summer 1999 to sell its 75 per cent stake in this business or buy Richard Branson's 25 per cent. In 1997, WHS rejected an offer of £135 million from Branson, and Branson reduced his offer to £105 million after the WHS restructuring plans were announced. However, by June 1998 the sale to Branson was agreed at a price of £140 million, taking the Virgin Megastores and Our Price outlets back into Virgin ownership.
- *The Family Treasure* – by November 1998, the urge to sell had even extended to the £3 million art collection built up in the 1970s and 1980s, through a series of auctions.

Strategic acquisitions

- *John Menzies Retail* – Bill Cockburn had agreed a price of £50–55 million for the Menzies retail chain with David Mackay in summer 1997. With Cockburn's departure, WHS did not go ahead. In January 1998, faced with the prospect of Menzies selling its retail arm to a third party, Richard Handover resumed negotiations with Menzies and agreed a price of £68 million for the 230-unit Menzies chain (and some freehold properties) in March 1998. The 140 Menzies outlets in England and Wales were to trade as WH Smith stores, while the Scottish outlets retain the Menzies brand under indefinite licence.

- *The Internet Bookshop* – in June 1998, WHS became the first mainstream UK retailer to take over an Internet shopping service with the purchase of bookshop.co.uk, operator of the Internet Bookshop (claiming to be Europe's largest Internet bookseller) and CD Paradise, for £9.4 million. The price was more than four times bookshop.co.uk's 1997 sales, and its losses were running at around £0.5 million a year. The acquisition is to be 'ring-fenced' and left in the hands of existing management. By January 1999, WHS was talking to investors about selling not just books, but music, videos and e-commerce services through this business.

'WHS became the first mainstream UK retailer to take over an Internet shopping service'

- *Helicon Publishing* – in January 1999, WHS acquired Helicon Publishing for £5.6 million to strengthen its new Internet venture. Helicon – with Microsoft as a 23 per cent shareholder – publishes consumer and educational reference books in print and electronic forms. Handover described this as an opportunity for the WHS Internet venture to publish own-brand material. Analysts speculated that Handover was planning to compete with Dixons as an Internet service provider, with encyclopedia reference sites provided by Helicon and a home shopping service.

The outcomes?

In July 1998, Handover announced a 15 per cent increase in profits with group sales growth of around 6 per cent to £2.1 billion: the high street retail stores achieved 6 per cent growth, overshadowed by 17 per cent growth in the UK travel-based outlets and a 47 per cent improvement in profits. Results in the US operation were disappointing.

The sales of non-WHS businesses and the forays into electronic commerce had driven WHS share price as high as 675p in January 1999, from its price of around 376p when Handover became CEO. However, early signs are that the integration of the WHS and Menzies retail operations is not proceeding smoothly, particularly in terms of integrating diverse supply sources and internal systems and processes.

Renewal at John Menzies

The sale of the Menzies retail newsagents chain to WHS signalled the new Menzies CEO David Mackay's intention to exit from retailing altogether after 165 years. The problematic Early Learning Centre chain was to go as well (though to be retained until it could be sold as a going concern), as well as the Smythsons stationers. This would allow the company to refocus on its successful operations in wholesaling and distribution, as well as developing interests in airport ground-handling services. Mackay's strategy review had led him to conclude, 'Ninety per cent of our profits are from distribution. It's two-thirds of our turnover. It's cash, it's profitable, it's non-seasonal and it offers real growth opportunities.'

> *'Ninety per cent of our profits are from distribution. It's two-thirds of our turnover. It's cash, it's profitable'*

Early successes in the refocused strategy were a three-year contract worth £4.5 million for cargo handling at Heathrow for SAS, the Scandinavian airline; a £3 million deal with Canadian airlines; a £13 million contract to run DHL's freight operations; and a joint-venture partnership arrangement with Lufthansa.

Year-end results in July 1998 pushed share price back up to its 1996 570p level from less than 400p in January 1998. Mackay announced at this time he was looking at spending £100 million on acquisitions – the first likely to be in the home delivery area. In December 1998, Mackay was looking at acquiring Servisair, his rival in airport ground handling.

Two steps forward, one step back . . .

Mid-year results announced in January 1999 saw successes in the transport business overshadowed by problems in the distribution business. THE Entertainment – the book, video and music distribution business – lost two major contracts: Boots and WH Smiths because of uncompetitive quotes and inefficiencies in stocking. These contracts were worth £40 million a year out of divisional turnover of £200 million. Mackay is spending £15 million to cut staffing, management and stocks. Other parts of the business were performing satisfactorily, even the Early Learning Centres looked likely to have reached break-even for the year as a result of massive sales of the 'Furby' electronic doll at Christmas 1998.

Sources

Hamilton, Kirstie (1998), 'Virgin and WH Smith Are Near Deal On Our Price', *Sunday Times*, 14 June.

Hollinger, Peggy (1997), 'WH Smith With Waterstone's Wood – Would it Be Good?', *Financial Times*, 15 October.

Hollinger, Peggy (1998), 'John Menzies To Pull Out of Retailing', *Financial Times*, 22 January.

O'Connor, Brian (1999), 'WH Smith Poised To Cash In On Net Shopping Frenzy', *Daily Mail*, 13 January.

Olins, Rufus (1995), 'Behind the Times', *Sunday Times*, 4 June.

Olins, Rufus (1997), 'WH Smith Stalls On The Road To Nowhere', *Sunday Times*, 31 August.

Olins, Rufus (1997), 'WH Smith Fights To Sell Its new Chapter to City', *Sunday Times*, 19 October.

Olins, Rufus (1998), 'WH Smith Sells Music Chain for £28m', *Sunday Times*, 2 November.

Osborne, Alistair (1999), 'Internet Fever Gives Boost To WH Smith Share Price', *Daily Telegraph*, 16 January.

Piercy, Niall (1998), 'Changing Times', unpublished working paper.

Potter, Ben (1998), 'Menzies Bows Out From Newsagents', *Daily Telegraph*, 1 January.

Price, Christopher (1997), 'Sums On Smith's Parts', *Financial Times*, 19 August.

Price, Christopher (1997), 'More Questions Than Answers at WH Smith', *Financial Times*, 25 August.

Vander Weyer, Martin (1997), 'The Shop That Time Forgot', *Daily Telegraph*, 30 August.

Voyle, Susannah (1998), 'John Menzies Plans £10m of Acquisitions', *Financial Times*, 8 July.

Voyle, Susannah (1999), 'WH Smith Acquires Helicon for £5.6m', *Financial Times*, 16/17 January.

Waples, John (1997), 'Smith's Shuns Waterstone Potion', *Sunday Times*, 5 October.

Wright, Robert (1998), 'Waterstone's, Dillons and HMV Bound In £800m Deal', *Financial Times*, 26 February.

Wright, Robert (1998), 'WH Smith Buys John Menzies' Retail Side', *Financial Times*, 10 March.

Wright, Robert (1998), 'WH Smith Takes Over Internet Bookshop for £8.8m', *Financial Times*, 9 June.

PART IV

Reflections on the Stories

CHAPTER 17

Commentaries

This is the part where I get to mouth off about what I think is most interesting and insightful in the tales and stories told here. It is here for two reasons.

If you are reading the book alone and your reaction to one of the stories is 'so what?', then the commentary here will let you know why the story was included and why I think it matters. Try reading the stories and then look at the commentary. Maybe your ideas about the significance of the events described will be better than mine,* but you won't know unless you try.

If you are using some of the material from the book in a training or education context, then the commentaries may be useful as a first cut at shaping discussion of the story or as feedback to people after a discussion.

British Airways

BA is a fascinating story of a major corporation that is in the midst of the revolution and reinvention that the rest of us face.

---

* In which case, please feel free to let me know by writing to me at Cardiff Business School (Cardiff, CF1 3EU) or send an e-mail to me at piercy@cardiff.ac.uk

'revolutionaries and reinventers may not win popularity polls'

The story underlines dramatically two facts: revolutionaries and reinventers may not win popularity polls, as Robert Ayling would probably agree, and certainly put their jobs on the line; and making it happen is not as easy as strategy textbooks say.

'making it happen is not as easy as strategy textbooks say'

First, can anyone answer me two questions? When was it that someone decided that the new rule of competition was that you have to tell your competitors what you are going to do before you do it, in case they don't like it? When was it we decided that the strategic response to competition was to roll over on your back and wave your legs in the air like a two-year-old in a temper tantrum, until nice Uncle Regulator comes along and says, 'There, there . . . I'll make that nasty old BA leave you alone'? I ask because

'The story of BA's strategy dramatically underlines the increasing reduction in strategic freedom'

that is sort of what the airline business in Europe is beginning to look like. The story of BA's strategy dramatically underlines the increasing reduction in strategic freedom that constrains strategic choice and the ability to execute strategy, as well as the growing role of regulator as arbiter of first choice. This is a very different competitive situation to the one assumed by most conventional strategy analysts.

The US and European airline industries are described as 'deregulated'. This is an interesting use of the word 'deregulated' which I have not previously encountered. It apparently means that every move you make will be scrutinized and challenged by the UK government, a rabid European commissioner, and the US transportation and justice departments.

The BA story raises some other questions as well, which may be interesting in all sectors, not just the airline business.

- What is the impact of transparency on the ability to make and implement strategic decisions?
- Does BA have a strategy that is internally consistent?
- Does BA have a value-driven strategy?
- What are the implementation barriers Ayling faces?

Transparency

'Will strategy in the new realities have to be made in a public forum?'

How different is competing going to be when your plans and strategies are leaked to the financial press before you can implement them and your competitors' knee-jerk reaction is to run straight to the regulator or court? If that court or regulator wishes it can demand complete and public disclosure of your plans and decisions. Compliance is not optional. Will strategy in the new realities have to be made in a public forum?

Strategic consistency

Since they are so public, we can ask some searching questions about the internal consistency of the strategy BA is following. If you tease out the major elements of the BA strategy they look something like this:

- *Vision* – the vision statement published is generic (it could describe the goals of just about any company). When Ayling talks about the company he tends to focus on cost cutting, and on the core operations network and alliance – maybe this is closer to his real vision?
- *Brand* – the re-branding has been a debacle. It raises questions about why you would want to change the British image if it is actually something the most **'the re-branding has been a debacle'** important customers, the alliance partners, the staff and the shareholders seem to like ('consumer research' notwithstanding). More importantly, look back to the comments about the move from brand and relationship focused strategy to value-based strategy. Is BA clinging to an outdated concept as the mainstay of its strategy? For example, will 'Oneworld' really impress customers, who know they are going to be dumped onto umpteen different airlines to reach a foreign destination, even though they bought a BA ticket? The question is whether the half-way house BA now occupies between the old brand and the new brand leaves it vulnerable, and without the support of customers or employees.
- *Globalization* – the company has no choice but to pursue globalization. The question remains: is the current brand and partnership path the best and only way to achieve this?
- *Alliance* – this is the chosen route to globalization. It is stalled by regulators. In fact, the price demanded by the regulators (the Heathrow slots) is probably unreasonable. On the AA strategy, BA now finds itself a hostage in the open skies negotiation between the USA and Europe, which is not the company's fault but which was predictable. The issue is whether the whole strategy now unravels because BA cannot have the foundation of the AA alliance **'The issue is whether the whole strategy now unravels'** in the near future. And anyway, the company does not have a great track record in managing partnerships (ask the CEO of USAir, if you disagree). Has BA

been drawn into managing through alliance, when it is weak in the skills needed to deliver customer value through partner organizations?

- *Leaning* – this is a polite way of describing Ayling's cost-cutting programme. Efficiency is a high priority to stay in profit in this sector. However, you have to ask if a leaned BA will be able to deliver its service promise to customers, let alone re-establish a service and quality superiority over competitors. The timing is not good – probably the best way to enduring efficiency is through individual staff productivity. Alienated staff who resent the changes and fear for their jobs are less likely to make those extra efforts.

- *Virtual organization* – whatever Ayling says, he is following a path to a hollow or virtual business. The question arising increasingly is whether the cash income from selling assets and cost savings from outsourcing actually creates vulnerabilities that are deadly? To believe that BA can operate as a brand and a network, you have to believe two further things: first, that brand strength will hack it in the marketplace with customers (particularly value-oriented business customers); and that you can *manage* a network of partners and suppliers to deliver service and efficiency. Is BA in danger of selling/outsourcing things that are actually its core capabilities? Will it have to rethink its strategy to operate effectively as a virtual airline?

'Is BA in danger of selling/outsourcing things that are actually its core capabilities?'

- *Market segmentation* – this is not made explicit by the company. In effect, BA is dealing with two segments: premium passengers and the rest. BA has focused its efforts on the premium segment and is highly dependent on these passengers – they are the ones who get the benefits in the loyalty programme, the upgraded facilities, etc. BA has two major problems here: this may be a non-growth part of the market (many business travellers fly economy now, even long-haul – Ayling is not the only CEO who is cost-cutting) and BA facilities have been equalled by competitors such as Virgin and Singapore; and the brand switching by business class passengers is absolutely frightening. BA may be trapped in dependency on a market segment that is more value-oriented and less loyal. For the economy class passenger, BA facilities are appallingly bad and competitors are superior in service and/or price. The BA response has been to launch Go as a new low-cost brand in a separate division. This is a high-risk move: it risks devaluing BA as a brand and cannibalizing the customer base, i.e. putting BA in competition with Go for the same customers. This has been handled badly for a company that believes in the power of the brand.

- *'A–Z services'* – financial services are a red herring. **'financial services**
Like every other corporate BA wants the secondary **are a red herring'**
income of selling financial services to its customer
base. Fine. It is secondary income, not a strategy of becoming
a global player in financial services. The links with other
transport modes are potentially more important and should be
watched as a route to new and distinctive types of travel
product for BA. Right now they are a long way off. The
question is whether BA will survive in a good shape so it can
exploit these new opportunities.

Is this a value-driven strategy?

The answer is probably 'no'. It is mainly a brand-based strategy
with a strong relationship marketing approach in one segment.
This is conventional textbook stuff. It also looks very tired. Can we
really believe that this company has in place the strategies that
will be effective in the new realities it is facing?

What are the implementation barriers?

The easy answer is probably that there are four implementation
barriers: the alienated workforce; the regulators; Virgin; and
Robert Ayling. However, BA is particularly interesting as an
illustration of the real relationship management challenge in
managing the implementation of strategy. The BA strategy rests on
a set of relationships, shown in Figure 17.1. These relationships
underpin the strategy. Each set of relationships also impacts on the
others. BA management has performed badly in each area and has
unleashed the interactions, e.g. poor employee relationships
impact on customer service which influences the regulators
adversely, strengthens the competition, causes problems in
partnerships, which makes life less pleasant for employees who
then deliver less good service, and so it goes on . . . BA's
future depends on untangling these hidden relation- **'BA's future**
ships and rebuilding them. The company has followed **depends on**
much of the conventional wisdom – build the brand, **untangling**
use strategic alliances, focus on core competencies, **these hidden**
become a global player, and so on. No one ever **relationships and**
mentioned the foundation on which the strategy would **rebuilding them'**
rest – successfully managing relationships. The ques-
tion is when will BA master this problem and move forward?
Rebuilding the morale and commitment of the BA people is
probably going to take more than glossy internal communications

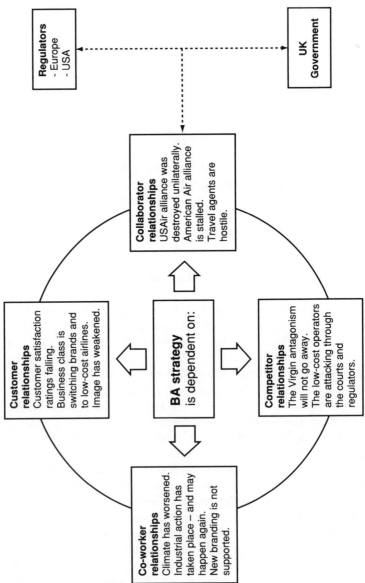

Figure 17.1 The hidden relationship failures underpinning BA's strategy

programmes, however prettily they are done. Without the support of those people the current strategies cannot be implemented. The regulators remain hostile to BA, to a degree that questions their ability to be even-handed. This remains a constraint. There is no sign that Virgin is going to go away – BA has so mismanaged this competitive relationship that it is probably in the position where it has to factor the 'Virgin issue' into every decision it makes, which provides a further restriction on freedom of choice and ability to implement. Finally, there is the question of Ayling himself. His position is weak. He has a very limited time horizon to produce results that impress investors.

Broadly it seems that BA's management has greatly under-estimated the degree of organizational stretch that is involved in implementing this strategy. Renewal of this business will surely rely on rediscovering the company's implementation capabilities. In the meantime, Robert Ayling's position remains vulnerable.

Dell Computers

This is a simply amazing success story. To defy industry conventions, to invent a new way of doing business, to offer lower prices and simultaneously higher customer choice and service levels, to have a business model that is set-up to exploit new electronic commerce opportunities and avoid involvement in low margin 'commodity' segments of the market, to build a new-style organization based on information exchange and partnership with suppliers and customers, and at the same time to deliver incredible profitability and shareholder value – *'this is what* this is what revolution and reinvention is all about. *revolution and*

There are, none the less, some interesting questions *reinvention is all* to consider about the Dell situation at the end of the *about'* 1990s:

- Is the direct business model really robust?
- Can the competitors catch Dell?
- Can Dell 'own' Internet selling of PCs?
- Is the 'virtual integration' of the organization sustainable?

The robustness of the direct business model

What are the real strengths of Dell's direct business model and which can be imitated by competitors in the industry? This is not just about direct selling – anyone can do that – what is awesome is what this has evolved into. (An interesting extension of this question is to consider what other sectors with traditional selling and distribution structures could be attacked with the same type of innovation, though the answer depends on what you believe are the real strengths of the model.) Perhaps the most important aspect of the model is its learning charac- teristics: the Dell model has evolved and is evolving on the basis of the new understanding and experience gained. This is probably the hardest thing for a conventional competitor to emulate.

'Perhaps the most important aspect of the model is its learning characteristics'

Competitive retaliation

How can existing competitors such as Compaq and IBM regain the advantage in the corporate market? Will consolidation in the industry change the competitive threats to Dell? What is the role of Microsoft and Intel going to be in this battle? Certainly, Dell's direct model is based on exploiting other people's technology. What might happen if that access was threatened? It should be remembered that Microsoft has been accused of (and vehemently denies) supplying the Windows operating system cheaper to 'friends' such as Dell and Compaq who toe the Microsoft line, as opposed to 'non-friends' such as IBM and Gateway.

'What is the role of Microsoft and Intel going to be in this battle?'

Internet selling

Is Dell going to be able to continue dominating Internet-based sales? If this is just a natural extension of the direct business model and if it accounts for a growing proportion of the market, then how can Dell be beaten? Perhaps the critical issue is whether a competitor can create a new way of doing business through the Internet that does not create disruption in its own distribution channels by competing with its own resellers. Could Microsoft create a new type of Internet-based reseller with a higher value offer to corporate customers and existing manufacturers?

The new organizational form

Can Dell continue to operate its 'virtually integrated' organization now it is a global player? It has grown successfully through collaboration with suppliers and customers and it is at the centre of what is a form of hollow or networked organization. Is this stable? Is it a prototype of what global organizations will be in the future, i.e. hollow structures based on partnerships of varying duration and held together by information exchanges?

This is a fascinating and evolving story, which is well worth watching over the next few years, to see what happens and what we can learn. The point is that the unthinkable can happen and if a reinvented business model can catch out even sophisticated and capable competitors such as IBM, Compaq and Hewlett-Packard, then we should all be watching for the revolution in all marketplaces.

> *'a reinvented business model can catch out even sophisticated and capable competitors'*

New marketing channels

The experience of firms in diverse activities, varying from car distribution to flower selling to book marketing to the music industry, underlines a number of important questions that are worth teasing out. They are worth teasing out for a very simple reason: the underlying forces that are reshaping those businesses are affecting *all* businesses. Some of the critical questions to consider are:

> *'the underlying forces that are reshaping those businesses are affecting all businesses'*

- How does electronic commerce affect a business?
- What do these revolutions and reinventions do to our traditional definitions of markets and products/services?
- Can conventional suppliers and manufacturers survive this process of revolution?
- Does electronic commerce and the Internet spell the death of the conventional middleman or distributor?
- How are these phases of reinvention unfolding and what new opportunities are being created?
- Is there any market, industry, product, service or distribution channel anywhere which cannot or will not be affected by the Internet?

How does electronic commerce affect a business?

At one level these stories of a number of different types of business are illustrations of the power of electronic commerce using the Internet to undermine conventional ways of doing business, but more fundamentally that the technology facilitates and stimulates the

> *'technology facilitates and stimulates the development of new business models'*

development of new business models that offer customers superior value in their own terms. In the businesses described here, we might well ask:

● *How different is car distribution going to be?* All the ingredients are there for a massive process of reinvention, probably driven by direct marketing and the Internet. However, even more interesting is the Huizenga business model, which may be developed into something radically different from the conventional car business. It is impressive how that business model is being tested, adapted and refined. This case is also interesting because it shows the dynamics impacting on the 'middleman'. Conventional distributors are under threat and many are likely to disappear, but the intermediary role may be reinvented by Internet-based brokers and integrated branded operations such as Huizenga's plan.

● *Has Calyx & Corolla made any difference?* In the total flower market selling marketplace, C&C is small. However, the C&C model has been significant for the larger players in offering faster delivery of fresher flowers. C&C's positioning is strong also in focusing on an attractive niche (probably the most profitable – 'flower lovers' who buy big and regularly), and building the whole operation on a hollow model of collaboration with growers and FedEx. As Anita Roddick of The Body Shop noted, if you think being small means you have no impact, try spending a night in a tent with a mosquito! C&C has redefined not just how it sells flowers, but also the standards for its competitors.

● *Can Amazon.Com survive?* It is astounding that a business with this market valuation has yet to make a profit. There is little doubt that Amazon has redefined the standards, prices and choices that book buyers expect. The direct marketing of books from an Internet site provides a powerful business model with many competitive advantages. The issue is whether this model provides a sustainable competitive advantage or whether conventional competitors can successfully imitate it. But the important underlying point is: has Amazon used the technology to create a new business form, the 'Wal-Mart of the Web' or an information broker for shoppers? The Amazon model also gives the lie to the conventional view about diversification (there are high risks in getting into areas you do not know). Amazon is not really a specialist retailer; it is some kind of technology-led information exchange, which means it can move easily from books, to music, to videos, to shopping search services. The

'has Amazon used the technology to create a new business form'

intriguing thing is that just about anyone can launch a web site to sell books: Amazon's business model has gone far beyond this and this is what cannot easily be imitated.

- *What is really happening to the music business?* The music business example is an even better illustration of the impact of e-commerce in driving the creation of new business models. To begin with, the Internet was little more than an alternative, direct distribution channel competing with conventional retailers. The power of the model was enough to draw conventional retailers onto the web. A critical change was when record producers were also drawn in direct selling on the web, undermining the future of conventional distribution. Even more critical is the acceptance of downloaded digital music as a replacement for conventional CDs and tapes. This opens the way for music to reach listeners from musicians not from record companies. These phases of change may be what we expect to see unfolding in many other areas, leading to the reinvention of the industries concerned.

What happened to conventional product and market definitions?

In many cases, conventional categories become obsolete and firms not recognizing this are wide-open to attack. If Tesco sells cars, Republic Industries creates an integrated flexible car operation with more in common with car rental than distribution; if Calyx & Corolla can apply direct marketing expertise to sell fresh flowers from a catalogue; if Amazon.com ends up competing with Wal-Mart not Barnes & Noble or creates a unique type of consumption community; if music is consumed without CDs or record shops or record companies; if the music industry is reshaped by IBM and AT&T, then what possible use are traditional definitions of those industries?

'conventional categories become obsolete and firms not recognizing this are wide-open to attack'

For example, another sector that is being reinvented by electronic commerce is travel. The big players are not traditional travel agents who have moved onto the web. The major competitors are Microsoft, with its online travel service Expedia, and Sabre, the world's biggest provider of computer services to airlines is now selling £600 million of travel a month in the US through its Travelocity site. The next major entry is Air Miles, which is planning to exploit its relationship with travellers who collect Air Miles to cut out travel agents and sell direct to the public and to its corporate customers. For similar reasons, British

Telecom is planning to sell holidays direct to the public through its Yellow Pages web site.

Traditional definitions of products, markets and competitors do not stop the 'rule breakers' entering where they believe they can create value better than the existing players.

Can conventional suppliers survive?

The answer is almost certainly that they can but life is going to be very different. They are being forced to find areas where they can deliver superior value in different ways, for example the bookshop as a 'socialization centre' does things the Internet sellers cannot. Peter Martin in the FT argues that 'the challenge posed by the era of digital business is this: what parts of your value chain does it make redundant – and how much does that damage your competitive advantage?'. He argues that value chains are fragmenting, as in electricity supply where production and distribution of power are now separated and competitive advantage in distribution is more related to strength in customer relationship management than being good at producing cheap electricity, hence the multiple 'retailers' of electricity are emerging.

'value chains are fragmenting'

For example, if home-based Internet purchasing of groceries becomes a significant part of the grocery business, super-markets are facing major changes to the way they manage supply chains to meet individual orders from a wholesale level, with distribution depots close to consumers not stores. (The early approach to online grocery sales by Tesco was to fax the consumer's Internet order to the store closest to the consumer's location, have a member of staff go round the store with a trolley to 'buy' the goods required, then queue at a checkout to 'pay' and then arrange delivery. This somewhat low technology approach was the only way to cope with individual consumer orders from the web conflicting with supply chain efficiency in delivering in bulk to stores.) Tactical shopping and store-switching driven by the Internet is also likely to dramatically increase demand volatility at the store level, causing major problems in the supply chain designed to service stable demand at the store level. Even if home-based shopping for groceries attracts only a minority of customers, it is likely to affect prices for all customers.

This leads to a recurring theme: clinging to a traditional business model when others are reinventing the business is not an option attractive to those who want to survive.

Is the Internet the end for the middleman?

Electronic commerce has been associated with 'disintermediation' – the replacement of conventional intermediaries such as retailer and distributors by direct selling from producer to customer. However, what we are also seeing emerging is 'reintermediation' – the creation of new kinds of brokers acting as 'brokers' or 'infomediaries' in the purchase process. Amazon.com is an example. Alan Mitchell describes this as the rise of new middlemen who will gather information about their customers and use it on their customers' behalf to get a better deal of some kind; shopping around between alternative suppliers to find the best on the basis of the customer's information about requirements and preferences. They will, in effect, 'sell' their customers to suppliers. This is not restricted to selling books, there are few markets where this concept could not lead to a new route to superior customer value.

'"reintermediation" – the creation of new kinds of brokers acting as "brokers" or "infomediaries"'

The only 'certainty' is that distribution channels are going to be different.

Phases of change and new business models

Although it is crude, the music industry (and maybe soon the publishing industry) provides an illustration of phases of technology-driven change fundamentally changing the nature of an industry, making traditional business models weak if not obsolete, inviting new competitors to enter and changing the relationship between buyers and seller. It underlines the dangers in clinging to conventional strategies and business models when a market is revolutionized. An attempt to summarize these phases of change is shown in Figure 17.2.

The music industry is not the only one where this change process may create revolution. It has long been possible to download obscure author-published books from the Internet as computer files. At Christmas 1998, Barnes & Noble offered more than 150 book titles that can be downloaded and read on the $500 NuvoMedia Rocket eBook or the $300 Softbook (lightweight electronic book readers). Currently, electronic books are restricted to the leisure reading market, but the potential for reference books and manuals capable of regular updating is huge – a flatscreen electronic reader weighing 3 lb is an attractive alternative already to a 100 000 page aircraft maintenance manual. Projectable readers offer yet more possibilities.

Phase one changes	Example
Doing the same things in a different way	Selling records, CDs, tapes direct
Phase two changes	**Example**
Technology provides a new way of doing the same things	Selling records, CDs and tapes from the Internet
Phase three changes	**Example**
Technology provides a new way of doing new things	Music is downloaded from the Internet onto the customer's computer/music player
Phase four changes	**Example**
The technology changes the product	Customized music/video/text products of new kinds are created on the Internet and accessed by customers to download onto CDs and other recordable media
Phase five changes	**Example**
The technology becomes the product	Music makers and music listeners communicate directly without conventional commercial intermediaries

Figure 17.2 Phases of technology-driven reinvention

Is there any market the Internet cannot affect?

Probably not, even if it just provides enhanced information search by customers or new types of distributor.

For example, they used to say that consumers would not buy from unknown names on the Internet, only from trusted brands. Tell that to Amazon.com.

They said you could not sell things such as clothes on the Internet – people wanted to see and touch their purchases and try them on in the shop's changing room. By 1998 the online clothes market was already worth $100 million a year. The Gap has gone global with its Internet site. Land's End has increased its Internet product range from 100 to 800 items in two years, and says the web customers are new to Land's End, not switching from the traditional catalogue. It seems that a lot of customers do not value the shopping experience for clothes very highly, contrary to conventional retailers' beliefs it appears that significant numbers seem to hate it and do not have the time to spend anyway.

Then they said that you could not sell 'low ticket' items over the Internet – books and CDs were about the lowest ticket items that would work. Well, 1998 saw the launch of Sparks.com selling greetings cards over the Web with prices as low as $2.75. Felicia Lindau from Amazon's advertising agency has shown that greetings cards have low ticket value but very attractive margins. Sparks.com offers wider choice, convenient access and the consumer gets the cards for normal retail price mailed to their homes. Cards can be personalized by laser printer or hand-drawn calligraphy and can be accompanied by gifts such as book tokens. The system works with any 'small, thin things', e.g. tickets, vouchers, books, disks and so on. What turns out to be the lowest ticket price that can sell off the Internet page is likely to be extremely significant to the whole world over the next ten years.

Similarly, NetGrocer in the USA is selling a limited range of packaged supermarket goods to consumers, with the Internet as its *only* channel of distribution.

It is an interesting game to choose an industry where e-commerce has not yet impacted and to brainstorm the ways in which it may operate in that industry, the likely players and the effects on the existing suppliers and distributors. The only rule is that no one from that industry is allowed to play, because they are always the last to see how reinvention changes the rules and invalidates the assumptions that the industry 'experts' habitually make. Booksellers did not forecast Amazon, flower sellers did not believe that Calyx & Corolla would work, and so on.

'reinvention changes the rules and invalidates the assumptions that the industry "experts" habitually make'

Reinventing the airline business

The story of the emergence of low-cost, no-frills airlines to challenge the existing carriers is a great example of a value-based strategy, which beats all the industry conventions in terms of brands, loyalty programmes and relationship marketing strategy in attracting customers of a particular type. There was nothing marginal about the change in value offered to the customer – it was a truly awesome step-change in the value equation for short-haul flying. It may also show the type of strategy that appeals to the more sophisticated buyer – a surprisingly large proportion of the European low-cost business is with business travellers. The story underlines the fact that processes of reinvention can occur anywhere, even

'processes of reinvention can occur anywhere'

(perhaps especially) in conventional industries dominated by large companies. It demonstrates the advantage that goes to the rule-breaker that abandons industry norms and conventions.

The story also illustrates a number of very significant issues that should exercise the minds of those who want to reinvent and revolutionize an industry:

- Can an imitative, 'me-too' strategy be robust?
- Can conventional competitors destroy the innovators?
- Does the new model give a sustainable competitive advantage?
- Where do regulators come into it?
- Will the 'no-frills' model endure?

Imitative strategy

Imitation is flattering to the imitated, but can you be sure you have imitated the right bits? Southwest in the USA survives as the model of the low-cost, no-frills airline with very low fares. However, there is more to Southwest than low costs. The company has a unique approach to management and staff development and wins awards for customer service as well. How can we be sure that the European low-cost airlines have not just replicated the low costs and low fares without having the other impact of Southwest? Have they just copied the trapping of Southwest's strategy without the real substance? If so, they are vulnerable – anyone can reduce prices (at least for a while).

Competitive retaliation

'The rule makers do not like the rule breakers' The rule makers do not like the rule breakers. As soon as the low-cost providers started hurting BA, reaction was inevitable: either BA's entry to the low-cost market by acquiring an existing firm or by starting its own low-cost operation. The low-cost operators were caught out by their own success: involvement in the low-cost market is a big risk for BA, but the no-frills operations were too successful to be ignored. The resulting competition is fierce and antagonistic. It is likely it will destroy at least some of the low-cost competitors.

'Rule breakers need sustainable competitive advantage to survive'

Sustainable competitive advantage?

Rule breakers need sustainable competitive advantage to survive. Southwest is unique and had cash reserves as it expanded. Ryanair 'owns' routes that it has developed from nothing and dominates. What do the rest have to sustain them through the competitive war with Go?

The regulators' role

Regulators do not like the rule makers. This story illustrates how the reality of competition has changed radically in some industries. The regulators have turned into arbiters of market share. Every move BA/ Go makes is automatically challenged. Issues of commercial confidentiality and privacy have disappeared. The demand is for total transparency. We are having to learn to compete under new and arbitrary rules imposed by legal sanction and exploited to the full by competitors. The largest part of the competitive response to Go's entry to the low-cost market has been legal action to attempt to deny them the right to compete.

'Regulators do not like the rule makers'

Stuck-in-the-middle firms lose out both ways. If the low-cost/no-frills basis for competitive differentiation weakens as the frills are added back in, is this not the classic stuck-in-the-middle problem described by Michael Porter? As the low-cost firms add in services and extras, they risk losing out on price to the remaining low-cost operators, as well as on service to the full fare carriers. This is probably the most vulnerable position in the market. It seems to be what most of the European low-cost operators are doing. It is not what Southwest does. Have they lost their nerve?

'Stuck-in-the-middle firms lose out both ways'

Robust strategy

Is the no-frills strategy in the airline business in Europe a robust strategy, or simply a short-term ploy that will soon disappear? This is the most important question and the least easy to answer. The answer will probably depend on what the low-cost operators learn and how they refine the model to pursue what gives superior value to their different customer segments.

Treasure Island

Probably the most important questions to ask about these stories are:

● What do we think about the strategies being pursued by firms in the grocery and motor trades to maintain high prices in the UK?

- Can these strategies be sustained, and if not why not?
- What are the most likely outcomes for the large supermarket companies and car manufacturers, and who might be attracted into these industries as they reinvent?

What do we think about high price strategies?

The first reaction of most people to the facts in this area is surprise and anger. We are all consumers, so we are all paying the inflated prices for our food, cars and so on. This is a good and useful reaction. It is good and useful because it provides a reminder about how customers feel and maybe how *our customers* feel about *us*, if they do not think we are giving them good value. This is worth hanging onto.

*'We **would all like** to do what the supermarkets and car producers are doing'*
The second reaction from managers tends to be more cynical. *We* would all like to do what the supermarkets and car producers are doing and make higher profits wherever we can, all the better if we can dominate a market and control customers. This raises some interesting points about what the cost of a strategy like this may be in the longer term and whether it is worth it. For example:

- Loss of customer goodwill when they find out what we have been doing may be a barrier to new strategies. When Tesco started dual pricing in 1998 (i.e. cutting grocery prices in poor areas to benefit less affluent consumers), the reaction was not praise for the company's social responsibility, but demands they should cut prices *everywhere*.
- There is accumulating evidence (for example from the Marketing Forum early in 1999) that if you want a 'citizen brand' (one that is high value but also sympathetic in environmental and social terms) that is durable and stretches to new areas, you have to be trusted by customers, and companies appear to be trusted on everything or nothing. After a 1998 of public attacks on its high prices, Dixons scored 22 per cent on the question about being trusted to be honest and fair in its dealings, compared to 91 per cent for M&S, and only 17 per cent on trust them to use personal information responsibly and confidentially. If customers are persuaded to turn against you, you may lose the value and sustainability of your brand.
- Advocates of the stakeholder view of business point to the 'global goldfish bowl' in which firms operate and the erosion of credibility and trustworthiness they risk if seen to be exploiting market power against customers.

- The ability to sustain such a strategy lasts only as long as the market barriers that prevent new competitors and new types of competition from breaking the control of the dominant. The biggest threat to the cosy UK car market is undoubtedly the availability of car information and purchase through the Internet and the 'legalization' of grey imports.

  'The ability to sustain such a strategy lasts only as long as the market barriers'

- You may invite unwelcome attention from regulators, which can lead to crude controls which may be very difficult to live with.

Are high price strategies sustainable?

The answer here is probably different for the grocery and car markets and is underlined by the amazing interconnectedness, i.e. supermarkets moving into the car distribution business.

The protections and barriers around the grocery business in the UK remain pretty strong. They are reinforced by the nature of the product: few consumers will willingly travel very far to buy grocery products (the occasional splurge on duty-free booze or the ferry to Calais excepted). They are also held in place by the efforts of the established players to make sure that they are the ones who dominate new channels such as direct marketing of groceries and Internet-based shopping. The costs of entry for new competitors are also high. There has been no emergence of 'grey imports' in food with cheap products being brought in from Europe on any serious scale.

The grocery supermarkets are also pursuing a brilliantly effective strategy to sustain their ability to earn high margins on food. Pressure from government, media and consumer groups is being managed in the following type of way. The supermarkets are repositioning themselves in the customers' minds – they are not reinventing the industry, they are reinventing the debate. The stages are:

'they are not reinventing the industry, they are reinventing the debate'

- *Stage 1 – Denial.* In the short term all you can do when you have been caught charging higher prices is to deny it. Produce figures that 'prove' you are not charging more than supermarkets overseas, argue that wages and site costs in the UK are higher than elsewhere, make noises about the high employment numbers in retailing and the threat to jobs if you are forced to cut prices and so on. This muddies the pool and buys you time.
- *Stage 2 – Shift the attack.* Move the pressure from grocery prices to other areas. It is entirely coincidental that while Tesco was

so accommodating about helping Peter Mandelson with his Millennium Dome project (to the tune of some £12 million), it should happen to be the same Peter Mandelson (then trade and industry minister) who launched the attack on personal computer pricing in Dixons. The large retailers must have been more upset than most when Mandelson was sleazed out of ministerial office. The government has also been very helpful in supporting supermarkets in winning the right to cut the prices of branded products such as clothes and cosmetics.

- *Stage 3 – Repositioning.* If the pressure is now on non-food pricing, the supermarkets can demonstrate that they are cutting prices all over the place, e.g. computers, books, cosmetics and clothes. The supermarkets are repositioning as the consumers' champion against brand owners and other retailers. And anyway, who cares about a penny or two on a tin of beans if Tesco gives you a pound off a paperback book, twenty pounds off a pair of branded jeans or a couple of hundred pounds off a new computer?

'you can design a strategy that makes the high price strategy sustainable in grocery supermarkets' It would seem that you can design a strategy that makes the high price strategy sustainable in grocery supermarkets. The repositioning also fits well with the portfolio strategy emerging (food as the cash cow to build growth in non-food). The only thing that could disrupt this situation is the entry of an effective new competitor, and the rumour is that Wal-Mart is on the way. . . .

It is here that the underlying position is different for the car manufacturers. The conditions that allowed the manufacturers to make the UK a high price market are rapidly changing. Also, the product is different. While few people will travel or willingly suffer inconvenience to get their cars serviced, if you separate servicing from purchase, people may easily travel farther to buy a car, put up with inconvenience, or use new channels like the Internet or even the supermarket. The new car is the second largest purchase most people ever make.

In addition, the ability of car manufacturers to continue dictating prices to independent distributors is unlikely to survive. In an industry where supply outstrips demand (or threatens to), it is likely that prices will fall, at least closer to the European level. There does not seem any way that the high price strategy is sustainable in the long term. The short-term defence includes:

- *product variants* – if you can say that the cars sold in the UK are different to those sold in Europe (technical specifications, etc.), then you may justify a higher price for a while

- *brand strength* – the pressure downwards on price will take longest to work for the strongest brands, where customers are less price sensitive and more loyal to the brand
- *informal pressures* – you can continue to make life difficult for customers and distributors who are 'unco-operative', but if you get caught by the regulators the cost may be high (ask Volkswagen)

'the pressure downwards on price will take longest to work for the strongest brands'

However, it seems unlikely that these policies will sustain the high price strategy very long for most manufacturers. For the global manufacturers this is not that big a deal anyway, they have enjoyed enhanced margins in the UK, but the UK market is not all that big compared to the rest of the world. It may simply not be worth fighting for.

Perhaps most fundamental is the fact that high price strategies in both these sectors rely above all on one thing: that your customers believe they have to choose between low prices and high service and quality. The day they realize that they can have *both* (because a new-style competitor with a different business model shows them they can), then your strategy is finished. For the grocery supermarkets, that competitor may be Wal-Mart.

The likely outcomes

This is more speculative. The strategy of supermarkets in becoming general stores seems well in place and likely to continue, and there seems little reason to expect that these firms will cut grocery prices (unless they are forced to by a new competitive entry). The car industry is likely to see more complex channels and increasing inability for manufacturers to maintain high retail prices in the UK: there are just too many pressures to resist.

The biggest threat to the status quo is probably that the high margins in the UK are an invitation for new competitors to enter with new business models, e.g. direct channels for cars, such as Daewoo, service and quality plus low prices in food, such as the Wal-Mart model. The message from consumers is becoming clearer: if you ask them whether they want service, quality and convenience or low prices, the answer is 'yes'.

BT International

BT has developed into a fascinating, successful and awesomely complex company from the very unpromising origins of an inefficient state enterprise. It is also in the midst of a marketplace that is changing and reinventing so fast that anything written about the competitors and the technology is out of date as soon as the ink dries. Whole teams of BT-watchers are employed at investment banks and financial commentators just to try to keep up, so they can advise investors. However, if we stand back from the dynamics of the technology, there are some strategic issues underpinning BT's progress that are well worth debating in the search for insights into what strategy is all about in the real world. Some of the interesting questions to ask about BT's strategic pathway are:

- Is globalization the best strategic choice for developing the company?
- Was the concentration on the USA the best direction to take the business?
- What went wrong in the MCI deal?
- What are the things to watch and manage in the AT&T alliance?
- What do the experience of Vallance and Bonfield illustrate about the new problems in building strategy in large organizations?

Globalization as a strategic choice

The BT strategy of expanding internationally has been challenged by some BT investors, who would rather see BT investing in its domestic market and improving services to customers there. There was some resentment in 1999 when Concert reduced prices for its corporate customers making their phone calls substantially cheaper than those for residential customers in the UK. This has become a serious shareholder issue.

'BT had no choice other than build the international business or learn to downsize'

In fact, the question is a 'no-brainer'. BT had no choice other than build the international business or learn to downsize. In common with all the other local carriers, its domestic market has been opened to external competition and its market share is eroding. The choice was a strategy to be a world player or wait to be taken over by a world player. Only the world players have the clout to integrate the technology (though it is clear they do not drive the technology). This was clear even from the time of privatization. The issue was not whether to be global but how to implement the global strategy.

If there is a failure underlying this question, it lies in not communicating the strategy to employees and investors sufficiently that the question was ever raised. Underestimating the power of shareholders to exert influence had much to do with the MCI failure. In fact, BT has a lengthy record of investment in its local market, which is continuing, particularly now in the mobile phone market and Internet services. The accusation of treating the domestic market as a second-class citizen is largely untrue, so why do people believe it to be true?

Concentration on the US market

The focus on the USA was dictated by the size of that market, its dominance in the multinational corporate market, and the fact it is the home of much of the technological drive that is transforming the industry. This too is a 'no-brainer'. BT had no choice but to have a linkage to the US market. Again the real issue was how to implement that strategy.

BT would not be the first company to have been seduced into investing in the USA because of the sheer size of the market, without considering enough whether they had the differentiating capabilities to take a worthwhile position in that brutally competitive market. This would be an illusion strategy, where you end up taking a weak and unprofitable position in a very attractive market. In spite of the views of its critics, BT has avoided that trap, even though the early investments in Mitel and McCaw looked like it was falling right into it.

'BT had no choice but to have a linkage to the US market'

The position taken in alliance with AT&T looks smart: combining resources to focus on the corporate market, with the potential for further co-operation in areas such as mobile telephones and Internet services, but without getting involved in the domestic market with its need for network enhancement and tumbling prices. It looks to exploit BT's differentiating capabilities in the market where these can pay off, and avoids being drawn into the commodity end of the marketplace.

Also, it is easy to exaggerate the extent to which BT is actually focused on the USA. Right from the outset Vallance, and later Bonfield, had a clear strategic goal of positioning in the US market, and the achievement of this goal has been tough. However, during the same period BT has invested heavily in its European operations and in collaboration-led growth in Asia.

The MCI failure

The MCI deal failure was a public humiliation for BT's senior managers and left the company looking very

'The MCI deal failure was a public humiliation'

vulnerable for a time. In fact, many investors disliked the deal from the outset, and Vallance and Bonfield obtained a hugely advantageous package from WorldCom to walk away from the deal.

The 'fit' between BT and MCI looked good: they had been working together since BT took a stake of MCI in 1993, there was a strong technology case for merger from both sides' point of view. There were signs, however, that there was some mismatch between the cultures of the two companies. The collapse of the MCI merger was triggered by the BT investor reaction to the fall in MCI profits. Bonfield and Vallance had no choice but to find a way to make MCI a lower bid. It was always unlikely that a lower price would be acceptable to MCI, if only from a 'pride' point of view. There is also the fact that the strategic paths of the two companies did seem to be diverging: MCI determined to attack the local phone market and BT concerned that these resources should be used for international development. The deal fell apart for entirely human and cultural reasons, even though the technology made sense.

The MCI interlude is indicative of some of the new risks that we all face in driving and implementing strategy:

- This whole industry is being driven by alliance, partnership, merger and acquisition activity. The industry may contain some of the smartest technologists in history, but the evidence is that neither they nor we have yet got a handle on the requirements for managing successfully through partnership-based networks. What is apparent is that alliance and partnership can offer huge advantages faster than any other strategy: access to resources, access to markets, access to technology, access to capital. The link between MCI and BT made much sense in terms of technology and market access for both sides. Those potential gains bring substantial risks as well.

'Alliances and partnerships are fragile'

- Alliances and partnerships are fragile. Agreements are broken by 'partners' who see advantage in moving from one alliance to another. The alternative of cross-ownership and integration may mean building more permanent links with those who are not going to be good partners. The need is for better ways of evaluating the 'fit' between members of alliances and better ways of monitoring their stability and effectiveness.
- The MCI experience also identifies another issue to consider about alliances: if they fail at any stage and fall apart, you may be left extremely vulnerable. When WorldCom took MCI, BT walked away with a substantial profit. It was also left with a

massive hole in its ability to implement its main strategy and no obvious ways to fill it. The trauma left the company drifting for a short period, Bonfield was vulnerable to a campaign to take his job away, and just suppose Ebbers had mounted a bid. . . .

- Indeed, if they succeed, forming alliances can stimulate competitors into renewed efforts (e.g. Cable & Wireless versus BT in Europe – hell hath no fury like a CEO scorned).
- They can also mean that the role of the regulators becomes paramount and aggressive competitors are likely to do their best to stimulate regulators to be as picky as possible.

The AT&T alliance

In some ways the same fears exist with respect to the AT&T alliance. It may be undermined by clashes of culture and competing strategic goals, rather than a poor technology or financial logic. However, BT has learned enough to evaluate the culture issue very seriously and to map out very clearly how the joint venture is expected to operate. It is a different deal: a jointly owned venture rather than a take-over and is going to be managed by an outsider recruited for the job, not by someone from AT&T or BT.

However, there are still risks. Neither partner has a great track record in collaboration. If it does crash, then Bonfield and BT are going to look very vulnerable.

The new problems of strategy

It follows that one of the new problems is that strategic choice may be far more limited than we like to think. BT had no choice over whether to globalize or whether to go after the US linkage. There were choices over the forms of those strategies, but not much else. The fundamental issue for senior management was *implementation* and developing the new type of organization that would support the strategy.

'strategic choice may be far more limited than we like to think'

It is also clear that some of the implementation strategies that seem unavoidable may carry huge and unfamiliar hidden risks. Alliances and partnering are seen as a way of coping with this type of business environment and yet they bring great strategic risks.

BT is also obliged to make its choices very publicly and under detailed scrutiny, from investors and the financial press, from competitors, from regulators, and from its own employees. This type of transparency is increasingly common, and we are just beginning to see it may be a major constraint on strategic freedom: shareholders killed the MCI deal, disgruntled competitors run to the regulator, and so on.

'People issues make and break strategies'

Lastly, BT underlines a central paradox about fast-changing high technology industries such as telecommunications. People issues make and break strategies. Relationships determine what happens. Customer demands for value in their terms drive technological convergence and market invasion on a massive scale. Even with a technology moving so fast it is difficult to even understand how it is unfolding, the primacy of value-driven strategy and its drivers remains central.

Retail banks

This somewhat polemical piece is about the obsolescence of a particular organizational and business type in a specific market, i.e. retail banks in financial services. It is a safe bet that

'few professional bankers will like what is written here'

few professional bankers will like what is written here and will give a hundred reasons why it is wrongheaded nonsense. The significance of the story is not really the demise of retail banks (for which many of us have little sympathy anyway), it is the impact of revolution in transforming the way a business operates, recognizing the impact of fundamental change and responding positively. This story has lessons for all of us in all sectors – next time it may be us.

The history of customer dissatisfaction with banks also underlines why it is important that even monopolistic firms with customers as 'hostages' need to worry about customers – because if you don't sooner or later they will get their revenge.

'Brands and relationships may even lull you into believing that retained customers are loyal, instead of just hostages'

The experience of this sector also illustrates the growing significance of value-based competition, superseding conventional attempts to compete through branding or 'relationship marketing'. Brands and relationships may even lull you into believing that retained customers are loyal, instead of just hostages. The test is what do those customers do when they have *real* choices of better value, made easier to access by lower information and search costs and lower switching costs.

The banking sector also illustrates the vulnerability of established firms in being tied to traditional systems and ways of doing business. The pursuit of economy of scale and standardization of service creates inflexibility. It also tends to create a fixed 'mind-set', which denies the importance of external changes. It is illustrative that the reaction of the traditional banking firms to most of the new forms of competition and new competitors has been scorn and complacency:

- They said building societies could never operate as banks because they lacked the skills and experience – but they did, and then most became banks.
- They said companies such as Virgin Direct were a disgrace, selling sub-standard investment products to the naïve – as customers flooded towards simple, transparent products that were easy to buy.
- Now they say that supermarkets and insurers cannot survive as banks.
- They seem to believe that customers will never trust 'outsiders' operating on the Internet, because they are not proper bankers.

How often do you have to get it wrong, before you realize that the world has changed?

Interesting questions worth dwelling on about this business include the following:

What does reinvention do to market definition?

This business is an excellent illustration of the way in which traditional market definitions – enshrined in planning and information systems – can be positively harmful to corporate health. Markets consist of customer needs and different ways of meeting them. Defining markets around existing 'me-too' competitors and existing products and services is dangerously short-sighted. Anyone responsible for planning and strategy should be searching for new and insightful ways of defining the market. At least then you might stand a chance of spotting the new sources of competition you are going to face.

'Defining markets around existing "me-too" competitors and existing products and services is dangerously short-sighted'

What about market sensing, customer focus and corporate complacency?

How can banks have become so unresponsive to market change? Banks are information-rich, high-technology institutions. This is not the same thing as understanding customers and the way things are changing. If you do not have superior market-sensing capabilities, then it is hardly surprising if complacency takes over, and you will pay the price that is always paid by the complacent. Maybe sheer complacency is why the traditional banks are not dominating electronic commerce and developing new products for under-served customer markets, or driving collaborations to deliver high-value financial services through new distribution channels – all these things are being driven by others.

'sheer complacency is why the traditional banks are not dominating electronic commerce'

What are the role of brands, relationships and value?

An interesting debate is whether the banks have clung to the idea that if they invest in brand development and build 'relationships' with customers, then they will dominate the market and cross-sell to their hearts' content. If so, they have been caught out by two things: the growing sophistication of customers; and the impact of value-based strategies (where value is defined by customers not companies).

What is the implication of loss of initiative and obsolete business designs?

'the traditional business design shared by banks has reached the end of its life cycle'

There seems little doubt that the traditional business design shared by banks has reached the end of its life cycle, and the vulnerability of banks is to those with new business designs that offer superior value to customers. In the short term the banks are protected by history and regulation and are just experiencing a loss of initiative in the marketplace. In the longer term, this loss of initiative may translate into a more serious loss of profitability and shareholder value. We wait and see. . . .

Marks & Spencer

Apart from all its many attributes of excellence, the M&S story tells us something else, no one gets it right all the time, notwithstanding the sign on Sir Richard Greenbury's desk which reads, 'I have many faults, but being wrong is not one of them'. The question is whether you have the robustness to recover from the mistakes, to learn and to move on to something more successful.

Some of the more interesting questions for consideration include the following:

- What are the factors underpinning M&S success up to the end of the 1990s?
- What has changed to cause the problems in 1998 and 1999?
- Is the strong M&S culture a strength or a weakness as the company faces up to the new challenges?
- Is the fight over management succession at the top the signal for the end of M&S' success?
- Can you have a long-term strategy in a situation which the City judges you on quarterly results and investors shape your decisions?

'Is the strong M&S culture a strength or a weakness'

Factors underpinning M&S success?

The development of M&S compares favourably to the value-driven model of strategy discussed earlier:

- *Value* – M&S built a unique value position with the British consumer based on the high quality of all products sold under the St Michael brand. Never the cheapest on the market, M&S provided something better for a good price and products and services that could be trusted. It pioneered a no-questions exchange policy when such a thing was anathema to British retailers.
- *Management leadership and vision* – for generations M&S was a prototype of a company with strong leaders and a distinctive way of doing things.
- *Market sensing and organizational learning* – M&S developed customer closeness and intelligence collection way ahead of any other British retailer. They sometimes got things wrong – some fashion seasons were disasters and some of the early international ventures went badly wrong. However, they learned and improved.

'for generations M&S was a prototype of a company with strong leaders'

- *Differentiating capabilities* – M&S always did things differently and brought new products to new markets for fifty years, outperforming the rest in quality and customer trust and loyalty.
- *Relationship strategy* – M&S understood supply chains before anyone coined the term – the company was renowned for its, sometimes brutal but always effective, control over suppliers. Employee relations were advanced in British terms

'M&S understood supply chains before anyone coined the term'

from the earliest days. The family involvement until the 1980s kept the company close to the major shareholders. Competitors could not get even close to the relationship M&S built with its customers.

'M&S created a hollow organization – a "manufacturer without factories"'

- *Reinvented organization* – M&S created a hollow organization – a 'manufacturer without factories' – that abandoned traditional retail models decades ago.

M&S was frequently cited as the prime example of a robust strategy. The trouble is if you lose the underpinning characteristics of robustness, things may change dramatically. . . .

The impact of change?

'the rest of the world has learned the lessons that M&S taught'

The most significant change facing M&S is clear: the rest of the world has learned the lessons that M&S taught – about service to customers, about innovation in products and services, about managing supplier relationship through partnering and control. Competitors in many areas have caught up with M&S.

This did not show until other changes made it matter: the recessions in the British economy undermining sales and profits at home; the Asian crisis affecting overseas earnings adversely; unexpectedly high costs in Euro-conversion, staff training, stores upgrades and so on.

The impact of change is that M&S core businesses still offer excellent value to customers in customer service, but they do not have the *superiority* in value that M&S enjoyed for years. Also the marketplace had changed.

Add to this the fact that customer value has migrated in the clothes business. Branded designer clothes and cheap discount clothes have flourished and this is the value that key customers are buying in 1999, and that are provided by aggressive competitors. This leaves M&S stranded in the middle of the market offering neither branded designer clothes (such as Debenhams and smaller players) nor cheap clothes (such as the growing discount retailers).

'This leaves M&S stranded in the middle of the market'

Is a strong culture good or bad?

M&S has a very distinctive culture which underpins its innovation, learning and its demands on suppliers.

That same culture can be smug and inward-looking. *'culture can be* Greenbury, for example, is deeply suspicious of out- *smug and inward-* siders, as well as being hostile to the financial press *looking'* and City analysts. It is also a culture of conservatism and relatively slow change. Most executives have been developed from within the business. This did not provide a good foundation for the radical international expansion and rapid UK redevelopments unveiled by Greenbury in 1998.

M&S culture under Greenbury has been introverted and hierarchical, and respectful of strong and forceful central management. This was a good mind-set for a 'command and control' organization led by an autocrat. The question is whether it will be a sound basis for the more flexible and responsive organization Salsbury wants to create.

Is the boardroom fight the end of M&S success?

Having a public battle for control is never a good idea, *'Having a public* but the M&S experience underlines the transparency *battle for control is* and openness in which senior managers must increas- *never a good idea'* ingly operate. The battle also probably marks the end of an era for M&S when management succession was family-dominated and involved the 'baton' being passed from generation to generation. (Neither Rayner nor Greenbury were actually members of the founding families, but maintained the traditional approach.)

However, the struggle between a number of exceptionally talented managers to achieve a lifetime goal of running one of the world's most successful businesses is hardly likely to damage the business, in spite of the vast number of column inches devoted to the subject at the time by the financial press. In fact, if anything the fuss probably underlines the short termism of City investors more than anything else. The incident does, however, underline the new realities of making decisions in a 'goldfish bowl', where everything is under critical observation – this is the reality of the new demands for 'transparency'. Transparency does not just mean that people want to *know* what you are doing, it means they want to know so they can *change* what you are doing. As Greenbury demonstrated in his attempts to keep the succession private: you can be as forceful as you like, you can threaten people with the sack if they talk to outsiders, you can accuse your suppliers of treachery for revealing your buying plans, you just cannot keep things secret any more.

A contrast exists between how M&S have suffered from mismanaging these realities and the skilful way that Ian (now

Lord) MacLaurin managed his way out of the leadership role of Tesco over a two-year period and transferred control in a way that protected City confidence and share values. It would be ironic if MacLaurin did, indeed, take Greenbury's role at M&S.

If there are any major serious outcomes for the company from the management changes, they are probably:

- the loss of the finance director at a crucial time
- the possibility of lasting internal dissension and conflict, and the potential for further 'coups' in the future, instead of the traditional M&S management transition
- that Greenbury may have had to make his move earlier than he wished, and could have handed things over in better shape if he had been able to wait
- that Salsbury may not have the experience to lead the company out of its crisis and to drive the new strategy
- that the company was being battered and bruised by a fight inside the organization, when it should have been obsessing over its customers outside the organization
- however, the most serious issue is timing – Greenbury has built a strategy to take the business forward and may have needed more time to firmly embed the new plans in the company and build the new capabilities needed. The timing of the hand-over to Salsbury was forced on him by events and he may not have had the time he needed to prepare Salsbury or the company for what was to follow. This is potentially extremely serious

The alternative view, of course, is that Greenbury stayed too long, and that Oates was acting in the company's best interests to resolve the leadership issue and to start building a way out of the company's trading crisis.

'the process of renewal may be painful' The events of November 1998 do underline another point as well: the process of renewal may be painful. Some feel that Greenbury stayed in the top role too long and that the succession should have taken place earlier when it could have been managed quietly in the traditional 'M&S way'. One way or another, the changes needed to renew may be major and unwelcome to the incumbents of senior posts in a company.

Can you have a long-term strategy in a short-term world?

Probably the most serious limitation on Greenbury's ability to implant the new strategy is the determination of financial analysts and investor groups to focus on short-term margins. His expenditure of £2 billion was, after all, only two years' profits at the level to which he had taken M&S profitability. Critics suggest that Greenbury should have been more skilled in managing City relationships, and in selling the need to take a profit hit in the short term to build a stronger long-term position.

None the less, it seems predictable that a company like this will continue to be plagued by pressures towards short-term performance at the expense of long-term position, and this is a major threat to the implementation of the Greenbury strategy. There is actually no easy way around this, as many British CEOs will attest. Ultimately it may be the biggest threat to M&S renewal, and trigger the rounds of management change and restructuring seen in other companies, but always avoided by M&S.

The result is that Salsbury is left with a very short time horizon to reshape the M&S culture, cut costs and build profitability, while regaining M&S' underlying ability to understand its customers, before City pressure costs him his job or a corporate predator strikes. However, if he does do this turnaround he will be everybody's hero.

Skoda Cars

The Skoda story is an excellent example of renewal of a company and a brand. However, an underlying theme that may be of even greater significance is the issue of customer expectations and satisfaction. Skoda is one of the few demonstrations of the fact that if customers have relatively low expectations, then mediocre or average performance may produce high satisfaction and loyalty. If customer expectations are high, exactly the same performance standards may produce customer dissatisfaction, as shown in Figure 17.3.

This is of interest for one very important reason: conventional marketing, advertising and brand development drives you towards making high promises to customers and hence raising their expectations. This probably leads for most of us to average performance perceptions in the customer's eyes and we have little competitive advantage. If then at any stage something goes wrong for the customer – as it is liable to do – then the high expectations we have built up will kill us: the customer is disappointed at the broken promise and blames us and our brand. Skoda did not have this problem in its renewal, the general perception was that the cars were cheap rubbish. In fact, the quite acceptable cars greatly exceeded this perception and

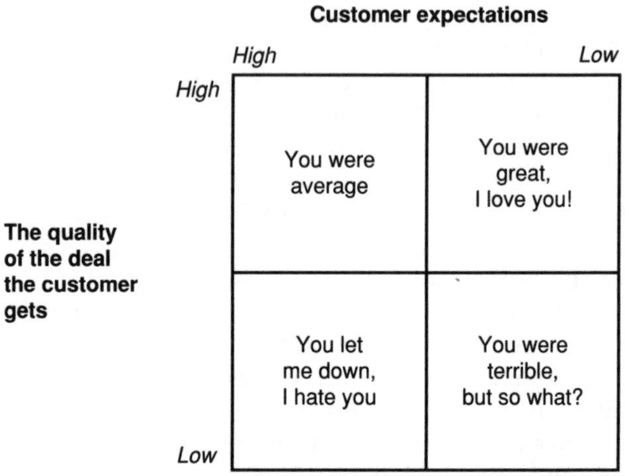

Customer expectations

Figure 17.3 Customer expectations, satisfaction and loyalty

achieved very high levels of satisfaction and loyalty. There may be something in this that offers a more general lesson, maybe there is a positioning strategy which flies in the face of conventional wisdom, which involves managing customer expectations *down* instead of *up?* I think we should call this the 'Skoda Advantage Ploy'.

'customer value is defined by customer perceptions, not by engineers and "experts"' The Skoda story also underlines other recurring themes in value-based market strategy: customer value is defined by customer perceptions, not by engineers and 'experts'; and different customers buy different value. The much-despised Skoda Favorit was a popular vehicle in its limited budget market, achieving high customer satisfaction and loyalty.

However, remember what they say about pushing in to the front of the queue in a Glasgow pub: you can do it, but only once ... The problem facing Skoda now may be that customer perceptions and expectations have changed: they know the cars are good quality and value. So where does the competitive advantage come from now?

Some of the questions worth considering about the Skoda story include the following:

- Now that the low expectations of quality have been replaced by higher expectations, where is Skoda's competitive advantage? The days of selling a £6000 car, where the owner was likely to be over the moon if it started in the morning, have gone.
- Skoda has in effect moved from one market to another. The budget car market for the Favorit and the early Felicias has

been abandoned in favour of head-on competition with the main suppliers in the middle of the market with the enhanced Felicia and the Octavia range. The worry is that in the UK market, Skoda has given up a strong position in a small market where they had no competition, for an average position in a much larger market, which is full of competitors. Currently, its only advantage here is price. Maybe Skoda is at the start of its renewal not the end?

- Where do the distributors stand? Skoda in the UK has stuck with its existing distributor network of small family-run garages. Is this going to be a good platform to compete with Volvo and Rover in the middle of the market? With a growing Internet channel for cars, will a traditional distributor network actually kill Skoda's chances of further progress?

- If you took away the price advantage, would the Octavia still sell? That is, has the Skoda brand really been transformed, or has it just surprised people who now want to see more?

Answering these questions is highly speculative. However, they underline an important point: robust strategies involve constant innovation and improvement through superior market sensing. We wait to see if Skoda has this quality. If it does, then maybe the Skoda joke will turn out to be a prototype of value-based strategy beating brand-based strategy.

'robust strategies involve constant innovation and improvement through superior market sensing'

The Body Shop

There is no doubt that as new CEO, Patrick Gournay has been asking questions like: What kind of business does Body Shop want to be? How can it extend its brand to new areas? How should it manage its complex manufacturing distribution systems? How big a business can it be selling alternative therapies and massage? How can supply chain inefficiencies be overcome to get new products to market faster? How can Body Shop rebuild its differentiation in the face of competitive imitation? What is more debatable is whether he has come up with the right answers.

'How can Body Shop rebuild its differentiation in the face of competitive imitation?'

However, the fascinating story of the Roddicks and the creation of The Body Shop, suggests four major strategic questions to me:

- Is The Body Shop an outdated business design?
- Does the company have the formula in place for renewal and recovery?

- What are the core competencies of this business and are they being ignored or exploited?
- Where does Anita Roddick stand in all this?

Is the business design outdated?

I admit that I was one of those who waxed lyrical about The Body Shop as a prototype for the future business organization. The combination of social responsibility with commercial success, an entrepreneur's vision creating a new market position out of nothing, a 'hollow' organization using franchising to grow rapidly internationally and so on. Yes, I did regret saying these things when the share price fell to less than £1!

'The Body Shop got complex, too quickly for its management systems'
Probably at the heart of the problem is simply that The Body Shop got complex, too quickly for its management systems. In May 1998 Gordon Roddick noted: 'This business is so complicated. It has a manufacturing, wholesaling and retailing arm, as well as Body Shop Direct. There are company-owned stores and franchised stores. All this across 47 countries and 18 languages made more difficult by the overlay of social responsibility . . .'

However, it may be that the real problem is that in creating a complex international supply chain, The Body Shop has lost sight of its business theory, rather than clinging to one that is outdated. A lot depends on what you think are The Body Shop's real distinguishing competencies and capabilities. Indeed, you could ask how the business design could be outdated when so many competitors are imitating it?

This said, there does seem an urgent need for The Body Shop to be more adaptive in its products and operations for overseas markets, particularly given that less than 10 per cent of its outlets are in the UK. It was always a paradox that an ethical and socially aware company should be somewhat insensitively exporting British retailing and British products with little adaptation to local market needs. In the past, it got away with this because of its other strengths – this is no longer true.

A formula for recovery?

What was being put in place in 1998 looked sensible and made a lot of sense in terms of *operational effectiveness*. However, this is a long way from concluding that The Body Shop has a strategy for recovery. Perhaps the most critical thing is whether the US operation can be rescued and if the approaches adopted there provide a model to be applied elsewhere in the company.

The really worrying question is whether these policies are the right ones to refocus on The Body Shop's core capabilities and use them to rebuild market position. By 1999, Gournay has committed to a very specific, and very conventional, view of what The Body Shop should be – a retailer.

The Body Shop's core competencies and capabilities

In judging if he is right, a lot depends on where you think The Body Shop excels. Conventional analysts always like conventional categories and so they categorize The Body Shop as a retailer and talk about the company as a 'global retail brand'. The Body Shop is not really a retailer, indeed there are many signs that it is not particularly good at retailing.

'The Body Shop is not really a retailer'

The company survived its retailing and supply chain deficiencies because it was good at something else, which no one else could do. It is not easy to capture the uniqueness of what the Roddicks created. The best I can do is 'creating and bringing to market unique socially responsible products to promote well-being'. The new hemp and bergamot product lines are a good example: they are original, unique and very difficult for competitors to emulate.

If you follow this logic, the opening up of new routes to market such as direct selling, non-conventional retail outlets and Internet-based marketing make a huge amount of sense. Indeed, the direct operation is outperforming the stores in the UK already.

What does not make sense is the determination to refocus on conventional retailing. This sounds like investing heavily in an area where there is no likely sustainable competitive advantage, quite possibly to the detriment of what makes The Body Shop unique. Anyone can open retail outlets selling 'ethical' cosmetics (Virgin Vie and Boots have proved that, along with lots of other smaller imitators and Virgin Vie is struggling to make a living as a retailer in this sector). What they cannot imitate is the magic that the Roddicks created that differentiated The Body Shop from everyone else.

However, Gournay has now committed to a strategy that focuses everything on becoming a better retailer – closing/selling production units, looking for outside manufacturers, moving away from franchising and the wholesale role of The Body Shop. This is profoundly unoriginal.

A deeper understanding of the company's real uniquely distinguishing capabilities would probably lead away from some of these recovery strategies now being put in place. Conventional City analysts talk about the desirability of turning The Body Shop into something more like Boots or Marks & Spencer. This would undoubtedly be the end of The Body Shop dream, but the City would probably be delighted. However, at its simplest, if the challenge is to create and implement new ideas to meet new competition, becoming a better conventional retailer does not look like the way to do it.

In fact, as a limiting case, should The Body Shop *'should The Body* withdraw from conventional retailing altogether? If *Shop withdraw* Body Shop products reach the market through direct *from conventional* channels such as the Internet, home parties, cata- *retailing* logues, outlets in leisure complexes, hotels and air- *altogether?'* lines, then why do you need the conventional shops?

In fact, if you retain the brand and its cause-related identity, what would you lose by selling the brand through department stores and pharmacies?

The real point is that identifying the real core competencies of a business does not mean accepting conventions and assumptions – it may lead to challenging the fundamental structure of a business.

Where does Anita Roddick stand?

It is tempting to say right behind Patrick Gournay, with a large bergamot in her hand. However, in reality she has been surprisingly supportive to the new structuring and allocation of responsibilities – at least, so far.

However, the serious answer to this question is actually critical. If the new structures facilitate the continuation and extension of Roddick's innovation and creativity, then the company has a chance of rebuilding. If the new structures stifle that flow of ideas and creativity, then The Body Shop is probably dead in the water, and if it survives it will be as a conventional cosmetics company competing on a 'me-too' basis with all the rest. In fact, if you kill the Roddick uniqueness, you are probably just left with a chain of small shops, which will probably be bought by Boots or Virgin.

Kellogg's Cornflakes

However you read the present situation, it should not be forgotten that Kellogg is an old brand, one of the biggest in the world, and one which inspires high levels of consumer trust. The company has done much to associate its products with healthy nutrition and healthy living. There is no way that this brand is going to die. But in an era of value-driven strategy, this story illustrates some of the problems that traditional brands – and traditional marketing – are having to confront. This comes down to the issue of whether traditional brand-based competition can survive against value-driven strategies. Some of the interesting questions to ponder are:

'There is no way that this brand is going to die'

- How much were the traditional marketing strategies pursued responsible for Kellogg's downfall?
- What is the underlying cause of the loss of market share for Kellogg?
- Has the company responded in appropriate ways?
- What else can it do?
- Is the answer a take-over or merger?

The effects of traditional marketing strategy

Although the cereals market was a nice place to be for many years (if you were one of the big three manufacturers with a stable market share and high profits), it was never going to last forever. The market has changed fundamentally (see below) but there is some evidence that conventional brand marketing actually fuelled that change, and blinded Kellogg to the need for new strategy. In particular:

- The excessive use of coupons (which is after all no more than a very expensive way of cutting prices temporarily) actually trains consumers in being price-sensitive and in switching from one brand to another on the basis of prices and discounts. So great was the coupon promotion level that it probably opened the way for the private labels to grow. The consumer accustomed to having a coupon to get cheaper cereal might well switch to the permanently lower priced private label product, the first time she or he does not have your coupon.
- The proliferation of new brands and products is likely also to be responsible for eroding brand loyalty and building consumer resistance because so many of the new products failed.
- The regular and predictable price/promotion cycle led consumers to stockpile and buy only at times of promotions, not to increase consumption.

'The proliferation of new brands and products is likely also to be responsible for eroding brand loyalty'

'The thinking of every competitor was driven by market share'

- The thinking of every competitor was driven by market share – traditional marketing usually does this. The real issue was market growth – actually the lack of it and the absence of strategies to build new markets.

This raises the question of whether Kellogg has truly caught up with the idea that competitors are doing different things and that the days of 'price up and spend back' are gone. The plans for 1999 look terribly familiar. . . .

The cause of market share loss

On the face of things there are three underlying causes: strong branded competitors building expertise and strength through the high margins of the 1980s; strong low-cost competitors supplying retailer own labels; and market change.

However, what this seems to be about really is *value* as the basis of competition:

- The branded competitors have innovated new products with uniques that Kellogg cannot imitate, that create value for customers and achieve higher average revenue per unit sold.
- The own-label manufacturers have exploited volume advantages and low operating and marketing costs to provide retailers with products of comparable quality that sell at much lower prices and provide higher value in this sense.
- Consumers are changing their breakfasting habits, so the things that create value for them have changed. Value has migrated to more easily consumed breakfasts for those in a hurry or more distinctive products for others. Kellogg seems, incredibly, to have failed to sense or understand how the market has changed.

Company responses

'The Kellogg responses have been totally conventional'

The Kellogg responses have been totally conventional and in some cases highly damaging:

- *Price cutting* – the brand strategy dilemma is what you do when confronted by low-price competition and price cutting. Brand theory says you should be protected from these attacks by consumer loyalty to the brand and its distinctive values. This means if the only thing you can do to hold volume against price cutters is to cut your own prices, then maybe your brand is not as strong and valuable as you believed? This is exactly what Kellogg did, and paid a high price in lost profits and declining share value.

- *Promotion* – an equally conventional marketing response to competitive inroads is to try to buy market share back by aggressive advertising spends and sales promotions of various kinds. The twin threats are destroying the profitability of the operation, as competitors retaliate to restore the status quo, and devaluing the brand further. This too seems central to what Kellogg is doing.
- *Management restructuring* – if the blame for poor performance is an inward-looking culture and weak management performance, then a traditional and possibly reasonable policy is culling and restructuring. However, rebuilding to improve performance is one thing – restructuring as a substitute is another.

'the blame for poor performance is an inward-looking culture and weak management performance'

What else can it do?

Well, that is the $64 000 question, or rather more, actually. Perhaps the biggest issue is whether to focus on traditional breakfast cereals or to spread the brand onto other food areas. Although don't forget that when the company tried to become the 'king of breakfast' a few years ago with juices and other products, it did not work. In breakfast cereals, Kellogg is probably going to have to accept that the market has changed and has become more competitive as well.

The theory is clear – the question is what differentiating capabilities does Kellogg have that will produce superior value for customers? The competitors have already done this at the top and bottom ends of the market in price terms. The Kellogg search has to be for the part of the market where it can offer better value than others.

Take-over or merger?

The process of renewal is often painful for companies. The new chief operating officer has a certain amount of time to try and recover the situation.

However, even the brief account given here suggests that it may be very difficult for an insider to make radical changes in a strong and established culture. It may be that the best way forward for this company may be through alliance and merger with another organization to get the new ideas and challenges to conventions that it needs.

Laura Ashley

'the major response of the company seems to be continual rounds of management change and restructuring'

'is the business model just too tired and out of date to survive?'

This is a sad story of a spectacularly successful business that has fallen on (very) hard times. It has lost its core markets to competitors, it is pouring cash into loss-making businesses, it has been fighting to survive in the brutal US retail marketplace, sales are falling, share value has hit the floor, and the major response of the company seems to be continual rounds of management change and restructuring. Perhaps the really interesting question is: can this be fixed or is the business model just too tired and out of date to survive? Some of the interesting questions to consider include the following:

- Was the company doomed after the death of its main founder, Laura Ashley?
- What are the core strengths of this business?
- How much of the problem can be traced to the company's market choices?
- To what extent does lack of technology and infrastructure explain the company's decline?
- Is the problem the brand?
- Is Laura Ashley really a retailer?
- What is the future likely to be?

The death of Laura Ashley

There is no particular reason to accept this as a reason for the company's problems, although it is frequently trotted out as an excuse. The founder had established the design concept for the business and the extension of the brand into a range of new areas, but did not personally create the designs and the company did not ever manufacture more than a fraction of its total sales. What the company did lose was perhaps the vision and leadership of its founder and exchanged it for the somewhat dogmatic and fiery management approach of her husband.

Perhaps the issue is more the transition from a family-owned business to a public company operating a complex global business. This would not be the first time a company had problems in making this transition.

Core strengths

This leads to the question of what capabilities and resources Laura Ashley has as the basis for renewal. The core seems to be a design concept embracing clothes and furniture that appealed to a particular type of female consumer and provided a unique brand identity. This is very different from skills in retailing or manufacturing or managing global supply chains.

'The core seems to be a design concept embracing clothes and furniture that appealed to a particular type of female consumer'

The trouble is this design concept has been diluted and partly abandoned as out of date and unfashionable by successive CEOs and merchandisers, who have seen the business primarily as a retailer. It follows if you hire retail specialists to run the business, they will try to run the company as a retail business. It may be that this conventional view of the business underpins many of the problems – if you define the business as a design house, then why would you go on opening stores and building stocks (shops you cannot supply and stocks you cannot sell, incidentally)? In some ways, the original business model has been abandoned and a conventional retailing model substituted. Laura Ashley gives a good impression of being a very poor retailer in operational or strategic terms.

'if you hire retail specialists to run the business, they will try to run the company as a retail business'

'the original business model has been abandoned and a conventional retailing model substituted'

It is more than possible that renewal will depend on rediscovering the core strengths of the business and not attempting to become a generic retailer. There is little sign of this recognition by management.

Market choices

One core issue is the company's market choices and how they have developed. There has been a consistent tendency to target markets because they are large and attractive (e.g. the USA), with too little concern for the company's capabilities for taking a strong position in those markets (demonstrably poor in the US example). This has drained many of the company's resources.

At a more detailed level, the company shows signs of abandoning traditional buyers of the brand, in an attempt to reach a new, larger female fashion shopper market. Conventional marketing would suggest that this was the best way to grow the business. In reality, Laura Ashley lost its long-standing customers (who went to Marks & Spencer and John Lewis) to plunge into a market with fierce competition for younger shoppers (Oasis,

Monsoon, etc.) and strong branding for older shoppers (Ralph Lauren, Gucci, etc.). Specialist, niche retailers do not prosper in head-on competition with stronger players and yet this is exactly what was attempted. They have been trapped in a cycle of price discounting as a result.

At no point in the 1990s does Laura Ashley seem to have genuinely gone back to basics and focused on the core markets where it still had a strong position. Instead, it abandoned them.

In addition, the move into home furnishings largely made sense only as a way of taking a higher proportion of the spend by the Laura Ashley customer. On their own, the furnishings have problems facing up to the tough competition in furnishings and home products. If you lose the Laura Ashley shopper, you have effectively lost your entry point into this marketplace. To then move towards more generic, less 'Laura Ashley style' products in these markets, means you lose even more touch with the remaining Laura Ashley loyal customers, but have no differentiated basis for gaining new customers.

Technology and infrastructure

Is managerial incompetence in managing operations the real cause of the company's problems? Certainly to continue opening-shops, when you have already proved your supply chain cannot provide them with products to sell does not look smart. Indeed, this is a low-technology company: it has no web site and no effective direct selling capabilities to rival its competitors. The absence of even supplementary direct sales through 'L.Ashley.Com' is a serious missed opportunity.

However, these problems are not worth fixing until you decide what you want the business to be.

The brand

'If all this company has is its brand, then it is probably dead'

If all this company has is its brand, then it is probably dead. The brand looks dated and the company has done much to undermine the brand values by its own actions. It has also had an over-optimistic idea about the stretching of the brand to new markets, for example, the USA.

The issue is whether the company can move from a brand-based strategy to create superior value in its core markets, and it is difficult to see how it can do this.

Retailing versus design and manufacture

Some conventional commentators have suggested that the real problem was that Laura Ashley was a smallish company trying to be a manufacturer and a retailer in dozens of different countries, all at the same time. Conventional advice was to do exactly what Iverson did – to focus on retail operations. This has proved to be a poor strategy.

If you see the brand more as a design capability, then these retailing developments make less and less sense. A design house would surely be better advised to develop and consolidate the brand, to franchise the brand to related areas, to source and manufacture through alliances, to develop a direct marketing and electronic commerce capability.

The future?

The prognosis is not good at the time of writing – the company seems determined to do more of the same, in spite of the evidence that it is doing the wrong things. The debatable issue remains whether the business can be fixed and this depends on how you read the underlying problem:

'the company seems determined to do more of the same, in spite of the evidence that it is doing the wrong things'

- Is the brand dead? In which case the future is as an 'also-ran' retailer of generic products with limited value-creation and probably struggling to make a profit.
- Is the business model obsolete or has it just been abandoned by successive short-term occupants of the CEO position?
- Could the business be renewed by going back to the original business model (a kind of branded design house) or developing a new one (for example, as a hollow organization built around the core brand values with sourcing and direct marketing capabilities along with franchised areas in shops run by others)?

It is interesting to apply the value-driven strategy model to the history of this company to understand how much would have to be done to rescue it.

Boots the Chemists

Boots provides a remarkable story of disaster to renewal, which raises a number of interesting questions worth dwelling on:

- Why did a business this sophisticated get drawn into the disastrous diversification of the Ward White acquisition?
- What does Boots tell us about the importance of shareholder value as a management focus?
- What are the keys to the renewal and reinvention that Blyth is driving in this company and do they make sense?
- What has the company's history got to do with anything?
- What is likely to happen next?

Why did a business this sophisticated get drawn into disastrous diversification?

'no matter how smart you are, there is always scope to drag defeat from the jaws of victory'

At its simplest, because no matter how smart you are, there is always scope to drag defeat from the jaws of victory. Let us be clear on one thing: Lord Blyth is nobody's fool, and no company takes lightly the investment of nearly a billion pounds of shareholder money. There is a very good chance that many of us brought up on a diet of conventional tools of strategic analysis would have made exactly the same choice. Some of the issues surrounding this question are:

- *The heat of battle and Pyrrhic victories* – mergers and take-overs are emotional as well as rational and involve big risks. There is always a danger in a contested bid that the determination to win becomes a stronger force than the attractiveness of the purchase. If this was the case with the Boots' acquisition of Ward White, then Lord Blyth will be neither the first nor the last CEO to win a take-over battle that was not worth winning.
- *Valuing acquisitions* – most approaches to placing a price on an acquisition are driven by historical information. At the end of the 1980s, the DIY and home decorating markets looked attractive: they had grown consistently and at impressive rates and the competition did not look strong.

'Historically based forecasts are not good when there is a revolution in a marketplace'

Unfortunately, things changed, the markets nosedived with the housing and property market, and the main competitors got their acts together to defend their market leadership. Historically based forecasts are not good when there is a revolution in a marketplace.

- *Strategic fit* – a compelling case can still be made in conventional terms for the fit of the Ward White businesses with Boots. Boots had a strong brand name and a massive consumer market presence. Having entered into a variety of products for the home – giftware, some household linens, ornaments, etc. – extending the product range into home improvement and refurbishment looks like a good fit. It is a classic product development strategy: sell more products to an established customer base where you have a foothold. What else could be the logic for Marks & Spencer to move from clothes to household products to furniture to finance?

- *Portfolio modelling* – anyone who has been on a course of strategic management will wax lyrical about the importance of cash cows (low market growth, high market share) parts of the operation being used to fund the acquisition and development of stars (high market growth, high market share) operations. You could still run those models on the computer, and with the information available at the time they would still urge you to go for it. Unfortunately, portfolio models tend to be nice models that take little account of marketplace change and real synergy (or lack of it).

  'portfolio models tend to be nice models that take little account of marketplace change and real synergy'

- *Branding* – for the assumed synergy to work, the acquisitions would have had to be rebranded as Boots businesses. Conventional logic says this would have been a huge risk to the Boots brand, and could have undermined the core business, so it was never done. Customers never knew that Payless or Do-It-All were Boots' businesses, so how could the brand values possibly transfer?

Quite simply, the Ward White acquisition made much conventional sense at the time – that is why conventional analytical tools can be so dangerous.

What does Boots tell us about the importance of shareholder value?

It tells us that, however much a company benefits by focusing on building superior customer value and being an enlightened employer, there are many stakeholders in a business and the owners want value too. Probably the major gains from the value-based management at Boots approach have been:

- *A new discipline* – the approach has given Blyth a new way of reshaping the business and re-orienting management thinking, that has proved highly appropriate for the company.
- *Culture change* – one of Boots' problems comes from its long history, corporate philosophy and traditions and the strong

culture it has produced: one which is oriented towards pharmacy, social responsibility and welfare. Blyth needed an approach to shift some of these values for the future and this gave him one.

- *Shareholder returns* – to achieve such impressive returns to owners at a time when the company had problems was a brilliant way to retain City and shareholder support for management.
- *Surprises* – giving shareholders nice surprises in the form of extra dividends and bonuses has another effect; your owners are a lot more forgiving about the things that you get wrong, because they can see very tangibly how much you are getting right.

What are the keys to Boots' renewal and reinvention?

Probably the most important lessons from the Boots story of renewal are along the following lines:

- *Sorting out the mess* – Blyth has had the courage to take the losses and the criticism and get out of the loss-making businesses, which did not fit with the Boots operation.
- *Customer understanding* – unlike many of the companies operating 'loyalty schemes' Boots has used the data it collects through the loyalty card to enhance its market sensing and build new directions for the business. It is one of the first British companies to understand the real power from this superior market and customer understanding. This is proving far more effective in identifying new areas to develop, than the old type of 'assumption' that because customers buy healthcare products from you they will buy home improvement products from you as well (just because you happen to own the home improvement outlets).

> 'Boots has used the data it collects through the loyalty card to enhance its market sensing and build new directions for the business'

- *Refocusing the retailing* – the potential gains in the transformation of the retail outlets from chemists shops with some general merchandise into personal care and healthcare centres are massive. This is a genuine reinvention that is designed to play to the company's strengths internally and with customers.

> 'This is a genuine reinvention that is designed to play to the company's strengths'

- *Emphasizing the products* – the company has traditionally been seen as a retailer, but in reality it is much more: it is also a leading developer and producer of over-the-counter medicines. The potential from unleashing this potential as a separate business with a global remit is already being realized.

What influence has the company's history?

The history of the company is the source of its culture and values. This is a hidden but powerful influence on management's ability to implement new strategies. One of the attractions of the renewal is that it plays to the company's traditional strengths and values. It may be a 'soft' factor, but it should not be underestimated.

What is likely to happen next?

At the very least this is a company worth watching to see what does happen over the next few years. A first issue is that Lord Blyth retires in 2000, and the business has to survive a leadership transition, with a new CEO who may have a different vision (although it seems likely that Blyth's successor will be from within the business and is likely to share much of Blyth's philosophy).

A second issue is acquisitions and disposals. A major question mark can be placed alongside Halfords. This is a successful business that is growing and contributes to profits. However, its links to the rest of the operation are tenuous and it seems a likely candidate for disposal if a buyer appears. It seems likely that growth of the UK retail business by further acquisitions is likely to be limited and most of Europe remains closed because of the legal restrictions on the ownership of pharmacies. It will be interesting to see if Boots has managed its way into Japan and the Far East at a time of lasting decline in those economies. Probably the most interesting acquisitions will be in acquiring further channels of distribution for Boots Healthcare International in Europe and beyond and growing this part of the business further. It is possible to make mistakes here though, the company has had to withdraw from its Russian operation because of bad debts.

A third issue is the reinvention of the chemists' shops and general stores into services-oriented health-care and personal care centres. This is exciting and visionary, but the question is whether it will work. There is also the fascinating speculation of what additional services and facilities can be added to extend the concept further. Certainly, Boots seems the first of the retail chain to be effectively exploiting the *'the first of the retail chain to be effectively exploiting the loyalty card programme as a strategic tool'* loyalty card programme as a strategic tool rather than just a promotional device and this may be significant in identifying new developments that exploit the strong customer relationship.

WH Smith and John Menzies

The story of these companies' experiences in recent years suggests a strategic principle. If you are in a hole . . .

1 Stop digging.
2 Look for a ladder.

Having been wrong-footed by underlying changes in their core markets driven by new-style competitors and a change in the behaviour of value-seeking customers, as well as introverted company cultures driven by the past, both companies have taken drastic actions to reinvent and rebuild their businesses. It is too soon to see if these actions will be effective, though it is pretty clear that trying to stay with the old business model would have been disastrous in any case. There are a number of interesting questions to consider:

'both companies have taken drastic actions to reinvent and rebuild their businesses'

- Has WHS built the path to its renewal?
- Does John Menzies have a superior approach?
- What is likely to happen next?

The WHS path to renewal

WHS is a large organization with an introverted and embedded culture, which has developed a history of snatching defeat from the jaws of victory. Building a process of renewal in such an organization is not simple. However, examining the path they have chosen raises a number of points:

- *Have they really refocused or are they just doing more of the same?* – the retail high street chain has been extended with the Menzies acquisition, and there has been a flurry of store refurbishments, with some rationalization of duplicating outlets. The management distraction of the non-core, non-WHS businesses has largely gone (The Wall, Virgin Our Price, etc.). However, there seems no sign that the retail business is actually doing much different. There is an old rule in mergers:

if you take two low performers and merge them, you most likely end up with one big low performer. If the UK retail business design is obsolete, the Menzies acquisition does not look healthy. Tim Waterstone had a major point in the proposals he made to WHS which they rejected – reinventing the retail stores involves more than repainting them, they have to become 'destination stores' again with exciting and distinctive product ranges and flair. The lack of real change in this part of the operation raises many questions about the future. Why, for example, given the superior performance of the Travel retail units (with their protection against supermarket and convenience store competition and the specialist niche retailers) is that model not being extended (e.g. into hotels, leisure complexes, hospitals, and so on)?

'reinventing the retail stores involves more than repainting them'

- *Is the WHS future in electronic commerce?* – the explosion of WHS share value in the Internet feeding frenzy may actually be unhelpful in blinding management to the real issues. Two small investments do not make a company an 'e-tailer'. There is, however, a serious danger that these small operations will further distract management from sorting out the really big problem they have – the retail chain.

'Two small investments do not make a company an "e-tailer"'

- *Is there a middle-market left?* – the WHS vision for the high street stores is based on occupying the middle-market, with wide-choice specialists on one side of them and cheap supermarkets and convenient local shops on the other. Apart from the fact that this sounds like a classic 'stuck-in-the-middle' posture, which loses out to every type of competitor, there is some question about whether there is going to be any middle-market for much longer. As the US chains and Internet book and music sellers expand from one side and the voracious, diversifying supermarkets advance from the other, why would anyone want to be in between them?
- *If you have to sell something, why sell the profit makers?* – disposing of businesses because you cannot make them pay is fine. The logic for selling the highest performing unit in the group – Waterstones – is difficult to comprehend. The effect is to lose the growth potential in specialist bookselling and at the same time to help in the creation of a powerful competitor – HMV Media. (The answer to this question is probably because those are the only bits anyone would buy for a decent price.)
- *Why let Menzies have a free shot at distribution?* – WHS has much in common with Menzies, in terms of heritage and capabilities. If WHS has underlying strengths in distribution, then does it make sense to back off and allow Menzies to build

its business in this area? The implication is that WHS is going to let Menzies build its expertise in this area until the point when Menzies offers for the WHS distribution business.

- *Maybe the break-up made sense?* – WHS has achieved some deliverables: money returned to shareholders in particular and some useful divestments. It remains difficult to see a new business emerging. It is difficult to see reinvention as opposed to repetition. In retrospect, maybe the full-blooded break-up made sense, selling the specialist businesses to specialists and the retail chain to a supermarket or effective high street performer such as Boots.

'At best, WHS is at the very start of its renewal process'

At best, WHS is at the very start of its renewal process. Once the dust has settled from the de-mergers and acquisitions, and the Internet adventure, then the search will be for a way forward. It has not yet been found.

The John Menzies approach

The Menzies approach to meeting the crisis was more radical than that at WHS, but it may be more firmly grounded in the company's capabilities and strengths – their retailing skills were not enough to sustain the shops when the going got tough in terms of competition and customer demands. The stores were simply badly run with out-of-date retail methods. However, if your conclusion is that the old high street formula has passed its sell-by date, then why would you want to spend time and money fixing the retail operation? Interesting aspects of the rebuilding at Menzies are:

- *Radical pruning* – abandoning the retail operation was a necessary shock to the Menzies' culture. It frees Mackay from the stopgap costs of fixing an operation that is probably never going to return to high levels of performance. It also lands the problems of sorting them out on a competitor. The sooner he can shift the Early Learning Centres the same way the better – hopefully he will not be deterred by the return of ELC to profitability.

'Mackay has set out to exploit the underlying strengths of Menzies in distribution'

- *Creating freedom to manoeuvre* – leaving the retail problem with WHS has also distracted that traditional rival from throwing its weight behind a distribution strategy and getting in the way of Mackay's strategy.
- *Leveraging differentiating capabilities* – Mackay has set out to exploit the underlying strengths of Menzies in

distribution and to use these to extend the distribution services offered. There have been some early problems, but these look to be soluble, if the City allows Mackay enough time.

- *Building relationships* – there is the start of a move towards joint venturing and partnering with others in the distribution field such as Lufthansa, which should provide a new set of capabilities.
- *Strategic clarity* – for better or worse, Mackay seems to have a clear idea of what he wants to turn Menzies into, and is pursuing that vision doggedly, and not being distracted by side issues.

The test will be the next 2–3 years. If Mackay achieves what he says he wants, and learns and refines the model along the way, there is a good chance that the Menzies company will soon be almost unrecognizable as the failed newsagents of the 1980s.

The future

This is speculative, but ask of the two companies:

- Is there evidence of management vision of how to reinvent and renew?
- Are they closely in touch with their markets and anticipating trends and changes?
- Are they exploiting their differentiating capabilities?
- Are they developing relationships with customers, employees, collaborators and competitors that support their customer strategies?
- Are they restructuring and rebuilding their organizations to achieve new things?
- Are they working towards building superior value for their different types of customers?

Your views of how the two companies are building those qualities of robustness may suggest that they are in very different stages of transition from being the dinosaurs of the high street to become world-class service providers. They may not both make it.

CHAPTER 18

Final thoughts . . . for now

*'strategy making
exists in an
environment of
revolution and
reinvention'*

*'A single well-told
story may reveal
more insights for
managers than a
hundred surveys or
models'*

This book was built on two major thoughts: that strategy making exists in an environment of revolution and reinvention that has largely been ignored by those who talk about strategy, rather than actually making it; and, that maybe we can learn more by looking at the experiences of real companies in real marketplaces, than by theorizing and model-building. A single well-told story may reveal more insights for managers than a hundred surveys or models.

The underlying logic was that making sound choices that lead to sustainable and robust strategies has become more vital than ever – strategic clarity is high on the agenda for senior managers everywhere. But conventional theory with its thousand-and-one arbitrary 'rules' and simplified 'models' just has not caught up with the realities than real managers have to face:

- the market has become the dominant issue because that is where the revolutions are taking place, and market-based strategy is taking priority over traditional strategic planning, i.e. 'strategising' not planning
- the search for operational efficiency is vital, but it is not strategy
- the power of reinvention and the creation of new business models make much of the strategic wisdom of the past obsolete

- operating in a familiar 'competitive box' of your own making makes you all the more vulnerable and you will not even see the revolution coming
- increasingly sophisticated customers are making new demands for value and transparency
- brand and relationship marketing is giving way to new ideas of value-driven strategy
- value-driven strategy is built upon new management vision, superior market sensing and organizational learning, competing through differentiating capabilities and it is implemented through relationship strategy and the reinvented organization

'value-driven strategy is built upon new management vision, superior market sensing and organizational learning'

The stories of revolution, reinvention and renewal told here add weight to this view of building robust strategy:

- *Management vision and leadership* – the creative reinvention of traditional businesses with innovative business models by Michael Dell at Dell Computers, Jeff Bezos at Amazon.com, Stelios Haji-Ioannou at easyJet and Ruth Owades at Calyx & Corolla underlines the significance of visionary leadership. The instability and lack of clarity in current leadership goals at The Body Shop, Laura Ashley, British Airways and Marks & Spencer is equally illustrative of the risks of a management vacuum at the top of an organization.
- *Market sensing and organizational learning* – there is little doubt that Dell or Owades or Bezos did not start out with a complete and perfect model of the companies they created. The process of reinvention is continuing and based on learning and experience, and provides the basis for translating competitive differentiation into a sustainable advantage that competitors cannot easily overtake. It may even be that what we are seeing is the rate and effectiveness of organizational learning as the key corporate capability that drives value-driven strategy forward. The retail giant, Marks & Spencer is a company rediscovering the need to stay close to customers, in its search for renewal, while WH Smith clings to an illusion of occupying the middle of a market that has disappeared while it was looking the other way. Conventional retail banks still struggle with the realization that their customers are looking to new types of competitor for superior value, even though they are not 'proper banks'.

'The process of reinvention is continuing and based on learning and experience'

- *Differentiating capabilities* – successful new business models underline the power of superiority over

'new business models underline the power of superiority over competitors in the areas that create customer value'

competitors in the areas that create customer value. The stories of Skoda Cars and the 'no-frills airlines' demonstrate the impact of being best at something that provides a step-change in value for a specific group of customers. The failures at The Body Shop and Laura Ashley demonstrate the disastrous effect of losing differentiating capabilities in the areas that matter most to customers. Kellogg underlines the message that traditional branding may no longer be enough to protect companies from value-based competitors and value-oriented customers.

- *Relationship strategy* – the importance of managing an infra-structure of relationships – with customers, employees, competitors, collaborators, regulators and shareholders – to drive strategy is illustrated by the continuing problems at British Airways and the crisis that BT survived, as well as the 'virtual integration' of Dell with its customers and suppliers.

- *Reinvented organization* – the complexity and mixed forms of the organizations needed to drive strategy in the new reality are illustrated by the stories of BT and BA. The creation of new hollow or virtual forms as part of building competitive advantage through superior value is seen at companies such as Dell and Calyx & Corolla. The development of even more radical and unfamiliar organizational forms is central to the development of companies such as Amazon.com and the new music businesses. We do not even have a word for some of these new forms yet, although some talk of them as 'info-mediaries'. The penalty for clinging to outdated structures can be seen in companies such as The Body Shop and Laura Ashley.

'compelling evidence that robust strategy is indeed value-driven, but that the meaning of value is always created by customers'

- *Value-driven strategy* – in overview, the stories provide compelling evidence that robust strategy is indeed value-driven, but that the meaning of value is always created by customers. The manoeuvring and struggles of the supermarkets and car companies described in Treasure Island have been driven by the new transparency and changing sources of customer value, challenging conventional abilities to control markets. The robust companies may make mistakes but can renew themselves by searching out new avenues to customer value where their differentiating capabilities give them a competitive advantage. The processes of renewal and rediscovery at Boots are a powerful illustration, while we wait to see if the same can be said about the progress of the struggling companies, WH Smith and John Menzies.

There will be those who dislike the approach taken in this book. That is their privilege. I urge managers, however, to take seriously the messages here about the inevitability of *revolution* in the industries and markets where you have to survive, about the power of *reinvention* in the form of new business models that create superior value for customers, and the search for *renewal* by those whose business methods have become obsolete and who have been wrong-footed by new competitive forces. Use the picture built here as a framework for studying your own company's position and comparing it with competitors and the forces driving customer value. The alternatives to building and using these new insights have been clearly illustrated in the stories told here.

Index